Taking Stock
Belize at 25 Years of Independence

Taking Stock:
Belize at 25 Years of Independence

Barbara S. Balboni and Joseph O. Palacio
Editors

Contributors:
Jaime J. Awe
Candy Gonzalez
Crucita Ken
Melanie McField and Nadia Bood
Antoinette Moore
Joseph O. Palacio
Michael J. Pisani
Robert B. Richardson
Michael Rosberg
Michael Stone
Jerome Straughan
Richard Wilk
Colin A. Young and Robert Horwich

CUBOLA BOOKS / BELIZE

Published by:
Cubola Productions
35 Elizabeth Street
Benque Viejo del Carmen
Belize, C.A.

First Edition, September 2007

Photography by Crissie Ferrara (cover); Sarah Weeden (pp. 19 and 97); Tim O' Malley (p. 281) and Richard Holder (p. 173)

ISBN: 978-976-8161-18-5

Printed and bound in Mexico

This book is dedicated to all those Belizean patriots-women and men-who throughout history, regardless of race, class, and religious or political affiliation, have stood for truth, justice, and freedom.

From the publisher

A few years ago when I started to work on a book to commemorate Belize's 25 years of independence, I approached experts for contributions. Many responded with an enthusiasm that matched my own; some could not deliver, but others dedicated long hours to write the essays collected in this book.

I'm very grateful to the Belizean scholars who, in spite of receiving very little support for doing research and publishing, have dedicated much time and effort to writing these essays. I hope this publication will help them achieve the recognition they so rightly deserve and encourage others to contribute to the second volume.

I'm also indebted to the researchers from other countries who sent their work and who for many years, some for decades, have come to Belize to conduct their research. Their work has helped us to better understand Belize. We are united, not by place of birth, but by our desire to add to the growing body of knowledge about Belize.

Belize is a very small country; the essays in this book have not been constrained by society or by the tinted glass of politics, but are based on our contributors' capacity to analyse, interpret, and evaluate. This represents a change. Their essays are a bid for independent thinking, and their contributions represent an important exercise in democracy.

September 2007
Montserrat Casademunt
Publisher

Contents

PART 1

ECONOMY

PART 2
ENVIRONMENT

PART 3
SOCIETY

Introduction

This volume does what the title suggests–it "takes stock" of Belize as it makes its way along the continuum from its first 25 years as an independent nation into the regional, international, and global arena. Belize's proximity to Mexico, Guatemala, and the United States, its close relations with Canada and England, and the fact that it is English speaking have drawn scholars worldwide to its shores to analyse its caves and ancient sites, its flora and fauna, natural environment, society, and culture. Often the data gathered and work produced–scholarly reports and papers, theses and dissertations–are published abroad and are not accessible to Belizeans. This volume breaks that trend. All but one essay have been written for this collection and with the forth-coming volume two, present for the first time since independence an analysis of the "state-of-the-state" of Belize.

This collection is a tangible indication of not only our intellectual maturity but also our ability to "tease apart" issues, critically analyse them, and make concrete suggestions that stakeholders, decision-makers, and government officials can use. Scholarly in the depth of their analysis, the essays in each section are straightforward and accessible. The main reason the people of Belize supported independence was they wanted the country to have political control over national affairs, which in turn would empower them to improve their economic, social, and cultural well-being. The convergence between the social welfare and the performance of the economy is the topic of analysis by Robert Richardson, Michael Pisani, and Crucita Ken.

Richardson's essay is a snapshot of Belize from its economic beginnings in logging to its foray into the fledgling oil industry. Whether he is discussing GDP, GNP, or GINI, or the less well-known HDI, human development index, Richardson's analysis is clear and concise. Those unfamiliar with economic terms will relish the ease with which they are able to negotiate the data and tables depicting the correlations between aid, investments, and trade and the data on imports, exports, and the trade deficit. Within the comparative picture that Richardson portrays of our economic well-being, the following are worthy of note. The HDI created by the United Nation Development Programme places Belize below the average Latin American and Caribbean states; furthermore, the

HDI has been declining since 1980. Belize is currently facing decreases in foreign aid. More particularly, our national debt and its servicing are at a level much higher than those of our regional peers. The question that will arise in the reader's mind is "Is this economic strategy sustainable?" After reading his and the other two essays in this section, you will be able to assess Richardson's economic argument that Belize is making "two steps forward, two steps back."

Equally accessible is Michael Pisani's analysis of Belize's foreign trade performance since independence. He explores the nature and composition of Belize's foreign trade basket since independence by focusing on foreign trade and how it can be improved to meet the rigorous demands of a small and emerging independent state. His meticulous collation of the import and export data from 1970 provides readers for the first time with a picture of what Belize's "trade deficit" really looks like. Of particular concern are the inherited neo-dependent trade relationships, such as the commodity export base; the industrial, finished, and consumer goods import basket; the primary trade links with countries outside the region; and the structural balance of the trade deficit. Utilising globalization and dependency frameworks, Pisani analyses the Belizean trade performance and concludes his paper with recommendations to counter Belize's neo-dependency and propel us forward into a non-dependent trade insertion and growth. Pisani's title, "Belize's foreign trade performance since independence: Neo-dependent challenges and opportunities," is a call to action, a call to forge ways to sustainably meet the challenges and opportunities in Belize's economic future.

When Belize achieved full independence, the northern region of Corozal and Orange Walk, once the most important economically, was going through an economic crisis with debt burden and traditional export price reductions. Crucita Ken analyses how the region faced major challenges that prompted the government of Belize to introduce fiscal incentive programs to alleviate the increasing unemployment and decreasing economic activity. During the 1980s and 1990s, because of its proximity to Mexico the region experienced the effects of the Mexican peso devaluation. Ken assesses the role that Mexico played in Belize's economy, especially as the major market for the Commercial Free Zone. Like her fellow economists, with clarity and precision Ken walks the reader through implications of informal and formal trade between the two countries, the export and re-export of sugar, and the effects of unemployment and lends a critical and realistic eye to the high expectations associated with the establishment of the Commercial Free Zone in Corozal.

Environment

Certainly one of the most profound changes during the past 25 years has been a shift from a public perception of wanton exploitation of the physical environment to its stewardship as a common good for the benefit of future gener-

14

ations. This shift has not taken place smoothly, as vested interest groups have often locked horns on which part of the physical environment is to be preserved, who should be the beneficiaries, and what should be the nature of public policy in the short and long term.

Candy Gonzalez analyses the evolution of public policy toward the environment as a composite of natural resources in her essay with the telling title "The environment—preserve, reserve, plunder." In capsule form she summarises her analysis using the following chronological benchmarks, "In 1981, Belize incorporated into the preamble of our Constitution the expectation that ...The people of Belize.... require policies of State which... protect the environment.... Nearly a decade later, in 1992, the first such policy was enacted with the passage of the Environmental Protection Act....The first environmental regulations followed in 1995, and the first civil environmental case in 2001."

Gonzalez argues that civil society needs to maintain its guard to keep in check the government, given its proclivity to sacrifice environmental well-being for quick and unsustainable benefits proffered by multilateral development projects. Grounded in environmental law and in the commitment in the Preamble of the Constitution to "protect the environment," Gonzalez highlights the turning points in the environmental life of Belize from preserving and reserving the environment to impoverishing it for the future. Gonzalez's analysis will seem almost understated when viewed against the overwhelming evidence that the environment is in danger. Readers are left to assess the full impact of her title.

Another example of "for the first time ever" is Dr. Young and Dr. Horwich's essay. "The history of protected area designation, co-management and community participation" is a veritable "what is what" of protected areas in Belize. The topics include the types of protected areas; the integration of conservation, co-management, and community participation; and the recently announced National Protected Areas Policy and Systems Plan. With Young and Horwich, readers will wonder how well protected, how sustainable are Belize's "protected areas." Scholars, teachers, and students will relish the numerous Belize-specific sources in the reference section. The essay ends with sorely needed recommendations on how to strengthen and make sustainable the community co-management of protected areas.

The Belize Barrier Reef System is undoubtedly one of Belize's crown jewels. Melanie McField and Nadia Bood do it justice by providing some answers to the question "Our reef in peril—can we use it without abusing it?" As do the others, the authors begin with the historical context, which lays the foundation for what follows. McField and Bood supplement their description of the reef—its use and economic importance—with data on lobster and whole fish production. They highlight the threats to this critical part of the environment; they address the health and well-being of the reef, what is being done to preserve and protect it

15

within Belize and the region, and its sustainability. The conclusions of the essay elevate the reef to a heightened degree of significance that normally escapes most Belizeans.

Society

Any assessment of a country in transition would be incomplete without assessing the elements of social control, crime, and violence. Youth perpetrated criminal behaviour is of primary interest to all Belizeans, especially in urban communities. Michael Rosberg covers this topic not in the usual knee-jerk and quick fix fashion to which we are accustomed, but in a sociological manner complete with primary data and an analytical framework going back to Émile Durkheim, the founder of modern day sociology. Rosberg reminds us that although Belize was one of the first countries to ratify the Convention on the Rights of the Child, as a society we have not extended to all parents the support they need to provide for their youth and children. Addressing this larger problem is a prerequisite that needs serious attention. He gives concrete suggestions arising from his research and long term involvement with youth and adults in Belize, and he incorporates suggestions from a joint UNICEF and Community Rehabilitation Development study. Rosberg ends his essay by referring back to his title–the pot is Belize; its contents, security-seeking citizens who are "boiling;" and the rocks on the lid are increased repressive measures. Readers may disagree with his argument that these measures will fail to "quiet the Belizean pot," but all will agree that the debate is greatly needed.

The large scale outflow of Belizeans for economic improvement had been an endemic characteristic of colonialism. In his "Emigration from Belize since 1980," Jerome Straughan uses information from his recently completed doctoral dissertation to discuss emigration primarily to the United States, especially to Los Angeles, before independence, and three other periods–at independence, in the 1990s, and 2000 and beyond. In addition to providing statistics on the numbers of Belizeans who have emigrated, he describes the characteristics of these Belizeans as they have changed and adjusted to life in the "states." He analyses the changing factors promoting emigration and the overall impact of emigration on the homeland. As does the essay by Young and Horwich, Straughan's references provide excellent sources for students and scholars.

Culture

The field of cultural aesthetics is greatly diffused, especially in a multicultural society such as ours. Michael Stone amasses a great deal of information and forges them into an analytical framework in his essay "Cultural policy, local creativity, and the globalization of culture in Belize." Among others, his topics include culture; internationalization and globalization; cultural development in Belize; and Belizean music in the post-independence era. Together these topics describe the thorny issue of where Belize currently fits within the borderless world of cultural expression. Finally, Stone provides a comprehensive description of cultural policy considerations in Belize and makes recommendations on elements that should be integrated into cultural policy. It is critical that policy makers understand culture, which can serve to unify and divide societies, when designing and implementing cultural policies. This essay should help them in this all-important task and readers will delight when they read the names of favourites in the visual arts, dance, and music.

As a scientific discipline, a public administration system, and now a primary driver for tourism, archaeology in Belize has steadily matured during the past 25 years. Jaime Awe's essay, "Coming of age: Reflections of 25 years at archaeology" chronicles the expansion of the Department of Archaeology into the Institute of Archaeology. This expansion is reflected in the Institute's numerous foreign-funded projects, on-going research, contributions to print and visual media, organising and hosting international symposiums, and leadership in the burgeoning field of integrating archaeology with tourism.

Richard Wilk's surprising and informative "Independence, globalization, and rice and beans" integrates many of the issues addressed in the essays that precede it. Using of all things Belize's national dish rice and beans, Wilk unearths the changes to not only this staple, but to other material and immaterial elements of our culture. He traces the evolution of food dishes as a symbol of our efforts to carve out a unique socio-economic and cultural identity over time. Wilk crafts a wholistic perspective in which material and symbolic culture combine seamlessly and recommends that Belize take a serious look at the implications of the trade deficit through its food industry.

The authors "take stock." They let history, statistics, data, laws, and the effects of individual, corporate, and governmental actions tell the tale. We hope that readers will be inspired to continue the discussions and be propelled into action.

Barbara S. Balboni, Ph.D.
Joseph O. Palacio, Ph.D.

Part 1
Economy

1. Economic Development in Belize: Two Steps Forward, Two Steps Back

Robert B. Richardson

Introduction

The economy in Belize has its origins in the logging trade from the days of colonialism, and it has expanded over the decades through the cultivation, production, and exportation of sugar cane, citrus products, bananas, farmed shrimp, and several more specialized crops, as well as through the development of a successful nature-based tourism sector. Despite erratic growth that has taken an overall positive course, the accumulated wealth has not been realized throughout the country, as poverty and its afflictions restrain a significant portion of the population from the advances of a rapidly-changing world. The path of economic development in Belize has resembled the paths of the country's political, environmental, and social development; it could be characterized by notable advances as well as acute setbacks, sometimes with both occurring contemporaneously. Saddled with unsustainably high levels of public debt, reduced credibility, and a more competitive global trade environment, the government of Belize is in a highly-precarious position in its 25th year of independence. This essay begins with a brief overview of economic history in Belize and continues with an analysis of several indicators of economic development, followed by a discussion of the opportunities and challenges that the country faces as it looks to the next 25 years of its independence.

Economic history: from logging to bananas

Economic history in Belize since independence can be best understood in the context of its colonial past. Like much of the Central America and Caribbean regions, Belize was entangled in a colonial contest between European powers in the 16th, 17th, and 18th centuries, where islands and territories were played like pawns in a quest for land, slaves, and resources. In the early years of the 17th century, Spain effectively controlled the region, although British wood-cutters and former buccaneers had begun to settle near the coast of what is now known as Belize.

The British were interested primarily because of mahogany and logwood, and forest products dominated the economy for three centuries. British pirates raided Spanish ships for logwood beginning in the 17th century. Logwood (also *Campeche* wood, dye wood, and *palo de tinte*) was used as a coloring matter by the British woolen industry to produce a variety of shades (Shoman, 1994; Rocas, 2003). The British penchant for the prized logwood led to numerous struggles with the Spaniards for possession of forested land and the eventual settlement of what became Belize City. After numerous attacks on the British settlers, Spain eventually began permitting English logcutters to claim land and establish "logwood works" to cut logwood in 1763. The right to establish mahogany works was accorded in 1786; mahogany produces one of the finest known woods and rivaled logwood for importance and value for furniture and ship-building in Europe (Shoman, 1994; Rocas, 2003). Logcutters set up temporary camps along the coast and rivers, and the mouth of the Belize River became a trading port where "bark logs" were floated for export. The humble British settlement became known as "Belize in the Bay of Honduras," and later, "British Honduras."

The population of Belize increased ten-fold during the 19th century, due in great part to immigration to the northern and southern ends of the country. Agricultural production for export had been prohibited according to treaties between Spain and Britain, but with British sovereignty assured by mid-century, the cultivation of sugar cane fields proliferated. Sugar exports expanded rapidly, nearly tripling from 1865 to 1866 alone. However, the expansion was short-lived, and the industry suffered a steep decline prior to the end of the century (Shoman, 1994).

After more than a century of British occupation and conflict over the struggle for power and authority, Belize was officially made a Crown Colony in 1871. By century's end, the growing economic influence of the USA had surpassed that of Britain, due in part to its closer proximity for trade. The majority of exports were shipped to the USA by the early 20th century, the most significant of which was chicle for the production of chewing gum. In 1896, chicle exports reached one million pounds, a dramatic increase from less than 5,000 pounds a few years earlier; by 1912, shipments averaged three million pounds per year. Land settlement policies in the southern districts favored the development of a banana export industry, which attracted thousands of immigrants from other Central American countries seeking work (Shoman, 1994).

By 1950, forest products comprised about 85% of total export earnings, but the industry declined rapidly because of decades of excessive colonial exploitation. A decade later, the economy had shifted from forestry exports to agriculture; agricultural policies promoted large-scale production for export, which were based on preferential trade agreements with the developed economies to the north. Since 1959 exports of both sugar and citrus products have exceeded that of forest products (Shoman, 1994). The Commonwealth Sugar Agreement (1959) provided for an export quota for sugar to Europe (Barnett, 1999).

By 1961 political developments within the country eventually led to the agreement that Belize could attain independence from Britain at any time, but this process was delayed because of the territorial claim of Belize by Guatemala. In 1963 Belize was offered "full internal self-government," which did much to increase national pride and optimism (Shoman, 1994). After a lengthy process of international negotiations, involving Britain, the USA, Mexico, the United Nations, and CARICOM, Belize resisted pressure to cede land to Guatemala, and by 1980, independence for Belize seemed inevitable. Independence was formally granted on the 21st September 1981.

Beyond independence: from tourism to oil

Since independence, the economy of Belize has maintained its focus on exports, although like many developing nations in the tropics, after the forests were exploited, large-scale plantation-type agricultural production followed (Central Bank, 1999). The economy has followed a course of instability that is defined by a vulnerability to a narrow range of export products, dynamic global market forces, and a heavy reliance on imports for consumption. At the time of independence, sugar had returned to prominence, accounting for 63% of total exports, but rapidly plummeting market prices resulted in lower export earnings and a profound economic crisis (Shoman, 1994). The predominance of sugar and citrus exports suggests an extremely narrow and vulnerable economic base (Barnett, 1999); the Belizean economy has remained vulnerable since that time, due in part to rising import prices and declining prices for its export products.

The exportation of agricultural products remains an important component of the Belizean economy. Domestic exports declined from a peak of BZ$420 million in 2000 due in part to falling prices, but have partly recovered because of hefty increases in the production of citrus products, marine products, and bananas. The value of citrus products exports comprised more than one-fourth of total domestic exports in 2005. Exports of cane sugar and bananas have fluctuated in recent years, but their respective contributions to total exports have been remained between 12% and 17%. Marine products have historically played an important role in Belize's export base, but mushroomed to nearly 29% of exports in 2003 with additional investments in aquaculture, or the farmed production of seafood species such as shrimp and fish. Table 1 (see next page) presents historic data for major domestic exports from 2000 to 2005.

Table 1: Major domestic exports, 2000-2005
(millions of Belize dollars)

Export Product	2000	2001	2002	2003	2004	2005
Bananas						
Tonnes	63.73	50.14	41.83	73.02	79.43	76.08
Value	$65.82	$42.80	$33.50	$52.58	$52.99	$51.08
Price per unit	$1.03	$0.85	$0.80	$0.72	$0.67	$0.67
Garments						
Tonnes	1.7	1.38	1.42	1.44	1.77	1.57
Value	$39.58	$31.01	$30.44	$30.91	$37.10	$34.56
Price per unit	$23.28	$22.47	$21.44	$21.47	$20.96	$22.01
Grapefruit concentrate						
Millions of gallons	0.89	0.81	0.73	0.77	1.81	1.24
Value	$13.41	$15.70	$13.95	$12.52	$23.82	$19.31
Price per unit	$15.07	$19.38	$19.11	$16.26	$13.16	$15.57
Marine products						
Tonnes	3.18	4.07	3.33	7.74	8.34	9.25
Value	$70.44	$66.42	$70.36	$110.16	$107.33	$85.74
Price per unit	$22.15	$16.32	$21.13	$14.23	$12.87	$9.27
Orange concentrate						
Millions of gallons	5.45	4.9	3.62	4.92	6.45	8.4
Value	$95.25	$68.85	$53.49	$66.24	$55.49	$87.81
Price per unit	$17.48	$14.05	$14.78	$13.46	$8.60	$10.45
Papayas						
Tonnes	5.2	6.25	11.1	16.57	25.22	17.14
Value	$11.45	$10.26	$15.51	$16.75	$22.82	$26.87
Price per unit	$2.20	$1.64	$1.40	$1.01	$0.90	$1.57
Sugar						
Tonnes	109.33	95.51	104.94	100.15	113.93	79.47
Value	$74.39	$59.37	$65.98	$73.75	$81.53	$69.9
Price per unit	$0.68	$0.62	$0.63	$0.74	$0.72	$0.88
Other						
Value	$50.43	$31.03	$33.44	$21.73	$29.04	$39.2
TOTAL	$ 420.78	$ 325.45	$ 316.67	$ 381.41	$ 410.13	$ 413.27

Source: CSO, Belize, 2006.

Figure 1: Price per unit of citrus and marine products in Belize, 2000 - 2005

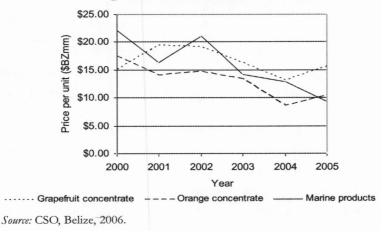

Grapefruit concentrate ·······   Orange concentrate – – – –   Marine products ————

Source: CSO, Belize, 2006.

Despite significant increases in production and exportation, particularly in citrus and shrimp production, the value of domestic exports in Belize has remained mostly flat because of declining market prices. From 2000 to 2005 exports of marine products have nearly tripled from 3.2 to 9.2 tonnes, but average market prices have fallen by nearly 60% over that period (see Figure 1); the decline is primarily driven by world shrimp prices that have fallen by more than half, while lobster and conch prices have risen. Prices of grapefruit and orange concentrate followed a similar downward trend, but in 2005 rebounded slightly. Papaya production is a relatively nascent industry in Belize, and production tripled between 2000 and 2005; prices (see Figure 2), however, have followed a

Figure 2: Price per unit of papaya, banana and sugar exports in Belize, 2000 - 2005

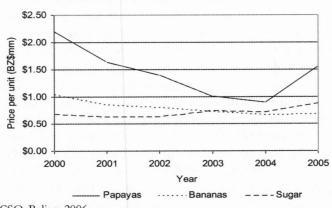

———— Papayas ······· Bananas – – – Sugar

Source: CSO, Belize, 2006.

Table 2: Arrivals of overnight tourists by nation of origin, 1998-2005

Nationality	1998	1999	2000	2001	2002	2003	2004	2005
USA	87,991	92,695	104,717	106,292	104,603	127,288	137,376	145,977
Europe	25,638	24,746	27,674	29,115	29,115	33,530	32,770	33,466
Canada	9,416	8,430	9,205	9,492	9,185	9,831	11,925	13,580
Belizeans living abroad	13,104	14,545	14,106	12,999	11,896	7,799	7,698	7,705
Guatemala	9,631	12,162	17,313	15,652	21,184	17,632	15,949	13,907
Mexico	8,877	8,258	8,688	7,739	8,413	6,312	6,851	5,893
Other	21,397	19,959	14,062	14,045	15,126	18,182	18,272	16,045
TOTAL	176,054	180,795	195,766	195,955	199,521	220,574	230,832	236,573
Annual Change		2.7%	8.3%	0.1%	1.8%	10.6%	4.7%	2.5%

Source: Belize Tourism Board.

downward trend similar to that of citrus products. Since 2000 banana prices have fallen by 35%. Prices of sugar exports have been less erratic due in part to preferential trade agreements that guarantee the industry above-market prices for its products.

Perhaps one of the most significant developments in the Belizean economy since independence has been the growth of the tourism sector, which originally had its roots in small-scale, adventure or nature-based recreation activities. Belize is particularly well endowed with tourism resources, including the longest barrier reef in the Western Hemisphere, numerous limestone caves, and tropical rainforests. The barrier reef was one of the earliest attractions, and the islands of Ambergris Caye and Caye Caulker have hosted visitors for snorkeling, underwater diving, and other water sports enthusiasts for decades. Significant resort and hotel development in the town of San Pedro has made it the country's largest tourist destination, and more recently, a destination for foreign retirees and migrant expatriates. Tourism has expanded rapidly in recent years in the Cayo District, particularly near the twin towns of San Ignacio and Santa Elena, where tropical rainforest walks, medicinal plant trails, Maya archaeological sites, and limestone cave tours entice adventure-seekers traveling between Guatemala and the Caribbean coast. National parks and protected areas such as the Blue Hole National Park and Cockscomb Basin Wildlife Sanctuary attract wildlife viewers and bird watchers hoping to spot elusive jaguars or keel-billed toucans.

Average annual growth in overnight visitors was more than 4% from 1999 to

Table 3: Economic impact of tourism in Belize, 1998-2005

	1998	1999	2000	2001	2002	2003	2004	2005
Tourist expenditures (BZ$ millions)	216.6	222.9	240.4	241.0	265.6	311.4	345.3	349.4
Tourist expenditures (% of GDP)	15.7	15.2	14.5	13.9	14.3	15.9	16.7	15.8
Tour operators	n.a.	51	129	130	171	200	204	209
Tour guides	n.a.	706	929	907	1,098	1,005	1,127	1,113

Source: Belize Tourism Board.

2005, although growth has slowed since a peak of 10.6% in 2003 (Belize Tourism Board, 2006). More than half of overnight tourists (61.7%) come from the USA (see Table 2), where nearly all international air passenger service to Belize originates. The second most important region of origin for tourists in Belize is Europe, which constitutes 14.1% of visitors. In the last decade the overall number and share of Mexican tourists have sharply declined.

Tourism is the single largest contributor to gross domestic product (GDP) and the largest source of foreign exchange earnings for Belize. In 2005, tourist expenditures reached nearly BZ$350 million, which equates to nearly 16% of GDP (see Table 3). The escalation in the numbers of tour operators and registered guides has outpaced the growth in arrivals, but given the continued increase in tourist spending, this may be because of changes in the type of tourist and the preferred recreation activities. The popularity of cave tours in the Cayo District has flourished, and because of the risks to personal safety and fragile artifacts, many of these sites require booked tours with certified tour operators.

The continued success of the industry is evidenced by hotel occupancy and revenue data (see Table 4, next page). Hotel capacity has increased with the growth in tourist arrivals, and hotel occupancy rates and revenues have increased generally during recent years. Hotel revenues dipped in 2002 despite increased tourist arrivals, but recovered in 2003. For the 1998-2005 period, growth in hotel revenues has considerably outpaced growth in tourist arrivals. Average hotel revenue per tourist visitor has risen significantly (nearly 75% since 1998), suggesting an increase in the proportion of high-end tourists and a willingness to pay higher prices for the amenities and activities offered in Belize. Average revenue per hotel has increased by nearly as much (72% since 1998), suggesting rising profits for property owners. These data depict a dynamic industry that has matured far beyond the image of budget backpacker destination with which Belize has long been associated.

Growth in the tourism sector escalated in recent years, primarily because of

Table 4: Hotel data for Belize, 1998-2005

Hotel Data	1998	1999	2000	2001	2002	2003	2004	2005
Hotels	408	390	391	418	437	466	506	557
Rooms	3,921	3,963	4,106	4,463	4,705	5,050	5,151	5,593
Beds	6,617	6,810	7,045	7,187	7,902	8,166	8,722	9,327
Occupancy (%)	29.9	31.4	41.7	44.8	40.1	41.3	40.7	40.6
Revenues (BZ$ millions)	$43.9	$49.5	$57.3	$66.7	$61.2	$78.9	$92.5	$103.2
Average revenue per visitor (BZ$)	$249.36	$273.79	$292.70	$340.38	$306.73	$357.70	$400.72	$436.23
Average revenue per hotel (BZ$000)	$107.6	$126.9	$146.5	$159.6	$140.0	$169.3	$182.8	$185.3
Employment	2,203	2,570	2,769	2,934	3,074	3,447	3,770	4,045

Source: Belize Tourism Board.

the upsurge in arrivals of cruise ship passengers, which increased more than six-fold in 2002 to nearly 320,000, and reached over 850,000 in 2004 (see Table 5). The expansion and promotion of cruise ship tourism has been controversial; although it has increased the country's visibility among international tourists, its economic impact has been lackluster. The average expenditure for cruise ship visitors is US$45.00, approximately 57% below the average level for the Caribbean region (Belize Tourism Policy, 2005). There is a general concern that the expansion of cruise ship tourism may threaten the early ecotourism niche that originally brought notoriety to Belize as a travel destination as well as the fragile coral reef ecosystem on which much of the country's tourism depends.

In the very year of the 25th anniversary of independence, all eyes are on the

Table 5: Tourist arrivals in Belize, 1998 – 2005

Visitor Category	1998	1999	2000	2001	2002	2003	2004	2005
Leisure	166,743	172,292	186,883	185,705	186,097	207,930	218,506	224,772
Business/official	9,311	8,503	8,883	10,250	13,424	12,644	12,326	11,801
Total, overnight	176,054	180,795	195,766	195,955	199,521	220,574	230,832	236,573
Cruise/port	14,183	34,182	58,201	48,164	319,890	575,511	851,842	800,701
Total visitors	190,237	214,925	253,897	244,071	519,211	795,770	1,082,268	1,036,904

Source: Belize Tourism Board.

oil wells in Spanish Lookout in northwest Cayo District. This recent twist on the development of the Belizean economy is set against the backdrop of soaring oil prices and great instability in the Middle East. Truckloads of sweet crude oil are being pumped from the rich tropical soil from wells in Spanish Lookout and are shipped off to the USA for refining. Previously, despite the granting of numerous licenses for petroleum exploration over several decades (Peedle, 1999), only dry wells were found. Petroleum deposits of commercial quantity had not been found until Belize Natural Energy, Ltd (BNE) began pumping oil in July, 2005. As of mid-year 2006, the Irish-backed investment group and its partner, CHx Limited Liability Company, were producing nearly 3,000 barrels a day in the region; although optimistic forecasts predict higher production levels, seismic tests suggest that oil deposits in Belize may be smaller than those of neighboring countries (Economic and Financial Update, 2006). The oil is of exceptional quality; while API gravity ratings average 15-25° for oil from surrounding countries, the sweet, light crude coming out of Belize is 40° (by comparison, refined diesel is just 42° API) (Leahy, 2006).

The agreement with BNE is a royalty-tax arrangement, which is viewed by oil companies as more attractive than a production sharing contract since it does not commit the contractor to a share of production in advance in order to recover costs (*Colombia Trade News*, 2006). There is much skepticism about the potential contribution of oil to the development of the economy. A string of corruption scandals have left the general public somewhat jaded about the likelihood of an equitable distribution of the wealth generated by the country's natural resources, especially oil (Romero, 2006). Much of the cynicism about the government's ability to manage the process has stemmed from its agreement to royalties of 7.5%, far below the world average for crude oil. The low royalty was designed to encourage speculation, but now is viewed by many as a giveaway. The realization seems to have resonated with the national government, which is currently embroiled in a revenue-sharing dispute with BNE; recent proposals to impose a 40% sales tax have been met with threats from BNE to pull out altogether.

In hopes to curry good favor amongst Belizeans, BNE had already pledged 1% of revenues to an environmental protection fund. Unfortunately, the recent addition of crude oil to Belize's export offerings has been accomplished with a similar level of legal and contractual instability and low returns that have been associated with other economic developments, such as privatization of public assets. Along with several other foreign-owned sectors of the economy, the petroleum example supports the notion of an ongoing trend that Belizeans are too frequently denied fair returns for their own resources. The economic impact of this development is yet to be realized. Meanwhile, a legal challenge by the Sarstoon-Temash Institute for Indigenous Management (SATIIM) has slowed down the efforts by Texas-based US Capital Energy, Ltd. to explore for petrole-

29

um deposits in the Toledo District, in Belize's second largest national park. The potential effects to the fragile ecosystems of the area as well as the land rights of the Maya and Garifuna people of the region have raised international concern (Global Response, 2006; SATIIM, 2006).

GDP growth before the turn of the century was impressive—the average GDP growth rate between 1997 and 2003 was 7.2% (Trade Policy Review, 2004). Domestic savings began a sharp decline while public debt mounted to record levels, which raised concerns among financial institutions and commercial creditors about the economy's vulnerability and resistance to shocks. Compelled by the IMF and USAID as early as the 1980s, the government embarked upon a structural adjustment program, which included the privatization of many public assets, trade liberalization, and the promotion of foreign investment. Unfortunately, some of the adjustment provisions had unintended consequences and have left the economy with great uncertainty in the country's 25th year of independence. By 2004, the government had completed its privatization program, which included the sale of the port authority, airport, printery, telecommunications, electricity, and water services sectors (Trade Policy Review, 2004). Privatization of public assets is intended to reduce the role of government promoting market competition, but the small size of Belize's population and the scale of the economy make competition somewhat infeasible. In effect, privatization has transferred control of public assets from government to a few investors (many of whom are foreign) whose objectives are to generate profits for shareholders rather than to protect public interests. The end result is that some of the most basic infrastructure needs have been traded to firms with significant monopoly power; the effects of monopolies are known to include price exploitation, inefficient production levels, and inferior quality of services due to a lack of incentive to innovate (Sharp, et al., 2004). Although privatization proceeds were significant (3.5% and 2.5% of GDP in fiscal years 2000-01 and 2002-03 alone) (IMF, 2005), their contributions to fiscal improvements were not apparent in 2006; they seem to have been diluted amid soaring public debt, an increasing trade imbalance, and mounting financial losses from negligence at the Social Security Board and the DFC.

Economic development

Development is defined generally as an increase in the well-being of residents—a worthwhile objective, but a difficult concept to quantify or measure (Yarbrough & Yarbrough, 2003). Economic development has been traditionally measured by growth in per-capita GDP or gross national product (GNP), both of which represent the market value of output or all of the goods and services produced within a given period of time. GDP is often criticized for its weak-

**Figure 3: GDP growth rates in Belize,
1991 - 2004 (CSO, 2005)**

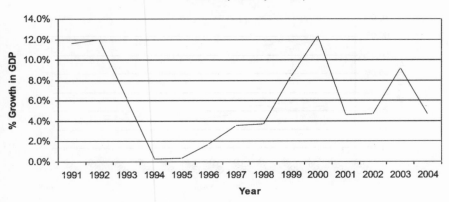

Source: CSO, Belize, 2005.

nesses as an indicator of development, in that it primarily measures total output, but ignores levels of informal economic activity, environmental damages, the distribution of income, and quality of life issues (e.g., crime, health, and mortality rates) (Yarbrough & Yarbrough, 2003). However, it has the advantage of being measured widely and frequently throughout the world, which facilitates the global monitoring and analysis of economic development within and between countries and regions.

GDP in Belize grew at an average rate of 5.9% between 1990 and 2004. The growth rate of GDP peaked near 12% in the early 1990s (due primarily to growth in the services sector, mostly tourism) and again at the turn of the century (due primarily to the expansion of aquaculture production in the fisheries sector, and continued growth in the manufacturing of food products and in the construction sector). Declining activity in the forestry and textiles sectors contributed to very low GDP growth in the mid-1990s. Figure 3 presents GDP growth rates for this period and illustrates the sporadic path of economic growth in Belize.

Figure 4 (see next page) illustrates the changes in the composition of GDP in Belize since independence. The contributions of both primary activities (e.g., agriculture, forestry, and fishing) and secondary activities (e.g., manufacturing, energy, and construction) have fallen from nearly 30% of GDP to roughly half that level in 25 years, while the contribution of tertiary activities (e.g., retail trade, hotels, restaurants, and business services) has increased from approximately 45% to over 60% of GDP. These trends reflect in part the declining importance of forestry and manufacturing, and the steady growth in retail trade and tourism.

The calculation of real GDP removes the effects of price changes by holding prices constant at some base year in order to highlight only the effects of

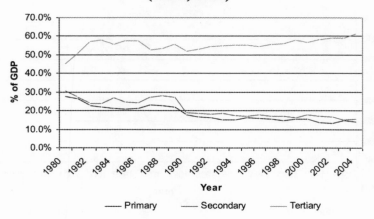

Figure 4: Contributions to GDP 1980 - 2004
(CSO, 2005)

Source: CSO, Belize, 2005.

changes in production. Real GDP is presented in Table 6 (see p. 33) for the period 1998-2004, based on prices in the year 2000. Of particular note is the rapid expansion of the fisheries sector—its contribution to GDP more than doubled in 2003, primarily because of investment in aquaculture. Tourism is considered to be the largest single contributor to GDP at approximately 18% (Belize Tourism Board, 2006), but given the unique characteristics of the sector, it is not identifiable as an industry from these data; rather, it is obscured across the trade and repairs, hotels and restaurants, and transport industries.

In 2004 per-capita GDP was BZ$7,329 (Central Bank, 2005), but this statistic should not be misconstrued as an indicator of household income, since national income is not distributed equally. As mentioned previously, this statistic fails to account for the distribution of income. Despite reasonably healthy economic growth rates since independence, significant portions of the Belizean populace live in poverty. The 2002 Poverty Assessment Report (PAR) was based in part on a Living Standards Measurement Survey of Belizean households conducted that year. Table 7 (see p. 34) presents some poverty statistics by district. The report reveals that more than one third (33.5%) of Belizeans have a standard of living that falls below the poverty line, and more than 10% are classified as indigent. The indigent line is defined as the minimum cost of food required for healthy existence; the poverty line incorporates non-food expenses such as housing and clothing. Poverty rates are highest for the Toledo (79.0%), Orange Walk (34.9%), and Stann Creek (34.8%) districts, and are higher for rural areas (44.2%) than for urban areas (23.7%). The poverty gap measures the disparity between poor households and the poverty line and is an estimate of the minimum cost of eliminating poverty; the national poverty gap is

Table 6: Real GDP (millions of Belize dollars, 2000 prices), 1998-2004

Industry	1998	1999	2000	2001	2002	2003	2004
Agriculture & forestry	165.1	172.6	181.6	178.0	183.9	212.4	237.6
Fishing	38.6	50.0	62.2	64.9	60.3	126.9	133.0
Mining & quarrying	6.8	7.3	9.0	9.3	8.8	8.8	9.3
Manufacturing	120.6	128.2	159.2	158.1	160.5	159.8	179.1
Electricity & water supply	47.7	51.6	58.5	58.6	60.2	65.3	64.3
Construction	51.1	59.6	82.8	83.9	87.0	71.5	74.7
Trade & repairs	222.5	241.5	270.5	290.2	301.8	306.1	305.0
Hotels & restaurants	47.2	52.9	58.5	6.4	68.0	77.9	90.0
Transport & communications	112.0	125.3	141.7	152.9	163.7	177.0	187.6
Financial & intermediation	68.3	79.7	103.7	103.8	131.1	172.5	178.8
Real estate & business services	91.7	101.1	98.2	110.9	121.7	123.1	129.4
Community, social and personal services	97.1	99.1	100.7	102.2	106.5	110.6	113.6
Government services	154.2	155.0	164.8	174.4	181.2	191.4	192.7
Taxes, subsidies, and adjustments	143.7	158.0	173.4	187.9	188.9	187.6	187.5
GDP at market prices	1,366.7	1,481.9	1,664.7	1,741.5	1,823.7	1,990.9	2,082.6

Source: CSO, Belize, 2005.

11.1%, but the estimate for the Toledo District (44.4%) is four times the national average (PAR, 2002). The Gini index measures the distribution of income across the population; index values vary between 0.0 (representing equal distribution, where income for every household is equal to per-capita income) and 1.0 (representing unequal distribution, where one individual receives all of the income) (Yarbrough & Yarbrough, 2003). District-level estimates of the Gini index indicate that income is distributed least equitably in the Belize District (PAR, 2002).

Belize is considered to be a developing country, but the great disparity among developing countries is obfuscated by this classification. The World

Table 7: Poverty statistics by district

District	Monthly Poverty Line	Poverty Percent of Population	Indigent Percent of Population	Poverty Gap (%)	Gini Index
Corozal	$192.32	26.1	6.2	7.0	0.4
Orange Walk	$178.82	34.9	7.1	9.3	0.2
Belize	$222.77	24.8	4.9	6.2	0.6
Cayo	$150.89	27.4	4.8	6.6	0.3
Stann Creek	$179.03	34.8	5.6	8.6	0.3
Toledo	$236.81	79.0	56.1	44.4	0.2
National average	n.a.	33.5	10.8	11.1	0.4

Source: Poverty Assessment Report, 2002.

Bank classifies countries into four groups, based on per-capita gross national income (GNI, expressed in US dollars) calculated using the Atlas method.[1] The country classifications are low income ($875 or less), lower-middle income ($876 - $3,465), upper-middle income ($3,466 - $10,725), and high income ($10,726 and higher) (World Bank, 2006). Per-capita GNI for Belize in 2004 was US$3,940, which places the country on the low end of the upper-middle income group.

The United Nations Development Programme (UNDP) publishes the Human Development Report, which calculates the Human Development Index (HDI) for nearly 200 countries. This composite index expands upon the measurement weaknesses in the per-capita GDP and GNI (or GNP) figures; it provides indicators of development by incorporating additional measures of well-being. The HDI is based on the model of three dimensions of human development: longevity, knowledge, and standard of living (UNDP, 2005). Longevity is measured by life expectancy at birth, which is intended to represent the extent to which a country's population lives long and healthy lives. Knowledge is measured by both the adult literacy rate and the combined gross enrollment ratio for primary, secondary, and tertiary schools. Standard of living is measured by per capita GDP, adjusted for purchasing power parity, or price differences among nations. The HDI is calculated for 177 countries, including 175 U.N. member

---

[1] Gross national income (GNI, formerly gross national product) is calculated by the World Bank using its Atlas conversion factor, which accounts for exchange rate fluctuations in comparisons of national incomes (World Bank, 2006).

Table 8: Human Development Index data
for Belize and peer nations, 2003

Human Development Indicators	Belize	Latin America & the Caribbean	All Developing Countries
Human Development Index (HDI)	0.753	0.797	0.694
Life expectancy at birth (years)	71.9	71.9	65.0
Adult literacy rate (% for ages 15 and above)	76.9	89.6	76.5
Combined gross school enrollment ratio (%)	77	81	63
GDP per capita (PPP US$)*	6,950	7,404	4,359

Source: UNDP, 2005. *Purchasing Power Parity

nations plus Hong Kong and the Palestinian Territory. HDI values may range between 0 and 1; higher indices represent higher levels of human development.

The 2003 HDI for Belize is 0.753, which places the country 91st out of 177 countries, and just below the world median of 0.755. The 2003 HDI represents a decline from the 2000 calculation of 0.776 (rank of 47 out of 117 countries). Belize ranks below the regional average for Latin American and Caribbean states (0.797) but well above the average for all developing countries (0.694). Belize's rank as low among its regional peers but high among all developing countries is consistent throughout all of the HDI dimensions, as illustrated in Table 8.

The HDI for Belize has been measured on five-year intervals since 1980, and an analysis of historical data yields some insight into the overall trend of human development. Although the HDI for Belize rose continually between 1980 and 2000, it fell in 2003, and its ranking among other countries has declined generally since 1980, as illustrated below in Table 9.

Table 9: Human Development Index for Belize,
trend analysis

HDI for Belize	1980	1985	1990	1995	2000	2003
Human Development Index	0.707	0.717	0.747	0.768	0.779	0.753
Rank	46	47	54	52	47	91
Total number of countries	113	121	136	145	117	177

Source: UNDP, 2005.

Table 10: Human development indicators for Belize, trend analysis

Human Development Indicators	1970 – 1975	2000-2005
Life expectancy at birth (years)	67.6	71.9
Infant mortality rate (per 1,000 live births)	56	33
Under five mortality rate (per 1,000 live births)	77	39
Total fertility rate (births per woman)	6.3	3.2

Source: UNDP, 2005.

Despite the recent slip in the HDI for Belize and its rank among countries, there has been considerable progress in specific development objectives, including increasing life expectancy and decreasing birth rates. As compared to the early 1970s, Belizeans are living longer, child mortality rates are lower, and fertility rates have dropped dramatically (see Table 10).

Economic development in Belize is constrained by high debt and decreases in aid, as illustrated below in Table 11. Official development assistance (primarily loans and grants) fell from 7.4% of GDP in 1990 to 1.2% in 2003, but still exceeds the average for peer nations in the Latin American and Caribbean region (0.8%). Net direct foreign investment decreased slightly to 4.0% of GDP, but still remains quite high relative to regional peers (2.1%). Of greater concern is national debt–debt service rose sharply from 4.9% of GDP in 1990 to 13.6% in 2003. Debt service remains much higher than debt service levels of regional peer nations (8.6% of GDP) and for all developing countries (4.7% of GDP), and in 2003 it reached nearly one-fourth the level of exports. High levels of debt severely restrict economic development, as debt service consumes greater portions of national income, leaving less for the provision of essential social services such as education and health care.

Table 11: Aid, investment, and debt, 1990 and 2003

Aid, Investment, and Debt Data	1990	2003
Official development assistance (as % of GDP)	7.4	1.2
Net direct foreign investment inflows (% of GDP)	4.2	4.0
Total debt service (% of GDP)	4.9	13.6
Total debt service (% of exports)	7.0	24.9

Source: UNDP, 2005.

Opportunities and threats in the next 25 years

As Belize marks its first quarter-century of independence, great uncertainty about economic development abounds. The elements of this uncertainty bring into question the very meaning of independence, although the nation is politically and administratively independent of its former colonial power, its present economic situation can be characterized by a kind of dependency that is not entirely different from colonialism. In 2006, public debt owed to foreign and commercial creditors hovers around US$1 billion–roughly the equivalent of annual GDP. With the USA as destination for over 50% of Belizean exports and the source for roughly 38% of imports (CSO, 2006), the economy is highly vulnerable to market shocks that may affect the value of the US dollar or trade with that country. The preferential trade agreements that have buoyed the country's export-based economy are beginning to erode because of globalization and international rules of trade, and the small scale of agricultural production in Belize is unlikely to be competitive under world market prices. The value of the Belizean dollar, pegged at a rate of 2:1 to the US dollar since 1976, has been increasingly difficult to maintain as international reserves are drained to service public debt; by year-end 2006, reserves are forecast to be only about BZ$86 million, enough to cover only one month's worth of imports (Economic and Financial Update, 2006).

While numerous challenges lie ahead, three significant concerns threaten the economic development of Belize as the nation looks toward its next 25 years. Trade liberalization, access to capital, and global environmental change pose significant risks to the financial and economic outlook for Belize. The approach in response to these risks will determine whether or not they are realized as opportunities or threats.

Trade liberalization

The development of exports throughout most of Belize's history has been based on preferential trade agreements for sugar, citrus products, and bananas, which guarantee above-market prices for export to various countries, including the USA, the UK, and the European Union (EU). Belize is ranked among the most vulnerable middle-income countries in terms of vulnerability to trade because of expected erosion of preferential market access (IMF, 2005). The EU's banana and sugar agreements with African-Caribbean-Pacific (ACP) countries (to which Belize belongs) were challenged with the World Trade Organization, and reductions of these agreements are expected to begin in 2006. Regional trade agreements such as the North American Free Trade Agreement (NAFTA) and the Central American Free Trade Agreement (CAFTA) have added pressures to the erosion of these special agreements. Because of economies of scale, it is highly unlikely that Belize could be competitive in many of its export markets if world market prices were to prevail. Belize's trade position is made even more precarious by its product concentration ratio (citrus, shrimp, and sugar comprise nearly 60% of exports) and its destination concentration ratio (exports to the USA, UK, and European Union comprise over 85% of exports), which leave the country highly vulnerable to market shocks (IMF, 2005). Smaller, burgeoning export sectors such as papayas may offset some of the losses from trade liberalization. Unlike many other export products, the value of papaya exports has escalated; growth in export revenues averaged more than 28% between 2001 and 2005 (CSO, 2006).

As a small, open economy, Belize faces many obstacles in the game of international trade. Its neighboring countries in Central America produce many of the same export products, but at a far lower cost. Without the security of the preferential trade agreements, Belize has few choices other than economic integration. As a former British colony, Belize is more closely aligned with the English-speaking island nations of the Caribbean Community (CARICOM), and has chosen to integrate with these partners rather than its Central American neighbors. Belize joined the membership of the Caribbean Community and Common Market on 1 May 1974 (Trade Policy Review, 2004). In 1989, CARICOM agreed to establish the Caribbean Single Market and Economy (CSME), which took effect 1 January 2006. The CSME allows for the free trade (without tariffs or duties) of goods and services and the free movement of capital and labor between CARICOM nations. In this way, it represents a higher level of economic integration than NAFTA or CAFTA, which only provides for free trade of goods and services. The CSME presents a potentially significant economic opportunity for Belize in terms of new export markets and sources of foreign investment. A potential threat lies with the fact that many CARICOM nations produce a similar palette of products (e.g., sugar, bananas), which may limit the potential for gains from integration. In 2005, exports to CARICOM nations amounted to just 11% of total exports; imports from CARICOM were only 2.3% of total imports (CSO, 2006). Furthermore, the CSME and bilateral and multilateral trade agreements are likely to reduce import tariff revenues, which have traditionally been an important source of revenue. Additional concerns surround the possible employment effects, since CARICOM nationals are permitted to pursue jobs in Belize under the CSME.

Given the threat of eroding preferential trade agreements for agricultural exports, opportunities for continued economic development in Belize lie mainly in the growth of the tourism sector and in niche markets such as organic produce. However, given its foundation in natural resources-based recreation activities, the tourism sector is extremely vulnerable to future climate change, and this vulnerability necessitates a strategy for diversification of tourism products. Green & Black's USA, Ltd., a unit of British-based Cadbury Schweppes, produces an organic chocolate bar under the Maya Gold label and buys all the organic cacao produced in the Toledo District, guaranteeing farmers a minimum price for their produce and supporting a range of social projects and agricultural extension programs (Purvis, 2006). Demand for organic chocolate products is increasing rapidly: industry revenue in the USA alone is presently about US$70 million and is growing at 40% annually (Olivari, 2006). Organic chocolate is made from cacao produced without herbicides and pesticides, and the market for these products helps to sustain environmental quality as well as the livelihood of some of Belize's poorest rural communities. Similar opportunities for development of new niche export markets exist with organic honey, garlic, and fruits, where global production cannot keep pace with growing demand. Worldwide demand for organic products is increasing at approximately 20% annually, outstripping growth in supply, which is about 10 to 15% (Austrade, 2006). The potential for export expansion is significant: consumers in Japan spend over US$3 billion annually for organic products; sales in the USA are about US$7 billion. The UK imports roughly 70% of its US$450 million organic product consumption; Taiwan, already an important economic partner to Belize, imports 100% of its organic products, and Canada imports 80% (Lohr, 2001).

Access to capital

In 2006, Belize faced an unprecedented economic and financial crisis that severely limited its access to capital for years into the future. Declining export prices, unsustainable debt levels, rising energy and fuel costs, and gross fiscal mismanagement have led to a declining confidence in government among citizens and international and commercial creditors. Despite moderate economic growth, the budget and current account deficits have remained at unsustainable levels, and the stock of public debt has swelled to about the size of annual GDP. Credit rating agencies downgraded Belize credit and foreign currency to the lowest ratings given. Standard & Poor's Rating Service lowered its ratings for Belize twice in 2006 because of doubts of the ability of government to service its debt obligations (S&P, 2006). The ratings report warns that the risk of default is "extremely high," which has brought into question the country's credibility for prudent fiscal management and severely limited prospects for access to capital.

Government policies to promote the housing sector through the DFC largely failed; loan defaults and questionable governance forced the government to assume more than BZ$400 million in loans, and this resulted in a tripling of public debt between 1999 and 2004 (IMF, 2005). The stock of public sector debt swelled to over US$1.05 billion in 2005, approximately 95% of GDP; the figure rose to approximately US$1.1 billion in 2006, which was roughly equivalent to 100% of GDP partly because of a slowdown of economic growth. More than half of public debt is owed to private sector creditors (Economic and Financial Update, 2006), which are frequently less flexible than bilateral and multilateral lenders. For Belize nearly one-third of current external receipts are consumed by debt service; this ratio, along with the ratio of debt to GDP, is the highest among Caribbean and Central American nations. The government's approach to the debt crisis has been to pursue frequent refinancing and restructuring measures, which have led to a rise in the costs of borrowing. The effective weighted-average interest rate on public debt in 2006 was 11.25% (Economic and Financial Update, 2006), and interest on public debt rose from its previously stable level of 2% of GDP in 2000 to 6.5% in fiscal year 2005-06 (Glenday & Shukla, 2006).

The fiscal and current account deficits have been strained further by costs of past hurricane damages and sharp increases in fuel and energy costs. The current account deficit has expanded from 3.8% of GDP in 1994 to an average of about 20% of GDP during the 2000-2005 period (Economic and Financial Update, 2006). Belize is highly vulnerable to oil price shocks; imports of fuels and lubricants represented about 10% of GDP in 2005 (CSO, 2006). Rising oil prices increased the cost of imports by about BZ$100 million in 2005 (Economic and Financial Update, 2006); given the political and economic instability in the Middle East, oil prices are expected to increase through 2006 and beyond.

Complicating financial matters is a long string of alleged corruption and political scandals that have tarnished the nation's international reputation. Like a cruel birthday gift to Belizeans, the 25th year of independence has been riddled with revelations of financial negligence at the DFC and the SSB, and a sense of powerlessness pervades the populace as millions of dollars seep through the cracks of a weak and neglectful financial regulatory system. Nonperforming loans at the DFC reached 47% in 2005 and its asset base continues to deteriorate, placing a heavy burden on the already stressed public sector. The SSB has been investigated repeatedly in recent years for its questionable investments and the misappropriation of assets of the Social Security Fund, and in 2005 a Senate Select Committee (2006) handed down a harsh review of its findings that included recommendations to terminate several SSB positions and enact legislative reform.

Corruption is defined as the misuse of entrusted power for private gain (Transparency International, 2006). It constitutes a major obstacle to democracy, it hinders the development of fair economic markets, and it distorts competition and the rule of law. Furthermore, it has been shown to undermine people's trust in government, institutions, and political leadership. The Corruption Perceptions Index (CPI) measures perceived levels of corruption for over 150 countries as determined by expert assessment and opinion surveys

Table 12: Corruption Perceptions Index for Belize, 2003-2005

CPI for Belize	2003	2004	2005
Corruption Perceptions Index Score	4.5	3.8	3.7
Corruption Perceptions Index Rank	46 out of 133	60 out of 145	62 out of 158

Source: Transparency International, 2006.

of business people and country analysts. The CPI ranges between a score of 10 (highly clean) to 0 (highly corrupt). The 2005 CPI score for Belize was 3.7 (rank of 62 out of 158 countries), a decline from the 2004 and 2003 scores (the only years the index has been calculated for Belize). CPI scores and rankings for Belize are presented in Table 12. While the measurement of corruption is somewhat subjective, implications of the declining index, coupled with other economic, financial, and governance problems, have diminished Belize's credibility among international interests.

In late 2005 the government began a contractionary economic program that aimed to increase revenues, reduce public expenditures, and bolster international reserves. The regressive general sales tax (GST) was introduced in July 2006, and places a 10% tax on most items, including food and clothing; in general such taxes most significantly impact the poor.

Global environmental change

Global environmental change has emerged as one of the most important international concerns since the dawn of the 21st century. The Intergovernmental Panel on Climate Change (IPCC) uses "climate change" as a general term associated with rising global temperatures, rising sea levels, and an increase in the frequency and intensity of extreme weather events such as tropical cyclones (2001). As a low-lying nation facing the Caribbean Sea, Belize is particularly vulnerable to tropical cyclones or hurricanes that form in the Atlantic Ocean. The hurricane seasons of 2000-2002 brought flooding and wind damage that severely affected the agriculture and tourism sectors, and reconstruction costs reached over BZ$50 million (IMF, 2005).

Belize is considered a small island developing state (SIDS) because of its low-lying coast, its coastal communities, and its open vulnerable economy (UNDESA, 2005; NAR, 2003). Small island states are considered "extremely vulnerable" to climate change and rising sea levels from an economic, social,

41

and physical perspective (IPCC, 1997). As a small, open economy, Belize depends on imports for many basic goods and relies heavily on tourism for foreign-exchange earnings to meet the demand for imported goods. Because of its small size, land resources are constrained. SIDS are often already at risk from other environmental hazards such as flooding, tropical storms, and deforestation; the effects of climate change are expected to exacerbate these risks and introduce new ones (Tompkins, 2005).

Coral reefs are particularly vulnerable to changes in sea surface temperatures. The IPCC (1997) notes that the reefs of the Caribbean Sea already live near their thresholds of temperature tolerance. Higher seawater temperatures impair reproductive functions and lead to increased mortality. The adaptive capacity of mangroves is expected to be reduced as well. Coral reefs and mangroves in some areas are already stressed by factors such as pollution and coastal development, and climate change is expected to exacerbate those stresses (IPCC, 1997). Coral mortality, or "bleaching," from climate change threatens the future of the tourism industry, which depends heavily on the barrier reef system as a tourist attraction.

A recent study by the UN Food and Agriculture Organization (FAO) predicts that developing countries will experience an 11% decrease in the amount of cultivable land and an associated decline in agricultural production because of climate change, and the most significant declines are anticipated for sub-tropical regions, including Central America (2005). The FAO also includes the spread and emergence of diseases in livestock and plant pests among the impacts of climate change. These findings have significant implications for the narrow range of agricultural products on which the Belizean economy depends.

Climate scientists warn that the main hurricane problem facing that country is the rapidly expanding concentration of population and wealth in vulnerable coastal regions (Emanuel, et al., 2006). Indeed, coastal populations in Belize have outpaced the national rate (IPCC, 1997). The risks of climate change pose an urgent need for leaders of government and industry to evaluate building practices, land use, insurance, and disaster relief policies that have served to exacerbate vulnerability to hurricanes. This problem implies serious threats for Belize, particularly the tourism sector, much of which is concentrated on a few offshore cayes and along the mainland coast. Rising sea levels and increased storm activity are expected to lead to increased erosion in coastal areas and possible loss of land area for many islands.

The problems of climate change cannot be ignored—their impacts are profound and ubiquitous. Economic diversification to adaptive crops and less vulnerable industries could partly shield against the anticipated costs of climate impacts. Construction of sea walls and the restoration of natural defenses such as mangroves have been suggested as viable physical adaptation measures.

Conclusion

The development of Belize's economy prior to and since its political independence from colonialism can be characterized by many successes, including higher national income, improved access to education, longer life expectancy, and the emergence of several new industries in response to market changes. The development of public infrastructure such as highways and telecommunications systems has facilitated gains to commerce, education, and economic opportunities. While there have been numerous obstacles in the path of development, most have been overcome either by resilience or innovation.

However, in the few years prior to the 25th anniversary of independence, a combination of political and economic disorder have saddled Belize with a range of unprecedented challenges that must be confronted with concerted and coordinated effort because of their interrelated nature. Unsustainably high stocks of public debt along with a deteriorating trade imbalance have placed enormous pressures on international reserves, which have already been depleted to minimal levels; declining export prices and rising energy costs merely intensify those pressures. None of these challenges can be resolved without consideration of the others.

Three particular challenges offer potential opportunities, but may threaten the country's economic security if they are not addressed comprehensively. First, trade liberalization and the certain erosion of the preferential agreements that have sustained the economy for decades will almost surely bring about changes in the composition of the economy, but opportunities such as the CSME may very well open new export markets and strengthen regional integration with CARICOM nations. Second, access to capital is essential for future development, and the scope of the public debt problems along with concerns of fiscal mismanagement have already degraded the country's financial credibility; a transparent restructuring of debt and a renewed commitment to good governance could potentially recover some of the lost integrity and restore some confidence in public officials. Finally, the dynamic issues related to global environmental change are worldwide in scope and, given Belize's size, mitigation of the effects of a changing climate is not a viable concern for the country. However, a comprehensive adaptation strategy could ease some of the more disastrous economic impacts, and the development of international carbon markets could present a new opportunity for strategic economic gain.

In conclusion, the 25th anniversary of independence is a cause for celebration on many fronts, but it is a time for serious reflection about the economic uncertainties that will likely determine the path of development in the coming 25 years.

References

AUSTRADE. (2006). Organics overview. Australian Trade Commission. Retrieved 13 November 2006 from http://www.austrade.gov.au.

BARNETT, CARLA. (1995). Looking beyond the year 2000: The implications of developments in Belize's economy in the 1980's and 1990's. *Belizean Studies 22(1)*, 3-14.

BELIZE TOURISM BOARD. (2006). Tourism statistics. Retrieved 4 August 2006, http://www.belizetourism.org/statistics.html.

BELIZE TOURISM POLICY. (2005). Belize Draft Tourism Policy. Prepared by Launchpad Consulting for the Belize Tourism Board, March 2005.

CENTRAL BANK OF BELIZE. (1999). *Understanding our economy*. Belmopan: Central Bank of Belize.

CENTRAL STATISTICAL OFFICE. (2006). Foreign trade statistics. Belmopan: Central Statistical Office.

CENTRAL STATISTICAL OFFICE. (2005). General indicators. Belmopan: Central Statistical Office.

COLOMBIA TRADE NEWS. (2006). Colombia's energy industry: Recent developments and new opportunities. Washington, DC: Embassy of Colombia. Retrieved 23 July 2006, http://www.coltrade.org/doingbusiness/energyindustry.asp.

ECONOMIC AND FINANCIAL UPDATE. (2006). Government of Belize, July 2006.

EMANUEL, KERRY. (2006). Position paper on tropical cyclones and climate change. Cambridge, MA, USA: Massachusetts Institute of Technology. Retrieved 27 July 2006 from http://wind.mit.edu/~emanuel.

FOOD AND AGRICULTURE ORGANIZATION. (2005). *Special event on impact of climate change, pests and diseases on food security and poverty reduction: Background document*. Report on the 31st session of the Committee on World Food Security, 23-26 May 2005, Rome.

GLENDAY, GRAHAM & SHUKLA, GANGADHAR P. (2006). *Belize: A review of public expenditures*. Prepared for the Inter-American Development Bank.

GLOBAL RESPONSE. (2006). Stop oil development in national park/Belize: Region: Central America. Campaign #2/06. Boulder, CO: Global Response. Retrieved 13 November 2006 from http://www.globalresponse.org.

HUMAN DEVELOPMENT REPORT. (2005). *International cooperation at a crossroads: Aid, trade and security in an unequal world*. New York: UNDP. Full report available at: http://hdr.undp.org.

INTERNATIONAL MONETARY FUND. (2005). Belize: Selected issues. *IMF Country Report* No. 05/353. Washington, DC: International Monetary Fund. (For items related to the IMF and Belize see: http://www.imf.org/external/country/BLZ/index.htm.)

INTERGOVERNMENTAL PANEL ON CLIMATE CHANGE. (2001). *Climate change 2001: Synthesis Report*. Geneva: Intergovernmental Panel on Climate Change.

INTERGOVERNMENTAL PANEL ON CLIMATE CHANGE. (1997). *The regional impacts of climate change: An assessment of vulnerability*. Cambridge, UK: Cambridge University Press.

LEAHY, ENDA. (2006). Has mind guru's teaching paid off in a giant oil strike? UK: *The Sunday Times*, April 9, 2006.

LOHR, LUANNE. (2001). Factors affecting international demand and trade in organic food products. *Changing Structure of Global Food Consumption and Trade*. WRS-01-1. Economic Research Service, U. S. Department of Agriculture.

NATIONAL ASSESSMENT REPORT. (2003). *National assessment report for the BPoA+10 Review*. Belmopan: Government of Belize.

OLIVARI, NICK. (2006). Organic chocolate taking a bite out of the US market. *Reuters*, 10 November, 2006. Retrieved 10 November 2006 from http://today.reuters.com.

PEEDLE, IAN. (1999). *Belize: A guide to the people, politics and culture*. New York: Interlink Books.

POVERTY ASSESSMENT REPORT. (2002). *2002 Poverty assessment report*. Belmopan: Government of Belize.

PURVIS, ANDREW. (2006, May 28). How a £1.50 chocolate bar saved a Mayan community from destruction. *Observer Guardian*. Retrieved 28 May 2006 from http://observer.guardian.co.uk.

ROCAS, ANIBAL NIEMBRO. (2003). Species descriptions. In J. A. Vozzo (Ed.). *Tropical Tree Seed Manual*. Washington, DC: USDA Forest Service.

ROMERO, SIMON. (February 21, 2006). Touched by oil and hope in Belize. *The New York Times*.

STANDARD & POOR'S. (2006). *Sovereign risk indicators*. New York: Standard & Poor's. Retrieved 7 August 2006, http://www.standardandpoors.com.

SARSTOON-TEMASH INSTITUTE FOR INDIGENOUS MANAGEMENT. (2006). Oil discussions heat up in Toledo. *SATIIM's Advocacy Update, 1(1)*, August 2006.

SENATE SELECT COMMITTEE. (2006). Report of the Senate Select Committee investigating the Social Security Board. Belize City: Government of Belize.

SHARP, ANSEL M., REGISTER, CHARLES A. & GRIMES, PAUL W. (2004). *Economics of social issues*, 16th edition. New York: McGraw-Hill/Irwin.

SHOMAN, ASSAD. (1994). *Thirteen chapters of a history of Belize*. Belize City, Belize: The Angelus Press, Ltd.

TOMPKINS, E. L., NICHOLSON-COLE S. A., HURLSTON, L., BOYD, E., BROOKS HODGE, G., CLARKE, J. GRAY, G., TROTZ, N. & VARLACK, L. (2005). *Surviving climate change in small islands: A guidebook*. Produced for the Tyndall Centre for Climate Research. Norwich, UK: University of East Anglia.

TRADE POLICY REVIEW. (2004). *Trade policy review–Belize*. Trade Policy Review Body, World Trade Organization. WT/TPR/G/134.

TRANSPARENCY INTERNATIONAL. (2006). *Corruption perceptions index*. Berlin: Transparency International. Retrieved 7 August 2006, http://www.transparency.org.

UN DEPARTMENT OF ECONOMIC AND SOCIAL AFFAIRS. (2005). *Small island developing states*. New York: United Nations Department of Economic and Social Affairs, Division of Sustainable Development. Retrieved 27 July 2006 from http://www.un.org/esa/sustdev/sids/sids.htm.

WORLD BANK. (2006). *World development indicators 2006*. Washington, DC: The World Bank.

YARBROUGH, BETH V. & YARBROUGH, ROBERT M. (2003). *The world economy: Trade and finance*, 6th edition. USA: Thomson South-Western.

2. Belize's Foreign Trade Performance Since Independence: Neo-Dependent Challenges and Opportunities*

Michael J. Pisani

Introduction

Political independence has not changed the structural economic dependence of Belize within the larger global economic community. This is clearly evident in Belize's trade relationships and trade performance, recently characterized by an International Monetary Fund (IMF) visitation team as "small," "open," "export-dependent," "vulnerable," and facing imminent "preference erosion" (IMF, 2005a; IMF, 2005b). Belize's economy is small compared to its neighbors–in 2005, Belize's economy was only a fraction of the size of Guatemala's at 4.0%, Honduras' at 13.7%, and Mexico's at 0.2%. Regionally, the size of the Belizean economy in 2005 was 11.7% of Jamaica's, but minuscule at 0.008% compared to its largest trading partner, the United States. Belize's economy is also very open as total trade (imports and exports) represents over 70% of total economic activity.

Export dependent refers more to the limited types and destination of products exported–sugar, bananas, citrus, and marine products, primarily to the US and Europe–than to the contribution that exports make to the overall economy (about 20%). Vulnerable suggests the undiversified nature of the economy (primary product production and tourism, both of which are very weather dependent), is subject to weather and commodity price shocks. Lastly, the commodity-laden export basket currently enters the global marketplace through a system of

* Special thanks go to Dr. Jana S. Pisani for critically reading and commenting on an earlier draft of this paper. Financial support for continuing field research in Belize was provided by the Faculty Research and Creative Endeavors Committee, the Department of Management, and the College of Business Administration at Central Michigan University.

preferential access which is set to expire (e.g., the ACP [African, Caribbean, and Pacific colonies]–EU Contonou Agreement ends January 1, 2008) or diminish in importance in the face of new trade relationships (e.g., the Central American/Dominican Republic-US Free Trade Agreement may displace Belizean exports to the US currently accessed through the US Caribbean Basin Initiative).

In spite of the IMF accounting of the economic challenges posed by the external sector, Belize is nonetheless a relative success story in Central America enjoying a moderately stable democracy (in a region known for civil strife) and a middling-level standard of living as measured by per capita income. In fact, Belize has a higher 2005 per capita income at purchasing power parity prices than El Salvador (44.7% higher), Guatemala (44.7% higher), Honduras (134.5% higher), Jamaica (54.6% higher), and Nicaragua (134.5% higher), and nearly the same as Panama (5.6% less), lagging behind only Mexico (32.0% less) and Costa Rica (38.3% less).[1] So the situation is not bleak, but the external sector concerns are genuine and worrisome. The free market ideology and one-size-fits-all recommendations of the IMF, however, do not allow for individual (and sovereign) solutions to national development. As a late entrant into the family of nations, Belize's economy and external sector are conditioned by the prevailing conditions of the global economy. Its development path should be cognizant of and structured to overcome these global structural barriers.

This chapter seeks to put into perspective the historical trajectory and context of Belize's trade performance since independence. Special consideration is given to the macro-level trade performance, product-level trade performance, and historical trade linkages. The chapter ends with a summary and recommendations for non-dependent trade insertion and growth for Belize.

Historical trajectory and context: globalization and dependency theory and frameworks[2]

The "trappings" of globalization are evident throughout Belize: satellite television and Internet; intense consumerism through imports; and the international movement of people, such as Belizean emigration and tourism in Belize itself (Sutherland, 1998). The economic history of Belize has been shaped by its colonial past as a peripheral state in a core imperial British Commonwealth (Bolland, 2003; Shoman, 1994). This colonial past has been described by Moberg

---

[1] Belize's per capita income is 16.3% of the United States'.
[2] The section is derived from the author's, "Neo-Dependent commercial exterior relations? An analysis of the Belizean export basket since Independence," *Journal of Belizean Studies*, 2006.

(2003) as being controlled by "a close-knit oligarchy of timber companies and expatriate merchants [who] ruled the territory as a virtual fiefdom, often in defiance of the Colonial Office in London" (p. 145).

For example, Moberg's (2003) study of United Fruit, the infamous US banana conglomerate that dominated markets and sovereign nations in the Western Hemisphere, and the introduction of mass banana production in British Honduras in the late 1800s and early 1900s, provides perceptive insights into the colonial extractive agricultural legacy of contemporary Belize. Moberg (2003) systematically describes United Fruit's ascension to dominate the banana trade and the colony's banana and general export markets. Through market penetration pricing, United Fruit secured its monopoly position in the colony. At its peak before 1920, United Fruit sourced three percent of its bananas from British Honduras while banana exports accounted for more than 70% of colonial export earnings (Moberg, 20003). The power asymmetry was not lost on either party. Once a free market monopoly was established, United Fruit sought and received government favors–the alternative for British Honduras was economic blackmail. That is, if government favors were not granted to United Fruit, then United Fruit would threaten an immediate pull out of the colonial economy potentially triggering widespread economic crisis. This strategy gained United Fruit monopoly power not only in banana exports, but also in steamer transportation, mail delivery, and control of the colony's twenty-five mile railroad, built at colonial expense to serve the banana producing enclave in Stann Creek. According to Moberg (2003), United Fruit's treatment of British Honduras was on par with its treatment of Honduras and Guatemala–a dubious distinction indeed. As quickly as United Fruit appeared in British Honduras, it left when Panama disease destroyed the banana producing region of Stann Creek shortly after World War I. British Honduras was certainly worse off for the experience with United Fruit than if United Fruit had never come to the colony. Moberg (2003) concludes: "In their pursuit of alternative export markets, however, administrators subjected the colony to a costly and humiliating dependence on the corporation that dominated those markets" (p. 146). He also suggests, "The common dependence of Central American nations on North American capital during this period highlights the limited sovereignty of states whose economic power is dwarfed by the corporation that exports their primary products" (Moberg, 2003, p. 147).

Contemporary research on globalization in conjunction with dependency analysis like that of Moberg (2003) provides many insights into the economic condition of Belize.

Globalization

The most parsimonious definition of globalization is offered by Wolf (2004) as "the integration of economic activities, across borders, through markets" (p. 14).[3] Ohmae (2005) takes his definition of globalization beyond the confines of the nation-state, stating "globalization is nothing but liberalization of the individual, consumers, corporations and regions from the legacy of the nation-state in which they belong" (p. 122). The economic philosophical foundation for the literature on globalization is David Ricardo's (1817) seminal text on comparative advantage. Briefly, comparative advantage is the specialization in the production of goods in which a nation is most efficient. With specialization, nations engage in international trade to acquire goods that they do not produce efficiently (relative to other nations) in exchange for the goods that they have previously specialized in producing. For David Ricardo, this was simply an extension of Adam Smith's free market ideology (or invisible hand) from domestic interests to international interests. Scholars today separate the process of globalization from the ideology that has been labeled globalism (see for example Steger, 2002 and Veseth, 2005).

The most popular writer today on globalization is *New York Times* foreign affairs columnist Thomas Friedman (2000, 2005). Friedman (2005) finds a world that is becoming "flatter" all the time, that is "the global competitive playing field [is] being leveled" and "flattened" (p. 8). Friedman's (2005) message for the developed world embodied in a chapter concerning the United States argues that "America as a whole will benefit more by sticking to the basic principles of free trade, as it always has, than by trying to erect walls" (p. 27). Definitely David Ricardo redux. Directing his comments at the developing world, Friedman (2005) urges:

> that more open and competitive markets are the only sustainable vehicle for growing a nation out of poverty, because they are the only guarantee that new ideas, technologies, and best practices are easily flowing into your economy and that private enterprises, and even governments, have the competitive incentive and flexibility to adopt those new ideas and turn them into jobs and products. (pp. 314-315)

Friedman (2005) suggests that for developing countries to increase their standard of living they need to implement a two-stage reform package: stage 1 opens the economy to free market forces, export-led growth, privatization, and labor reforms; stage 2 deepens the process to include upgrades in infrastructure, education, regulatory institutions and culture (i.e., making friends and partners abroad).

---

[3] The focus of this paper is mostly economic relations; a more inclusive definition of globalization is "an unprecedented compression of time and space reflected in the tremendous intensification of social, political, economic, and cultural interconnections and interdependencies on a global scale" (Steger, 2002, p. ix).

Dependency analysis

Formulated in the neo-Marxist tradition, dependency theorists suggest a causal link between the nature and structure of the global economic system and persistent underdevelopment in Latin America. Dos Santos (1970) defines dependence as "a situation in which the economy of certain countries is conditioned by the development and expansion of another economy to which the former is subjected" (p. 231). Furthermore, a transfer of wealth occurs from the dependent (peripheral) nations to the wealthy (or developed core) nations through a systematic and structural process of unequal trade relations and restraint of peripheral internal markets.

Dos Santos (1970) cites three historic forms of dependence: 1) colonial dependence or mercantilism that is trade export focused; 2) financial-industrial dependence or neo-mercantilism that is still outwardly focused through the domination of "big" capital in dependent nations focused on exports (e.g., foreign-oriented development); and 3) technological-industrial dependence created and sustained by multinational corporations' (MNCs) penetration of the internal markets of dependent nations. Dos Santos (1970) argues that within the first two forms of dependence, the global economic system geared the economies of the periphery towards exports. In doing so, the argument continues, this circumscribed the development of the internal economies of the periphery nations.

Dos Santos (1970) suggests further that the final form of dependence propagated by MNCs relies on the acquisition of foreign (globally-traded) currency to buy inputs for industrial development and puts pressure on the nations' balance of payments and MNCs themselves as they hold a technological monopoly in the marketplace. The need to buy inputs (intermediate goods) requires the preservation of the traditional export sector to earn foreign currency; this focus on traditional exports curtails the development of dynamic internal markets as capital flows to maintain the traditional export industries. According to Dos Santos, these traditional export industries tend to be commodity-based in which the value of production over time declines, in essence requiring more exports just to maintain a constant level of earnings.[4] This need for foreign inputs and the nature of commodity-based exports necessitates foreign financing (borrowing) to cover the needs created by the global economic system, hence the creation of a spiral of borrowing to maintain the system that itself is not maintainable. And this is before the repatriation of profits from MNCs as well as economic rents extracted from their technological monopoly.

---

[4] This condition is also known as a declining terms of trade.

Table 1: Belizean exports by value (BZ$1000s)

| | Total Exports | | | Total Exports | |
Year	Exports	% Change	Year	Exports	% Change
1970	31,334	—	1988	232,504	13.0%
1971	31,687	1.1%	1989	249,096	7.1%
1972	40,887	29.0%	1990	258,098	3.6%
1973	52,686	28.9%	1991	239,274	-7.3%
1974	76,862	45.9%	1992	282,239	18.0%
1975	120,397	56.6%	1993	263,131	-6.8%
1976	94,041	-21.9%	1994	302,083	14.8%
1977	124,164	32.0%	1995	323,361	7.0%
1978	159,565	28.5%	1996	335,000	3.6%
1979	173,462	8.7%	1997	352,699	5.3%
1980	221,295	27.6%	1998	342,067	-3.0%
1981	238,014	7.6%	1999	372,110	8.8%
1982	183,839	-22.8%	2000	426,415	14.6%
1983	155,559	-15.4%	2001	338,812	-20.5%
1984	186,390	19.8%	2002	340,941	0.6%
1985	180,258	-3.3%	2003	409,175	20.0%
1986	185,250	2.8%	2004	424,587	3.8%
1987	205,665	11.0%	2005	413,270	-2.7%

Source: CSO, Belize.

Globalization and dependency–a synthesis

Globalization and dependency are not new to former colonial states. Together, globalization and dependency provide an excellent context for Belize's insertion into the global economy. At harmony with globalization are Belize's offshore banking regulations, legislation to attract First World retirees, and Belize's world class tourism industry most recently augmented by the arrival of mass cruise ship tourism. On the other hand, most of Belize's hard (globally accepted) currency earnings, needed to pay back a burgeoning national debt and trade deficit, come from traditional extractive commodities such as sugar, bananas, citrus (orange and grapefruit) juice concentrate and marine products, or

Figure 1: Belizean exports by value (BZ$1000s)

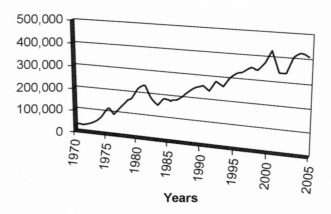

tourism, which is primarily in the hands of foreigners–a recipe for dependency. And for nations with a high-risk profile and debt service needs like Belize, oftentimes the IMF is the international lender of last resort. The IMF will assist and in return the IMF seeks to set the economic agenda for the economy. As Belizeans know all too well, Belize has had many "painful" dealings with the IMF as well as other international lenders. One hopeful remedy to dependency has been Belize's participation in the Caribbean Community; however, this regional trade body is of little significance at the present time. Next we turn specifically to Belize's trade performance since independence.

Macro-level trade performance

This section provides an historical and macro-level overview of Belizean imports and exports, balance of trade, and trade as a component of the overall economy.

Macro-level overview of exports

From 1970 to 2005, average annual growth of Belizean exports was 9.0%. Yet, nearly all of this relatively high growth occurred before independence and has declined each decade thereafter. Export growth rates per decade are as follows: 1971-1979, 3.2%; 1980-1989, 4.7%; 1990-1999, 4.4%; and 2000-2005, 2.6% (see Table 1, the next page). The average increase in exports since independence (1981-2006) has been 3.4%. By value, exports have increased from BZ$31.3 million in 1970 to over BZ$413.3 million in 2005 (see Figure 1).

Table 2: Belizean imports by value (BZ$1000s)

| Year | Gross Imports | | Year | Gross Imports | |
	Imports	% Change		Imports	% Change
1970	55,611	—	1988	361,948	26.6%
1971	58,590	5.4%	1989	431,390	19.2%
1972	69,257	18.2%	1990	422,498	-2.1%
1973	72,323	4.4%	1991	501,501	18.7%
1974	109,182	51.0%	1992	545,392	8.8%
1975	159,227	45.8%	1993	561,621	3.0%
1976	161,510	1.4%	1994	516,190	-8.1%
1977	180,151	11.5%	1995	517,027	0.2%
1978	212,991	18.2%	1996	511,114	-1.1%
1979	263,675	23.8%	1997	580,016	13.5%
1980	299,509	13.6%	1998	595,067	2.6%
1981	323,934	8.2%	1999	746,561	25.5%
1982	256,000	-21.0%	2000	1,029,670	37.9%
1983	223,582	-12.7%	2001	1,021,927	-0.8%
1984	260,373	16.5%	2002	1,049,034	2.7%
1985	256,333	-1.6%	2003	1,104,174	5.3%
1986	243,925	-4.8%	2004	1,028,215	-6.9%
1987	285,885	17.2%	2005	1,185,830	15.3%

Source: CSO, Belize.

Macro-level overview of imports

Imports have grown at a faster annual rate of 10.2% than exports over the period 1970-2005 (see Table 2). Similar to exports, the greatest decade of growth for imports occurred before independence (20.0%). However, after an impressive rise in the decade before independence and drop off in the 1980s and 1990s, import growth has inched upward toward the average rate in the new millennium, with the following period increases: 1971-1979, 20.0%; 1980-1989, 6.1%; 1990-1999, 6.1%; and 2000-2005, 8.9%. By value, imports have increased from BZ$55.6 million in 1970 to over BZ$1.2 billion in 2005 (see Figure 2, next page).

Figure 2: Belizean imports by value (BZ$1000s)

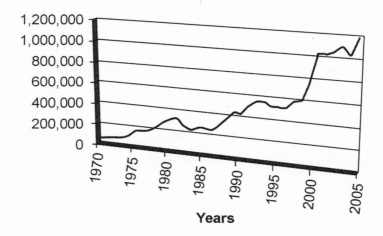

Years

Balance of trade

The balance of trade (BOT) measures the value difference between exports and imports. The balance of trade is an integral component of the balance of payments. The balance of payments (BOP) is a double entry accounting mechanism that tracks legal international business transactions within an economy.

By definition, the BOP must be in balance—neither deficit, nor surplus—at period's end. The BOP is comprised of four major accounts: the current account (or balance of trade going in and out of the country); the capital account (or balance of money going in and out of the country); the reserve account (the nation's on-hand foreign currency savings); and the errors and omissions account (an accounting mechanism to force the balance of small discrepancies). The balance of trade for Belize has been negative for every year since 1970 (the first year of the present study, see Table 3, next page) and has been growing rapidly.

When a country runs a persistent negative balance in its trade (exports minus imports), the BOT is said to be characterized by a structural (i.e., persistent) trade deficit. Since Belize runs a large structural trade deficit (see Figure 3, on page 56), Belize must maintain a surplus in one or more of the remaining BOP accounts. Though Belize typically experiences more inflows than outflows of money, it is not enough to cover the trade deficit. Hence, the nation must borrow from abroad to maintain its current level of imports as the country's reserve account is inadequate to cover the trade deficit after capital inflows.

Table 3: Belizean balance of trade (exports-imports) by value (BZ$1000s)

Year	Balance of Trade	Year	Balance of Trade
1970	-24,277	1988	-129,444
1971	-26,903	1989	-182,294
1972	-28,370	1990	-164,400
1973	-19,637	1991	-262,227
1974	-32,320	1992	-263,153
1975	-38,830	1993	-298,490
1976	-67,469	1994	-214,107
1977	-55,987	1995	-193,666
1978	-53,426	1996	·-176,114
1979	-90,213	1997	-227,317
1980	-78,214	1998	-253,000
1981	-85,920	1999	-374,451
1982	-72,161	2000	-603,255
1983	-68,023	2001	-683,115
1984	-73,983 .	2002	-708,093
1985	-76,075	2003	-694,999
1986	-58,675	2004	-603,628
1987	-80,220	2005	-772,560

Source: Author's calculation from CSO data.

Trade and the overall economy

Belize's economy is an open one, where total trade has averaged 70.9% of gross domestic product from 1980-2005 with a period high of 87.5% in 2000 (see Table 4, on page 57). Since independence, the trend in total trade as a percentage of GDP has increased by decade, with the 2000s exhibiting a sharp increase in economic openness to the rest of the world (see Figure 4, on page 58). This increase in total trade openness is a result of rapidly increasing imports which make up 56.4% of GDP in the present era (and average 45.7% from 1980-2005). On the other hand, exports have continued to decline in overall importance as they contribute to gross domestic product, comprising about

Figure 3: Belizean trade deficit (BZ$1000s)

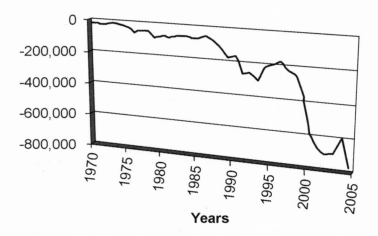

one-fifth of GDP in the 2000s. As a result of surging imports and declining exports measured by relative share value, the trade deficit has widened significantly to over one-third (35.7%) of GDP since 2000. The historical average (1980-2005) of 20.5% for the trade deficit is misleading in this case as the present trend clearly indicates a very large and growing structural trade deficit.

Product-level trade performance

Moving from the macro-level environment of trade flows to micro-level product groups, this section examines the products which make up the export and import baskets.

Export basket by product group[5]

Primary products best characterize the nature of the Belizean export basket. Since 1980, four export products–sugar, bananas, citrus concentrate, and marine products–have made up between 66.9% and 82.3% of domestic export revenue (see Table 5, on page 59). The average of these four products over this 26 year time span is 75.2% of total exports. Individually, citrus has consistently made up about 20% of exports with sugar steadily declining in relative export

---

[5] The section is derived from the author's, Neo-Dependent commercial exterior relations? An analysis of the Belizean export basket since Independence, *Journal of Belizean Studies*, 2006.

Table 4: Belizean trade as a percent of Gross Domestic Product (GDP)

Year	Imports as a % of GDP	Exports as a % of GDP	Trade Deficit as a % of GDP	Total Trade as a % of GDP
1980	45.5%	33.6%	11.9%	79.1%
1981	48.2%	35.4%	12.8%	83.7%
1982	38.3%	27.5%	10.8%	65.9%
1983	34.0%	23.7%	10.4%	57.7%
1984	38.9%	27.9%	11.1%	66.8%
1985	38.2%	26.8%	11.3%	65.0%
1986	35.3%	26.8%	8.5%	62.0%
1987	37.0%	26.6%	10.4%	63.6%
1988	44.0%	28.3%	15.7%	72.3%
1989	46.3%	26.7%	19.6%	73.1%
Average (1980-1989)	*40.6%*	*28.3%*	*12.3%*	*68.9%*
1990	41.2%	25.2%	16.0%	66.4%
1991	47.4%	22.6%	24.8%	70.0%
1992	47.0%	24.3%	22.7%	71.3%
1993	45.5%	21.3%	24.2%	66.9%
1994	41.8%	24.5%	17.3%	66.2%
1995	41.6%	26.0%	15.6%	67.6%
1996	40.5%	26.6%	14.0%	67.1%
1997	44.4%	27.0%	17.4%	71.4%
1998	43.9%	25.2%	18.7%	69.2%
1999	50.7%	25.3%	25.4%	75.9%
Average (1990-1999)	*44.4%*	*24.8%*	*19.6%*	*69.2%*
2000	61.9%	25.6%	36.2%	87.5%
2001	58.7%	19.5%	39.2%	78.1%
2002	57.5%	18.7%	38.8%	76.2%
2003	55.5%	20.6%	34.9%	76.0%
2004	49.4%	20.4%	29.0%	69.8%
2005	55.2%	19.2%	36.0%	74.5%
Average (2000-2005)	*56.4%*	*20.7%*	*35.7%*	*77.0%*
Average (1980-2005)	*45.7%*	*25.2%*	*20.5%*	*70.9%*

Source: Author's calculation from CSO data.

Figure 4: Belizean trade as a percentage of Gross Domestic Product

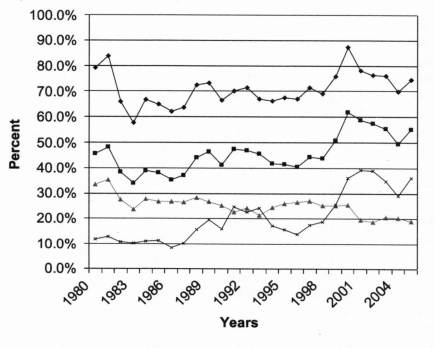

- ← Total Trade as a % of GDP —▲— Exports as a % of GDP
- —■— Imports as a % of GDP   —✕— Trade Deficit as a % of GDP

share and importance from nearly two-thirds of exports to just under one-fifth of all exports most recently (and 34.6% over the period, 1980-2005). Molasses and sawn wood are very small contributors to exports with neither product making up more than 4.2% of the value of exports in any given year, with recent performance of the two products together generating about one to two percent of export revenues. Bananas did not reach ten percent of export revenues until 1993, but have since averaged about that amount (10.5%) over the study period (1980-2005). Since 1993, bananas have on average contributed about 15% of export earnings with a high of 18.7% in 1996. As with sugar, marine products have seen the most drastic change in export share, in this case a positive one, since 1980. Marine products make up over one-fifth of export revenues today, up from five percent in 1980. The two major marine exports

Table 5: Domestic exports by product value (BZ$1000s), 1980-2005

Year	Sugar	Molasses	Bananas	Citrus Con.	Marine Products	Garments	Sawn Wood	Other	Total Exports*
1980	95,403	4,377	6,987	12,738	8,421	28,342	2,335	5,117	163,720
1981	85,227	2,419	4,311	13,004	14,405	22,128	2,394	5,584	149,472
1982	66,673	1,790	4,265	13,964	13,330	13,639	3,697	5,059	122,417
1983	70,927	1,213	4,818	12,600	15,045	16,771	2,706	6,306	130,386
1984	65,072	2,280	6,286	19,546	13,417	31,240	1,985	5,892	145,718
1985	45,857	1,725	6,605	24,240	15,002	31,050	993	3,378	128,850
1986	62,908	986	9,199	22,221	14,780	32,439	491	5,924	148,948
1987	62,622	1,069	14,312	32,008	16,856	31,238	4,228	11,510	173,843
1988	70,028	955	17,233	34,582	16,158	37,271	5,447	8,668	190,342
1989	68,128	1,258	18,071	38,936	13,344	34,673	4,659	8,900	187,969
1990	85,528	6,535	19,738	44,346	10,354	28,642	3,778	10,175	209,096
1991	83,319	7,481	14,674	17,923	11,650	35,077	5,855	14,667	190,646
1992	75,208	4,542	20,497	54,763	22,431	33,568	4,821	16,727	232,557
1993	82,912	9,623	24,178	27,800	26,029	40,634	4,242	13,215	228,633
1994	80,621	10,428	45,919	33,565	26,405	36,505	7,631	13,937	255,011
1995	95,503	5,609	44,074	58,291	31,142	29,106	3,930	18,186	285,841
1996	94,292	11,025	57,401	58,889	24,338	35,649	2,726	22,535	306,855
1997	91,890	6,638	52,215	48,116	35,033	37,005	5,236	41,742	317,875
1998	89,026	2,233	49,376	43,082	43,514	39,359	5,327	38,542	310,459
1999	86,616	436	56,834	54,886	55,566	39,259	4,168	41,470	339,235
2000	74,232	268	65,815	94,474	67,603	39,808	4,722	53,037	399,959
2001	59,370	1,649	42,805	88,554	63,712	30,367	2,314	33,746	322,517
2002	65,981	2,678	33,547	81,737	69,821	30,586	2,590	29,730	316,670
2003	71,177	2,466	52,580	79,873	110,224	30,869	3,563	30,625	381,377
2004	79,682	1,766	52,991	83,078	107,370	37,103	2,981	43,306	408,277
2005	69,900	n/a	51,080	107,120	85,740	34,560	n/a	34,870	413,270

Source: CSO, Belize.
*These total export figures may differ from those presented earlier in the paper as CSO does not include re-export values when reporting exports by product class.

Figure 5: Export share by value of primary Belizean exports (1980-2005)

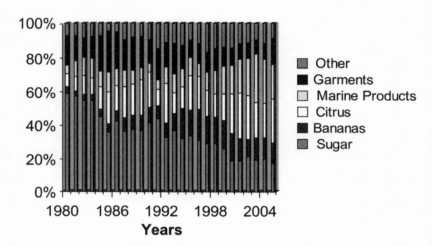

are white farm shrimp and lobster. The only non-agricultural export contributor of any significance is garment production, which has averaged about 15% from 1980-2005, with a high of 24.1% in 1985 and a low of 8.1% in 2003. The trend, however, shows garment export revenue quickly fading as a share of total exports and in line with the expiration of the World Trade Organization's multi-fiber agreement that governed global textile trade until the end of 2004 (see Figure 5).[6]

Import basket by product group

Imports are grouped by the Standard International Trade Classification (SITC) system which has ten major categories: food and live animals (0),[7] beverages and tobacco (1), crude materials, inedible, except fuels (2), mineral fuels, lubricants and related materials (3), animal and vegetable oils, fats and waxes (4), chemicals and related products (5), manufactured goods (6), machinery and transport equipment (7), miscellaneous manufactured articles (8), and commodities (9). The Central Statistical Office (CSO) in Belize generally follows these same headings, with data available in aggregate form since 1990,[8] and as of

---

[6] Asia, especially China as a producer and exporter, has benefited the most from the termination of the multi-fiber agreement.

[7] These numbers in parentheses represent the SITC general classification code.

[8] Additionally, narrower SITC data incorporating years before 1990 are available from the United Nations comtrade database.

Table 6: Domestic imports for Belize by classification & product value (BZ$1000s), 1990-2005

Classification	1990	1991	1992	1993	1994	1995	1996	1997
Food & Live Animals	87,106	92,753	97,952	82,123	76,363	80,392	86,009	90,423
Beverages & Tobacco	11,007	12,923	12,954	13,846	15,377	14,391	13,887	18,409
Crude Materials	2,406	3,316	8,401	5,504	4,711	3,439	2,359	2,728
Minerals Fuels & Lubricants	54,410	76,857	65,049	62,382	58,651	59,306	58,045	73,746
Oils & Fats	871	1,124	3,814	3,017	3,213	3,457	3,896	3,863
Chemical Products	40,575	44,058	50,390	64,178	55,780	55,473	58,939	62,604
Manufactured Goods	73,310	97,132	95,184	112,920	104,642	92,313	92,778	104,965
Machinery & Transportation Equipment	99,372	118,373	135,326	148,249	133,335	133,552	128,224	147,746
Other Manufactured Goods	50,919	62,995	78,655	69,500	67,570	72,007	63,821	64,488
Other Commodities	2,610	2,954	772	204	218	101	3,005	3,452
EPZs	n/a	n/a	n/a	n/a	n/a	n/a	n/a	n/a
CFZ	n/a	n/a	n/a	n/a	n/a	n/a	n/a	n/a
Personal Goods	n/a	n/a	n/a	n/a	n/a	n/a	n/a	n/a
Total	422,586	512,485	548,497	561,923	519,860	514,431	510,963	572,424

Classification	1998	1999	2000	2001	2002	2003	2004	2005
Food & Live Animals	99,317	107,074	106,270	118,770	107,840	118,720	109,230	120,680
Beverages & Tobacco	9,826	10,960	7,540	7,650	8,330	8,940	9,850	17,440
Crude Materials	3,794	5,410	8,010	11,570	7,530	6,690	7,260	9,100
Minerals Fuels & Lubricants	68,095	118,664	173,990	154,520	115,540	132,820	154,650	195,660
Oils & Fats	3,651	3,812	3,960	3,200	3,050	3,300	3,180	3,190
Chemical Products	63,293	73,088	84,790	71,690	85,000	82,660	76,310	88,750
Manufactured Goods	113,515	113,139	143,830	136,200	128,190	128,670	136,850	138,850
Machinery & Transportation Equipment	152,228	200,429	237,130	230,480	208,470	203,660	175,910	199,770
Other Manufactured Goods	75,099	86,495	64,490	75,840	80,450	103,220	81,810	101,110
Other Commodities	3,850	20,228	450	410	250	910	10	50
EPZs	n/a	n/a	100,560	87,020	80,010	130,700	113,910	124,710
CFZ	n/a	n/a	114,490	132,030	221,170	180,500	156,620	183,800
Personal Goods	n/a	n/a	3,070	4,290	3,190	3,400	2,630	2,720
Total	592,668	739,299	1,048,580	1,033,670	1,049,020	1,104,190	1,028,220	1,185,830

Source: CSO, Belize. n/a = data not available.

Table 7: Domestic imports for Belize
by product share value & classification

Classification	Period Average, 1990-1999	Period Average, 2000-2005	Period Average, 1990-2005
Food & Live Animals	16.5%	10.6%	14.3%
Beverages & Tobacco	2.5%	0.9%	1.9%
Crude Materials	0.8%	0.8%	0.8%
Minerals Fuels & Lubricants	12.5%	14.4%	13.2%
Oils & Fats	0.6%	0.3%	0.5%
Chemical Products	10.3%	7.6%	9.3%
Manufactured Goods	18.3%	12.6%	16.2%
Machinery & Transportation Equipment	25.3%	19.5%	23.1%
Other Manufactured Goods	12.6%	7.8%	10.8%
Other Commodities	0.6%	0.0%	0.4%
EPZs	n/a	9.8%	3.7%
CFZ	n/a	15.3%	5.7%
Personal Goods	n/a	0.3%	0.1%
Total Share	100.0%	100.0%	100.0%

Source: Author's calculation from CSO data.
n/a = data not available.

2000, CSO has added detailed information as to export processing zones, Corozal Free Zone, and the import of personal goods (see Table 6, on page 61). The import shares are reported in Table 7 indicating a heavy reliance on industrial and manufactured products and fuel imports,[9] imports destined for re-sale (e.g., CFZ), and food imports.

A more refined look at imports is possible with five products illustrating the general increase in imports generally since independence. These products (and the SITC codes) are road vehicles (79), medicines and pharmaceutical products

---

[9] Even with the recent commercialization of oil production in Belize, Belize lacks the ability to refine oil, hence refined fuel imports will remain a mainstay of the import basket for the foreseeable future.

Table 8: Selected imports, 1980-2003 (BZ$1000s)

Year	Road Vehicles	Medicines	Live Poultry	Footwear	Vegetables/Fruit
2003	61,382	17,982	340	6,424	11,899
2002	62,445	15,949	368	6,351	11,441
2001	70,478	14,933	250	6,825	12,101
2000	71,414	13,599	n/a	5,309	11,045
1999	11,590	1,029	321	581	25,062
1998	34,047	11,728	370	3,242	13,622
1997	30,040	9,741	322	3,480	12,976
1996	31,897	8,743	271	2,751	10,154
1995	31,187	8,237	298	2,577	9,113
1994	29,877	8,728	209	3,394	7,555
1993	37,079	9,523	186	3,672	9,696
1992	37,189	8,951	152	3,815	13,703
1991	n/a	n/a	n/a	n/a	n/a
1990	22,351	7,071	104	3,576	10,672
1989	22,283	6,683	111	3,195	9,136
1988	19,230	5,818	99	3,150	7,902
1987	13,986	6,705	76	2,488	7,744
1986	10,426	4,516	70	2,767	7,842
1985	9,706	5,578	49	2,696	6,830
1984	11,170	4,264	83	3,407	6,802
1983	10,121	3,706	125	2,870	7,025
1982	8,777	7,091	107	2,264	6,579
1981	n/a	n/a	n/a	n/a	n/a
1980	11,227	4,132	118	3,592	6,942

Source: United Nations Comtrade Database.

(54), live poultry (0014), footwear (85), and vegetables and fruit (05). These common household products–vehicles, medicines, poultry, footwear, and vegetables and fruits (see Table 8)–reflect import increases of 546.7%, 435.2%, 288.4%, 178.9%, and 171.4%, respectively, comparing 1980 data against 2003 data (though these increases are even larger in select years). It is not surprising that Belize imports large quantities of vehicles, medicines and some footwear, but the imports of live poultry and large amounts of vegetables and fruits reflect local production (and earnings) forgone.

Figure 6: Percent annual price fluctuations of major Belizean exports, 1990-2005

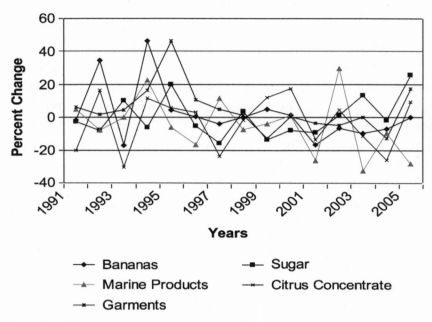

Source: CSO, Belize.

Terms of trade

The terms of trade take into consideration the price composition of the export and import baskets over time. This trade ratio or terms of trade becomes especially important when export prices decline while import prices remain steady or increase (e.g., the recent price increases in fuel). Belizean exports are mostly primary commodity products subject to wide ranges in price variation. An overview of price performance (1990-2005) for the five major export earners—bananas, sugar, marine products, citrus concentrate, and garments—reveals wide swings in annual price changes (see Figure 6). The aggregate swings throughout the period range from 41.5% for sugar and 63.5% for bananas (see Table 9). A declining price garnered for two of five of the products, marine products and citrus concentrate, decreased over time at average annual rates of -4.6% and -3.1%, respectively. Sugar exhibited essentially no price growth (0.3%) from 1990-2005. Bananas and garments displayed positive, though modest, average annual price increases of 1.9% and 5.1%, respectively.

Hence, in light of a declining terms of trade for Belizean exports, it is much more difficult for Belize to reduce its trade deficit as well as to afford its current

Table 9: Percent annual price fluctuations in major Belizean exports

Year	Bananas	Sugar	Marine Products	Citrus Concentrate	Garments
1990*	—	—	—	—	—
1991	-1.87	-2.58	4.84	-20.14	6.44
1992	34.31	-7.73	-7.65	16.43	1.74
1993	-17.11	10.24	0.08	-30.37	4.32
1994	46.40	-5.90	22.36	11.48	16.30
1995	4.71	19.75	-6.01	6.02	46.17
1996	0.53	-5.38	-16.74	3.20	10.67
1997	-3.98	-15.72	11.63	-23.64	5.07
1998	0.13	3.40	-7.37	-1.89	1.41
1999	4.83	-13.52	-3.75	12.15	-12.76
2000	1.33	-8.01	1.12	17.23	0.71
2001	-16.75	-9.19	-26.33	-13.61	-3.48
2002	-6.70	1.61	29.47	4.50	-4.60
2003	-9.82	13.27	-32.64	-11.38	0.13
2004	-6.87	-1.80	-9.66	-25.93	-12.71
2005	0.20	25.79	-28.30	9.32	17.48
Annual Period Average	1.95	0.28	-4.60	-3.11	5.13
High	46.40	25.79	29.47	17.23	46.17
Low	-17.11	-15.72	-32.64	-30.37	-12.76
Variation	63.51	41.51	62.11	47.60	58.93

*1990 = first year of time series.
Source: Author's calculations from CSO, Belize data.

level of import consumption with either increases in export output and/or reduction in imports.

Historical trade linkages

This section reports the historical linkages for exports, imports, and total trade by destination and origin of trade.

Export destination

Belizean exports are structurally tied to the developed world, primarily with the United States and Europe. More specifically, the USA and England have al-

Table 10: Belizean exports by destination (BZ$1000s)

Year	USA	UK	Other EU	CARICOM	Canada	Mexico	Central America	ROW^	Total*
1990	102,995	69,488	2,747	16,703	11,141	3,792	305	9,740	216,911
1991	94,024	56,205	5,780	13,384	7,549	6,242	63	13,829	197,076
1992	111,354	78,230	12,105	12,583	7,090	7,545	48	9,463	238,418
1993	101,538	94,137	8,393	9,928	15,776	6,209	25	1,870	237,876
1994	98,659	102,827	12,257	9,804	20,342	9,657	188	1,161	254,895
1995	93,736	131,763	28,527	10,872	13,404	1,438	262	5,730	285,732
1996	124,883	140,193	18,057	9,124	8,394	4,545	288	1,617	307,101
1997	143,526	105,503	34,640	14,553	11,572	3,075	605	4,642	318,116
1998	118,857	115,022	21,808	22,819	6,974	2,299	2,108	22,771	312,658
1999	140,990	110,597	44,525	19,530	6,431	1,921	1,079	14,193	339,266
2000	205,030	121,030	44,740	19,590	5,910	2,720	1,030	20,730	420,780
2001	169,370	78,830	22,570	21,850	1,340	2,040	2,610	26,840	325,450
2002	168,200	77,930	29,650	22,450	2,340	3,810	2,660	9,630	316,670
2003	211,630	93,520	20,590	35,020	600	5,540	1,140	13,370	381,410
2004	226,170	80,600	41,410	46,640	860	5,550	1,780	7,120	410,130
2005	216,050	90,910	28,770	45,540	230	17,630	3,020	11,120	413,270

Source: CSO, Belize.
^Indicates the rest of the world.
*These total export figures may differ from those presented earlier in the paper as CSO does not include re-export values when reporting exports by product class.

ternated leadership as to the primary destination of Belizean exports, with the US averaging the receipt of 46.1% of exports and the UK averaging 32.0% of exports from 1990-2005 (see Table 10). Together the two nations receive on average more than three-quarters of Belizean exports with a range of 74.1% to 86.3% since 1990. Regional exports to Central America, Mexico and the Caribbean comprise just 8.0% of all exports.

Import origin

Belizean imports originate from a slightly more diverse pool than the destination of Belizean exports; nonetheless, since 1990 Belize has imported more than half of all its goods from a single country, the US (50.3%). Reflecting loca-

Table 11: Belizean imports by destination (BZ$ 1000s)

Year	USA	UK	Other EU	CARICOM	Canada	Mexico	Central America	ROW^	Total*
1990	243,261	34,715	30,107	26,007	9,778	28,688	13,474	36,556	422,586
1991	301,800	40,379	44,442	13,776	11,496	42,291	17,761	40,540	512,485
1992	310,179	46,834	37,488	21,735	10,859	48,429	22,819	50,154	548,497
1993	317,735	39,331	25,523	21,776	11,558	53,864	24,355	67,781	561,923
1994	276,172	37,791	21,523	22,347	12,033	49,901	27,846	71,986	519,860
1995	276,789	32,378	21,784	25,528	15,849	57,040	21,794	63,340	514,431
1996	280,615	23,689	21,713	21,346	7,933	62,558	24,714	73,057	510,962
1997	294,666	30,526	17,050	22,057	15,635	72,464	24,846	90,022	572,424
1998	318,928	27,719	22,208	21,462	11,827	69,675	30,297	81,336	592,668
1999	381,375	30,902	31,424	26,104	10,887	89,763	41,050	133,162	739,299
2000	507,090	28,100	26,056	29,400	16,110	88,120	94,020	233,430	1,048,570
2001	474,460	32,640	52,300	43,750	13,480	86,710	121,400	220,830	1,033,640
2002	442,710	32,890	40,370	32,160	17,160	82,130	174,260	215,330	1,049,030
2003	469,600	28,060	56,400	30,130	13,680	87,300	183,610	235,390	1,104,170
2004	398,210	23,910	39,910	26,270	12,470	106,000	197,280	224,010	1,028,060
2005	463,850	18,560	60,850	28,440	15,810	111,100	230,930	256,290	1,185,830

Source: CSO, Belize.
^Indicates the rest of the world.
*These total import figures may differ from those presented earlier in the paper as CSO does not include re-export values when reporting exports by product class.

tional advantages, Mexico and Central America have also been important sources of goods for Belize with a period average of 9.7% and 8.6%, respectively, (see Table 11).

Total trade by destination and origin

Yet Belizean trade remains highly concentrated in and dependent on a handful of nations and regions (see Table 12, next page). The developed world accounts for nearly 90% of Belizean exports and contributes more than three-fifths of Belize's imports with the US predominate. Regional exports are small, reflecting a generally similar export basket and the non-competitive nature of much of Belizean exports (e.g., citrus, sugar, bananas). Regional imports are be-

Table 12: Concentration of exports and imports, 1990-2005

| | 1990-2005 Average | | |
Country/Region	Exports (%)	Imports (%)	Total Trade (%)
USA	46.1	50.3	47.9
UK	32.0	5.0	12.2
Other EU	7.1	5.0	5.5
Canada	2.8	1.9	1.9
Developed World	*88.0*	*62.2*	*67.5*
CARICOM	6.4	3.7	4.4
Mexico	1.8	9.7	7.2
Central America	0.3	8.6	7.5
Regional	*8.5*	*22.0*	*19.1*
ROW^	3.5	15.8	13.4
Total	100.0	100.0	100.0

Source: Author's calculation from CSO data, Belize.
^Indicates the rest of the world.

coming more important, a function of proximity advantages (e.g., transportation) and trade arrangements (i.e., CARICOM, SICA, and Plan Puebla-Panama[10]). For total trade, the developed world comprises over two-thirds of activity for Belize with regional partners contributing just under one-fifth of all trade.

Summary and recommendations for non-dependent trade insertion and growth

This section summarizes the trade data presented in the paper, offers an analysis within the globalization and dependency dialog, and proposes recommendations for non-dependent trade insertion and growth for Belize.

---

[10] See Pisani (2004) and Pisani, Yoskowitz, and Label (2003) for a fuller discussion of this issue of trade arrangements.

Summary

In summary, the paper has described Belize's participation in the global economy through an examination of its trade basket. Belize is fully inserted into the global economy. Since independence, exports have comprised about one-quarter of GDP, imports nearly one-half of GDP, while overall trade accounts for just over two-thirds of GDP.

Over a 36 year time period (1970-2005), exports have grown at an annual rate of 9.0% with a tapering off of growth over each subsequent decade. In the new millennium (2000-2005), export growth has averaged only 2.6%. Imports on the other hand, have grown at an average annual faster pace of 10.2% (and from a higher base) with an upshot of growth over the 1980s and 1990s in the 2000s. Concomitantly, the negative balance of trade has worsened to over one-third of GDP in the 2000s.

Four products make up the lion's share (approximately three-quarters) of exports: sugar, bananas, citrus concentrate, and marine products. Of these four major export products, only bananas have shown much of a positive annual increase in price since 1990 (with sugar prices steady on average though facing imminent preference erosion). Marine products and citrus concentrate have diminished significantly in price over the same period. The averages downplay the wide annual fluctuations in price, with period variations ranging from -32.6% to 46.4% (a 79.0% price spread).

Imports reflect an economy dependent upon foreign energy supplies, intermediate goods, manufactured goods, household consumer goods, and goods for re-sale (i.e., CFZ). While it is not practical in the near-term for Belize to become a manufactured goods or technology exporter due to limitations associated with infrastructure, relative high wages, education, industrialization, and trade diverting trade agreements, the widening trade deficit is not sustainable without creating a lot of dislocation and hardship (e.g., increased taxation and debt) within the local economy. In this light, more sustainable trade relations and policies need to be created.

The concentration of export destinations and import origins are dramatic as well. More than three-quarters of exports are sent to two countries, the United States and Great Britain. The country of origin of imports is slightly more diversified, though the aforementioned countries dominate here as well (making up 60.1% of imported products).

Analysis within the globalization and dependency dialog

As a legacy of colonialism, primary or commodity-based exports have not fared well in terms of price performance. The three largest contributors to export earnings–sugar, marine products and citrus concentrate–have all fallen or remained steady in price since 1990, requiring more (quantity of) exports just to maintain the approximate value of export earnings. This reflects worsening terms of trade, a bad position for a nation such as Belize in which trade comprises such a large portion of the economy, making economic development and progress precarious. For example, 92 long tons of sugar were exported in 1990 earning BZ$85.5 million; by 2004 114 long tons brought in BZ$79.7 million. The 24% increase in product (sugar) exports brought in 7.3% less in earnings, comparatively. Though not as obvious because the overall export earnings for marine products are up, the price for marine products have fallen 4.6% per year on average since 1990. The increased marine products' earnings have come from rapidly expanded production. Hence, more exports are required in a declining price environment to induce greater export earnings. Like marine products, citrus concentrate needs to produce more to keep up the earnings pace. For example, 2003 exports of 5.7 million gallons earned BZ$78.1 million, whereas, 7.8 million gallons in 2004 exports (a 26.9% increase) barely earned 1.5% more at BZ$79.3 million than the 2003 exports.

The good news for Belizean export earnings has been bananas and garments, as their prices have increased in price over the study period. The bad news is that these two products make up less than 25% of the export basket and more importantly, bananas and garments are products that are being squeezed by globalization. With the termination of the Multifiber Agreement at the end of 2004, the formal barriers to the textile trade have been eliminated, prompting a global re-ordering in textile production to China, India, and Southeast Asia to the likely detriment of future Belizean garment manufacturing. Additionally, the trade in bananas as well as sugar and citrus concentrate has been heavily subsidized by European price supports and guaranteed quotas, a preferential system that is nearing its end. And roughly three-quarters of Belizean orange concentrate qualifies for the United States Caribbean Basin Initiative, a preferential policy that will most likely change with the implementation of CAFTA (the US-Central America plus the Dominican Republic free trade agreement)

Compounding the worsening terms of trade faced by the handful of commodity-based Belizean exports is the concentration of export trade in only two major world regions: North America (US) and Europe (primarily the UK). This non-diversification of export destinations and asymmetrical trade power (Belizean trade to North America and Europe are insignificant to their trade calculus) reinforces the dependent relationship Belizeans find in their export markets. For example, bananas, sugar, textiles, citrus, and shrimp are all hot political trade issues in the US. The US sugar lobby came within a single vote in the House of Representatives of derailing US ratification of CAFTA in June 2005 because of fears of greater competition from Central America. Florida orange growers and Gulf of Mexico shrimpers (Texas and Louisiana) are vocal opponents of freer trade at the federal level, trying to safeguard their own US market share. And large US banana multinationals (Dole, Chiquita, and Del Monte) have fought hard and have won through the WTO to eventually eliminate European preferences for banana supports to former colonies of Europe (including Belize) so that the US banana MNCs may have fair access to the European market. Although the trade in textiles is supposedly free, the US (and Europe) have asked for and received voluntary export restraints from China in 2005 and 2006.

Two streams of thought–globalization and dependency–have been suggested to shed light on Belize's trade relations highlighted above. Globalization with its focus on comparative advantage, open competition, and a flat world economy argues for complete and unfettered access to markets and a reliance on strong institutions and modern infrastructure for development and prosperity. Dependentistas (advocates of dependency theory) suggest it is just that open access to global markets that impoverishes national economies, particularly those economies emerging from recent colonial or neo-colonial pasts. Both ideologies compete for prominence in Belize; however, the track record of Belizean foreign trade, especially Belize's export performance, suggests dependency theory as the more appropriate analytical tool to analyze export performance.

As far as Thomas Friedman's suggestion that free trade is the answer, this may work in environments in which the terms of trade and the machinations of global institutions are favorable, but in Belize the terms of trade are negative and they are structurally so in conjunction with global trading rules designed for First World economic powerhouses. The two major markets for Belizean products exist because of distortions in the international trading system whereby citrus concentrate finds preferential access to the US through the Caribbean Basin Initiative and bananas and sugar receive preferential access to British and European markets through the ACP. Yet preference erosion is a real and imminent threat to the current composition of the Belizean export basket. The ACP agreement with Europe ends in 2007 and the Caribbean Basin Initiative has been supplanted in part by the recent Central American (plus the Dominican Republic) Free Trade accords with the US.

Belize suffers from the classic first and second forms of dependence as described by Dos Santos (1970), 1) colonial dependence (mercantilism); and 2) financial-industrial dependence (neo-mercantilism). The evidence is overwhelming: dependent trade relations subject to hegemonic preferential access; declining terms of trade for much of the export basket; high level of dependence on the trade sector for the economy as a whole; balance of payments difficulties due to an over-indulgence in consumption (imports); IMF borrowing and conditionality (i.e., structural adjustment programs); and asymmetrical power in global trade forums.

71

Recommendations for non-dependent trade insertion and growth

Yet, Belize operates in the reality of the global economy and complete retreat from the vagaries of the global economy is not possible or practical. And protection under the economic grouping of choice, CARICOM, provides minimal relief for Belize in a "flat" world. In this present global environment, new comparative advantages must be created in an open, global economy while transitioning from extractive exports experiencing preference erosion. Three areas for non-dependent trade insertion and growth are offered; these recommendations fall under the sub-headings of promising products, re-focused domestic policy, and enhanced foreign economic policy.

Promising products refer to the development of goods and services that make use of Belize's natural and constructed comparative advantages. Promising products and services include hot pepper sauce, papayas, petroleum and natural gas, medicinal herbs, and tourism in its many manifestations (e.g., ethno-tourism, adventure tourism, cruise ship tourism, eco-tourism, and archeological tourism), but not beyond the ecological carrying capacity of the nation.[11] The national language may also be used for comparative advantage: for English as a second language training; as a comfortable, language-friendly, and hospitable site for Americans studying abroad; and for English business language training. Even short term and artificial development such as commercial free trade zones may provide short term niche growth opportunities.

Re-focused domestic policy suggests that the national government can and should do more to make Belize competitive in the global economy. First, operating globally, particularly given Belize's trade relationships and Western Hemispheric location, requires access to the US dollar. To this end, the trade deficit must be winnowed and access to US dollars made easier (to de-pressurize fre-

---

[11] Beyond the ecological pale lie the important millennium development goals promulgated by the United Nations that Belize has begun to address.

[12] Compounding the trade deficit is the large central government budget deficit, providing a double necessity to borrow abroad. This dual predicament is similar to the one found in the contemporary US economy where the US economy is dependent on the willingness of others to lend it money. Unlike the US, Belize is not privileged as an international borrower and does so at a very large premium, thereby provoking intervention and conditionality from the IMF. Furthermore, this premium includes debt repayment in hard currency (i.e., the US dollar) which only comes from exports, capital inflows, and borrowing—creating a vicious downward spiral of foreign exchange (hard currency) scarcity and rationing within Belize as the demand for hard currency continuously outpaces available supply, with the gap between demand and supply growing over time. This is in part reflected in the vibrant black market and the black market exchange rate. Nonetheless, this structural or permanent trade deficit since nationhood is both a legacy of neocolonialism and current economic policy making.

quent balance of payments crises).[12] As such, borrowing for import consumption should be curtailed to a "pay-as-you" go environment with unfettered use of the US dollar through parallel or complete dollarization.[13] Not all borrowing is bad, however; and borrowing, particularly state-sponsored (e.g., through the Small Farmers Business Bank) for export and job creation at the micro-, small-, and medium-sized business level may be very beneficial. Nonetheless, this must be done in an environment of transparency given the rising level of corruption within Belize.

Furthermore, critical and costly production inputs such as gasoline should not be taxed beyond that level needed to create, maintain, and upgrade the transportation infrastructure. Though taxing gasoline and related products is an easy and efficient way to collect government tax revenue, the tax places an undue and non-competitive burden on the business sector–the sector that is most needed to help Belize compete globally. Other factors must all receive adequate investment, such as the educational system to enhance the human capital stock of the nation as well as physical infrastructure networks.

Enhanced foreign economic policy provides an opportunity to utilize and harness the global economic and political system to re-position Belize into a more advantaged situation. For example, Venezuela and Taiwan, for political reasons more than concerns for fraternity and solidarity, have recently assisted Belize. The former in terms of easy credits for petroleum purchases and the latter in terms of technical assistance and cash grants. In return, Belize supports the political aspirations of Taiwanese independence from mainland China and Venezuela's (under Hugo Chavez) ambition to lead Latin America contra to Washington's will. Belize needs to capitalize on such geopolitical interests not only in securing its own claim against Guatemala, but also in its drive towards development. The recent announcement (June 2006) that the government of Belize and the state-run Venezuelan petroleum agency (PDVSA) will partner in the development of Belizean oil is a very positive development in light of Belize's neo-dependent past. Additional initiatives created outside of the developed world core (e.g., the US, Europe, East Asia), such as the Plan Puebla-Panama under Mexico's leadership,[14] should also be nurtured. All of this is intended to diversify and better balance Belize's trade relationships.

---

[13] See Pisani and Yoskowitz (2002) for a discussion of the ramifications of dollarization in Belize. As an aside, the tourist sector makes up about 20% of GDP; and tourists, mostly from America, inject large sums of US dollars in the form of cash into the economy that somehow do not make it into the formal banking system, but instead find their way into private coffers. Dollarization would legalize this currency conversion practice that has mostly benefited the well-healed and tourist-focused.

[14] See Pisani, Yoskowitz, and Label (2003) for a discussion of Belize and the Plan Puebla-Panama.

Nonetheless, the government of Belize has chosen to integrate with the Caribbean Community (CARICOM) as a means of offsetting its power disadvantage in the global economy. Unfortunately, many members of CARICOM have similar export baskets, limiting integration benefits.[15] This is readily evident from the small share of intra-CARICOM trade as well as Belizean trade with CARICOM members. As such, new avenues for regional integration (e.g., Central America) should be explored if the benefits outweigh the costs. Targeted, desirable, and sustainable foreign direct investment should be emphasized. And Belize should work to create a longer transition mechanism as it loses preferential access in its important export markets for its primary export earners. Hope for increased economic prosperity in the future may also lie in developing a greater Meso-American region-state à la Ohmae (2005) based on excellence in education; solid infrastructure (roads, ports, airports); superior telecommunications and information technology; strong, transparent, and clean democratic institutions; and safe living conditions. In the end, Belize need not be flattened by the global economy.

References

BOLLAND, O. NIGEL. (2003). *Colonialism and resistance in Belize: Essays in historical sociology*, 2nd Edition, Benque Viejo del Carmen, Belize: Cubola Productions & University of The West Indies.

DOS SANTOS, THEOTONIO. (1970). The structure of dependence. *American Economic Review, 60(2)*, 231-236.

FRIEDMAN, THOMAS L. (2005). *The world is flat: A brief history of the twenty-first century*. New York, NY: Farrar, Straus and Giroux.

FRIEDMAN, THOMAS L. (2000). *The Lexus and the olive tree*. New York, NY: Anchor Books.

INTERNATIONAL MONETARY FUND (IMF). (2005a, September). Belize: 2005 Article IV Consultation-Staff Report; Staff Statement; and Public Information Notice on the Executive Board Discussion. *IMF Country report No. 05/352*. Available online at http://www.imf.org, accessed on June 8, 2006.

INTERNATIONAL MONETARY FUND (IMF). (2005b, September). Belize: Selected Issues. *IMF Country report No. 05/353*. Available online at http://www.imf.org, accessed on June 8, 2006.

MCBAIN, HELEN. (2001). Open regionalism: CARICOM integration and trade links. In Victor Bulmer-Thomas (Ed.), *Regional integration in Latin America and the Caribbean: The political economy of open regionalism*. (pp. 275-294). London, UK: University of London, Institute of Latin American Studies.

---

[15] Overall, CARICOM has a net negative effect on economic welfare within the member states as trade diversion trumps trade creation (McBain, 2001).

MOBERG, MARK. (2003). Responsible men and sharp Yankees: The United Fruit Company, resident elites, and colonial state in British Honduras. In Steve Striffler & Mark Moberg (Eds.), *Banana wars: Power, production and history in the Americas* (pp. 145-170). Durham, NC: Duke University Press.

OHMAE, KENICHI. (2005). *The next global stage: Challenges and opportunities in our borderless world.* Upper Saddle River, NJ: Wharton School Publishing (Pearson Education, Inc.).

PISANI, MICHAEL J. (2006). Neo-Dependent commercial exterior relations? An analysis of the Belizean export basket since independence. *Journal of Belizean Studies, 26(1),* 57-74.

PISANI, MICHAEL J. (2004). A preliminary assessment of the proposed Belize-Guatemala Free Trade Agreement. *Journal of Belizean Studies, 26(2),* 3-15.

PISANI, MICHAEL J., YOSKOWITZ, DAVID W., & LABEL, WAYNE A. (2003). Belize and the Plan Puebla-Panama: Prospects and challenges. *Journal of Belizean Studies, 25(2),* 3-17.

PISANI, MICHAEL J. & YOSKOWITZ, DAVID W. (2002). Dollarization! *Journal of Belizean Studies, 24(2),* 19-27.

RICARDO, DAVID. (1817). *On the principles of political economy and taxation.* Available online at www.econlib.org.

SHOMAN, ASSAD. (1994, 2000). *Thirteen chapters of a history of Belize.* Belize City, Belize: The Angelus Press Limited.

STEGER, MANFRED B. (2002). *Globalism: The new market ideology.* Lanham, MD: Rowman & Littlefield Publishers, Inc.

SUTHERLAND, ANNE. (1998). *The making of Belize: Globalization in the margins.* Westport, CT: Bergin & Garvey.

VESETH, MICHAEL. (2005). *Globaloney: Unraveling the myths of globalization.* Lanham, MD: Rowman & Littlefield Publishers, Inc.

WOLF, MARTIN. (2004). *Why globalization works.* New Haven, CT: Yale University Press.

3. Belize's Northern Region; Its Economic Performance in the Post-Independence Period

Crucita Ken

In 1981 when Belize attained its independence, other countries in the region were also celebrating anniversaries: Mexico its 171st anniversary, Jamaica its 19th, Guatemala its 160th and Honduras its 159th Independence in the voice of then-Prime Minister George Price was the attainment of political and economic freedom. Although this political move was met by scepticism by some, many were betting on better times to come, higher standards of living, and improved political participation.

On that 21st day of September the Belizean people faced a challenging future, since the neighbouring Central and South American regions were at the verge of falling into debt crises. Guatemala, El Salvador, and Nicaragua were in the midst of civil wars—battling with guerrillas and civil revolutions, and at the same time international trade was restructuring with respect to traditional exports, which affected the whole region.

The economic performance of Belize was, and continues to be, connected to its relations with the United States, the Caribbean, and to a lesser extent to its Latin American neighbours, with the exception of Mexico, which has played an important role in Belize's development. This brief description of Belize's post independence performance highlights Belize's economic relations with Mexico, in particular that segment that deals with the border region that they share.

Belize enjoys warm relations with its neighbour to the north. As early as 1958, Mexico stated its desire for a resolution of Belize's territorial problem with Guatemala and supported initiatives that respected the freedom and independence of the Belizean people. Mexico also provided critical support in favour of Belizean independence and territorial integrity in 1977. Although Mexico claimed parts of Belize during the nineteenth century, it signed treaties with both Britain and Guatemala in the course of that century to set the border definitively between Mexico and Belize. One such treaty, and probably the most important, is the Spenser St. John-Mariscal signed on the 8th of July 1893 and its amendment on the 26th July 1897. Part of this amendment included an agreement to guarantee Mexico, in perpetuity, transit rights through Belizean waters (*Tratado sobre límites*).

Quintana Roo is the most southeastern state in Mexico and borders Belize. Its capital city is Chetumal. Quintana Roo and other Mexican states in the region,[1] Belize, Guatemala, and Honduras all share a common heritage initiated and perpetuated by the great Maya civilisation. The Maya people, their heritage, culture, and language today serve as tourist attractions in a broad project carried on by the Mundo Maya Organisation (Mundo Maya).

Economic relations between Belize and Mexico can be analysed at least on two levels: national and local. At the national level we share the benefits of international trade and socioeconomic agreements with respect to motor vehicle transit, education, culture, the fight against drug trafficking, and dependency, preservation of archaeological sites, preservation of natural resources, among others (Secretaría de Relaciones Exteriores). At the local level there are cultural and economic relations between the inhabitants of the border region. The published accounts of these relationships are many (Ken, 1994a, 1994b, 1994c; Ken & Hernandez Trueba, 1992; *Iniciativa*, 1992a, 1992b; CIQRO, 1994a, 1994b); however, our interest is in how these relationships have evolved since the independence of Belize in 1981.

The major events affecting the border region during this period are (1) the devaluation of the Mexican peso in 1982, (2) the closure of the sugar factory at Libertad, Corozal District in 1985, (3) the entry of Mexico in the World Trade Organisation in 1984, (4) the signing of the North American Trade Agreement in 1994, and (5) the opening of the Commercial Free Zone at Santa Elena, Corozal District, also in 1994. These events have influenced the relations between Belize and Mexico, both at the national and local level, in particular the latter.

Devaluation of the Mexican peso

Northern Belize and southeastern Mexico share a common Maya culture. During the colonial era, the early inhabitants of northern Belize came from Mexico, bringing with them the Spanish and Maya language, traditions, and other elements of culture, including the cultivation of sugar cane. Cultural[2] and later economic ties with Mexico have therefore been present from years back. Mexico, unlike Guatemala, gave its sup-

---

[1] Yucatán, Campeche, Quintana Roo, Tabasco, and Chiapas.
[2] Historical accounts of cultural and economic ties between inhabitants of Mexico and Belize can be read in O. Nigel Bolland, Grant Jones, and Paul Sullivan.

Table 1: Devaluations of the Mexican peso

Year	Pesos per $US(average)	Percentage of devaluation
1976-82	70.00	240%
1982-88	2.285	3,164%
1988-94	3.45	51%
1994-00	9.45	174%
2000-	11.63	23%

Source: Banco de México.

port to Belize in the negotiations for independence. Mexico voted in favour of the United Nation's General Assembly resolution that called for the necessary steps to be taken to lead Belize to independence with territorial integrity (Mexico voted in favour, 1981).

However, during the early 1980s Mexico was going through economic problems that led to continued devaluation of the Mexican peso as shown in the table above.

Devaluations have an effect on the balance of trade by making imports expensive and exports more attractive. This translated to weakening of Mexico's purchasing power of foreign goods. Both at the national and in particular at the local level, this event caused significant economic changes in Belize and Mexico.

In 1972 the city of Chetumal was designated a free zone area. Being the only such territory in southeastern Mexico, its fame as a commercial centre was well known in the region. Manufactured items from Panama were imported through the deep water port in Belize. Reciprocally, Belizeans have used Mexican highways to travel from the USA bringing along goods and used vehicles for sale in Belize. As a Free Commercial Territory, Chetumal flourished with the sale of imported merchandise such as electrical equipments, canned food, and clothing.

Informal trade

During the 1970s Northern Belize, especially Corozal, also experienced an economic boom with Mexicans coming to buy from the East Indian, Chinese, and Belizean merchants. Among their favourite imported products were Dutch cheese, creamery butter, textiles, and many Chinese and East Indian products, a luxury for most Mexicans. Mexicans came in their private vehicles and by buses. This important injection of Mexican pesos in the northern Belizean economy helped to keep the Indian, Chinese, and local businesses vibrant, particularly in

Corozal. However the devaluation of the peso in 1982 reversed this benefit. Now with more pesos to the Belizean dollar, the monetary flow of Belizean dollars went north to the businesses in Chetumal, Mexico.

The devaluation of the peso marked the beginning of the small scale transborder trade conducted by Belizeans households and merchants, particularly from the Corozal and Orange Walk districts, of basic items purchased in Chetumal. This leakage was increased by the demand by Belizeans for medical and other services in southeast Mexico. Consequently, commercial activity in Corozal declined resulting in the flight of many foreign businessmen to other parts of Belize and to Mexico causing the town of Corozal to face a depression. Other businesses, such as cinemas, discotheques, and restaurants among others, eventually shut their doors, since most of the income available was being spent in the state of Quintana Roo's capital, Chetumal.

In an article in *Amandala*, "Devaluation in Mexico," I stated that the 1982 devaluation had a tremendous impact on the northern economy. The peso fell from 12 to 20, and then to 50 and eventually reached 70 to the Belize dollar. Belizeans flooded the Mexican supermarkets in search of basic food items and conducted business with gas stations, health centres, hotels, and restaurants. These transactions created an informal trade estimated to have reached an amount of BZ$6.9 million per annum (Ken, 1995). Between 1981 and 1991 estimated arrivals per day in Chetumal were 500 Belizeans. This represented a significant leakage for the Belizean economy. Belizean customers caused a financial boom for the city of Chetumal.

The flow of Belize dollars to southern Mexico increased with subsequent devaluations of the Mexican peso. From 1988 to 1994, this situation worsened. However, the effect of this trade in Mexico was the transfer of subsidy to Belizean consumers since most of the trade was concentrated in basic food items bought at the government-subsidised supermarkets, such as CONASUPO, SEDENA, and ISSTE (Pech Febles & Cruz Cáceres, 2000).

It is important to note that while the transfer of income over the border meant a loss to the Belizean economy, it helped the Belizean households of the northern region to stretch their dollars. The sugar industry was in a crisis, the business community was suffering, and the possibility of getting more for the few dollars circulating in Belize was there. The situation of the Mexican economy and its impact on northern Belize indicated a lack of interest by the national government: research was not conducted, the economic impact was not measured, and no contingency plan or solution was proposed. The economic crises experienced by the northern region illustrated the centralisation of economic[3]

---

[3] Economic issues such as commercial and price structures in Belize have not been studied sufficiently, but the existence of few companies in this activity can indicate the existence of duopolies.

Figure 1: Belize's imports and exports from Mexico

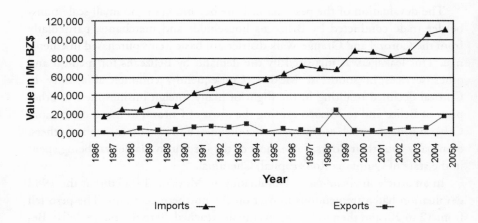

and political issues, since the concerns of this outdistrict were not given enough importance in the house of representatives and by the cabinet.[4] Prices of Mexican imported food items in Belize were many times higher compared to prices in the easily accessible Mexican bordering town of Chetumal. This stimulated contraband, and families made numerous border crossings to acquire basic food items (CIQRO, 1994b). This behaviour of the Belizean population at the Mexican border gave an insight into the commerce structure that maintains higher prices on imported food items.

Formal trade

Formal trade between Mexico and Belize are of two types: the normal imports and exports of goods and Belize's reexports to Mexico (see Figure 1).

Imports of Mexican products to Belize have steadily risen, while exports remained stable, with the exception of a sudden rise in 1999.

As a reexporter, Belize imports goods and then resells them in neighbouring countries, primarily Mexico, or merely transports them, collecting fees for port

---

[4] This is a result of the political structure of Belize. Research needs to be done to provide evidence of the effects of the centralization of accounts. During the 1990s, the move for political reform mandated by government and carried out by the Society for the Promotion of Education, Advocacy and Research (SPEAR) together with civil society, constitutes the initial platform towards the decentralization process.

Figure 2: Share of reexports

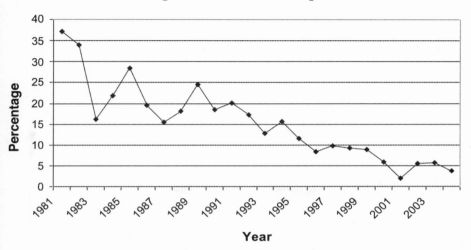

Year

Source: Abstract of Statistics, 1990, 2000, 2005, CSO and Central Bank of Belize.

and road facilities. The arrangement is attractive because of Belize's relatively low shipping costs. However, Mexico's economic payment crisis of 1982, which reduced Mexican imports, put a dent in Belize's foreign exchange earnings as well. Reexports had amounted to 37% of export earnings in 1981, but fell to 16% in 1983, contributing to a 35% drop in total export earnings during that period.

Reexports show a decline, particularly in 1993, 1996, 2001, and 2004 (see Figure 2). Most of these reexports are related to the economic performance of Mexico. However, the recovery in 1997 and 2002 as a whole may have been in response to the activity at the Commercial Free Zone at the Belize-Mexico border.

Restructuring of the sugar industry

To add to the economic crises already being suffered in the north during the early years of independence due to the devaluation of the Mexican peso, the sugar industry, Belize's number one foreign exchange earner, was also in crisis. The history of sugar cane in Belize starts on a commercial scale in 1964 when the small mill at Libertad was established by Tate & Lyle, a large British sugar conglomerate. This event accompanied the beginning of nearly twenty years of great profit.

During the 1960s and 1970s, Belize's economy grew rapidly, thanks to the extraordinary success of the sugar production. During the 1970s, sugar accounted for almost 70% of all export revenues. As a result of this high level of dependency, the Belizean economy, although prosperous, entered the 1980s insufficiently diversified and highly susceptible to external shocks. In the late 1980s,

Figure 3: Sugar exports

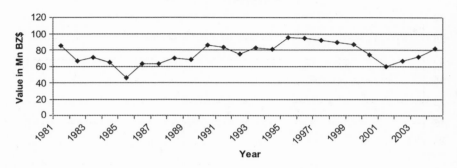

Source: Abstract of Statistics, 1990, 2000, 2005, CSO and Central Bank of Belize.

farmers of Corozal started to diversify into the production of papaya, soya beans, and other agricultural products (see Figure 3).

In 1980 the average world price of raw sugar was US$0.13 per kilogram. By 1984, that price had fallen to US$0.02. As sugar prices collapsed, Belize's terms of trade deteriorated, and from 1980 to 1985 GDP grew an average of only 1.2% per year. The crisis was compounded in 1982 when, for the first time since 1974, the United States government implemented a sugar quota system. The result was a reduction in total sugar exports from about 5 million tons in 1980-81 to about 1 million tons by 1987.

During 1984 it became clear that the combined effects of reduced US quota, low world prices, and unfavourable currency exchange rate resulted in financial losses for the Belize Sugar Industry (BSI) and would shortly lead the company into bankruptcy unless drastic action was taken. By mid-1985, the financial crises forced the restructuring of BSI which, unfortunately, had to include the closure of the Corozal Factory after the completion of crop in that year (BSI, 25th Anniversary Publication,1989).

Preferential trade agreements provide a reminder that trade liberalisation is a double-edged sword for all trade participants, developed and developing countries alike. For example, in the early 1990s the existing quota systems for the Belizean sugar industry provided distinct advantages. Quotas guaranteed that Belizean sugar would have access to markets in the European Economic Community (EEC) and the United States at prices far above world market levels. At the same time, it was also clear that a quota system was a unilateral act that limited market access and that it could be changed or eliminated by foreign powers at their will.

The sugar crises in the early years of independence created a production problem in the northern district of Corozal. As noted by Perry, Woods, and Steagall (1993):

82

Sugar industry leaders reacted rationally, trying to shift output to alternative markets as cultivation shrunk. Great Britain was able to absorb much of the excess supply, under the LOME Agreement, passing it through to world markets... Cane farmers in northern Belize also reacted rationally. Many of them shifted to the illegal cultivation of marijuana, adding to the problem of drug regulation facing the national government. (p. 49)

By December of 1986 the closure of the Libertad sugar factory had displaced hundreds of employees and affected the livelihood of cane farmers and their families. According to the BSI officials, the 41% reduction of the sugar quota from 16,200 to 8,500 long tons by the US Congress meant an $8 million loss in foreign exchange to the economy of Belize.

The sugar industry situation was the result of the world's trading conditions of that commodity as mentioned above. Similar experiences had occurred in many other regions; for example the henequen processing in Yucatan caused an economic crisis among the cultivators, the industry, and the government, which eventually led to the restructuring of the region's economy. It is important to state that the effective restructuring of the economy of a region depends largely on the government's insight and foresight of the industry and its communication with the stakeholders and the population at large. However, for political reasons, the situation of the sugar industry was not adequately shared with the people. The government kept on promising an increase in quotas, which led not only to increasing the existing quotas among the cane farmers, but making the situation even worse by giving quotas to new farmers based on political clientelism. After the closure of the Libertad factory the government promised to re-open it and to establish a new factory under an agreement with the Mexican sugar industry in the region. But indeed the sugar industry was and continues to be a declining industry worldwide.

In 1988 a new industry, Petrojam, opened at the Libertad factory to produce molasses. The government of Belize (GOB) records indicate:

As part of its first moves to address the situation, government increased the sugar quota—that is the amount of sugar cane both the Belize Sugar Industries (BSI) and Petrojam can grind each year... This increase has benefited cane farmers in the northern districts, especially Corozal. (Oct. 11, 1990)

Government is also exploring the possibilities of a joint venture between the Obregón Sugar Factory in Chetumal, Quintana Roo and Petrojam to produce sugar. Earlier this year, government signed a memorandum of understanding with Belize Bio-chemical Limited for the establishment of a sugar cane factory on 50 acres of land between Concepcion and Libertad Villages...to produce sugar and ethanol. (Oct. 11, 1990)

Petrojam opened, but only for a few years. The other projects mentioned by government were not successful. By November of 1989 the shortage of jobs was also causing frustration, especially among the young population. Then the news broke:

> We (the government) are looking into the possibility of establishing a pilot commercial free-trade zone in Santa Elena. Studies are presently being undertaken and we hope to get this project started as soon as possible. This would undoubtedly create jobs for more customs officers, clerks, managers, carpenters, plumbers, electrician and masons. Recently, a concession to open a bicycle factory has been signed by the Minister of Economic Development in Corozal. (*El Corozaleño*, 6th November 1989)

Because of the uncertain future of these traditional exports, efforts were made towards agricultural diversification, and a special focus was made on tourism and industry. Industrial development was encouraged through a number of incentives, which included the awarding by government of tax holidays and import duty exemption on imports of up to a maximum of 25 years to qualifying companies.

Tourism

With the decline of the sugar industry in Corozal, tourism started to become important as an alternative economic activity to generate the necessary income for the region. But unfortunately, with both Corozal and Chetumal's slow growth, it would take a couple of years for it to surge. To market tourism it is necessary to know your attractiveness and your market potential. The characteristics of the bay and the services available at the time in Corozal were underqualified for the type of tourists who visited the area. Much needed to be done to turn this into an income generating activity. However, proximity to San Pedro, Belize and Cancun, Mexico, meant that a potential market existed and efforts to link up with these two tourist sites would be a sound investment.

Thus in the early 1990s some projects were announced; one was the Consejo Bay Project to develop a multi-million dollar tourist resort on 550 acres of land in the Consejo Area about two miles north of Corozal Town. "The company plans to build vacation villas, condominiums, hotels along the seaside. The resort will have an 18 hole golf course and a harbour marina for pleasure boats" (On the Scene Report, 1990, p. 13). At the time Consejo already had the Adventure Inn Resort and was being promoted as a residential area for retired US and Canadian citizens. The resort eventually closed, but the residential area for retirees continues to grow slowly. The Consejo Bay Project was also aborted, and it is not quite clear if the extension of land proposed for development was sold to the company and what the future of it will be.

Belize's environmental resources create substantial opportunities in the na-

84

Figure 4: Unemployment rate Corozal District 1993-2005

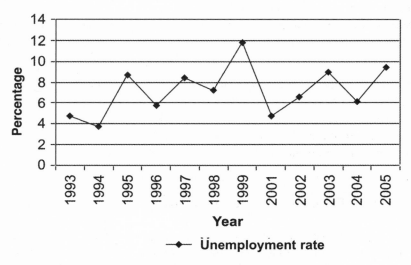

Source: Abstracts of Belize, 1990, 2000, 2005, CSO, Belize.

ture-based tourism market; the district of Corozal can participate in it, but much has to be done in regards to training in services, tourist guides, catering, marketing, among others. Again government policies play an important role in promoting tourism in the out districts; concentration of funds and activities and centralisation of policies will not help Corozal to diversify its economy.

A favourable initiative in 1990 was the creation of the Belize Tourism Board to carry out marketing plans. Its actions need to focus on all parts of the country.

Fiscal incentives to promote employment in Corozal

As mentioned above, Corozal suffered economically during the early years of independence; the devaluation of the Mexican peso and the closure of the sugar factory had adversely affected employment. However, for the 1980s period and early 1990s no data on the rate of unemployment in this district are available.

As shown above, in 1999 the highest unemployment rate was experienced, but the entire period shows instability of employment. The fluctuations were primarily because of the opening of new sources, such as the Export Processing Zone and the Commercial Free Zone, which offset some of the decline caused by other economic activities. In a move to bring stability to employment in the country of Belize, the government created an array of fiscal incentives.

The 1990 Fiscal Incentives Act provided tax holidays and duty exemptions for investments that would benefit the economy. The 1990 Income Tax Act granted tax relief to non-traditional exporters.

Several incentive schemes have been instituted to encourage and promote investment. The investment schemes are contained in the following legislations:

1. Fiscal Incentives Act No. 6 of 1990
2. Mines and Minerals Act, 1988
3. Export Processing Zone Act, 1990
4. Commercial Free Zone Act, 1994
5. International Business & Public Investment Act, 1990

The Export Processing Zone in Corozal

The Export Processing Zones (EPZ) Act exempted eligible firms from certain requirements concerning import licenses, quotas, import and export taxes, export licenses, price controls, and other regulatory mechanisms. The first export-processing zones (EPZs) were scheduled to be established in 1993. The concept required the designation or development of a physical facility (the zone) similar to an industrial park. As part of the effort to provide a more favourable environment for investment, Prime Minister George Cadle Price also introduced legislation that would lower corporate taxes from 45% to 35% in fiscal year 1992.

The EPZ Act's main focus was to encourage local and foreign investment in Belize in order to promote trade, foreign exchange earnings, employment, and transfer of technology. On July 18th, 1992, Belize's first EPZ was inaugurated at San Andres, two miles from Corozal Town. A total of two companies established themselves in Corozal under this fiscal incentive: Pleat-Tex Ltd and The Belize Bicycle Co. The expectation on the passing of the Act was for this EPZ to generate approximately 2,500 jobs, a goal never attained. In 1994 the EPZ Programme was amended, but the number of established companies did not increase in Corozal.

Transformation of the northern economy: the Commercial Free Zone in Corozal

The Corozal Free Zone project was a private initiative involving few citizens[5] interested in the development of the northern region. In its proposal phase, the CFZ project was discussed with the Northern Caucus[6] and the Corozal Business

86

Community. Once the proposal was written, the supporters of the CFZ lobbied nationally to get the approval of the Cabinet.

The Commercial Free Zone Act No 27 was passed in June of 1994 and was published in the Gazette on the 11th February, 1995. This was a much needed instrument to reverse the economic situation of Corozal as stated below:

> An Act to provide for the establishment and operation of commercial free zones within Belize to foster commercial trade and investment with neighbouring countries, to promote economic growth and development, to create new employment opportunities for Belizeans, and to provide for matters connected therewith or incidental thereto. (Act No 27 of 1994)

As defined in the Act, a commercial free zone means a geographic area in Belize designated as such by the Commercial Free Zone Management Agency (CFZMA), where investors may establish businesses and conduct trade and commerce free of the national customs regime.

One year later in June of 1995 the Corozal CFZ started to operate with the establishment of the CFZMA's office at the Santa Elena Border, situated at the foot of the bridge connecting Mexico and Belize. Its purpose was to establish a private sector driven commercial activity with internationally competitive laws for the attraction of trade and investment in Belize. This designated area can best be described as a tax haven. Its primary income was to be the administrative services offered to the businesses. Its location offered an advantage since it is within walking distance from the only bridge that connects Mexico and Belize, allowing Mexican residents to enter the zone without having to go through Belize's Immigration and Customs checkpoints.

Its strategic location made it attractive for tourism packages and offshore financial services. The signing of the North American Free Trade Area (NAFTA) gave it another competitive advantage; the slogan utilised to showcase it was "60 seconds to NAFTA territories." The objective was for the CFZ to serve, in addition to the NAFTA territory, the wider Asian and European market. The expected goods traded were automobiles, chemical products, electric and electronic equipment, iron and steel, textiles and leather, oil, fresh vegetables, computers, machinery parts, glass, cattle, fresh fruits, copper, photographic appliances, mining products, wood, shrimp, coffee, petrochemicals, canned foods and other products.

Although the performance of the Free Zone of Colon in Panama and in Miami, Florida served as models to design the CFZ of Belize, other experiences were welcomed to improve the operation of this pioneering project. Thus for the

---

[5] I was personally involved in the initial proposal of the CFZ and became the first Free Zone Business Association's General Manager in 1996.

[6] A group consisting of the People's United Party representatives and other interested citizens.

Figure 5: Commercial Free Zone businesses

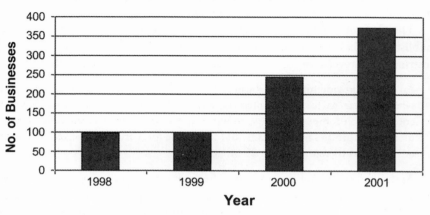

Source: Information and Statistical Office, CFZMA.

month of January 1996, experts from the Free Zone of Chile visited the CFZ of Belize to give their advice on its future development. They met with government authorities and other business officials in Belize and in Chetumal, Mexico. The specialists stated, "As a development alternative, this (CFZ) should be given priority in Government's economic policy and must be kept on the agenda until it becomes consolidated" (Ken, 1996).

The CFZ started with the businesses already established as "In bond" businesses and some new arrivals. The first businesses were Belizean-based companies. Few Mexicans businesses took up the challenge. As months went by, promotions were directed to Belize, Mexico, and the US; new investments started to flow both from Mexico and Belize (see Figure 5).

The promotion of the Affiliated Associates, small scale businesses, brought in many small business people from Belize and Mexico. The full package for company formation, including as optional the purchase of land, was US$12,500, among other expenses.

By the end of 1995, goods were already being imported to the CFZ; these included food items and cereals. Mexico at this time was going through economic restructuring since its entry in the GATT/WTO and the NAFTA agreement was eliminating its tariff advantages, and its privileged free zone territory was disappearing. The CFZ offered the Mexican businessmen an alternative to continue in the activity they knew well. This prompted their participation as businesses opened with very high expectations from the Mexican customers. By the end of 1996, and especially for its Christmas season, businesses at the CFZ made good sales. Mexican consumers were flooding the CFZ. It was precisely at this initial stage that the CFZ project gained the acceptance of the business community of both Mexico and Belize. From then on, the entry of businesses

Figure 6: Gross imports to CFZ

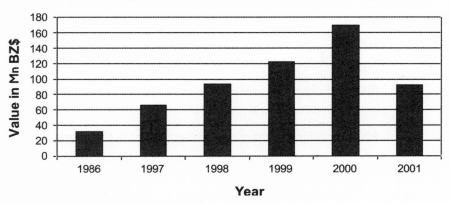

* 2001 is from January to July.
Source: Information and Statistical Office, CFZMA.

to the CFZ multiplied, attracting Mexican, Belizean, and other foreign investors; see Figure 6 above (Ken, 2000).

In the year 2000 there were a total of 372 registered companies, of which 215 were active. The type of economic activities at the time were manufacturing, consulting, importation and exportation, wholesale and retail, leases of business spaces, gas stations, restaurants, electric energy and construction.

In 2000 the major businesses sold commodities such as liquors, perfumes, foodstuff, gift items, electronics and appliances, household items, footwear, clothing, beverage, health and beauty aids, tires, cigars and cigarettes. At that time fuel distribution to Mexican clients was a substantial part of the zone's commercial activity. Also taking place were light industries such as the manufacturing of compact and optical disks, CD ROMs, plastic bottles, brooms, and mops.

The transit of Mexican vehicles to the CFZ in 2000 increased 30% in the first six months compared to the same period in 1999, stated the Mexican Customs Administrator at Subteniente Lopez. This represented an amount of 642,096 automobiles, including some that came from as far as the states of Campeche, Yucatán, Chiapas, Veracruz, and Tabasco. He stated that from Monday to Friday, an average of 3,304 vehicles crossed the border per day to shop at the CFZ; on Saturdays and Sundays there was an increase to 3775 vehicles. He recorded approximately 1 million vehicles to have crossed the border towards the CFZ in 1999 with at least 3 occupants that went shopping for food items, clothing, shoes, gasoline and electric appliances. (Notimex, 31st July 2000)

Taking into account the large amount of "walk over" customers, it was estimated that some 10 to 12 thousand Mexicans patrons entered the CFZ daily to shop in the growing number of establishments.

Figure 7: Comparison of gross imports

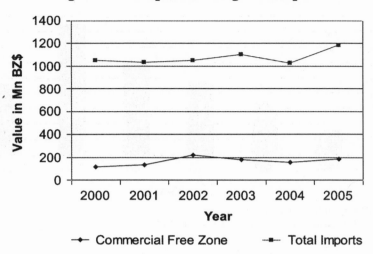

Source: Abstracts of Belize 2005, CSO.

Reduced prices for gasoline and commodities kept attracting Mexican consumers to the CFZ. In 2000 a total of 14,743,175 gallons of gasoline were imported to the CFZ, shared among five gas stations for a value of BZ$44,084,893.62. This was approximately 28% of the total volume of commerce of the CFZ.

All this activity at the CFZ meant an increase in imports registered in Belize. The graph below shows gross total imports and the amount that corresponds to the CFZ from 2000 to 2005. Imports to the CFZ increased from 2000 to 2002 and fell slightly in 2003, and more so in 2004. Total imports also show a reduction in that same year. Part of the decline of the CFZ imports in 2004 may be the result of the opening in Chetumal of the first mall and a department store. These took away part of the CFZ market. From that date to the present, businesses at the CFZ have suffered reduced sales. The only remaining attractive businesses are the casinos and a recently opened night club.

The year 2002 was a good year for the CFZ since it registered the largest amount of imports. The following years show a reduction of imports. The year 2004 also showed a reduction of total imports. "Gross imports (f.o.b.) contracted by BZ$83.2 million, with respective decline of BZ$58.7 million and BZ$24.5 million for goods imported into the customs' territory and the CFZ" (Central Bank of Belize, 2004).

In 2004 re-exports declined by 10.7% to BZ$232.4 million, reflecting reductions in sales from the CFZ and the customs' territory of 7.6% and 42.6% respectively. Cross-border sales at the CFZ fell as customs' regulations at the northern border further tightened and fuel prices in the Mexican border town of Chetumal remained lower than that in the CFZ (Central Bank of Belize, 2004).

Figure 8: Gross imports by type

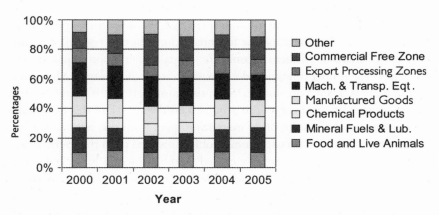

Source: Abstracts of Belize 2005, CSO.

The CFZ has impacted on the import structure of Belize. As shown above, we can see that importation to the CFZ is second in importance only after machinery and transport equipment. This infers important sales that should be vital in keeping employment and business activity. However, it is not known how much of these imports to the CFZ go back into the territory of Belize and how much to Mexico. These pieces of information are significant to measure the real impact of the CFZ in the border region.

A social cost was introduced at the CFZ imports of 1.5% on the aggregate value of general merchandise and 10% on fuel. This social cost was to finance research and infrastructural wear and tear in the country, as a result of the roads used to transport goods from Belize to the CFZ. Since the implementation of the cost, nothing has been said of the use of these monies, nor of the total amount collected to date. Further studies into the economic impact of the CFZ are needed, for there are many aspects of it that are not yet known.

The CFZ performance

The CFZ is a trap and is not a viable solution to economic development. Employment and increased incomes are needed, but dependency on one activity predominantly is dangerous. The delicate situation of the activities at the CFZ is exacerbated because of its border location. All borders are focal points where the concerned governments must have in place proper control on all types of trafficking for the benefit of the population at large.

The objective of the CFZ was to compete with the Miami International Free Zone and the Colon Free Zone in Panama with regards to the amount of imports and reexports. The retail business in the CFZ was important, but not to the extent of becoming the main activity.[7] This retail business created various problems for the CFZ: first, the amount spent by Mexican consumers was limited to US$50, which is the franchise for international border regions, according to the customs law of Mexico. Second, the migration situation required shoppers to have the proper migration documents to leave the country. Most Mexicans did no possess such documents. Soon the Immigration Office in Chetumal had long queues of citizens filing to acquire a border pass, and this occurred to such an extent that the solution of exempting them from this requirement was soon reached. Third, an infrastructural problem resulted from the traffic jams at the international bridge. These were caused by the numerous buses and private Mexican cars from central and southern Mexican territories, and pedestrians going toward Belize and the busses and the private vehicles, and pedestrians from Belize entering Mexico. Fourth, numerous security problems for vehicles and persons existed since many vehicles were damaged or hampered with and the insurance companies did not respond because the CFZ territory was considered in neither Mexico nor Belize. The CFZ was not prepared; eventually some of these problems were addressed with the implementation of security guards at the gates and the expansion of the CFZ territory allowing another gate to be opened.

As part of the expansion of the CFZ, the migration and customs offices at the Santa Elena border have had to relocate. Plans are also on way to build another bridge over the Rio Hondo to provide for a more fluid vehicle pass.

Effects on employment, investment, and growth in general

The CFZ has generated the much needed employment for inhabitants of the northern districts. Direct employment has been as shop keepers, attendants, and casino employees. Indirect employment occurs in companies and industries such as trucking, mechanics, retail stores, car rental agencies, insurance brokers, and construction material vendors. People work as contractors, masons, electricians, plumbers, engineers, architects, accountants, and landlords, among others.

In 2000, there were a total of 1,709 direct employees at the CFZ of which 307 are foreigners who are primarily administrative and technical personnel.

As stated above, more detailed studies need to be conducted to analyse the impact on direct and indirect employment, its effects on the growth and development of the border region, the growth of the CFZ businesses, its competitive-

---

[7] The retail business was implemented as a complementary activity (taken from the Chilean model) since the main activity at free zones around the world is the movement of great volumes of imports and reexports.

Figure 9: Calculations of Gini and Lorenz Curves for the district of Corozal

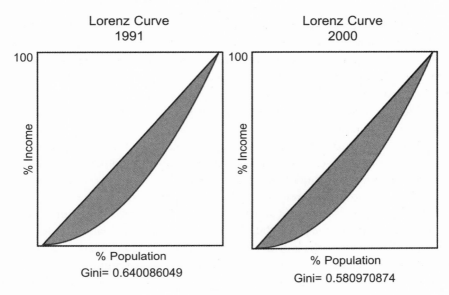

Lorenz Curve 1991
Gini= 0.640086049

Lorenz Curve 2000
Gini= 0.580970874

Source: CSO, Belize.

ness and its prospective. Some claims of low paying jobs and labour exploitation have been made by CFZ employees. These allegations were made public on some of the national radio stations. Some would argue that a badly paid job is better than none, but there are laws and regulations in Belize and at the CFZ, although the latter does not provide duration of work per day and wage level.

Improved income is evident in Corozal since new shops and hotels are flourishing. There is a certain degree of improvement in incomes demonstrated by the economic activity; however, there is still much needed to recover the economic activity of the 70s.

The way forward

The District of Corozal is part of a broader territory; therefore its economic performance is largely dependent on the national economic policies and programs. As we have seen, Corozal has gone from a buoyant economy when sugar cane cultivation was booming, to a state of depression due to the loss of jobs as a result of the closure of the sugar factory. There is a slight recovery, basically due to the operation of the CFZ. Other activities are needed to bring the desired diversification to the economy. Agriculture products with viable markets such as papaya are on the way; tourism needs proper attention to flourish; CFZ needs refocusing to compete in volume and value with the major free zones of the hemisphere; and most importantly adequate government policies are needed. Poverty has become a daily debate among the sufferers and the policy makers. The perception that the Belizean society is divided between the poor and the wealthy is accurate. This socio-economic stratification existed previously, but the gap was not as wide during the pre-independent period, at least not among native Belizeans. Although Corozal is not on the lower end, it does reflect the need for the national government to take the out districts into serious consideration in its planning process.[8]

The Lorenz curve and the Gini index are measures of income distribution. The Lorenz curve gives an indication of income distribution inequality with respect to a perfect distribution (45 degree) curve.

The Gini index measures the level of income concentration; the index varies between 0 (equal distribution) and 1 (greater concentration). The graph on page 93 indicates that for the year 2000, there is less concentration, although for both years, 1991 and 2000, the indices are very high, indicating a stronger tendency towards concentration. Further studies should be done to determine if the impact of the CFZ might have caused the Gini index to show a better position for 2000.

Given the above analysis, the CFZ has been eminently disappointing and not been the panacea that it was supposed to be; the prosperity that it was supposed to bring did not materialise.

References

ABSTRACT OF STATISTICS. (1990, 2000, 2004, 2005). Central Bank of Belize. (For the *Statistical Digest*, see http://www.centralbank.org.bz/dm_browse.asp?pid=19.)

BELIZE SUGAR INDUSTRIES LIMITED, 1964 - 1989, 25th Anniversary. Belize City: Belize Sugar Industries Ltd.

BELIZE TIMES, México voted in favour of the UN resolution. March 22, 1981.

BELIZE TODAY. Corozal bounces back! On the scene report. Oct. 1990.

CENTRAL BANK OF BELIZE. (2004). Commercial Free Zone Act.

CENTRAL STATISTICAL OFFICE, Abstract of Statistics: 1999, 2000, 2005.

CIQRO, CONACYT y Gobierno del Estado. (1994a). Estudios Socioeconómicos. Estudio Integral De La Frontera México-Belice, Tomo I,. Chetumal, Quintana Roo.

CIQRO, CONACYT y Gobierno del Estado. (1994b). Monografias de Belice. Estudio integral de la frontera Mexico-Belice, Tomo iii, Chetumal, Quintana Roo.

---

[8] This paper did not take into consideration social topics such as drugs, education, housing, medical care among others, but they all play an important role in the economic performance of every region.

EL COROZALEÑO, Corozal Bay. 6th November 1989.

GOVERNMENT OF BELIZE. (1994). Commercial Free Zone Act. Act No. 27 of 1994. Belmopan, Belize.

KEN, CRUCITA. (2000, octubre-diciembre). La Zona Libre Comercial de Belize: Historia y realidad actual. *Itzamná*. Revista de la División de Ciencias Sociales y Económico Administrativas. Universidad de Quintana Roo. Año 1. No. 3. Chetumal, Quintana Roo, México.

KEN, CRUCITA. (1996, February 4). Experts assess the commercial Free Zone of Belize, its development and its regional impact. *Amandala*. Belize

KEN, CRUCITA. (1995, January 27). Devaluation in Mexico: How it impacts on Belize. *Amandala*. Belize.

KEN, CRUCITA. (1994a, abril-junio). Realidad y perspectiva ante el nuevo modelo económico". *Caribe*, Año 1, Número 2, Chetumal, Quintana Roo.

KEN, CRUCITA. (1994b, julio-septiembre). Las economías fronterizas: Othón P. Blanco y Belice; perspectivas para la inversión privada. *Caribe*, Año 1, Número 3, Chetumal, Quintana Roo.

KEN, CRUCITA. (1994c, noviembre-enero). La inversión privada y el desarrollo económico del municipio de Othón P. Blanco y Belice. *Caribe*. Año 1, Número 0, Chetumal, Quintana Roo,

KEN, CRUCITA. (1992, junio). Belize: Paraíso fiscal. *Iniciativa*. Chetumal, Quintana Roo.

KEN, CRUCITA and HERNÁNDEZ TRUEBA, LEYDI. (julio 1992). "Las relaciones comerciales México-Belice". *Iniciativa*. Chetumal, Quintana Roo.

MUNDO MAYA ORGANISATION. (1992-2007). Retrieved from the World Heritage Centre/UNESCO webpage: http://whc.unesco.org/en/partners/35.

NOTIMEX. (31st July, 2000). Aumenta 30% afluencia de vehículos mexicanos a Zona Franca de Belize.

PECH FEBLES, REBECA and CRUZ CÁCERES, MARIA E. (2000). El impacto de la Zona Libre Comercial de Belice en el comercio de Chetumal. *Revista Itzamná.*, Año 1, No 2, Mayo - Septiembre de 2000, Universidad de Quintana Roo, Chetumal, Quintana Roo, México.

PERRY, JOSEPH, WOODS, LOUIS A. and STEAGALL, JEFFREY W. (1993) "Sugar consumption, sugar policy, and the fate of Belizean cane growers. *SPEAReport 9*. SPEAR, Belize.

SECRETARÍA DE RELACIONES EXTERIORES. Retrieved from Government of Mexico webpage:http://www.sre.gob.mx/cilasur/Assets/Images/ActasBelice/tratado mexbel1893.pdf.

TRATADO SOBRE LÍMITES ENTRE MÉXICO Y HONDURAS BRITÁNICA. (1893/1897). Retrieved from the Secretaría de Relaciones Exteriores, Government of Mexico Available from webpage: http://www.sre.gob.mx/cilasur/Assets/Images/Acta Belice/tratadomexbel1893.pdf.

Part 2

Environment

Part 2

Environment

4. The Environment: Reserve, Preserve, Plunder

Candy Gonzalez

Introduction

In the last few decades a greater knowledge and appreciation for the environment has evolved. To refer to the "environment" is to take in all aspects of the natural environment, including air, water, soil, flora and fauna, and the human environment, comprising indigenous and non-indigenous cultural heritage.[1] The concept of biodiversity demands equal importance for all living things.

The introduction of "the environment" as a separate area of concern is a fundamentally different way of thinking. It challenges the belief that everything inside the fence is ours (or someone's) and everything outside the fence is free to exploit; it calls for a rejection of the philosophical and legal principles that underlay the current social order.

It also requires a change on a more basic level. Traditionally, western thought (western civilization)[2] has assigned superior rights to human life viewing the natural systems as subservient, something to be manipulated, controlled, tamed, and/or conquered. The difficulty with environmental ethics, or environmentalism, is that it forces us to abolish the historic duality of how we think about humans and nature; it promotes the idea that natural systems have the same fundamental rights as humans.[3]

---

[1] See Convention on Biological Diversity, 1760 U.N.T.S. 79; entered into force December 29, 1993.

[2] The term "western civilization" is used to portray the philosophy that evolved in civilizations throughout the "white" world, which sees people vs. nature as opposed to people co-existing with nature.

[3] Indigenous peoples have a tradition of viewing people as a part of nature and seeing natural systems as sacred. The Maya were known as the Guardians of the Forest. This belief system was present in Belize and remains present in many indigenous cultures; unfortunately, to give it the attention it deserves is beyond the scope of this paper.

Environmental law refers to those laws directed towards protecting soil, air, water, and biodiversity. This includes environmental planning and assessment, natural resource management, pollution management, biodiversity conservation, and natural and cultural heritage. Belize's legal system is based on the protection of private rights, including private rights to property. Protecting the environment calls for a shift in thinking, away from protecting the rights of private individuals to protecting the wider public interest.[4]

Concern for the environment in relationship to development has become a major concern worldwide and in Belize. There is a growing acceptance that what is done in one area of the world has impacts in other parts of the world.[5] Since independence in 1981, Belize has experienced many of the growing pains of a non-industrialized nation and faces the constant push-pull between economic developments and developments that are sustainable in a changing world.

This essay reviews the evolution of environmental protection and environmental law over the past 25 years and chronicles significant events with an assessment of where we are and where we are going.

Background of environmental law in Belize

Colonialism is, by definition, a system whereby countries rule other nations or territories for their own benefit. The legacy of British colonial rule continues to be reflected in Belize's laws, Belize's values and beliefs, and Belize's way of thinking. The natural resources are viewed as something to control, own, sell, barter, or, in some way, exploit. The thinking goes like this: there is a tree, cut it; there is a bird, shoot it; there is a fish, catch it.

Protections put in place by the British and by the early conservationists were not problematic because there was plenty of land, plenty of resources. The provisions that were put in place were for the management and distribution of national lands, provisions for reservation of tracts of land as "reserves"[6] and as bird sanctuaries;[7] there were ordinances for protecting wildlife, such as the manatee that allowed for the governor to "...prohibit the killing or taking of any Manatee within any specified area or areas of the Colony..."[8]

---

[4] See generally Hunter, Salzman, & Zaelke. (2002). *International Environmental Law and Policy*, (2nd Ed.). Foundation Press.

[5] The international discourse on climate change is a clear example.

[6] This is more fully discussed in the essays by C. Young & R. Horwich and M. McField & N. Bood within this volume.

[7] Crown Lands Act, Laws of Belize, Revised Ed., 1980-1990, CAP 147.

[8] The Manatee Protection Ordinance (Ordinance 32 of 1935) Legislative Council of British Honduras, 3 October 1935, Gazetted 12 October 1935.

At independence, the only mention of the environment as something separate unto itself is found in the Preamble of the Constitution, adopted in 1981.[9] It states that the Belizean people require policies of state, which, among other things, "protect the environment...".[9]

Following independence, the major change in the laws was in name only, from being called "colonial" to being called "national" laws, leaving the legal framework virtually intact. By simply renaming, rewording, and updating the colonial laws we were left with a legal system with all the imperfections, inequities, and possibilities for abuse of the previous laws that gave unfair advantage to the colonial government. The system that was perpetuated is that of paternalism and subjugation. The Minister is presumed to know what is best for "the people," regardless of the provisions for advisory councils and committees. Land, among other things, is held in "trust" and implies total trust in the hands of the Minister.

No separate laws covered the environment; there was, and is, a patchwork of laws under a variety of ministries and departments dealing with natural resources, land use, pollution, health, water, etc. These laws, as they relate to the environment, evolved from British common law, statutes and subsidiary legislation, administrative policies, traditional laws, and from international law.

This early regime of laws concerning the environment can be viewed as laws for protection or for exploitation. The protection side can be "...described as those rules for the protection of the environment from undue degradation by human activity and rules for the conservation of natural, built, and cultural items within the environment. The 'exploitative component' may be described as those rules for the disposition of natural resources and rules which promote or facilitate development activity."[11] Most of the laws overlap, sometimes causing confusion over who has responsibility for a particular area of concern.

Early environmental protections–description of the laws

To demonstrate from whence we came, a description of some of the earlier laws, all of which are still in force, is instructive. It also demonstrates how fundamental a mind shift it is to establish environmental laws and regulations specifically for the protection of the environment. The laws are divided into those establishing protected areas, those protecting flora and fauna, those cover-

---

[9] The Belize Constitution Act, Ch. 4, Substantive Laws of Belize, Rev. Ed. 2003.
[10] Ibid.
[11] McCalla, Winston. (1995). *Compendium on Environmental Protection and Natural Resource Management Legislation in Belize*, (pp. 4-5). Ministry of Tourism and the Environment, Belmopan, Belize.

ing pollution and public health, and those covering land management and planning.[12]

Those laws that set aside areas for protection, conservation and/or reservation of natural resources are the National Parks Systems Act (to establish National Parks, Natural Monuments, Wildlife Sanctuaries and Nature Reserves),[13] sections of the Fisheries Act (to establish marine protected areas),[14] the National Lands Act (setting aside a buffer zone along bodies of water, rivers, etc.,[15] as well as covering Bird Sanctuaries), the Forest Act (to establish Forest Reserves),[16] and the Ancient Monuments and Antiquities Act (to establish archaeological reserves).[17]

The most egregious sections in each of these Acts are those giving the Minister complete discretionary powers to de-reserve or change the boundaries of the area(s) under protection.[18] No provisions exist for public participation when an area is declared "protected" or when "protected" areas are taken out of protection. Although instances exist where the public has been consulted, it is not mandated and therefore, it is discretionary. When decisions are made with no community or stakeholder consultation, animosity from the buffer communities can and does result. If there were provisions for community or stakeholder

---

[12] This does not purport to be a complete list; there are many sources where explanations and analysis of the laws can be found.

[13] Chapter 215 of the Substantive Laws of Belize, R.E. 2003. The Act provides for preservation and protection of highly important natural and cultural features, for the regulation of scientific, educational, and recreational use of the same. It defines four categories of protected areas: Nature Reserve, National Park, Wildlife Sanctuary, National Monument, along with the activities allowed within each.

[14] Chapter 210, Sec. 14 of the Substantive Laws of Belize, R.E. 2003. The Act states that the Minister responsible for fisheries may declare an area within the fishing limits of Belize a marine reserve for specific purposes of conservation of marine fauna and flora, preservation of fish breeding grounds and habitat, promotion of scientific study, natural regeneration of aquatic life in areas where it has been depleted and enhancement of beauty. This may include the incorporation of adjacent areas of land.

[15] Chapter 191 of the Substantive Laws of Belize, R.E. 2003, Sec. 12 states that land outside a city, town, or village that adjoins any running stream, river or open water shall maintain a 66 foot wide strip of land along the side that shall be left in its natural state.

[16] Chapter 213, Sec. 3 of the Substantive Laws of Belize, R.E. 2003. Forest Act allows for establishment of Forest Reserves on national lands with purpose of protection for controlled use to ensure an adequate and increasing supply of timber and other forest produce at a reasonable price. Conservation of fauna, flora, and ecosystems, tourism and environmental protection are also of concern.

[17] Chapter 330 of the Substantive Laws of Belize, R.E. 2003. The Minister may declare any national lands containing or adjacent to an ancient monument an Archaeological Reserve, with certain restrictions on use.

[18] Ibid., chapter 191, Sec. 6(2).

involvement, it may very likely lead to involvement of people in the monitoring, care, and protection of the area.

A need exists for an overall National Protected Areas System for all forms of protected areas within a national plan or scheme. Although many drafts of such a plan have been created, no such plan has been put in place.[19]

The other areas of protection include protection of the flora and fauna of Belize. The Wildlife Protection Act provides for conservation, restoration, and development of wildlife.[20] It seeks to regulate hunting and to protect many species from being hunted, captured, harassed, or held in the possession of individuals.

When the animals are dolphins, seals, whales or manatees, all listed under this Act because they are mammals, there are conflicts over who has the responsibility for their protection—Fisheries or Forestry. In November 2006, new legislation, long overdue, was reviewed to bring Belize into compliance with the Convention on International Trade in Endangered Species of Wild Fauna and Flora (CITES).[21] The Forest Act covers protection of trees and mangroves.[22] The Fisheries Act covers protection of marine life and corals.

The laws dealing with pollution, health, and a variety of other concerns relating to the environment are found in an array of laws, the main one being the Public Health Act.[23] This law provides regulatory power for the control of pollution in air, water, and on land if it affects the quality of human life. It addresses disposal of solid and liquid waste and the contamination of water intended for human consumption.

The laws concerning land use and planning are another area of laws that could be considered to deal with environmental protection. They include the National Lands Act, the Land Utilization Act (LUA), and the Coastal Zone Management Act (CZMA).

The National Lands Act[24] provides for the management and distribution of national lands, except those lands reserved as forest land, under the Forest Act. The Minister has the power to reserve "...to the Government of Belize the right of disposing of in a manner as for the public interests may seem best, such lands

---

[19] On 19 January 2006, the National Protected Areas Policy and System Plan was presented in Belize City. The Plan was said to have been approved by Cabinet but it has not been implemented at the time of this writing (author present at meeting).

[20] Chapter 220 of the Substantive Laws of Belize, R.E. 2003.

[21] If this legislation is not implemented this year, Belize becomes delinquent and may be punished by an export stop, which will hurt because it would stop export of both mahogany and conch (from a source in Forestry Department).

[22] Chapter 213 of the Substantive Laws of Belize, R.E. 2003. Forest (Protection of Trees) Regulations Sec. 5 and Forests (Protection of Mangroves) Regulations (Sec. 5).

[23] Chapter 30 of the Substantive Laws of Belize, R.E. 2003.

[24] Chapter 191 of the Substantive Laws of Belize, R.E. 2003.

as may be required as reserves, public roads or other internal communications, or commons, or as the sites of public buildings, or as places for the interment of the dead, or places for the education, recreation and amusement of the inhabitants of any town or village, or as the sites of public quays, wharves or landing places on the sea coast or shores of streams, or for any purposes of public defence, safety, utility, convenience or enjoyment, or for otherwise facilitating the improvement and settlement of Belize, or for special purposes."[25]

The Minister also has the power to de-reserve land, change or alter boundaries or impose terms or stipulations on any national lands.[26] The Minister's power to de-reserve (eliminate) or change the boundaries of an area previously reserved, without the need for public participation in the decision, is excessive and easily open to abuse.

The Land Utilization Act and amendments provide for measures to govern the use and development of land and to introduce measures for conservation of land and watersheds.[27] It requires that any proposed land subdivision get approval from the government prior to any activity. Originally it applied to rural land, but in 1990 was extended to all areas.[28] It gives broad powers to the Minister by virtue of the section allowing for the making of any regulations needed to better carry out the provisions of this law.[29]

Although the law itself does not establish a comprehensive legal regime for land utilization, it empowers the Minister to make regulations for a number of matters, including: demarcation of "water catchment areas or watersheds" and the prohibition of the clearing of vegetation within such watersheds; providing for the prevention of soil erosion; regulating the clearing of forests and the cutting of trees.[30]

The LUA also allows for the Minister (of Natural Resources) to declare Special Development Areas (SDA). Within an SDA, which is subject to development plans, the use of the area may be restricted to specific purposes. Thus, an SDA can be construed as a tool for land use planning and zoning and may include protected areas or zones.[31] Examples of established SDAs demonstrate the variety of stated purposes within this designation; they include tourism development; sustainable agriculture; urban development; maintaining forests; village expansion and economic development. This has been used to fill in the gaps for the lack of any overall zoning regulations. It has not often enough been used as

[25] Ibid., Sec. 6(1).
[26] Ibid., Sec. 6(2).
[27] Chapter 188 of the Substantive Laws of Belize, R.E. 2003.
[28] Ibid., Sec. 3.
[29] Ibid., Sec. 17. .
[30] Ibid., Sec. 19(a).
[31] Ibid., Sec. 19(d).

it could be to improvise a zoning plan for some areas that are developing quickly. In the end, it is still a patchwork approach; it does not have the benefits of an overall zoning plan.

The Coastal Zone Management Act established the Coastal Zone Management Authority and Institute whose role was to coordinate and to monitor activities in the coastal zone. Its goal was to develop an integrated coastal zone management plan that would preserve coastal resources by bringing together all the different agencies and interests, governmental and private, for the overall preservation and good of the coastal zone.[32] Management plans were developed for efficient and effective use and protection of the coastal zone, but those plans have not developed into a legal regime. One major problem is that the Act did not give the Authority the power to implement or enforce but only the power to advise and coordinate. In its advisory capacity, it has been very slow in making decisions; when action is finally agreed upon it is long after a problem has arisen, and sometimes, far too late to avoid damage.[33]

Laws related to the environment

Procedural rights are necessary to the legal system. Without procedure, laws cannot be applied. They are enabling rights in that they make it possible for people to participate in the business of government, to actively contribute and respond to activities that affect people's lives, including the protection of their environment.

For that reason, it is important to understand the right to information. Without proper access to information, we do not know what might be impacting an area or the people in that area. That is why the Freedom of Information Act (FOIA) is an important law related to environmental protection. The FOIA sets up a procedure for citizens to access information from the Government. The Minister is supposed to act in good faith with a duty to make the documents readily available to all who desire access to them. The request for information can be made to ministries of government and "prescribed authorities," including local authorities such as the city, town, village councils, a public statutory corporation, or a body established for a public purpose.[34] Private companies are NOT included in this Act and the agreements and contracts made between the Government and private companies are often hidden from public scrutiny.

---

[32] Chapter 329 of the Substantive Laws of Belize, R.E. 2003.
[33] Presentation by Vincent Gillett, *Natural Resource Management & Utilization*, at the 3rd National Symposium on the State of the Environment, Belize City, Belize, Jan. 13, 2000 (author present).
[34] Chapter 13 of the Substantive Laws of Belize, R.E. 2003.

Where there has been a decision to deny a request by a responsible minister or principal officer there is a process to apply for an internal review of that decision by the responsible minister or principal officer.[35] The other option is to apply to the Ombudsman to review the decision to deny access to a document requested. The decision of the Ombudsman can be appealed to the Supreme Court for review.

The environment in the laws of Belize

Although many countries had been enacting laws to preserve and protect the environment and to punish wrongdoers with regard to the environment, it was not until 1992 that the idea of environmental protection really took root in Belize and internationally with influence from the Earth Summit the same year. The Summit culminated in the *Rio Declaration on Environment and Development* (1992)[36] and by a global plan of action for balancing economic and environmental concerns in terms of sustainable development, a year earlier, referred to as Agenda 21.[37]

Belize's first environmental law, the Environmental Protection Act, was passed in 1992.[38] It created the Department of Environment (DOE), whose duties include: doing what is necessary for the preservation, protection and improvement of the environment; the wise use of natural resources; the prevention and control of pollution; investigation and inspection to assure that laws are followed; monitor environmental health; and advise, educate, and promote policies for the protection of environmental health and for protection of the environment, directly and indirectly.[39]

In the early years, the DOE had the freedom to do its job and there appeared to be a strong commitment to environmental protection. It also helped that funds from the Global Environmental Fund and other sources were coming in to help purchase equipment and strengthen the Department.[40] The environ-

---

[35] Appealing to the one who has denied the request may seem fruitless, but if persons want access the information and are willing to take the matter to court, they must first go through each of the required steps.

[36] *Rio Declaration on Environment and Development*, U.N. Doc. A/CONF 151/26:311 L.M. 874 (1992).

[37] Agenda 21, A/Conf. 151/26 (1991).

[38] Chapter 328 of the Substantive Laws of Belize, R.E. 2003.

[39] When the DOE was created, it was included in the portfolio of the Minister of Tourism, which is an indication of how the environmental protections were viewed in relation to the tourism industry.

[40] Interview with Jose Mendoza who held the position of Environmental Officer at DOE from 1993-2000.

mental regulations were developed and passed into law in 1995-96. Without regulations it would have been hard to carry out the functions of the DOE. The regulations laid out a process and guidelines for carrying out the mandates of the EPA.

The Environmental Protection (Effluent Limitation) Regulations apply to discharges of effluents into any inland waters or marine environment. The word "effluent" means sewage or liquid water or wastewater that comes from any activity or process that is taking place at any industrial or commercial place. It sets limits on the concentration of effluents that can be discharged and the treatment necessary before it is discharged. No new source of effluent discharge or a material change in the quality or amount of the discharge is to occur without the approval of the DOE.[41] It does not apply to non-industrial or non-commercial sources.

The Pollution Regulations cover pollution from any source: industry, cars, burning, water pollution, pollution to land, and noise pollution, and controls activities that affect these areas such as washing vehicles in rivers or streams. No one is allowed to release contaminants into the environment whether from the home, a business, agriculture, recreation, industry, or any other source. A contaminant is something that is likely to affect the life, health, safety, welfare or comfort of humans or cause damage to or impair the quality of the environment. Of course, there are circumstances in which such a release is considered necessary and a permit is needed from the DOE for that activity.

The Regulations allow for the DOE to make the user of land clean up the premises when a site is abandoned; the site is to be cleaned and the user is to restore the area to how it was, as much as it is possible. Of course the enforcement of the regulations is not always possible and there is a discretionary clause as well.[42]

The Environmental Impact Assessment Regulations include the procedures to determine if a proposed activity needs an Environmental Impact Assessment (EIA).[43] Before commencing a project or development, all persons, agencies, and institutions (public or private) must, before starting on a proposed project or activity, apply to the DOE who determines if an EIA is required. Some projects always need an EIA and some may need an EIA. These are listed in the Schedules at the end of the Regulations. A person who has submitted an EIA must publish a notice in at least one nationally distributed newspaper indicating: (1) the location and nature of the proposal; (2) that an EIA has been prepared; (3) where,

---

[41] Chapter 328 (Effluent Regulations), pp. 35-61 of the Substantive Laws of Belize, R.E. 2003.

[42] Chapter 328, Sec. 58, of the Substantive Laws of Belize, R.E. 2003 Pollution Regulations.

[43] Chapter 328, Environmental Impact Assessment Regulations, pp. 5-34 of the Substantive Laws of Belize, R.E. 2003.

when, and for how long the EIA can be seen by the public; (4) that anyone can make objections and representations to the DOE about the effects the proposed activity will have on the environment; and (5) the deadline for filing comments.

Many of the surrounding communities of the proposed project/development never see the EIA Notice and are unaware of the proposed projects or developments that may affect them. There is a lack of transparency and an absence of real participation from those directly affected and those concerned with the project.[44] This lack of transparency takes many forms. The EIAs should be: (1) stored in a place that is easily and readily available to the community members; (2) because of their huge size–some are thousands of pages long–interested parties should be able to borrow the EIAs for short periods of time; (3) the material should be reader-friendly. In other words, those affected by the proposed project should be able to–with reasonable effort–determine if their environment will be deleteriously affected and if they wish to participate further in the project. The EIA process should not be a game of "hide and seek."

The National Environmental Appraisal Committee (NEAC) reviews the EIAs. "The Committee is made up of

> (a) the Chief Environmental Officer or his nominee; (b) the Commissioner of Lands or his nominee; (c) the Housing and Planning Officer or his nominee; (d) the Chief Forest Officer or his nominee; (e) the Fisheries Administrator or his nominee; (f) the Chief Hydrologist or his nominee; (g) the Archaeological Commissioner or his nominee; (h) the Director of Geology and Petroleum or his nominee; (i) the Chief Agricultural Officer or his nominee; (j) two non-governmental representatives appointed by the Minister on the recommendation of the Department.[45]

The NEAC may advise the department to require the developer to conduct further work or studies, to supply more information, to amend the EIA accordingly, and/or to resubmit the EIA by a date mutually agreeable. If the damage to the environment is severe, the DOE can decide to reject an activity; to change how or where activity is done; to improve the plan, if they can; to approve the project despite the harm if it's believed to be in the best interest of the nation. DOE, on recommendation of NEAC, may require a public hearing about any project or activity where an EIA is required.[46]

In 1995, when the NEAC first convened, there was an optimism that the Committee would function as an independent and comprehensive, multi-field

---

[44] Thompson, T.W. "Ten Years of the EIA Process: Moving Forward With a Focus on People and Development." *Belize Audubon Society Newsletter*, Volume 37, No. 4. February 2006.
[45] Chapter 328 (Environmental Impact Assessment Regulations), Sec. 25(2).
[46] Ibid., Sec. 25.

group to seriously consider the impacts of all developments requiring an environmental impact assessment.[47] Those hopes turned sour when, in 1999, the NEAC rejected a proposal to reclaim land on the west side of Caye Chapel Resort for an 18-hole golf course. Exercising ministerial discretion,[48] and in opposition to the advice of the DOE and NEAC, the Minister overrode the decision allowing the project to proceed.[49] Disillusionment in the process grew.[50]

That event marked a shift in the underlying tensions between the preservation and conservation of the environment and economic development, which increased. It has become a generally held perception that politicians regard politics as an opportunity to amass personal fortunes. The view is that "they play the system" for what they can personally get out of it, including selling national land and supporting large developments that benefit foreign investors.[51]

Taking it to court

After a groundswell of opposition to the building of the Chalillo Dam on the Macal River in the Cayo District, the DOE granted environmental clearance. The Belize Alliance of Conservation Non-Governmental Organizations (BACONGO), an umbrella environmental organization for NGOs throughout the country of Belize, challenged the decision. The case brought to the fore the way decisions impacting the environment were being addressed and marked the first time an environmental case was heard by the Belize Courts.

BACONGO's complaint claimed that the NEAC and the DOE acted improperly in numerous ways, including the failure to genuinely consider the comments and concerns of those living downstream of the project and other stakeholders, including issues of health and safety; the failure to address the inadequate hydrological studies; the failure to address the faulty and misleading geology reports that identified rock at the site as granite, although it is softer sandstone and

[47] Personal communication, Jose Mendoza, Environmental Officer of DOE, 1993-2000 and two original members of NEAC.

[48] Chapter 328 (Environmental Impact Assessment Regulations), Sec. 27. Under this section, if the "Department has decided that an undertaking, project or activity shall not proceed, the developer may, within thirty days after the Department's decision, appeal to the Minister against the decision of the Department."

[49] Minutes of NEAC meeting of 7 August 1999 and notes related to the project, and on file at DOE; referenced 3 October 2006 on 7NewsBelize at http://www.7newsbelize.com/archive/10030602.html.

[50] Ibid. Referring to this decision and the owner of Caye Chapel Resort, the 7NewsBelize reporter said that the Minister's decision "seemed to come up again after Addington donated these sixteen pickup trucks to the Musa administration in 1999."

[51] These commonly held beliefs have been stated freely by dozens of Belizeans to author.

shale; the failure to address the safety issues related to the seismic activity in the area; the failure to properly take into account the destruction of large Maya sites that would be destroyed in the area of the Chalillo reservoir, and the area the power line corridor would go through would be a violation of the Ancient Monuments and Antiquities Act; the failure to address the detrimental impact of the project on the rare fauna and flora of the area, including a number of endangered species; and, the failure to hold a public hearing prior to a decision being made.

In addition, BACONGO raised concerns of an implied bias on the part of the Chairman of NEAC and all governmental representatives on NEAC because of these facts:

(i) prior to the decision complained of, the Prime Minister of Belize publicly announced his Government's support for the project; (ii) on 26 January 2001 the Government of Belize, BECOL, and BEL agreed to the terms of a Third Master Agreement wherein the Government of Belize committed itself to construct the access road to the Chalillo dam site, (iii) the Government of Belize also agreed to waive on behalf of BECOL and its Contractor all licenses, permits, consents and regulatory approvals in connection with the Chalillo project (the New Project) and to waive or cause to be waived all environmental laws, rules or regulations except those to which the Producer agreed to be bound.[52]

The Court, though recognizing the inadequacy of the EIA and a failure to precisely follow the letter of the EIA Regulations, ruled there was no adequate proof of impropriety and/or wrongdoing in the EIA process or on the issues of undue influence. The Court did decide there was no doubt that a public hearing was warranted and ruled:

I therefore direct that the DOE should hold a public hearing on the Chalillo dam project...In the circumstances of the present case, I realize, of course, that this order would, in effect, sound like putting the cart before the horse. In view of DOE's decision of 5th April 2002....though, in the round, I am not able to find in favour of the applicant, on all its complaints, the objections and challenges it has mounted...can not be regarded as de minimis or mere petty-fogging. They raised issues that touch and concern the responsibilities of NEAC and the DOE in relation to their consideration of the effects of a proposed development on the environment, and the application and implementation of the Environmental Protection Act and its regulations on the EIA submitted in relation to this project...[53]

The case was appealed to the Belize Court of Appeals who upheld the decision of the lower court but found that the issues raised were of significance and did merit review by Belize's highest Court of Appeals, the Privy Council of Eng-

---

[52] *BACONGO v Department of Environment*, Supreme Court of Belize Claim number 61 of 2002.

[53] Ruling in the case of *BACONGO v Department of Environment*, December 19, 2002.

land.[54] At the Privy Council, three out of five judges ruled that although the decision to approve the dam was flawed, it was not illegal.[55] The majority opinion noted the uniqueness of an important biologically diverse region that would be "drowned,"[56] as well as the unexplored archaeological sites.[57] In the end, they concluded that, "The Government of Belize...has the right to decide to destroy this area if it so chooses...the court challenge was about the adequacy of the EIA.[58] Despite the shortcomings in the information in the EIA, the NEAC accepted the document, which fulfilled the requirements of the EIA Regulations.[59] They relied heavily on the GOB's affidavits as to the ability of a monitoring regime and follow-up programs to address the errors and shortcomings of the EIA.[60]

In a strong dissenting opinion, two judges held that the failure of Belize Electricity Company Limited (BECOL) to disclose "highly relevant" matters of central importance to the Chief Justice of Belize as well as to the Court of Appeal of Belize,[61] "were incredible and should not be accepted."[62] This included the seriously flawed geology report and the existence of a major fault line in close proximity to the construction site of the dam.

BECOL's denial about the serious errors in the section on geology gradually shifted; it contended that the granite or sandstone issue was only a matter of nomenclature.[63] "While the report refers to the rock as granite, some believe the rock to be sandstone. The mineralogical composition of much of the rock around Chalillo is similar to granite." After all, what's in a name? American geologist Brian Holland says a lot.[64]

The Chairman of NEAC exercised pressure on the Committee to disregard

---

[54] In the Court of Appeal of Belize, A.D. 2003, Civil Appeal 1 of 2003. *BACONGO v Department of Environment*, 17 June 2003.

[55] Privy Council Appeal No. 47 of 2003 Ruling in case of *BACONGO v Department of Environment*, 29 January 2004.

[56] Ibid. ¶7.

[57] Ibid. ¶8.

[58] Ibid. ¶32.

[59] Ibid. ¶34.

[60] Ibid. ¶71.

[61] Ibid. ¶88.

[62] Ibid. ¶89.

[63] Ibid. ¶92.

[64] Brian Holland, an American geologist resident in Belize, who reviewed the geological data in the EIA for BACONGO responded to the statement on nomenclature. He is quoted, at ¶111, "The sandstones at Chalillo are...made up of transported and sedimented mineral particles that previously comprised the granite. However, this similarity does not make the sandstone equivalent to granite. This mineralogical similarity is only as to composition and has nothing to do with the physical strength of the rock. It is like coal and diamonds: both are composed of the element carbon, the physical properties, however, being very different."

"the question on the geology [because it] did not really affect the fact that the dam could be constructed..." The minutes also demonstrate that he "...urged NEAC to recommend the project and to defer further public consultation until after the decision."[65]

The dissent took note of the concern of one NEAC member who said, "...if the information on the geology is not accurate then this could raise concerns as to the credibility of the EIA preparers and the accuracy of other information contained in the document."[66]

The dissent concluded they would have quashed the DOE's decision to approve the project and would also "...grant an injunction restraining BECOL from continuing work on the project unless and until a corrected EIA is prepared for public consultation, and secures recommendation by NEAC and approval by the DOE."[67]

The dissent concludes

> Belize has enacted comprehensive legislation for environmental protection and direct foreign investment, if it has serious environmental implications, must comply with that legislation. The rule of law must not be sacrificed to foreign investment, however desirable (indeed, recent history shows that in many parts of the world respect for the rule of law is an incentive, and disrespect for the rule of law can be a severe deterrent, to foreign investment). It is no answer to the erroneous geology in the EIA to say that the dam design would not necessarily have been different. The people of Belize are entitled to be properly informed about any proposals for alterations in the dam design before the project is approved and before work continues with its construction.[68]

The strong dissent drew further attention to the concerns with the lack of transparency in the government's decision-making process and the disregard for public opinion, the failures to adequately address environmental, economic political and social issues as they related to development and the influence of foreign investors, and discredited the perception that Belize is a country of laws.

The BACONGO case forever changed the country's perception about the public's role [including the role of Non-Governmental Organizations (NGOs)] in environmental issues. The BACONGO case marked the first time an NGO was granted standing when it was not directly involved in the area at risk.[69]

---

[65] Ibid. ¶100 and ¶101.

[66] Ibid. ¶99.

[67] Ibid. ¶118.

[68] Ibid. ¶120.

[69] Standing can be viewed as the key to get in the courthouse door. In order for a complaint to be brought, plaintiffs must show they have an interest in the subject matter of the action that goes beyond the interests of other members of the public, usually by showing they have suffered some damage as a direct result of the subject of the complaint.

Community goes to court

Sarstoon-Temash National Park was designated a protected area in 1997.[70] It is co-managed by the Sarstoon-Temash Institute for Indigenous Management (SATIIM), whose Board of Directors includes representatives of the five villages surrounding the area (Crique Sarco, Sunday Wood, Consejo Creek, Midway, and Barranco). For the last decade, the indigenous Maya who live around the park have restricted their entry into and use of the Park's resources, in accordance with the law governing national parks.[71]

When the Government of Belize issued a permit to allow seismic testing for the exploration of oil in the Sarstoon-Temash National Park, SATIIM challenged the decision in the Supreme Court.[72] The grounds for the challenge were that: (1) the Chief Forest Officer did not have the authority to grant permission to permit anyone entrance to the park;[73] (2) since the Forest Department did not have power to make a decision on the permit, its issuance of the permit was outside their authority; (3) under the Environmental Impact Assessment (EIA) Regulations, oil exploration is an activity listed in Schedule I, which requires an EIA and no EIA was done;[74] and (4) because of the co-management agreement, SATIIM expected that decisions concerning the Park would only be made with their involvement.

The Court ruled that SATIIM was correct and that an EIA was legally required, and therefore the "permit" to do seismic testing was quashed.[75] In the matter of seismic testing: because it is an activity incompatible with the purposes of a national park, the Court interpreted the activity as an allowable scientific activity.[76]

On the grounds that SATIIM had expectations under the co-management agreement, the Court ruled this matter was premature. Since the agreement was

---

[70] Statutory Instrument No. 42 of 1994, under sec. 3 of the National Parks System Act.
[71] Under the National Parks Systems Act, a national park is defined as "any area established for the protection and preservation of natural and scenic values of national significance for the benefit and enjoyment of the general public."
[72] *SATIIM v Forest Department/ Ministry of Natural Resources*, Supreme Court of Belize Claim number 212 of 2006.
[73] SATIIM argued that the law states that "the Minister" or "the administrator" are the only persons allowed to issue a permit and the Chief Forest Officer is neither.
[74] Seismic testing is an aspect of oil exploration.
[75] Ruling in case of SATIIM v Forest Department, 27th September 2006. ¶19.
[76] "The Minister may at his discretion issue permits to bona fide organizations and scientists and other qualified professionals or specialists for cave exploration, collection of specimen of particular species of flora and fauna, group education activities, archaeological or phalaeontological exploration, scientific research and related activities." National Parks Systems Act, Sec. 7(1).

still in place and SATIIM still managed the Park, there was no breach of the agreement, yet.[77] On the actions of the Chief Forest Officer, the Court ruled he did not act outside his authority or capacity.[78]

The Court's decision that seismic testing is compatible with the purposes of a national park is what has allowed the oil company, US Capital Energy, to embark on doing an environmental impact assessment. If submitted and given environmental clearance, the company would be able to apply for a permit to do seismic testing within the national park.[79]

This case marked the first time communities directly affected by a project felt empowered to challenge the GOB.

Going international

With the promotion of cruise tourism and the growing number of ill-advised coastal development projects, Belize faces serious environmental threats to the coastal region and the reef. In 2004, when every form of proposal, from dolphin parks to leasing a portion of the reef, was being presented, the Belize Institute of Environmental Law and Policy (BELPO) sought an unusual way to gain more leverage to advocate for better, wiser, and more sustainable choices.

In collaboration with the Environmental Law Alliance Worldwide (ELAW) and the Climate Justice Programme, ELAW partners from Belize, Peru, and Nepal filed petitions with the World Heritage Committee in Paris to protect three distinct ecosystems: coral reefs in Belize, a tropical mountain range in Peru, and the majestic peaks of the Himalayas. Under the Convention Concerning the Protection of the World Cultural and Natural Heritage (World Heritage Convention) is a clause allowing for the listing of a World Heritage Site in Danger.[80] The petitions asked the World Heritage Committee to declare the sites "In Danger" and take remedial steps to protect them.[81]

The Belize Barrier Reef Reserve System (BBRS) provides critical habitat for threatened species, including marine turtles, manatees, and the American marine crocodile. The petitions recognize the need to reduce greenhouse gas emis-

[77] Ruling in case of *SATIIM v Forest Department*, 27th September 2006, ¶48-55.
[78] The Court ruled that there was never a permit issued, under Section 6 of the National Parks Systems Act. See ¶7 and that the permit that was issued was not beyond the scope of what the Chief Forest Officer could approve. Ruling in case of *SATIIM v Forest Department*, 27th September 2006, ¶20-47.
[79] At this writing, it is not clear whether that decision has been appealed by SATIIM.
[80] *Convention Concerning the Protection of the World Cultural and Natural Heritage.* 1972. Article 11(4).
[81] Information on the Petition is available at http://www.climatelaw.org.

sions to protect the World Heritage Sites for future generations.[82] An increase in sea temperatures and atmospheric concentrations of carbon dioxide has already damaged the reef along with the impacts of hurricanes.

The BBRS, already in a fragile state from forces beyond Belize's control, cannot withstand additional threats from pollution, especially through agrochemical run-off from banana and citrus plantations and shrimp farms, sewage from tourist and residential centers, solid waste disposal and industrial effluents, opportunistic diseases such as white band and black band coral disease, increased coastal development and tourism, including cruise ships as well as over-fishing. These weaken and will continue to weaken the resiliency of the reef system and compound the danger of global climate change by making the reef more vulnerable to its effects.[83]

It was hoped that bringing attention to the health of the BBRS would assist in making more sustainable and future looking decisions concerning development in the coastal zone and on the cayes. Though the petition is still pending at the World Heritage Committee, the idea of leasing the reef was abandoned.[84]

Sensitizing the courts

In June 2004, the United Nations Environment Programme (UNEP) convened a meeting to discuss the promotion of environmental law and sustainable development and how to build the capacity of the courts.[85]

At the conclusion of this event, the chief justices of the participating countries issued a statement, excerpted in part:

Recognizing the importance of the role of the judiciary in promoting sustainable development through strengthening the rule of law in the region for the effective implementation, development and enforcement of environmental law; Recognizing the importance of ensuring access to justice for the settlement of environmental disputes and acknowledging that there are significant obstacles to access to justice in environmental matters; ...considering that deficiency in knowledge, relevant skills and availability of information...is one of the principal causes that contributes to the lack of effective development, implementation and enforce-

---

[82] Climate change and greenhouse gas emissions were the unifying themes of the Petitions.

[83] Supporting science and references contained in the Petition.

[84] It might have been coincidental, or not. There is no proof either way, but the timing was fortuitous.

[85] The meeting was "The Role of the Judiciary in Enforcement and Implementation of Environmental Law: A Regional Assessment." Attendees were chief justices and senior judges from the Bahamas, Barbados, Belize, the Organization of Eastern Caribbean States (OECS), Guyana, Jamaica, Suriname and Trinidad and Tobago.

ment of environmental law...[therefore recommend that action be taken]...in developing and implementing judicial capacity-building activities in the field of environmental law...re-examination of the rules of standing...urge the consideration of possible solutions to other impediments to access to justice in environmental matters...[86]

In January 2006 the Chief Justice of Belize actively followed through on the recommendations when he helped promote the theme "Sustainable Development: Challenges for the Environment and the Law" as the subject for Belize's Seventh Annual Belize Bench and Bar Summit.[87] In light of the serious environmental threats Belize faces, the focus of the summit was seen as a step in the right direction, shedding light on the potential for motivated citizens to use the law to protect Belize's natural heritage. The chief justice said it was the only event of its kind in the Caribbean.[88]

The environment in context

Achieving sustained and equitable development is one of Belize's greatest challenges. When choices are presented to commit to large and questionable projects that will detrimentally impact the environment, the proponents often say that environmental protection is a luxury to be addressed later, but right now it only slows the engine of growth.[89] Is that really the case? Recent experience has demonstrated how hollow the promise of jobs has been.[90] With the number of jobless people estimated at 12,580,[91] those without work are hopeful that maybe this time the promise will be fulfilled. The Ministry of National Development reported that approximately one in three people in Belize are "poor" and one in every ten is "very poor."[92]

---

[86] Statement signed by the chief justices of the attending countries. The signatory for Belize was C.J. Conteh.

[87] The Bench and Bar Summit is a continuing legal education day for judges, magistrates, and lawyers.

[88] BELPO and ELAW-US co-hosted the event with the Belize Bar Association.

[89] Hunter, Salzman & Zaelke. (2002). *International Environmental Law and Policy*, (2nd Ed.). Foundation Press, p. 18.

[90] In the case of the building of the Chalillo Dam, Chinese and Nepalese workers were brought in to do the majority of the work, at extremely low wages.

[91] Belize Central Statistical Office. Retrieved December 2006 from http://www.cso.gov.bz/.

[92] Hugh O'Brien, CEO of Min. of Human Development, interviewed 6 September 2006 on 7NewsBelize, posted at: http://www.7newsbelize.com/archives/09060608.html. The National Human Development Advisory Committee, Belize: 2002 Poverty Assessment Report, 2004, defined "very poor" to mean those "more vulnerable to chronic poverty," p. 18. Full report is available at http://www.cso.gov.bz.

A commitment to protecting the environment and eliminating poverty are obligations to Belize's future. Belize has a high poverty rate and the majority of the population is young; one third of the population is poor and sixty percent of them are under 25.[93] Development is viewed as an avenue to provide opportunities for people to reach their full potential. Decisions made by Belize at 25 are decisions that will weigh heavily on over one half of the population who will be fifty or younger in another 25 years.

It is the poorest who suffer the consequences of environmental degradation and pollution; they cannot afford to protect themselves from things such as contaminated water; when the challenge is one of putting food on the table and surviving another day, it is no surprise that people cannot think of problems of climate change; they are trying to stay alive any way they can and this "...may drive people to unsustainable uses of land and other resources..."[94]

Belize has an opportunity to avoid many of the mistakes that have wreaked economic and environmental havoc in other countries. A chance still exists to employ preventive measures rather than rely in the future on curative measures and to preserve an eco-stability, but that opportunity is rapidly being lost. It is indeed unfortunate that the GOB appears to be unaware or unconcerned with the repercussions on the future of its present policies—policies that are putting Belize in a "race to the bottom," relaxing or failing to enforce the laws, including protection of workers, and a lowering of environmental standards in an attempt to attract developers.

Foreign investment contracts

In the process of attracting foreign investment, the GOB has entered into a number of financial investment contracts (FIC), or agreements.[95] Foreign investment contracts need to strike a balance between the legitimate interests of investors in stability for their investments on the one hand and, the pursuit of

---

[93] The poverty rate is 33.5%; 60% of those under 25. (33.9% were 0-17 years of age; and 39% were 14 to 24 years of age) National Human Development Advisory Committee, Belize: 2002 Poverty Assessment Report, 2004, p. 14.

[94] Hunter, Salzman, & Zaelke. (2002). *International Environmental Law and Policy*, (2nd Ed.) Foundation Press, p. 17.

[95] The term "foreign investment contract" is defined as an agreement between a foreign company or business and a state, or host country, for the purposes of an investment project in that state or host country. The agreement sets out terms and conditions applicable to the investment project. An investment contract is "foreign" when it is associated with a foreign business (which may or may not itself be a direct party to the contract) with capacity to control important management decisions or associated impacts.

sustainable development. All too often, the balance reflected in foreign investment contracts appears disproportionately to favor the foreign investor, not the host country government as keeper of the country's overall public policy goals.

The contracts generally include clauses relating to confidentiality, liability, property rights, taxes, and sections dealing with licenses and approvals from permitting agencies, as well as other benefits to the investors.

When there is a confidentiality clause, there is no transparency in what the government is doing; the public cannot access information, hindering input or review of the project. Transparency, access to information, and rights of public participation are core principles of sustainable development. Without them, no adequate mechanisms exist to guarantee the accountability of the parties, and they facilitate a breeding ground for corruption.

The contracts may have clauses to assist projects in getting licenses and clearances from regulating authorities. These have included changes to national legislation specifically to clear the way for controversial projects.[96] Such legislation results in giving foreign investors rights above and beyond those of the citizens and, in some instances, putting the investors above the Constitution.

The contract relating to the construction of the Chalillo Dam, the Third Master Agreement, became public during the course of the "BACONGO" case.[97] The terms of this Agreement,[98] not uncommon to FICs: (1) waive "any and all environmental laws, rules or regulations," whether in force or new, except those to which the investor specifically agrees to be bound;[99] (2) the GOB shall take care of any laws that might otherwise affect the project;[100] (3) BECOL is not responsible for any harm done to people and/or property, "...whether in

---

[96] When the BACONGO appeal to the Privy Council was being prepared, the GOB passed the Macal River Hydroelectric Development Act, 2003 (which was enacted and subsequently repealed). It attempted to sidestep any potential judicial review of the project. Section 4 (d) provided that: *"...[F]or the avoidance of doubt and for greater clarity, [the Belize Electric Company Limited] shall proceed with the design, financing, construction and operation for the Chalillo Project... notwithstanding any judgment, order or declaration of any court or tribunal, whether heretofore or hereafter granted, issued or made."*

[97] It is a contract between the GOB and Fortis Inc. of Newfoundland Canada, the majority owner of Belize's national utility who distributes electricity to the country, Belize Electricity Limited (BEL), and sole owner of Belize Electric Company (BECOL), the private hydro company. BECOL (also called Fortis-BECOL) operates the existing hydro facilities on the Macal River, the Mollejon dam, the Chalillo dam and reservoir, and is now in the first stages of constructing a third dam, the Vaca Dam.

[98] The Third Master Agreement is made up of a Power Purchase Agreement, Franchise Agreement, and an Amended and Restate Power Purchase Agreement.

[99] Franchise Agreement Sec. 7, p. 27.

[100] Franchise Agreement, Sec. 3.2, 3.3, pp. 24-5.

contract tort, negligence, strict liability or otherwise for any direct, incidental or consequential damages of any nature arising at any time or from any cause whatsoever;"[101] (4) BECOL has custody and control of the Macal River and all its tributaries;[102] (5) guarantee of profits, regardless of how the dams operate;[103] as well as concessions guaranteeing the right to operate tax–and duty-free under a special law written just for them,[104] with the exception of payroll taxes;[105] and assurance of annual rate increases.[106]

The contract between the Government and Belize Cruise Terminal Limited (BCTL),[107] known as the Carnival contract, has similar concessions to the investor.[108] It involves the development of a cruise ship port, free zone, and related facilities at the Belize Port at Port Loyola, Belize City. It states the GOB will use its best efforts to grant all licenses, approvals, permits, concessions, exemptions, and authorizations needed to complete the Project on an expedited basis; the GOB will also facilitate customs and immigration matters for the construction materials and labor needed to complete the project and process any necessary work permits "on an expedited basis."[109]

After completion of the BCTL Port, BCTL will control the scheduling of cruise ships coming to Belize, giving preference to Carnival cruise ships.[110] The GOB is guaranteeing to facilitate the approval of the project by pressuring or influencing the granting authorities. In addition, the agreement obligates the Government to promote cruise tourism;[111] that means the GOB commits the Belize Tourism Board (BTB), whose job it is to promote tourism, in general, to use its resources to promote Belize as a cruise ship destination.

A range of concerns about foreign investment contracts exists. The specific concerns are heightened by a general lack of transparency in the negotiation and accessibility of FICs and by their potential to undermine public policy goals re-

---

[101] Power Purchase Agreement, Sec.17.2, p. 17.
[102] Franchise Agreement Sec. 3.3, p. 25.
[103] BECOL can re-negotiate the contract in order to assure profits. Power Purchase Agreement Sec.3.2, p. 8
[104] Mollejon Hydroelectric Project (Exemption from Taxes and Duties) Title VI, Ch. 59 in the Substantive Laws of Belize, R.E. 2003.
for can re-negotiate the contracts to charge consumers more. Power Purchase Agreement Sec.3.2, p. 8).
[105] Franchise Agreement, Sec. 12.1, p. 29.
[106] Amended and Restated Power Purchase Agreement Sec.3.1(c), p. 6).
[107] In early October 2004 the agreement was leaked to the public by an unknown source.
[108] This is a company established as a joint venture by Carnival Corporation of Panama and Belize Ports Limited.
[109] Clause 9(b), Contract between BCTL and GOB. Signed April 2004.
[110] Ibid., Clause 10.
[111] Clause 9(a).

lated to sustainable development. New tools must be developed to facilitate the monitoring and evaluation of FICs through a sustainable development lens, the linking of provisions that allow foreign investment contracts to be reviewed, and the attaching of social and environmental conditions.

It is important to assess the sustainable development implications of these deals from the bottom up, applying a mix of "home" and "host" country expertise and political understanding.[112]

Pushing development

In 2006, Belize has entertained a large number of huge development projects, at a rapid pace, especially along the coast and cayes and often ignoring environmental laws and stakeholder concerns.

Despite its constitutional mandate to protect the environment and despite the mandate of the Environmental Protection Act and Regulations, there seems to be no end to these projects.

Cruise tourism

The growth of cruise tourism in less than ten years is astounding. In 1998, the cruise ship industry averaged about 1,400 cruise passengers per day.[113] By 2003, it was 575,000; and in 2005, another 800,331 cruise passengers came to Belize.[114] The BTB estimates that in 2006 one million cruise passengers will trek across a country that is 9,087 square miles.[115] Although the country's infrastructure has not grown to accommodate these growing numbers, the GOB is pushing for more.

The impact of cruise tourism on the country is becoming more obvious. At this writing, Belize is deciding on two cruise terminals in Belize City, each with the capacity to dock four cruise ships. To see the completion of these projects will involve the deepening of the waterways into Belize City, digging and cutting and gauging a pathway deep enough for the large cruise ships. What this will do to the marine environment and to the natural barriers has not been given proper consideration.

---

[112] See generally, IIED, Sustainable Markets: Briefing Paper, Number 1, "Lifting the lid on foreign investment contracts: The real deal for sustainable development." September 2005.
[113] *Tourism strategy for Belize*, Blackstone Corporation, June 1998.
[114] Belize Tourism Board website at http://www.belizetourism.org/cruise.html.
[115] From communication with a representative of BTB.

Coastal developments

From north to south, 2006 has seen numerous coastal development projects. Many of these projects threaten to destroy unique coastal ecosystems, mangroves, seagrass beds, coastal waterways, and the reef. It has also prompted many to ask whether it is wise to destroy coastal ecosystems to build tourist facilities, businesses, homes, and roads.

When development projects destroy ecosystems, the potential for storm damage during hurricanes increases dramatically. An overall Coastal and Marine Conservation Strategy is essential to evaluate the sustainability of these projects, but it does not look like it is on the horizon.

Oil

Aside from the proposed exploration of the Sarstoon-Temash National Park, Toledo District, oil exploration as well as oil exploitation is mushrooming across the country. Unfortunately, a great deal of activity is taking place outside the law.

Belize Natural Energy Limited has gotten environmental clearance to do a pipeline in Spanish Lookout, connecting their wells to a central storage area.[116] They have also gotten environmental clearance to explore for oil on the Hummingbird Highway, in the Belmopan area.

Belize Natural Energy Limited has not done an EIA for either of these activities; this is a violation of the EIA regulations and contemptibly ignores the Supreme Court's decision in the SATIIM case, which stated that oil exploration requires an EIA.

An Environmental Compliance Plan is done following approval of an EIA. Belize Natural Energy, Limited (BNE) has not submitted an EIA for any of their activities in oil exploration or oil exploitation. The DOE has informed the NEAC that BNE is submitting an EIA for the entire Spanish Lookout operation.[117] No EIA has been submitted.

No EIA has been submitted on oil exploration in the Belmopan area. An ECP has been completed for this activity as well. The Chief Environmental Officer signed it;[118] it violates the EIA Regulations and ignores the function of the NEAC.[119]

---

[116] Environmental Compliance Plan written by the DOE for Belize Natural Energy Ltd. Signed November 1, 2006.

[117] Minutes of NEAC meeting, October 11, 2006.

[118] Environmental Compliance Plan written by the DOE for Belize Natural Energy Ltd. Signed November 6, 2006

[119] According to Section 25 of the EIA Regulations, the NEAC "…shall be to review all EIAs; advise the Department on the adequacy of the EIA."

Where are we now?

As indicated earlier, underlying tensions exist between the preservation and conservation of the environment and economic development. But with intelligent and morally strong leadership and community support, a positive reciprocal relationship between the environment and development can be forged. Environmental problems can undermine a safe and healthy environment; strong environmental policies can support and strengthen development. This kind of relationship is not what we are seeing now.

Belize has moved from reserve (for future use), to preserve (for future generations) to plunder (no thought for tomorrow). How will we ultimately resolve the struggle between development and the environment?

Conclusion

We began this article with an explanation of how environmental ethics is a shifting of traditional thinking and how the protection of the environment connotes protection of the "commons," which is shared by all forms of life. Humans, like all species, depend on and are a part of the earth's changing and interdependent eco-system.

It is imperative that the actions taken today are viewed with the future in mind. Unless we become more forward thinking in how to advance, we will be left with little or nothing of what makes Belize special.

5. History of Protected Area Designation, Co-management and Community Participation in Belize

Colin A. Young and Robert Horwich

Introduction

Ever since the arrival in the early 17th century of the British into Belize, then British Honduras (Leslie, 1997; Bolland, 2004), the Belizean economy was primarily based on the exploitation of the country's bountiful timber resources. The logwood (*Haematoxylum campechianum*) was the *raison d'être* for the British; its trade flourished until the late 1700s, followed by the harvesting of mahogany (*Swetenia macrophylla*), cedar (*Cedrella mexicana*), rosewood (*Swartzia cubensis*), santa maria (*Calophyllum brasiliense*), and other hardwood species until the late 1800s (Bolland, 2004). Thus, for much of Belize's history, the exploitation of its forests continued to be the mainstay of the economy until 1959, when large scale agriculture began to replace forestry as the primary income earner (Leslie, 1997). Nonetheless, compared to our Caribbean and Central American neighbors whose economies were based on large scale agriculture, the historical dependence of forestry spared much of Belize's forest (Leslie, 1997) where today, the country boasts a forest cover of some 69% (Meerman & Sabido, 2001). The Government of Belize (GOB, 2005a) designated approximately 52% as protected areas. Recent data suggests that Belize's terrestrial protected area is actually only 34% (Meerman & Wilson, 2005). The situation is also changing because of the alarming deforestation rate, which is 2.3% annually–almost doubling the annual Central American deforestation rate of 1.2% (Di Fiore, 2002). At this rate, by 2020 if current trends continue unabated, the forest cover will be reduced to 58% (GOB, 2005a). The exploitation of timber resources (e.g., between 1797 and 1802 over 4.5 million board feet of mahogany were exported; Bolland, 2004) and the subsequent agricultural development have both exerted immense pressure on Belize's ecosystems. The exploitation of Belize's forest resources proceeded for much of our history with scant attention paid to the environment and the need for protected areas to conserve our rich biodiversity. This essay discusses the history of protected area designation and management in Belize from the 1920s to 2006 with emphasis on how this process has changed over time. It also discusses the role of co-management in Belize's Protected Areas System with a focus on community co-management. It describes some of the successes and failures of co-management and importantly provides some suggested directions for the future.

History of protected area designation in British Honduras/Belize

In an attempt to curb the monopolization of land and protect timber resources, in 1817 the Crown Land Ordinance (CLO) was passed (Leslie, 1997), which gave all unclaimed land to the Crown. While this CLO failed to curb the harvesting of timber species on Crown land, it provided a legal framework by which the colonial government could set aside land. For over a hundred years, the CLO remained the only significant legislation relating to the protection of the environment; in 1927, the Forest Ordinance (FO) was passed (CEP/UNDP, 1996; Leikman, Otis, Raymond, Sielken, & Sweeney, 2004), after which the Forest Department was established (GOB, 2005b). The FO provided the legal basis for the designation of protected areas (Hartshorn, et al., 1984; Leslie, 1997). Thus, the CLO gave the government control over all public or "crown" lands while the FO relegated authority to the appropriate government official to set aside forest reserves on an ad hoc basis (CEP/UNDP, 1996; Leikam, et al., 2004) for the purposes of timber exploitation (Hartshorn, Nicolait, Hartshorn, Bevier, Brightman, Cal, Cawich, et al., 1984).

Under these two pieces of legislation, the colonial government, then British Honduras (BH), made a series of attempts to conserve its land and natural resources:

- in 1920, Silk Grass Forest Reserve and the Mountain Pine Ridge Forest Reserve were designated (UNEP/WCMC, n.d);
- in 1927, the FO was passed; it was the first piece of legislation that regulated the use of forests despite the fact that the Forest Policy would not be passed until 1954 (GOB, 2005b);

124

- by 1930, under the FO, five forest reserves were designated–Silk Grass, Freshwater Creek, Sibun, Vaca, and Columbia River–and they became a part of the early protected areas network of Belize (GOB, 1998);
- in 1928, Belize's first nature reserve at Half Moon Caye was declared to protect the red-footed boobies (*Sula sula*) (Hartshorn, et al., 1984; CEP/UNDP 1996; Waight & Lumb, 1999);
- Half Moon Caye Preserve is significant because it was the first protected area in Belize set aside for wildlife conservation (GOB, 1998).

After 1930, the designation of protected areas (PAs) in BH entered into a hiatus for almost 40 years (Hartshorn, et al., 1984). BH's forests and wildlife faced numerous threats during this 40 year period (e.g., deforestation, hunting, agriculture) because of the increased exploitation of timber resources and agricultural expansion. Although no PAs were designated during this period, a number of legislations were enacted that, in many ways, set the foundation for the designation of PAs in the late 1960s:

- in 1944, BH passed the Wildlife Protection Ordinance and in 1945 passed a subsidiary legislation that provided the legal basis for the protection of wildlife (Hartshorn, et al., 1984);
- this act served as the basis for wildlife protection until it was replaced in 1981 by the Wildlife Protection Act (GOB, 2000);
- in 1948 the Fisheries Ordinance was established (FOA, 2005) and regulated the harvesting of fish species in all rivers and territorial waters (Hartshorn, et al., 1984);
- in 1954 the Forest Policy was instituted to add further protection of the forestry sector (GOB, 2005b);
- in 1958, the CLO and FO were revised to specifically include both the establishment and management of forest reserves within which timber extraction was allowed under strict regulations (Hartshorn & Green, 1985; Leikman, et al., 2004) in addition to the Fisheries Ordinance (Hartshorn, et al., 1984);
- under CLO and FO, BH designated 15 forests reserves covering almost 20% of the land by the time of independence (Hartshorn, et al., 1984).

The above took place while Belize was British Honduras. In the early 1960s, a constitutional review took place and from 1964 to 1981, Belize had internal self-rule. During the 1960s the fledgling government continued to take steps toward conservation:

- in 1964, with the coaxing by numerous international conservation organizations, Belize increased the number of PAs;

- in 1966, the National Parks Commission was created with the expressed purpose of identifying areas worthy of national park designation throughout the country;[1]
- assisted by the United Nations Food and Agricultural Organization (FAO), Belize hired national parks service consultant, William O. Deshler, to devise a national park system. As suggested by the National Parks Commission, the Deshler report strongly recommended passing appropriate legislation, such as a wildlife protection ordinance and national park legislation, providing environmental education about wildlife to both children and adults (Waight & Lumb, 1999), and providing data on which to create a protected area network.

In summary, Belize boasts a long history of setting aside protected areas for the conservation of biodiversity and the controlled extraction of resources. The above named ordinances–CLO, FO, and the Wildlife Protection Ordinance–were instrumental in providing the legal framework necessary for the designation of protected areas and the protection of wildlife in Belize. Cognizant of the need to protect Belize's rich biodiversity, in addition to the lobbying efforts of concerned Belizeans and international NGOs alike, the Government commissioned the National Parks Commission and the Deshler Report to provide data on which to create a protected area network. The recommendations of both reports proved integral to the rapid designation of protected areas that was to follow the post-independence years. However, much credit should be given to a new but steadfast group of Belizeans who would later organize into what was to become the Belize Audubon Society (Craig, 2006).

The role of Belize Audubon Society in protected areas designation

Not surprisingly, many of the National Parks Commission members later became instrumental in the establishment on February 9, 1969, of the Belize Audubon Society (BAS) as a branch of the Florida Audubon Society. The BAS was an environmental NGO whose expressed purpose was to study wildlife and conservation in Belize (Waight & Lumb 1999; Craig 2006). In fact, the five individuals cited below all became BAS board members. Using the knowledge they had gained from compiling the National Parks Commission's report and experiencing first hand the threats to Belize's biodiversity as they traveled throughout Belize, these individuals and BAS lobbied the government for the

---

[1] The Commission consisted of such notables as Henry Fairweather, Albert S. Grant, Louis Lindo, Ronald Clark, and James Waight; the Commission identified and strongly recommended a numbers of areas worthy of protection, and in 1968 submitted its report (Waight & Lumb,1999).

designation of national parks. As a result, the 40 year hiatus of park designation in Belize came to an end. Soon after its establishment, the BAS successfully lobbied the government, using the CLO and FO as their legal premise, to establish in 1968 Crown Reserves at Rio Grande and in 1973 Guanacaste Park (Hartshorn, et al., 1984; Belize Interim First National Report, 1998; Waight & Lumb, 1999).

BAS's two efforts to preserve the Rio Grande crown reserve eventually failed:

- in order to minimize erosion and siltation of the Rio Grande thus protecting the watershed, 3,644 hectares in the upper valley of the river was designated as a wildlife sanctuary and natural reserve (Hartshorn, et al., 1984);
- unfortunately, the area was later abandoned and the watershed was deforested for rice cultivation (Hartshorn, et al., 1984).

In 1968 the BAS, Florida Audubon Society, and Florida State University also unsuccessfully lobbied the government to designate 2,362 hectares of land set aside in the Columbia Forest Reserve as a wildlife refuge to be used for research and educational purposes. Even though the boundaries of the proposed wildlife refuge were demarcated and government had agreed to declare the area a wildlife sanctuary, the wildlife refuge succumbed to a rice cultivation project in the same area (Hartshorn, et al,. 1984; Waight & Lumb, 1999).

Guanacaste Park, consisting of 21 hectares near the confluence of Roaring Creek and the Belize River near Belmopan City (Waight & Lumb, 1999), on the other hand, was designated as a "Crown Reserve for the use as a national park" (Hartshorn, et al., 1984, p. 98) at the entrance to Belmopan City. The main attraction of the park was the large guanacaste tree (*Enterolobium cyclocarpum*), also called tubroose in Kriol, that supported an epiphytic flora of over 35 species as well as numerous bird species (Waight & Lumb, 1999). Guanacaste Park, at the request of the Ministry of Natural Resources, was BAS's first managed protected area (Hartshorn, et al., 1984) informally beginning a long history of co-management between the BAS and the GOB. However, since the National Parks System Act would be passed some eight years later, Guanacaste did not officially become a national park until April 2, 1990.

BAS's lobbying efforts continued, and in 1977 the Society persuaded the government to declare Crown Reserve Bird Sanctuaries on seven small cayes to protect the rookeries of numerous water bird species (Hartshorn, et al., 1984) under the Fisheries Regulations of 177 (FAO, 2005), one of the final pieces of legislation passed prior to Belize's independence (Hartshorn & Green, 1985). The Fisheries Ordinance, like its predecessor, the Forest Ordinance, ceded authority to the government to establish marine reserves, albeit on an ad hoc basis. Like Guanacaste Park four years earlier, BAS was given management authority of the park by the government.

While no other protected areas would be designated until after independence, BAS continued to lobby for the continued protection of Belize's biologically diverse ecosystems. Soon after Belize's independence, the government passed two landmark pieces of legislation–both of which were recommended by the National Parks Commission and the Deshler report–the National Park Systems Act (No. 5, 1981) and the new Wildlife Protection Act (No. 4, 1981), which set the stage for protected areas development in Belize. The National Park System Act provided the legal framework for the establishment of national parks, natural monuments, and wildlife reserves while the Wildlife Protection Act, greatly improved since the 1944 Ordinance, afforded protection to wildlife recognized under the Convention on International Trade in Endangered Species (CITES) and regulated the use and hunting of other species in need of protection (Hartshorn, et al., 1984). Both of these Acts delegated responsibility for their enforcement to the Forest Department (FD) in the Ministry of Natural Resources.

Because the FD lacked the capacity, personnel, and financial resources (Hartshorn, et al., 1984; GOB, 2005b) to adequately administer protected areas, the department was unprepared to deal with this new responsibility given to them under the two Acts. Recognizing its limitations, in 1982 the government approached the BAS and asked the Society to use its expertise and experience in protected areas management to manage and protect the six major national parks and wildlife sanctuaries (Belesky, 2004). Since then, the role of promoting conservation and management of Belize's protected areas increasingly fell to the BAS (Waight & Lumb, 1999; Craig, pers. comm.). In 1984 this co-management agreement between the government and BAS was formalized and solidified with the signing of an agreement that gave the Society the authority to collaborate with the FD and the GOB in the "protection and management of areas designated under the Forestry Acts and National Parks and Refuges Acts" as well as to draft management plans for government's approval for the said protected areas (Hyde, 1984). In 1987, the government ceded further authority to the Society to manage and protect protected areas "until further notice" (Neal, 1987). This co-management agreement continued until 1995 when BAS signed a five year tripartite agreement with GOB, and the FD that defined the Society's role in the protection of six protected areas (Waight & Lumb, 1999), five of which were terrestrial reserves. Later, the number of PAs under the auspices of the BAS was increased to eight protected areas totaling almost 64,000 hectares (Liekman, et al., 2004).

Around this same time, in 1984, when BAS's role in management of Belize's protected areas was solidified, the burgeoning tourism industry became an important source of foreign exchange for Belize (GOB, 1998). The partnership between tourism and conservation was soon realized and set the stage for increasing the number of protected areas in Belize.

Types of protected areas in Belize

Historically, protected areas (PAs) in Belize were designated primarily for the following purposes in order of importance: exploitation of timber resources (Hartshorn, et al., 1984), scenic value (Salas 1993), wildlife protection (Waight & Lumb, 1999), and rarely were protected areas designated for ecological or scientific purposes, although the latter purpose has become more common. The government's historical emphasis of extractive reserves (e.g., forest reserves) is evident by the sheer number of extractive reserves that currently exist in the protected area network. Of the 94 legally recognized protected areas in 2005 (see Fig. 1 on p. 134), 37 are designated as extractive reserves (20 forest reserves and 17 marine reserves) totaling some 13.1% of national territory versus 9.3% set aside for conservation and/or biodiversity purposes (Meerman, 2005a). Additionally, the majority of PAs designated for conservation purposes (e.g., Crooked Tree Wildlife Sanctuary) occurred post-independence due to lobbying efforts of both local and international conservation NGOs (e.g., BAS; World Wildlife Fund) and communities (e.g., Community Baboon Sanctuary) and private initiatives of concerned individuals (e.g., Runaway Creek Nature Reserve). Even though the number of PAs for biodiversity conservation has increased, the PA network suffers from gaps (Meerman, 2005a) that resulted from the historical ad hoc nature of PA designation. Consequently, the current system lacks integration and complimentarily of ecosystem types.

To increase complementarity and integrate the extensive protected area network, GOB recently commissioned a National Protected Areas Policy and System Plan (NPAPSP) to identify gaps and develop a tool for a systematic rationalization of protected areas designation (Meerman, 2005b). In addition to identifying gaps and espousing solid recommendations, the NPAPSP was a concerted effort to put biodiversity conservation at the forefront of PA designation together with social and economic development (Meerman, 2005a). Thus, if the recommendations put forth by the report are adhered to, for the first time, Belize will have a PA system that is informed by policy and gap analysis that is focused on an ecosystem approach and biodiversity conservation, rather than an ad hoc approach, which was focused on extraction of natural resources.

Integration of conservation, co-management and community participation

Following independence in 1981, and the implementation of the two major environmental laws that laid the foundation for the National Protected Areas System that was not to become a reality for 25 years, the young nation of Belize began exploring innovative types of conservation methods. By assigning BAS power to manage its early protected areas, the GOB began its history in co-management of protected areas as a way of tapping the resources of international conservation agencies that were anxious to help the young democracy that still had a great deal of its lands forested. As the GOB began expanding its PAs to include Half Moon Caye in 1982 (De Vries, Haines, Hufnagel, Laird, Rearick, Salas, 2003), Crooked Tree Wildlife Sanctuary (WS) in 1984 and Cockscomb Basin Forest Reserve (FR) in 1985, it began relying more on the BAS as a co-management partner; this co-mangement agreement was formalized in 1984 when GOB asked the BAS to manage six of its protected areas (Waight & Lumb, 1984).

In 1985, community participation in conservation began with the declaration of the Community Baboon Sanctuary (CBS). The concepts of co-management and community participation intertwined under the BAS when a great deal of exchange occurred between the CBS and Cockscomb Basin Forest Reserve, both of which were administered by the BAS. These early experiments in community participation and co-management were to presage the numerous future agreements the GOB was to sign with community groups, non-governmental organizations and private landowners.

The CBS began as an experiment in community involvement in land management whose mission was to protect the black howler monkeys (called locally "baboons") on the private lands of over 150 subsistence farmers. Each landowner signed a voluntary pledge to abide by a simple management plan for their farms (Horwich, 1990a; Horwich & Lyon, 1988, 1995, 1998). The main goal was to maintain aerial corridors for the howlers (Lyon & Horwich, 1996; Horwich & Lyon, 1998). The significance of the CBS in Belize was three fold: 1) it was the first time a community participated actively in conserving its land and protecting its wildlife, 2) the land being protected was private, and 3) the CBS was to act as a model for other communities country-wide. The step the seven communities of the CBS (Flowers Bank, Scotland Half Moon, Bermudian Landing, Double Head Cabbage, Willows Bank, St. Paul's Bank and Big Falls) took had a wide-ranging effect by encouraging other communities, directly and indirectly, to participate in conservation (Horwich, 2005) and to participate in the new ecotourism industry that was soon to become one of the leading industries in Belize's economy (Boo, 1990; Lindberg & Enriquez, 1994).

Protected Area management and community participation began to immediately influence each other. Under the direction of BAS' first Director, Walter Craig, the Cockscomb Basin Forest Reserve and the CBS histories became intertwined (Horwich & Lyon, 1999; Horwich, Murray, Saqui, Lyon, & Godfrey, 1993a). While the CBS was learning about traditional protected area management, Cockscomb Basin was utilizing local human resources from the adjacent village of Maya Center, hiring Ignacio Pop as the first warden and later Ernesto Saqui as the first director of Cockscomb Basin protected area. As the park expanded, so did the local staff and the economy of Maya Center became integrated with the protected area as economic benefits accrued from salaries and later from crafts sold to park visitors (Boo, 1990; Lindberg & Enriquez, 1994; Horwich & Lyon, 1999; Horwich, et al., 1993a). These benefits became so important that when, much later, a political representative of the area proposed deregulating the protected area to distribute lands to the people, the community objected and stopped it from occurring (Saqui, pers. comm.). Later in 1992-94, these two communities cooperated in translocating howlers from the CBS to create a new population in Cockscomb where they had been locally extirpated since the 1970s (Horwich, Koontz, Saqui, Saqui, & Glander, 1993b; Horwich, Koontz, Saqui, Ostro, Silver, & Glander, 2002; Koontz, Horwich, Glander, Westrom, Koontz, Saqui, Saqui, 1994).

The Community Baboon Sanctuary as a Belizean model

As the CBS became widely publicized nationally and internationally (ABC/Kane, 1991; National Audubon Society, 1991; Project Lighthawk, 1992; Lipske 1992; Koontz, 1993; Wildlife, 1994), it influenced other Belizean communities to become active in conservation activities (Anon., 1994; GOB, 1998). It first directly influenced Monkey River Village, when in 1988, the BAS and the Belize Tourism Industry Association (BTIA) took Fallett Young, the CBS' first manager to address community members about CBS's conservation efforts in the Belize River Valley (Placencia BTIA, 1988; Horwich, et al., 1993a). Because Monkey River had a significant population of howlers, residents soon saw the potential for Monkey River to participate in the growing conservation and ecotourism efforts that were developing. They eventually initiated the process to create Payne's Creek National Park in 1991 (Monkey River Village Council 1991; Horwich, et al., 1993a).

Three more efforts have been documented to duplicate the community work initiated by members of the CBS and their US advisors. The first was when Greg Smith, an expatriate living on Ambergris Caye, initiated a community effort based directly on the CBS method, organizing landowners of beach properties to protect turtle nesting beaches of Ambergris Caye in 1990 (Horwich et al., 1993a). When Horwich and Lyon, of the newly created Community Conservation (CC) organization, began to duplicate the CBS model in Gales Point, Manatee, (Lyon & Horwich, 1996) Smith moved his focus to work with the villagers of Gales Point to protect a significant population of nesting hawksbill turtles on the beaches on either side of the river entering the Southern Lagoon. Predators were destroying almost all nests. This project, managed by Gales Point villagers Kevin and Leroy Andrewin, an ex-turtle hunter, and Dickie Slusher, continues to the present and has released about 12,000 young turtles per year since its inception in 1992.

131

Two other projects were initiated using the CBS model: in 1991 the Slate Creek project (Bevis & Bevis, 1991; Slate River, 1997) and the Community Hicatee Sanctuary at Freetown Sibun on the Sibun River. The Slate Creek project involves private landowners and functions as an important buffer to the adjacent Mountain Pine Ridge Forest Reserve (Slate Creek Preserve, 2006). It has worked with local communities, including Siete Millas, in protecting its natural environment. Siete Millas also now works with Itzamna, a community-based organization co-managing the Eligio Panti National Park in the Maya Mountains (Garcia, pers. com.).

In 1994-5. the Community Hicatee Project (Anon., 2000) was stimulated by work carried out by John Polisar, a US student, on the endangered Central American River turtle (*Dermatemys mawii*), the hicatee, under the CBS (Polisar, 1995; Polisar & Horwich, 1994). This Community Hicatee Project, coordinated by Freetown Sibun chairman, Hubert Neil and later under the Sibun Watershed Association obtained a UNDP grant in 1997 (Neil, 1998) and created a visitor center but has been relatively quiescent to the present.

Indirectly, many rural communities in Belize, seeing the efforts of the CBS villages, realized that they too could participate in the growing conservation/ ecotourism movement. They saw the potential in having protected areas within their midst and began to initiate the process with the GOB to create protected areas adjacent to their communities (Horwich & Lyon, 1999). St. Margaret's village, led by expatriate Lee Wengryn initiated the establishment of Five Blues Lake National Park on Earth Day 1991 (Horwich & Lyon 1999). The Association of the Friends of Five Blues Lake NP formed in 1993, created a management plan draft assisted by CC (Gerlitz, 1994) and was the first community-based group to negotiate with the Forestry Department to co-manage a protected area (Agreement G.O.B., 1997). Community Conservation also initiated a community project in Gales Point with the help of the Ministry of Tourism and Belize Enterprises for Sustainable Technology (BEST) in 1991 (Horwich & Lyon, 1998, 1999; Horwich, et al., 1993a).

Recent history of protected areas, co-management and community participation

The late 1980s to early 1990s was a time of further protected area declaration. In 1988, Programme for Belize, a private NGO was established as the first private protected area (Programme for Belize, 2003). In 1989, the International Tropical Conservation Foundation of Switzerland followed suit creating the Shipstern Nature Reserve (Meerman & Boomsma, 1993) and in 1990 Monkey Bay Wildlife Sanctuary was declared a private reserve.

In 1990, the GOB created the Bladen Nature Reserve and expanded the

Cockscomb Basin Reserve Forest to over 100,000 acres (CBWS expanded, 1990). The original Cockscomb Basin, while created as the first sanctuary to protect jaguars, in reality, would have protected only a handful of those predators that normally require a large home range. Thus, the GOB now had a realistic protected area for jaguars. In 1991, Laughingbird Caye NP and Monkey Bay NP were created.

Toledo, often forgotten and a stronghold of the indigenous Maya community, was beginning to strengthen its organization and push for both indigenous rights and an indigenous voice in land use and conservation. As early as 1978, the Toledo Maya Cultural Council was created (Coc, 1989). More than a decade later in 1992, the Kekchi Council and Toledo Alcaldes Association were formed. When a proposal by Horwich, Chet, and Schmidt proposed a Toledo Biosphere to include protection of the Sarstoon-Temash area, Columbia Forest Reserve, and the Sapodilla Cayes (Horwich, 1990b), a number of the Maya villages were interested as were other communities; however, the GOB was not yet interested in the idea (Horwich, 2005).

In 1994, the GOB continued creating protected areas including Sarstoon-Temash, Rio Blanco NP and Payne's Creek NP. A pivotal year for government interest in community participation, 1994, the GOB seemed to respond to the community's interest in participating in conservation and ecotourism by sponsoring a conference on Ecotourism. This led to the production of a GOB-created video on some of the communities participating in community ecotourism, such as Gales Point and St. Margaret's village (Government Information Service, 1994a). They also produced a *Guide to Community Ecotourism* (1994b) advertising the facilities that many of the communities were producing and offering for tourists. But this peak of interest waned quickly and both the video and guidebook were not widely circulated. Later, although the GOB still talked about community ecotourism, most of the efforts went toward an economically higher level of tourism (Horwich & Lyon, 1999).

However, it was not only the GOB who left the communities dangling but conservationists as well. While talking about community participation, the conservation community as a whole was expecting too much from the untrained communities without providing them with the resources to play their part as co-managers. The conservation community and GOB were not providing these communities with either the financial resources or the training to be competent co-managers. Despite this, some community-based organizations such as the CBS were able to create a mechanism for financial stability. Others such as the Friends of Five Blues were able to establish relationships with foreign organizations and volunteers to struggle to maintain their CBO and co-management positions.

Despite the lack of training and finances, community interest continued and in 1995 the Association of Friends of Five Blues Lake NP signed a formal co-management agreement with the GOB. BAS signed agreements to co-manage six

Figure 1: Map of Protected Areas in Belize as of August 2005

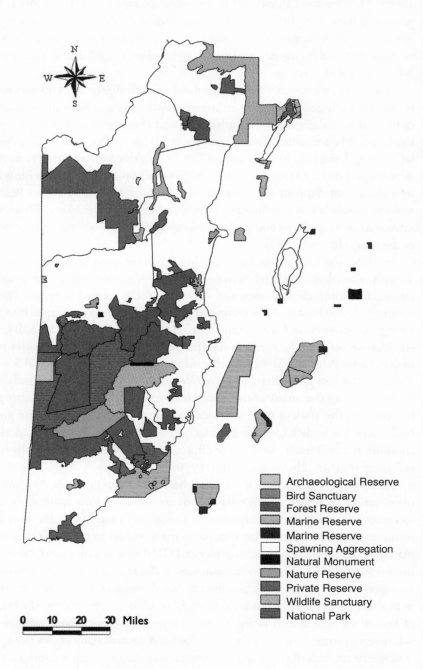

Archaeological Reserve
Bird Sanctuary
Forest Reserve
Marine Reserve
Marine Reserve
Spawning Aggregation
Natural Monument
Nature Reserve
Private Reserve
Wildlife Sanctuary
National Park

0   10   20   30   Miles

Source: Meerman, J. C., 2005. National Protected Areas System Assessment and Analysis: Protected Areas Analysis.

other PAs with the GOB a year later in 1996 (Leikam, et al., 2004). The GOB continued creating protected areas, particularly in the marine realm, creating in 1996 Bacalar Chico NP, Sapodilla Cayes, and South Water Caye MR.

In 1997, the Inuit Circumpolar Conference sponsored a co-management workshop in Belize City. In their promotional material, they featured the Community Baboon Sanctuary as an example of co-management (Kekchi Council of Belize and Inuit Circumpolar Conference, 1997; Inuit Circumpolar Conference and Kekchi Council of Belize, 1997). That same year, the Maya mapping project was carried out in which Maya villages in Toledo created maps of their villages (Toledo Maya Community Council and Toledo Alcaldes Association, 1997).

Later that same year, Community Conservation with the help of Judy Lumb, initiated the process for a stakeholders workshop for the Sarstoon-Temash NP (Anon., 1998a). Since the various stakeholder villages had little knowledge of the NP and its boundaries that had been established two years earlier, they were reticent to come to the meeting. Horwich and Lumb, accompanied by photographer Jim Beveridge and others, traveled to Barranco and then by foot to Midway, Conejo, and Sunday Wood to invite and convince the villagers that it was in their interest to attend this stakeholders meeting. The meeting, mediated by Sebastian and Fabian Cayetano, resulted in the publishing of the transcripts (Anon., 1998a) and, more importantly, laid the foundation for the participation of the villages in the management of the NP. Later, in 1998, SATIIM formed as an indigenous organization (Anon., 1998b) and helped organize the Sarstoon-Temash Stakeholder group with the help of a UNDP grant (Caddy, Ch'oc, & Paul, 2000).

In 1997, Cockscomb officially became a Wildlife Sanctuary (Leikam, et al., 2004), the Ya'axche Conservation Trust and the Aguacaliente Management Team were created and Toledo Institute of Development and the Environment (TIDE) was initiated as an independent group having originated as the Toledo office of the Belize Environmental Center directed by Lou Nicolait. In 1998, a number of other protected areas were created including three marine reserves (Caye Caulker MR, Corozal Bay MR, Blue Hole MR) and Aguacaliente WS. That year as well, the Golden Stream Preserve was created by Flora and Fauna International as a private protected area that would be eventually managed by the Ya'axche Conservation Trust (2004). A year later, BAS added two more PAs to its managerial responsibilities (Leikam, et al., 2004).

The stakeholders meeting for the Sarstoon-Temash (Anon., 1998a) became a pivotal time for community co-management. Shortly following that meeting, Horwich of CC realized that a larger grant was needed in order to involve a number of PAs and their community co-managers. Horwich conferred with Humberto Paredes of the Protected Areas Conservation Trust (PACT) and Richard Belisle of the Forestry Department to garner support in pursuing such a grant. Jon Lyon of CC took the lead in conferring with the NY office of

Table 1. A summary of NGO and CBO managed protected areas in Belize

Co-managed PA NGO Co-managed	Year Est.	Acreage	Co-managed Agency
Half Moon Caye NM	1982	9,771	BAS
Crooked Tree WS	1984	41,297	BAS
Blue Hole NP	1986	665	BAS with Armenia
Cockscomb Basin WS	1990	128,000	BAS
Bladen NR	1990	99,670	Bladen Consortium
Guanacaste NP	1994	58	BAS
Tapir Mountain NR	1994	6,744	BAS
Payne's creek NP	1994	31,676	TIDE
Sarstoon-Temash NP	1994	41,898	SATIIM
Blue Hole NM	1996	1,023	BAS
Laughingbird Caye/Gladden Spit	1996	10,119	Friends of Nature
Victoria Peak NM	1998	4,847	BAS
Port Honduras MPA	2001	96,731	TIDE
Actun Tunichil Muknal	2004	457	BAS
Man of War Caye	1977	13	BAS

CBO Co-managed			
Five Blues Lake NP*	1994	4,061	Assn. of Friends of Five Blues
Rio Blanco NP*	1994	100	Rio Blanco Mayan Assn
Monkey Bay NP	1994	1,799	Guardians of the Jewel
Sapodilla Cayes MR	1996	38,594	TASTE
Bacalar Chico NP*	1996	12,810	Green Reef
Freshwater Creek FR	1997	61,177	Friends of Freshwater Creek
Aguacaliente WS*	1998	5,492	Aguacaliente Mgmt Team
F and MR of Caye Caulker*	1998	94	FAMRCC
Honey Camp NP	2000	7,772	Assn of Friends of Freshwater Creek
Mayflower Bocawina NP	2001	7,107	Friends of Mayflower Bocawina NP
Noj Kaax Meen Eligio Panti NP*	2001	12,936	Itzamna Society
Billy Barquedier NP*	2001	1,500	STACA
GraGra Lagoon NP	2002	1,197	Friends of GraGra Lagoon
Spanish Creek Wildlife Sanctuary	2002	5,985	Rancho Dolores Environmental and Development Group
Swallow Cayes WS*	2002	8,970	Friends of Swallow Cayes
Davis Falls		94,156	Friends of Valley

Private			
Community Baboon Sanctuary	1985	12,980	Women's Conservation Group
Golden Stream	1998	15,038	YTC
Rio Bravo and C&MA	1988	259,206	Programme for Belize
Shipstern NR	1988	20,333	ITCF
Monkey Bay WS		1,150	Monkey Bay
Runaway Creek		7,124	(BB/ASF)
Boden Creek Ecological Reserve		7,600	Belize Lodge and Excursions
Aguacate Lagoon		284	
Block 127		9,232	TIDE

* Agreement signed after GOB (2005a; Leikam, et al., 2004).

UNDP and CC developed the original proposal. PACT, interested in taking the lead as the in-country NGO, worked with CC to develop the final proposal for a community co-managed park system (PACT, 1998) that was to include four potential community co-managed areas: Freshwater Creek Forest Reserve, Five Blues Lake National Park, Gales Point Manatee and Aguacaliente WS. The Sarstoon-Temash NP was also to be included but those stakeholders decided to pursue their own grant. The project was carried out between 1999 and 2001 (Ravndal, 2002).

In 1999 the PACT-CC partnership began the co-management grant with Horwich and Lyon and the newly appointed project manager, Lisell Alamilla, and by meeting with the four community groups and CC to create maps and compile histories for the four protected areas. By mid-1999, despite CC's original vision, a steering committee formed to oversee the project, decided to terminate CC's participation in favor of using Belize consultants and advisors. At the termination of the project, UNDP sent an independent party to evaluate the project (Ravndal, 2002). Ravndal's philosophy (pers. comm.) was that a project evaluation should have the expressed goal of improving the situation. She developed a list of critical barriers that she felt limited the success of the project. The GOB took these critical barriers very seriously and with other stakeholders met in 2002 to discuss how to proceed based on Ravndal's critique. This pivotal event led the GOB to create a Protected Areas System Plan in 2004 that was completed by the end of 2005 and presented to the conservation community in early 2006 (GOB, 2005a).

A second large grant followed in 2000 to BAS from the European Union with the intent to explore the potential for community co-management in Crooked Tree WS and Cockscomb Basin WS that were administered by BAS (Leikam, et al., 2004). That year, SATIIM initiated plans for an BZ$800,000 Global Environmental Fund grant to develop the Sarstoon-Temash NP that was carried out from 2002-5 (Caddy, et al., 2000; Horwich, 2005).

The barrier reef, one of Belize's most valuable national treasures, was not going unnoticed. The Mesoamerican Barrier Reef System Project was created in 1997 when Mexico, Belize, Guatemala, and Honduras committed to protect this important resource (Mesoamerican Barrier Reef System, 2006). The early 2000s marked a spurt in marine protection when the Project for the Conservation and Sustainable use of the Mesoamerican Barrier Reef System was launched in 2001. In 2000, TIDE signed the first agreement for a Marine Reserve (MR). The same year Port Honduras MR and Gladden Spit MR were created and Toledo Association for Sustainable Tourism and Empowerment (TASTE) was formed. TASTE quickly joined the ranks of co-managers by signing an agreement in 2001 with the Fisheries Department to co-manage the Sapodilla Cayes. Mayflower Bocawina NP was also created in 2001 followed by Swallow Cayes and Gra Gra Lagoon NP in 2002.

Community participation and the National Protected Areas Policy and Systems Plan

The late 1990s was a time of great conservation activity. The early beginnings of a National Protected Areas Plan occurred in the 1990s when WWF and US-AID collaborated in a National Resource Management and Protection Project (NARMAP). That resulted in an initial National Protected Areas System Plan (NPASP) published by Programme for Belize with assistance from the Inter-American Development Bank (Botnick, et al., 2000). The second major accomplishment was the creation of the Protected Area Conservation Trust (PACT) in 1996. PACT was established as a statutory body after several years of consultation and meetings with various non-government organizations, government departments, private sector and international conservation organizations. Through PACT, Belize was able to gain additional revenues for conservation from the increased ecotourism. A survey of tourists showed that they would be willing to pay as much as a $20US tax if they knew it would go toward the conservation of Belize (Spergel, 1996). Afraid that too high a tax would deter tourism, a modest US$3.75 tax was established instead with PACT as the recipient and distributor of the collected monies to the competing co-managers (Spergel, 1996).

Development of the more recent NPAPSP (GOB, 2005) serendipitously began with the proposal by Community Conservation in 1997, following the Sarstoon-Temash Stakeholders meeting, with the goal to strengthen the community co-management sub-system as a whole. Following the implementation of that UNDP grant in 1999-2001, a final evaluation noted a number of deficiencies in the system that prevented the success of the project (Ravendal, 2002). It highlighted the absence of an integrated national management plan for protected areas as a primary weakness (Salas, 2003). This led to a series of meetings in 2002-3, sponsored by BAS and UNDP, which included NGOs, CBOs government agencies and PACT, that led to a process of formulating a national policy and plan for protected areas (Salas, 2003). This involved a two year program involving a NPAPSP Task Force that ended in December 2005 and included guidelines and criteria for financial sustainability and co-management, together with the creation and de-reservation of terrestrial and marine protected areas.

Strengthening future community co-management of protected areas in Belize

During the past five years, a wide-range of activities has stimulated and created an environment that has produced a unique opportunity to explore and enhance the community co-management process in Belize. The key activities that have created this new environment include:

- the Protected Areas Conservation Trust (PACT) Co-management Project (1999-2002) added knowledge of community co-management (Lyon & Horwich, 2004; UNDP, 2002) and its evaluation (Ravendal, 2002; UNDP, 2002);
- the GOB and its communities took the lead in signing many community co-management agreements;
- the GOB developed a comprehensive Protected Areas Policy and System Plan (Briceño, 2004; GOB, 2003, 2005);
- the US Peace Corps-Belize created a revised Peace Corps project plan for Belize to support community co-management and community-based ecotourism initiatives (Miller, 2004).

As conservationists, researchers and government staff, we have not sufficiently helped community-based groups to achieve competence and empowerment to do their job as co-managers. We have expected them to perform with inadequate knowledge, training and finances. We must help them to obtain these necessities so they can participate fully and do the job we expect of them. Ravndal's report (2002) indicated specific critical barriers preventing effective co-management of protected areas in Belize. Many have been addressed in the last two years by creating a protected areas policy and system plan and by reviewing existing policy and legislation (Meerman, 2005a; GOB, 2005a). Others still need to be addressed to strengthen the community co-managers if the system is to work.

Defining co-management in Belize

What is it we mean by co-management and what do we expect of our community co-managers? Co-management of natural resources has been defined in numerous ways (Borrini-Feyerabend, et al., 2004). In its broadest sense, co-management can refer to any type of collaborative management between any number of parties including individuals, clans or other tribal units, non-governmental organizations or governmental entities. It can refer to the co-management of a great variety of resources including soil, water, agricultural systems, grazing lands, forests (Poffenbeger & Gean, 1998), fisheries (Berkes, 1989; Singleton, 1998), tree crops, wildlife (Murindagomo, 1990), coastal resources (Pomeroy & Goetze, 2003), wetlands, private property (Alderman, 1990) and protected areas.

In Belize today two basic types of co-management take place on public lands–NGO and CBO. There is also co-management of private protected areas by NGOs, private individuals, and communities. Examples of private co-management include the Ya'axche Conservation Trust management of Golden Stream Corridor Preserve, Programme for Belize's management of its Rio Bravo Conservation and Management Area, and management of recently acquired lands by Toledo Institute for Development and Environment (TIDE), Shipstern Nature Reserve and Monkey Bay Wildlife Sanctuary among others. Examples of co-management of public lands include Cockscomb Basin and other PAs co-managed by BAS and those PAs co-managed by community groups or other NGOs (see Table 1).

A simple working definition of community co-management of PAs is "the equal sharing of power and responsibility between government and a local community unit, with advisory involvement of an NGO where possible and desired, in the management of a protected area by members living on, near or adjacent to it." Often plagued with deficiencies, these community projects must be strengthened by addressing the following core issues.

Recommendations for strengthening co-managerial CBOs

1. Small seed money – Consistent seed money is necessary in initiating and maintaining small community-based conservation projects. This may seem obvious, yet many projects must continuously apply for yearly grants with no idea if their requests will be awarded. Thus, a great amount of time, energy and human resources are used by these groups in researching funding opportunities, proposal writing and other tasks connected to grant writing. The lack of success in obtaining continual funding creates funding gaps that can bleed enthusiasm from the project and cause discontinuity within the community organization. Integrated funding packages ought to include basic salaries and operating expenses to keep a project alive and functioning.

The Community Baboon Sanctuary was maintained on a continuum of small grants for its first five years–1985-1990 (Horwich & Lyon, 1995). In contrast, the Gales Point community effort experienced major gaps in funding (Horwich & Lyon, 1998). Had the money been spread over all of the years, arguably much more could have been accomplished without discontinuity in community motivation. The Association of Friends of Five Blues has had a similar challenge in funding. To offset this discontinuity in financial resources for salaries, they had success in attracting foreign volunteers as coordinators that has allowed them to continue at a low level without continuity in financial support.

One solution to this barrier is for government agencies, NGOs, and the parastatal PACT to work collectively with funding agencies to devise a plan to finance specific community projects on a 3-5 year basis. Thus, any such project would be given a chance to develop without the burden of focusing time and energy on seeking short term funding cycles. This could be either at a partial funding level, where they could also begin grant writing for complementary project activities or could be at a full funding level. Protected areas that might not have sufficient resources for financial sustainability might be chosen for longer term funding if the project and CBO are developing and performing successfully.

2. Financial mentor – A trend in Belize is that certain NGOs attract international donors who serve as a steady funding partner for them (DeVries, et al., 2003). To some extent these agencies have been more than just funders and have made a strong commitment to these local NGOs, including financial support, training and long term mentoring. Programme for Belize started this way in 1988 with the Massachusetts Audubon Society and later with The Nature Conservancy (TNC). TIDE has benefited greatly through its association with TNC. Flora and Fauna International (FFI) has helped purchase land and fund management of the Golden Stream Corridor Preserve and the local partner Ya'axche Conservation Trust. Friends of Nature (2004) attracts support from Conservation International, TNC and the Oak Foundation.

Most community-based projects have had much less success attracting external funding. Often community projects are only able to attract short-term grants that in many cases serve only to create funding instability in future years. Attempts should be made to connect community-protected areas with funding partners.

3. NGO mentoring – NGOs could serve as effective mentors to strengthen CBOs with the long term goal of "spinning off" these community groups as fully trained and empowered groups capable of managing their respective protected area. The role of NGOs in mentoring CBOs should be examined. While NGOs have been concerned mainly with their own projects, there is a potential win-win situation in maximizing the conservation success of NGOs while strengthening CBOs to take over co-management of the protected areas adjacent to their communities. Three cases in particular should be examined. Payne's Creek National Park was created by GOB due to petitioning of community groups representing Monkey River and Punta Negra Villages. Those same villages showed interest in co-managing the National Park (De Vries, et al, 2003). However, TIDE, which has been working with them, instead, is co-managing Paynes Creek with the GOB. TIDE's potential in mentoring those communities to manage that park could be a very positive situation. There is a great deal of work to do in the management of protected areas in Belize and with NGO mentoring, these villages could develop as responsible stewards and enable more benefits to accrue to local communities. Similarly, the Sarstoon-Temash Institute of Indigenous Management (SATIIM) is currently working toward a co-management of the Sartoon-Temash National Park. They are looking in the direction of expanding their sphere of influence to include community-controlled areas modeled on the Toledo People's Eco-Park Plan (Schmidt & Ack, personal comm.; Choc, personal comm.). The BAS looked at expanding the influence of the communities around the Cockscomb Basin Wildlife Sanctuary and Crooked Tree Wildlife Sanctuary (Leikam, et al., 2004). When the BAS offers those communities more autonomy over park management, perhaps it will free BAS to use its vast experience in protected area management to mentor other communities

141

to become better stewards of their nearby protected areas. As noted earlier, Programme for Belize has been mentoring communities in the Belize River Valley (Leikam, et al., 2004), and Friends of Nature of Placencia is looking to assist surrounding community efforts. In both cases, this mentoring will strengthen the protected areas system and facilitate integrated regional planning and communication.

In Belize, CC worked with WWF as an initial donor, the Milwaukee County Zoological Society as a secondary donor and the BAS as the in-county administrator until the CBS became independent. Currently, CC works with Stockton College in fund raising for the CBS and deals directly with the Women's Conservation Group from the CBS in advising them and providing them with books and posters for sale. As the effort in Belize expanded, CC worked with other community groups as well as the Peace Corps-Belize to further and strengthen community co-management in Belize.

4. Project support coordinator – A coordinator who can effectively work with a community group has been shown to help the whole community conservation process (McLain, 1997). It was the function that Horwich (1990a) served for the Community Baboon Sanctuary and is currently being served by Peace Corps Volunteers in a number of community conservation projects in Belize (Miller 2004; see Table 1 on p. 136). In the CBS, foreigners stressed their role as "transient catalysts" who would be ultimately replaced by local persons (Horwich & Lyon 1995). In the cases of Spanish Creek Wildlife Sanctuary and Mayflower Bocawina National Parks, support coordinators have worked well in providing training, grant writing, and general business development skills. Additionally, those communities become eligible for Small Project Assistance (SPA) grants through the Peace Corps. In the early stages of protected area formation and management, the BAS used such an approach in the Cockscomb Basin Wildlife Sanctuary and the Crooked Tree Wildlife Sanctuary (Horwich & Lyon 1999; Horwich, et al., 1993a). The project support coordinator serves as a mentor for skills transfer, connecting the community with both in-country and international resources and for general moral support. The role of the project support coordinator ultimately is temporary in that ideally the coordinator would train counterparts from the local community to replace them and assume the management support role.

5. Community training – Another critical barrier in community conservation projects is the lack of experience, knowledge and expertise for community members to act as empowered managers. Bernstein (2005) has determined 13 areas of training that would help strengthen community co-managers. These include: conflict resolution, natural resource and protected area management, organizational development, proposal/grant writing, meeting facilitation, project monitoring and evaluation, survey methods, business management, operation planning, biological monitoring, communications, and other related work skills such as tourism, environmental education, and empowerment. Only a long-term integrated training program can address this comprehensive need.

Working with the Peace Corps and the Belize Forest Department, CC initiated a series of training seminars for both Peace Corps support coordinators and community co-managers (Bernstein 2003). One idea for short-term intervention that came out of the 2004 Peace Corps in-service training workshop was that a team of Peace Corps volunteers with advanced training in business skills might function as a consultant team to train a number of communities. Volunteers could work intensively with one community at a time for up to three months and then continue to make themselves available on short-term consultant-basis as needed after the initial training period was over. Community training ought to be long-term, consistent, sustainable and designed to address the perceived needs and realities of each project in conformity with the National Protected Areas Policy and System Plan.

Conclusion

Even though Belize boasts a long history in setting aside protected areas for extractive purposes, the designation of protected areas for the preservation and protection of ecosystems and biodiversity is becoming increasingly common. Since independence, the number of protected areas in Belize has increased rapidly to 115 management units that include 94 protected areas (GOB, 2005a) accounting for 36% of Belize's national territory (Meerman, 2005b). Currently, protected areas declared for conservation purposes comprise 9.3% of national territory (Meerman, 2005b) and will most likely increase in the near future since numerous gaps in the protected area system were recently identified (Meerman, 2005c). At the same time, Belize has been exploring creative alternatives to traditional kinds of conservation and land management. These ideas and their inherent flexibility will help Belize in ensuring a more secure environment in its future. But the future is already displaying new complexities that will require creative solutions. According to Belize's Central Statistical Office (CSO), as Belize's population continues to grow at 2.7% per year, the population will double in only 26 years (Belize National Population, 2000). This drastic increase in population coupled with the simultaneous threats from climate change, cruise tourism, ecotourism, escalating poverty and crime, pollution (e.g., solid waste), and rampant deforestation will put immense strain of the country's natural resources and protected areas. Thus, new problems and challenges will begin to arise that Belize must be able to deal with and mitigate.

So how do we proceed in a way that will be sustainable in the future? The National Protected Areas Policy and System Plan has provided a roadmap of where we are and where we need to go in terms of protecting biodiversity and increasing the management of existing areas. Its findings and recommendations must be implemented. Additionally, the idea of co-management initially embraced by the GOB is a step in the right direction. Nonetheless, concrete and practical steps (e.g., seed money, financial mentoring, NGO mentoring, project support coordinator, and community training) must occur if co-management agreements are to become sustainable and aid in the conservation of Belize's abundant resources. The principles of sustainable ecotourism must be adhered to in order for communities to benefit economically. Furthermore, GOB must ensure that the playing field remains equitable to all Belizeans and not only for the fortunate few. Simultaneously, NGOs and other stakeholders (e.g., funding agencies) have an equally important role to play. They must ensure that CBOs have the capacity, experience, and financing to properly implement co-management agreements by fostering long-term mentorship and capacity building of community-based groups. Finally, a national initiative that will link and partner local NGOs and CBOs with each other to allow for the sharing of best practices and effective strategies must be undertaken. We believe that if communities are equipped with the relevant training and capacity, they will become empowered and work hard to mitigate the numerous challenges and threats that Belize's protected areas will soon face.

Acknowledgements

Special thanks to Meg and Walter "Mick" Craig for stimulating discussions of early conservation efforts in Belize and for making available hard-to-find literature on the subject area.

References

ABC/Kane. (1991). *A howler monkey village* (video).

Agreement G.O.B. and Association of Friends of Five Blues Lake. (1997).

ALDERMAN, C.L. (1990). *A study of the role of privately owned lands used for nature tourism, education and conservation.* Unpublished Report for Conservation International. Washington, D.C.

ANON. (1998a.) Sarstoon-Temash National Park. Transcript of Stakeholders workshop. Producciones de la Hamaca and Community Conservation Consultants.

ANON. (1998b, 1 Dec.). Belize: *BTIA Times*, Issue 1.

ANON. (2000). Hicatee (Central American river turtle) conservation. *Community Conservation Update*, 11(1), 4.

BELESKY, LES. (1998). *The ecotravellers guide to Belize and Northern Guatemala.* San Diego, CA: Academic Press.

BELIZE NATIONAL POPULATION AND HOUSING CENSUS 2000. (2000) Ministry of Budget Management. (Population Census 2000: Major Findings can be retrieved from http://www.cso.gov.bz/publications.html; accessed 23 June 2006).

BERKES, F. (1989). *Common property resources.* London: Belhaven Press.

BERNSTEIN, S.E. (2005). *Defining and building community capacity for co-management of protected areas in Belize.* Masters of science thesis, University of Wisconsin Madison.

BERNSTEIN, S. (2003). First capacity building workshop for protected areas management in Belize. Minutes in unpublished report.

BEVIS, J. & BEVIS, M. (1991). Slate Creek Preserve. Manuscript.

BOLLAND, O. NIGEL. (2004). *Colonialism and resistance in Belize: Essays in historical sociology.* Benque Viejo del Carmen, Belize: Cubola Productions/University of West Indies Press.

BOO, E. (1990). *Ecotourism: The potentials and pitfalls.* Vols. 1 & 2. Washington, D.C.: World Wildlife Fund.

BORRINI-FEYERABEND, G., PIMBERT, M., FARVAR, T., KOTHARI, A., & RENARD, Y. (2004). *Sharing power: Learning by doing in co-management of natural resources throughout the world.* Cenesta, Tehran, Iran: IIED and IUCN/CMWG.

BOTNICK, C., BUFF, J., CONGDON, L., MANTERNACH, J., MONTES DE OCA, L., & J. RENNICKS. (2000). *Examining the Belize Audubon Society's management of protected areas.* Masters of science thesis, University of Michigan.

BRICEÑO, J. (2004). Project launch of the national protected areas policy and system plan (keynote address). Can be accessed at http://www.mnrei.gov.bz.

CADDY, E., CH'OC, G. & PAUL, S. (2000, 10 Oct.). *The Sarstoon-Temash Institute of Indigenous Management: A grassroots initiative for social equity and sustainable development.* Manuscript presented at the IUCN World Congress, Amman, Jordan.

CBWS expanded, protected area now, 102,000 acres. (1990). *Belize Audubon Society Newsletter*, 22 (3): 1, 5.

CEP/UNDP. (1996). *Status of protected area systems in the wider Caribbean Region:*

Technical report No. 36. United Nations: UNDP. Report can be accessed at http://grid2.cr.usgs.gov/cepnet/pubs/techreports/tr36en/countries/beliz.html.

COC, P. (1989). *Proposed cultural homeland of the indigenous members of Belize in Toledo.* Manuscript.

DE VRIES, G.W., HAINES, M.F., HUFNAGEL S.B., LAIRD, A.K., REARICK, K.D., & SALAS, O.E. (2003). *Enhancing collaboration for conservation in Southern Belize.* Master of science thesis, University of Michigan.

DI FIORE, SONIA. (2002). *Remote sensing and exploratory data analysis as tools to rapidly evaluate forest cover change and set conservation priorities along the Belize River, Belize.* Master's Thesis, Columbia University, New York. (For full report, see http://www.wildlifetrust.org/content/difiore.pdf.)

FOOD AND AGRICULTURAL ORGANIZATION. (2005). FAO—Fishery country profile–Belize. http://www.fao.org/fi/fcp/en/BLZ/profile.htm; accessed 23 June 2006.

FRIENDS OF NATURE. (2004). *Summary of experience.* Manuscript. Website: http://www.friendsofnaturebelize.org/.

GERLITZ, W. (1994). *Five Blues National Park management plan* (draft manuscript).

GOVERNMENT INFORMATION SERVICE. (1994a). *Belize Today* (video on community-based tourism.) Belmopan, Belize: Ministry of Tourism and the Environment.

GOVERNMENT INFORMATION SERVICE. (1994b). *Guide to community-based ecotourism in Belize.* (1994). Belmopan, Belize: Ministry of Tourism & Belize Enterprise for Sustained Technology.

GOVERNMENT OF BELIZE. (1998). *Belize's interim national report.* Submitted to The Convention on Biological Diversity. Belmopan, Belize: Ministry of Natural Resources and the Environment.

GOVERNMENT OF BELIZE. (2000). Wildlife Protection Act, chapter 220, revised. See http://www.belizelaw.org/lawadmin/index2.html.

GOVERNMENT OF BELIZE. (2003). *National protected areas system for Belize: Executive summary.* Unpublished report. Belmopan, Belize: Ministry of Natural Resources and the Environment.

GOVERNMENT OF BELIZE. (2005a). *The Belize national protected areas system plan.* Belmopan, Belize: Ministry of Natural Resources and the Environment.

GOVERNMENT OF BELIZE. (2005b). *Forest department's five year strategic plan 2005-2010.* Belmopan, Belize: Ministry of Natural Resources and the Environment.

HARTSHORN, GARY, NICOLAIT, L., HARTSHORN, L., BEVIER, G. BRIGHTMAN, R. CAL, L., CAWICH, A., DAVIDSON, W., DUBOIS, R., DYER, C. GIBSON, J., HAWLEY, W., LEONARD, J., NICOLAIT, R., WEYER, D., WHITE, H., & WRIGHT, C. (1984). *Belize: Country environmental profile: A field study.* Appendix A: Archaeological Sites in Belize. Belize City, Belize: Robert Nicolait & Associates, Ltd.

HARTSHORN, G. S & GREEN, G. C. (1985). *Belize: Wildlands conservation in North-Central America.* International Union for the Conservation of Nature.

HORWICH, R. H. (1990a). How to develop a community sanctuary–An experimental approach to the conservation of private lands. *Oryx 24,* 95-102. For full report see http://www.communityconservation.org/documents/oryx.24.2.1990.pdf.

HORWICH, R. H. (1990b). *A Biosphere Reserve for Toledo District.* Manuscript.

HORWICH, R. H. (2005). Communities saving Wisconsin birds: North and south.

The Passenger Pigeon 67:1, 85-98. For full report see http://www.community-conservation.org/documents/Horwich.pdf.

HORWICH, R. H. & LYON, J. (1988). An experimental technique for the conservation of private lands. *Journal of Medical Primatology 17*, 169-176. For full report see http://www.communityconservation.org/documents/jmp.17.1988.pdf.

HORWICH, R. H. & LYON, J. (1995). Multi-level conservation and education at the Community Baboon Sanctuary, Belize. In S.K. Jacobson (Ed.), *Conserving wildlife: International education and communication approaches.* (pp. 235-253). NY: Columbia University Press. For full report see http://www.communityconservation.org/documents/educ.pdf.

HORWICH, R. H. & LYON, J. (1998). Community-based development as a conservation tool: The Community Baboon Sanctuary and the Gales Point Manatee project. In R. B. Primack, D. Bray, H. A. Galetti, & I. Ponciano (Eds.), *Timber, tourists, and temples: conservation and development in the Maya forests of Belize, Guatemala and Mexico.* (pp. 343-364). Washington, DC: Island Press. For full report see http://www.communityconservation.org/documents/cbsgpt.pdf.

HORWICH, R. H. & LYON, J. (1999). Rural ecotourism as a conservation tool. In T. V. Singh & S. Singh (Eds.). *Development of Tourism in Critical Environment.* (pp. 102-119). Lucknow, India: Centre for Tourism Research and Development/NY: Cognizant Communication Corp. For full report see http://www.communityconservation.org/tool.pdf.pdf.

HORWICH, R. H., MURRAY, D., SAQUI, E., LYON, J., & GODFREY, D. (1993a). Ecotourism and community development: A view from Belize. In K. Lindberg & D.E. Hawkins (Eds.). *Ecotourism: A guide for planners and managers.* (pp. 152-168). North Bennington,VT: The Ecotourism Society. For a full report see http://www.communityconservation.org/documents/ecotour.1993.pdf.

HORWICH, R.H., KOONTZ, F., SAQUI, E., SAQUI, H., & GLANDER, K. (1993b). A reintroduction program for the conservation of the black howler monkey in Belize. *Endangered Species Update* 10 (6), 1-6. For full report see http://www.communityconservation.org/documents/esu.10.6.1993.pdf.

HORWICH, R.H., KOONTZ, F., SAQUI, E., OSTRO, L., SILVER, S. & GLANDER, K. (2002). Translocation of black howler monkeys in Belize. *Re-introduction News*, 21, 10-12. Fir full report see http://www.communityconservation.org/documents/rn.21.2002_000.pdf.

HYDE, J. (1984). Belize Audubon Society: The first 30 years. In Waight, L., & J. Lumb (Eds.), (1999). Caye Caulker, Belize: Producciones de la Hamaca.

INUIT CIRCUMPOLAR CONFERENCE AND KEKCHI COUNCIL OF BELIZE. (1997). *Indigenous peoples and the application of co-management in Belize.*

KETCHI COUNCIL OF BELIZE AND INUIT CIRCUMPOLAR CONFERENCE. (1997). Co-management workshop. Manuscript.

KOONTZ, F, HORWICH, R., GLANDER, K., WESTROM, W., KOONTZ, C., SAQUI, E., SAQUI, H. (1994). *Reintroduction of black howler monkeys (Alouatta pigra) into the Cockscomb Basin Wildlife Sanctuary, Belize.* AZA Annual Conference Proceedings Wheeling West Virginia American Zoo and Aquarium Association, pp. 104-111.

KOONTZ, F. (1993, May/June). Trading Places. *Wildlife Conservation.* pp. 52-59.

LEIKAM, G., OTIS, S., RAYMOND, T., SIELKEN, N., & SWEENEY, T. (2004). *Evaluation of the Belize Audubon Society co-management project at Crooked Tree Wildlife Sanctuary and Cockscomb Basin Wildlife Sanctuary, Belize.* Master of Science Thesis, University of Michigan. Full report can be accessed at http://www.snre.umich.edu/ecomgt/pubs/bascm/complete.pdf.

LESLIE, R. (1997). *A history of Belize: A nation in the making.* Benque Viejo del Carmen, Belize: Cubola Productions.

LINDBERG, K. & ENRIQUEZ, J. (1994). *An analysis of ecotourism's economic contribution to conservation and development in Belize.* Vols. 1& 2. Washington D.C.: World Wildlife Fund.

LIPSKE, M. (1992, Jan-Feb.) How a monkey saved the jungle. *International Wildlife*, 22 (1), 38-43. For full report and pictures see http://www.communityconservation.org/documents/interwild.janfeb.1992.pdf.

LYON, J. & HORWICH, R. H. (1996). Modification of tropical forest patches for wildlife protection and community conservation in Belize. In J. Schelhas & R. Greenberg (Eds.), *Forest patches in tropical landscapes.* Washington, DC: Island Press. For full report see http://www.communityconservation.org/documents/patches.pdf.

LYON, J. & HORWICH, R. H. (2004). *Community co-management of protected areas in Belize: Cooperating to protect common ground.* Manuscript.

MCLAIN, L. A. (1997). *Community-based conservation plans: Local participation for empowerment and environmental protection in Gales Point, Manatee, Belize and the Kickapoo Valley,* Wisconsin. Master of Science Thesis, University of Texas, Austin.

MEERMAN, J. C. (2005a). *Belize protected areas policy and system plan: Result 2: Protected area system assessment & analysis.* Public Draft. Unpublished Report to the Protected Areas Systems Plan Office.

MEERMAN, J. C. (2005b). *Belize protected areas assessment & analysis: Protected area analysis.* Unpublished Report to the Protected Areas Systems Plan Office.

MEERMAN, J. C. (2005c). *Belize protected areas assessment & analysis: Gap analysis.* Unpublished Report to the Protected Areas Systems Plan Office.

MEERMAN, J. C & BOOMSMA, T. (1993). *Biodiversity of the Shipstern Nature Reserve.* Occasional Papers of the Belize Natural History Society 2(1), 1-7.

MEERMAN, J. C. & WILSON, J. R. (2005). *The Belize National Protected Areas System Plan.* Unpublished Report to the Protected Areas Systems Plan Office.

MEERMAN, J. C. & SABIDO, W. (2001). *Central America ecosystems map: Belize.* CCAD/World Bank/Programme for Belize.

MESOAMERICAN BARRIER REEF SYSTEM. (2006). Retrieved from www.mbrs.org.bz; accessed 15 April 2006.

MILLER, M. (2004). *Belize community conservation.* Unpublished Report to US Peace Corps, Belize

MINISTRY OF TOURISM AND THE ENVIRONMENT. (1994). *Community ecotourism* (video).

MONKEY RIVER VILLAGE COUNCIL. (1991). *Resolution*, No. 2 (91).

MURINDAGOMO, F. (1990). Zimbabwe: Windfall and campfire. In A. KISS (Ed.) *Living with wildlife: Wildlife research management and local participation*. World Bank Technical Paper No. 130. pp. 123-139. Washington, DC: The World Bank.

NATIONAL AUDUBON SOCIETY. (1991). *The environmental tourist: An ecotourism revolution* (video).

PROTECT AREAS CONSERVATION TRUST. (1998). *Creating a co-managed protected areas system in Belize: A plan for joint stewardship between government and community*. Manuscript.

Placencia BTIA meets on Monkey River pollution. (1988, 28 June). Belize: *Beacon*.

POFFENBERGER, M. and B. MCGEAN. (1998). *Joint forest management in India*. New Delhi, India: Oxford University Press.

POLISAR, J. (1995). River turtle reproductive demography and exploitation patterns in Belize: implications for management. *Vida Silvestre Neotropical 4(1)*, 10-19.

POLISAR, J. & HORWICH, R.H. (1994). Conservation of the large economically important river turtle *Dermatemys mawii* in Belize. *Conservation Biology 8(2)*, 338-342. For full report see http://www.communityconservation.org/ publications/ rivturt94.pdf.

POMEROY, R.S. & GOETZE, T. (2003). *Belize case study: Marine protected areas co-managed by Friends of Nature*. Caribbean Coastal Co-management Guidelines Project. Barbados: Caribbean Conservation Association. For a full report see http://cermes.cavehill.uwi.edu/publications/BelizeMPAscasestudy.pdf.

PROGRAMME FOR BELIZE. (2003). http://www.pfbelize.org; accessed 11 April 2006.

PROJECT LIGHTHAWK 1992. *Wings above the forest* (video).

RAVNDAL, V. (2002, Oct.) *Final project evaluation: Community co-managed park system for Belize*. UNDP/GEF Project funded by GEF and PACT.

SALAS, O. (1993). Belize Audubon Society: The first 30 years. In Waight, L., & J. Lumb (Eds.), (1999). Caye Caulker, Belize: Producciones de la Hamaca.

SALAS, O. (2003). Meeting of Protected Areas Management Organizations Proceedings.

SINGLETON, S. 1998. *Constructing cooperation*. The University of Michigan Press, Ann Arbor.

SLATE CREEK PRESERVE. (2006.) *Slate Creek Preserve News*. See www.belizeexplorer. com; accessed 11 April 2006.

SPERGEL, B. (1996). *Belize's protected areas conservation trust: A case study*. For Conservation Trust. For full report see http://www.ecotourism.org/WebModules/WebMember/MemberApplication/onlineLib/MemberApplication/onlineLib/Uploaded/Belize%20Conservation%20Trust.pdf.

TOLEDO MAYA CULTURAL COUNCIL AND TOLEDO ALCALDES ASSOCIATION. (1997). *Maya atlas*, Berkeley, CA: North Atlantic Books.

UNEP/WCMC. (n. d.). Mountain Pine Ridge Forest Reserve. http://sea.unep-wcmc.org/sites/pa/0563q.htm, accessed 23 June 2006.

UNDP. (2002). *Community Co-management of protected areas in Belize, reviewing lessons learned for the way forward.* Unpublished Summary Report of Meeting Proceedings.

USAID. (1988). Tropical forests/biodiversity. Annex to USAID/Belize FY 89-90 Action Plan, March.

WAIGHT, L., and LUMB, J. (1999). *Belize Audubon Society: The first 30 years.* Caye Caulker, Belize: Producciones de la Hamaca.

WILDLIFE (with Olivia Newton-John) (1994). *Baboons-Belize* (video).

YA'AXCHE CONSERVATION TRUST. (2004). Brochure. See http://www.yct.bz/display. php?menulevel1=1&menulevel2=74.

6. Our Reef in Peril-Can We Use It Without Abusing It?

Melanie McField and Nadia Bood

Overview

Belize is a nation blessed with a rich diversity of natural and cultural resources. Of paramount global renown is our magnificent barrier reef complex including the famous coral reef and associated habitats–extensive seagrass beds, lush mangrove forests, rich estuaries, and over 1000 islands or cayes (McField, Wells, & Gibson, 1996). The country is home to the longest barrier reef in the Western Hemisphere, extending approximately 280 km along its Caribbean coast and covering approximately 1,400 km². It is not, however, the second largest barrier reef in the world; New Caledonia, Fiji and several others are actually considerably larger barrier reefs than ours. Although many of our Caribbean neighbors (Bahamas, Cuba, etc.) have considerably more reef area than Belize (Burke & Maidens, 2004), ours is the longest in the region that meets the criteria of a barrier reef. Our reef complex actually contains a varied assemblage of barrier reef, lagoon patch reefs, fringing reefs, faro and off-shore atolls, which are probably our most notable claim to fame. Four offshore atolls (ring reefs surrounded by deep oceanic waters) exist in the North Western Caribbean, with three of these located in Belize.

The reef ecosystem is diverse, well-developed, and considered to be representative of the once flourishing reef environments of the Caribbean. These phenomenal ecosystems, along with their associated seagrass and mangrove nursery habitats, are critical to the life history of numerous species, including many with commercial significance. The diversity of coral reefs and fishes lures a wide variety of tourists and local recreational seekers to the crystal waters, including divers, snorkelers, and sports fishers.

From the lone fisherman hauling in his day's catch at a traditional fishing camp, to the affluent family enjoying the tradition of summering on St. George's

Caye, the lives of many Belizeans are intricately linked to the health of our coral reefs. Other Belizeans whose employment is not directly linked to marine resources may not recognize their dependence on the reef–until the onslaught of the next hurricane, whose battering waves have their initial, most powerful impact, slamming into our reef instead of our coastal homes and businesses.

Historical context and use of the reef

For centuries, coral reefs have been providing human inhabitants of this region with tangible cultural, ecological, and economic benefits. The Maya utilized marine resources for food (fish, turtles, and manatees), trade commodities (shells), and construction materials (coral foundations were used for some caye trading posts and homes). The reef also provided physical protection for these ancient Maya mariners and more recent historical mariners, including the famous (and infamous) Baymen and buccaneers of the 1700s.

In the colonial days as the city of Belize was being developed, corals, particularly the "pipe shank" or staghorn (*Acropora cervicornis*) and "pan tail" or elkhorn (*Acropora palmata*) varieties, were pulled from the reef and used as a sturdy material for road construction. Other than this destructive (although perhaps minor in scale) use of the reef, pre-independence use of the reef was primarily from fairly low-impact artisanal and commercial fishing.

In the last 25 years, we have seen some modernization of the fishing industry (boat engines, gear), although the total number of commercial fishers has remained approximately 2000 (Villanueva, 2006). Fishers today report a reduced abundance of fish, lobster, and conch, and the need to work longer hours and travel further distances to catch the same amount of fish. The most dramatic change in the coastal environment has been the steady expansion of the tourism industry, including intensive development and habitat alteration on many of the cayes adjacent to the reef.

It is sad to report that over the past 25 years, Belize's reefs have degraded from the vivid splendor of their past luxuriant coral growth and abundant fish, to their current average coral and fish abundances that are actually below the Caribbean average (Marks & Lang, 2006). A critical need exists for Belizeans to recognize the real and eminent danger of losing the ecological functionality of our reef–and ultimately the reef framework itself–if a sound coastal zone management plan is not developed and fully implemented.

Twenty-five years ago, coral reefs were not considered to be in great danger, and the global significance of Belize's reef was not well recognized by the Belizean people. As the Belize flag was raised on our first independence day few would have guessed the extent of future reef damage and the magnitude of conservation efforts that would be focused on this fragile resource. At independence, the main users of the resource were a couple thousand commercial fishers and the incipient marine tourism industry (first focused on sports fishing and then on scuba diving), based primarily in San Pedro, Ambergris Caye.

In 1981 marine conservation and management efforts were mainly based in the Fisheries Regulations (enacted through the Fisheries Department) and the protection of sea bird colonies through the efforts of the Belize Audubon Society and Forestry Department. In 1928, the Crown Reserves (small cayes protecting bird nesting areas) were established, followed by some expansion of these areas through the National Parks System Act established in 1981 (e.g., designation of Half Moon Caye National Monument to protect the famous red-footed boobies in 1982). The first marine reserve aimed at reef protection–the Hol Chan Marine Reserve—was not established until 1987.

Just as Belizeans began to enjoy their first taste of full independence including the initiation of some marine conservation measures, the entire Caribbean Sea experienced a basin-wide mass mortality of one of its most important residents, the long-spined sea urchin (*Diadema antillarum*). In 1983 a devastating disease outbreak wiped out 95% of these algae-eating echinoderms making this the largest marine mass-mortality recorded in modern times. Algal growth probably accelerated quickly in many areas, although the presence of abundant herbivorous fish helps to keep algae in check. Unfortunately there were not quantitative reef monitoring programs at that time to record all of these changes. Also in the 1980s coral disease (e.g. white-band) hit hard, and many elkhorn (*A. palmata*) and staghorn (*A. cervicornis*) corals, among the region's fastest-growing, were lost.

The International Year of the Reef (1997) marked a turning point for marine conservation in the region. Ten years after the establishment of our first marine reserve (Hol Chan in 1987), Belize celebrated the declaration of the Belize Barrier Reef World Heritage Site, and several international non-governmental organizations (NGOs) began setting up regionally focused conservation programs. On June 5, 1997, the presidents of Mexico, Guatemala, and Honduras and the Prime Minister of Belize signed the Tulum Declaration, formally acknowledging the exceptional global value of the reef (considered by many to be "relatively pristine" among Caribbean reefs at that time) and pledging to protect it for future generations.

The following year, 1998, was another extraordinary one–but for very different reasons. In a wicked twist of fate, the very next year Mother Nature provided a hard lesson in her destructive power. By September 1998, reef waters had warmed to unusually high temperatures and the most severe coral bleaching event in recorded history was underway. In late October, Hurricane Mitch slammed into Honduras, bringing torrential rains that produced catastrophic flooding and landslides. The result was tragic–more than 9,000 lives were lost. On the reef, the combination of bleaching and Mitch, plus chronic "background" stresses, led to dramatic reductions–almost 50% on average and even greater in some places–in live coral cover.

Over the past 25 years, the number and extent of marine conservation and monitoring programs in Belize have grown rapidly. The number of marine protected areas has increased from one in 1982 to 18 in 2006 covering approximately 250,000 hectares of sea. The increased global significance on Belize and the wider Mesoamerican Reef is evidenced by the establishment of a number of regionally focused projects and Initiatives: the Mesoamerican Barrier Reef System Project (MBRS), a Global Environment Facility/World Bank project now about to enter its second five-year phase; the World Wildlife Fund's Mesoamerican Reef Ecoregional Program; the Nature Conservancy's Mesoamerican Reef Program; the Wildlife Conservation Society's marine program in Belize; the International Coral Reef Action Network Mesoamerican Reef Alliance; and the Healthy Reefs for Healthy People Initiative, to name a few. The immense global value of coral reefs has recently become a popular subject of study and economic analysis, with conservation being only one of its many values.

Economic importance of the reef

Globally coral reefs are estimated to provide US$30 billion in net benefits in goods and services to world economies, including tourism, fisheries, and coastal protection (Cesar, Burke, & Pet-Soede, 2003). For the wider Caribbean the total value of goods and services provided by coral reefs are estimated to be between US$3.1 and 4.6 billion per year (Burke & Maidens, 2004). A full economic evaluation of Belize's reef will be conducted in 2007 (Burke, personal communication) although ballpark estimates are provided below.

Belize's growing tourism industry accounts for approximately 23% of the GDP (based on 2002 figures) with a total annual value of US$194 million (Burke & Maidens, 2004).

The fishing industry remains an important contributor to Belize's GDP (3.8% in 2005) (Villanueva, 2006) with export earnings of approximately US$34 million in 2005 (Ministry of Natural Development, 2006), although farm- raised shrimp accounts for US$25 million of this total. While farm-raised shrimp are not dependent on coral reefs, they are dependent on maintaining satisfactory water quality–a requirement shared by healthy reefs.

The lobster, conch, and finfish catches are all dependent upon coral reefs and associated mangrove and seagrass nursery habitats during some or all of their life history. Lobster has the highest export earnings of the wild caught fisheries products (approximately US$6M) followed by conch (US$2M). (Ministry of National Development, 2006).

One salient non-consumptive benefit provided by our barrier reef is its

154

role in coastal protection. The barrier reef runs along Belize's coast like a bulwark, protecting the nation's low-lying coastal areas from impacts associated with battering waves and storms. During catastrophic hurricanes this can equate to saving lives and property. The value of shoreline protection in Belize is roughly estimated at between US$35 and $100 million per annum—roughly estimated as 5% of the total Caribbean value calculated by Burke and Maidens (2004) because approximately 5% of the total reef area in the Caribbean is in Belize.

Using this same approach, the 5% of Caribbean reefs found in Belize have an estimated value of at least US$150 million per year in goods and services for Belize.

Without this vital function, a significant loss of land because of erosion will occur. This is of particular concern since most of eastern Belize is at or only slightly above sea level, and the country exists within the hurricane belt that increases the likelihood of being impacted by late season hurricanes. Belize's beautiful and economically valuable mainland coast and cayes might literally wash away without the protection of the reef.

A secondary benefit associated with the protection from wave energy is the creation of shallow lagoons and environments that foster the growth of seagrass and mangrove ecosystems, both of which are critical habitats and nursery grounds for numerous marine species, including threatened species such as manatees, Nassau groupers, golaith groupers, sawfish, green and hawksbill turtles, among others. Loss of these species at the local or global level would result in additional economic, scientific, and social losses.

Another benefit that is difficult to quantify in economic terms is the value of the genetic diversity of reef species and their vast potential in the development of new pharmaceuticals. Many important existing drugs have been developed from chemical compounds discovered in reef organisms, including those used to treat HIV, heart disease, pain, and a variety of cancers.

We also recognize a host of other values and benefits to Belizeans that are not easily quantified, such as the cultural, aesthetic, and recreational value (or potential value), that deserve consideration, if not quantification.

Threats to the reef

Although the reef complex continues to provide the nation of Belize with tangible ecological and socio-economic benefits, some of the same industries that benefit from the reef also threaten the reef, as do other activities occurring much farther inland, and even global environmental changes and natural events. The main threats to the reef can be grouped into the following categories: fishing, tourism and coastal development, land use, and agriculture, and global cli-

Figure 1: Lobster production

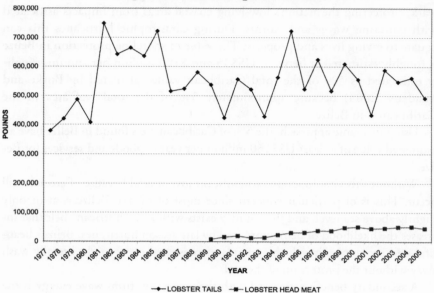

Source: Villanueva, 2006.

mate change. Also a number of "natural" disturbances have threatened the reef (e.g., coral bleaching events, hurricanes, diseases outbreaks), all of which may be augmented by global climate change and thus are not entirely "natural." Such events are not readily controllable at the local management level, while the other anthropogenic (human caused) threats are under local, national, or regional control.

Fishing (or over-fishing)

The distinction between fishing and over-fishing is not an easy or a trivial one to make. There is evidence that current fish stocks throughout the Caribbean (and the world) are already so over-depleted that any continued fishing represents over-fishing. However, the production of our main commercial species (measured as pounds of lobster) has remained fairly constant over the last two decades, indicating that populations may be able to maintain this level of production (see Figure 1). However, the average size of targeted species is said to be decreasing, while the effort required to catch similar quantities is said to be increasing. The production of fish and wild caught shrimp have declined in recent years (see Figure 2 on the next page).

The ecological results of over-fishing can be profound, particularly when

Figure 2: Fish production

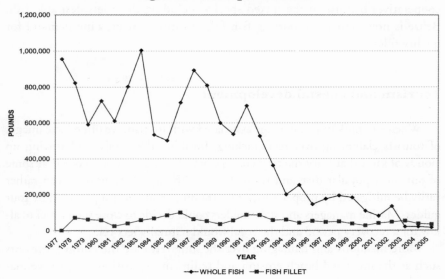

Source: Villanueva, 2006.

they involve the fishing of species that fulfill critical roles in the ecosystem, such as parrotfishes. Herbivorous fish play a critical role in the regulation of macroalgal (seaweed) growth that can overgrow or out-compete the corals on a reef if these grazers are not present. While most people think that our fishers are not taking many parrotfish, they are wrong. A recent study of the fishery out at Glovers Reef found that parrotfish were the second most frequently landed type of fish (barracuda was first), with our more favored snappers and groupers being more rare (Gibson & Hoare, 2006).

The growing resident and tourist population in Belize continues to place expanding pressure on our fisheries and offers more opportunity for direct sales of products to restaurants/hotels. These direct sales potentially bypass the fishermen's cooperatives that are responsible for collecting the data from fishers and enforcing size regulations at the point of sale.

Overall, Belize has good fisheries regulations, including size limits and closed seasons for the most heavily exploited species, and no-fishing zones in the marine reserves that serve as replenishment areas. However, there is inadequate financial support for full enforcement of these regulations with decreasing governmental financial support for the Fisheries Department, despite the increasing cost of enforcement, driven primarily by fuel costs. In addition Belize has no current regulations protecting the critical herbivores (parrotfish, tangs and surgeonfish) that are now being heavily fished because the more desirable fish are too scarce. The quality of these "fish fillet" is less desirable and many high-end restaurants report that they no longer buy fish fillet from the cooperatives because of the mixed species including these less desirable fish. Belize is now actually importing fish fillet to meet our growing demand for quality fillet.

Tourism and coastal development

When we think of reef damage associated with tourism we often have images of tourists clamoring over reefs kicking, breaking the corals, and stirring up clouds of sand that bury the tiny coral polyps. Such damages do occur at some of our most popular dive and snorkel sites, although these impacts can rather easily be mitigated by proper education, training, and control provided by tour guides. Marine managers and stakeholders could decide to close such a reef to allow for a recovery period and the coral would naturally recover.

More insidious and damaging over the long term are the chronic stressors such as the increased beach erosion and sediment deposition in sensitive marine habitats resulting from the loss of coastal vegetation (especially mangroves) and marine dredging operations that often destroy seagrass beds and wetlands that would naturally serve to trap sediments and pollutants. The increased number of tourists and resident human populations in sensitive coastal areas also result in increased pollution from sewage and solid waste disposal problems. Reef impacts from these factors are augmented during storms and hurricanes.

If reef decline associated with these factors is to be halted or minimized, sound management and monitoring procedures must be required to ensure that suitable water quality is preserved through environmentally sound coastal developments. Furthermore, penalties associated with contravention of regulations aimed at coastal and marine resource protection need to be increased. Current fines are so low and the permit procurement process so cumbersome that many developers choose to skip the lengthy permit process and pay instead the relatively quick and easy fines. Ultimately the fines and degree of planning required for development should be commensurate with the value of the natural resources impacted by the activity.

It is becoming increasingly evident that amplified tourist infrastructure development in sensitive natural areas, particularly given the absence of appropriate planning and local management controls, has become a major threat to the integrity of both ecological and cultural assets.

Global geo-political and social conditions can make over-dependence upon tourism a risky business. However, if adequately controlled, this growth can create significant opportunities for conservation and benefit local communities in Belize.

Land use and agriculture

All of Belize's land drains to the sea and activities occurring far inland can have negative impacts out on the reef. The fact that most of our reefs are relatively large distances from shore and the prevailing currents normally keep the coastal waters hugging the coastline with a southerly flow, saves the reef from receiving the brunt of the sediments delivered to the coast. However the fate of nutrients and chemicals that become biologically incorporated into ecological processes can be much more far ranging. Deforestation, agriculture, and aquaculture are currently considered the main land-based threats to our reefs, particularly in the south where the greater slopes and higher rainfall lead to more erosion and run-off.

According to the Reefs at Risk in the Caribbean study (Burke & Maidens, 2004), 29% of Belize's reef (mostly in the south and near Belize City) are highly threatened by sediments and inland pollution, while 51% have a low threat (primarily the offshore atolls), with the remaining 20% classified as being under medium threat.

The main problems associated with land use, deforestation, and agricultural practices are linked to the direct loss of forest habitat, especially riparian zones along the river banks, and increased contamination of rivers and coastal marine ecosystems with sediments, nutrients, pesticides and other pollutants. These sediments and nutrients cloud the waters and decrease the light available to corals, actually slowing their growth rates.

Increased nutrient levels in the water may also enhance the growth of fleshy algae, sponges, and other potential bio-eroding organisms that bore into the corals like termites into an old wooden house. Chemical contaminants, such as pesticides, may also decrease coral growth rates, and interfere with their reproductive success through many complicated larval and juvenile stages with chemically-mediated cues for settlement, metamorphosis, and growth.

Global climate change

Threats associated with global climate change are becoming more and more evident in Belize. Two threats that have been particularly noticeable in Belize are warming seas and extreme weather events. The 2004 and 2005 hurricane seasons, for example, provide strong evidence for adverse weather conditions, and the 1995, 1998, and 2005 mass coral bleaching events owed to increased sea surface temperature offer evidence for warming seas. All these events have resulted in some degree of impact to the reef systems. Current plans are to try to assist the protection of reefs through incorporation of reefs that are resistant (unaffected) and resilient (able to bounce back) to climate change impacts (e.g. bleaching) within Belize's Marine Protected Area (MPA) network system. Noteworthy, though, if policymakers and industry decision-makers do not confront the accelerating negative effects at a global level, the identification and inclusion of resistant and resilient reefs within MPA network systems will offer limited benefits.

An urgent need exists to confront environmental globalization synergistically with solving problems at local/regional scales. If these large-scale disturbance sources are not addressed, they will continue to kill even our most well managed and remote reefs. The best we can do to offset impacts from climate change is to invoke the precautionary principle and manage our reef resources with even more care, as a doctor would manage a patient with a serious illness.

As our environment continues to be influenced by climate change, continued impacts to reefs are inevitable. The additional stresses faced by the reefs coming from local decisions and careless actions may prove to be the tipping point for whether the reefs are to be or not to be in our children's future.

The ambient political climate and governance context also play a critical role in stabilizing or destabilizing environmental management efforts—as increasing levels of corruption and demoralization of government workers have a tremendous impact on the implementation of all environmental regulatory procedures.

There is a critical need to address multiple threats simultaneously since the detrimental effects of stressors such as over-fishing, pollution, poor land-use practices, and global warming are all interdependent and are acting synergistically to disrupt marine ecosystems.

A brief assessment of reef health over the last twenty-five years

Belize's coral reefs have been damaged by a combination of punctuated disturbance events and chronic stressors, leading to declining abundance of living corals and concomitant increases in the abundance of macroalgae in many areas. In fact, a few of our reefs appear to have undergone a phase-shift (meaning the ecological community seems to have shifted and remained in the altered state) from reefs being dominated by living corals to those dominated by macroalgae (seaweed). Hurricanes and more recent coral bleaching and disease events represent two of the main widespread disturbances (see Figure 3 next page).

The reefs of Belize only became the focus of serious investigations in the 1960s-70s. As Jackson (1997) argues, in the 1960s Caribbean reefs were far from pristine and that real baseline data from "pristine Caribbean reefs" are thus not available. Nevertheless, a brief review of some of the major historical studies provides insight into the current ecological status. The earliest expedi-

Figure 3: Generalized history of major reef disturbances in Belize

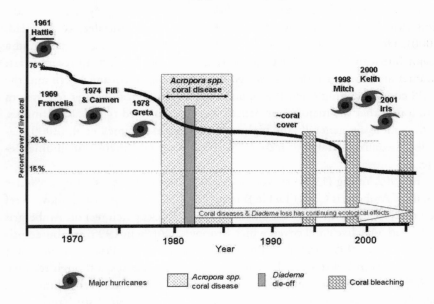

tion on this reef was the 1959-60 Cambridge Expedition (Stoddart, Thorpe, & Bregazzi, 1962), which focused primarily on the cayes. This project also produced the first description of reef zonation and dominant species from the area around Rendezvous Caye. Stoddart continued his studies in Belize, describing the structural formations of the three atolls (Stoddart, 1962) and the effects of Hurricane Hattie on the cayes and reefs (Stoddart, 1963; Stoddart, 1974).

Wallace (1974) describes coral-dominated patch reefs with 80% live coral cover in Glovers Reef atoll, and sampled lagoonal sediments and foraminifera populations. Purdy, Pusey and Wantland (1975) describe the Belize continental shelf in relation to hydrographic regions, sediments, basic reef development and molluscan assemblages. James and Ginsburg (1979) provide an early description of the morphology, sediments, and biota of the outer reef wall.

The Smithsonian Institution's research station on Carrie Bow Caye opened in 1972. Burke (1979) provides the first comprehensive descriptions of reef sites, with seven transects from Gallows Point reef to the Queen Cayes, in which bottom profiles, zonation of substrates and organisms were recorded. Rützler and Macintyre (1982) provide a compilation of early research conducted at the station, including descriptions of the reef at Carrie Bow Caye and taxonomic inventories. Although these early studies provide useful general descriptions of the reefs, they did not typically include what would now be considered standard quantitative ecological data. Thus, it is difficult to assess modern ecological changes relevant to these early studies.

Prior to 1998, Belize's reefs were thought to be in relatively "good" condition (McField, et al., 1996; Kramer, Kramer, Arias-Gonzalez, & McField, 2000). However, escalating threats, including coral bleaching, disease, and a major hurricane in 1998 have adversely affected Belize's reefs in recent years. Kramer and Kramer (2000) surveyed damages from hurricane Mitch and the 1998 coral bleaching event throughout the Mesoamerican barrier reef system and found that the majority of Belize's reefs had suffered significant damages, with coral losses generally the highest in the region. Kramer, et al. (2000) describe the current status of reefs in Northern Central America, including Belize.

In 1992 Young (1994) surveyed several barrier reef sites, finding 25% live coral off Ambergris Caye (Tackle Box site) and 20% live coral at Gallows Reef (Point 2) in 1992. In 1993 the shallow Mexico Rocks patch reef off Ambergris Caye had 84% live coral cover, which dropped to 66% in 1995, attributed primarily to the 1995 coral bleaching event (Burke, 1996). Prior to 1998, most reef impacts in Belize were thought to result from diseases, although regional nutrification, sedimentation, loss of *Diadema*, moderate over-fishing, and bleaching are also likely contributors. The 1998 multiple disturbance event (mass coral bleaching and a catastrophic hurricane) amplified these ongoing declines.

While the percent of live coral cover is only one measure of a reef's ecological status, it is the most commonly used indicator or "dip-stick" of reef health (McClanahan, 1997). The following studies can only be compared in a broad sense, as methods and depth ranges sometimes varied. Decreased coral cover has been noted at the few sites in Belize where long-term data are available. The earliest major declines are recorded from shallow patch reefs in Glovers reef atoll, which changed from 80% coral cover in 1971, to 20% in 1996 (McClanahan & Muthuga, 1998), to 13% coral cover in 1999 (McClanahan, McField, Huitric, Bergman, Sala, Nyström, et al., 2001). The inner forereef region at Carrie Bow Caye had 30-35% coral cover in the 1970s and declined to 12-21% in 1995 (Koltes, Tschirky, & Feller, 1995). The forereef at Channel Caye (3-15m. depth), an inner-shelf faroe, declined from 85% live coral in 1986 to 60% in 1996, attributable primarily to disease and loss of staghorn corals (*A. cervicornis*), with partial replacement by thin leaf lettuce coral (*Agaricia tenuifolia*) (Aronson & Precht, 1997). Subsequently, the bleaching event of 1998 devastated this reef reducing live coral cover to approximately 5% in 1999 (Aronson, Precht, Macintyre, & Murdoch, 2000).

The average live coral cover in Belize (about 13-15%) is now slightly less than the Caribbean average of about 20% (Marks & Lang, 2006; McField, 2002; and Figure 4).

Figure 4: Coral reef cover

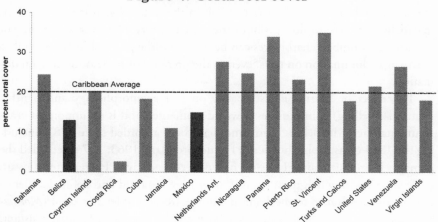

Source: Atlantic and Gulf Rapid Reef Assesment Database 1999-2004.

Reefs in distress across the Caribbean

Coral mortality, resulting from various disturbances in the 1960s to 1980s, has resulted in the "opening-up" of space for colonization by other organisms. In the 1970s, two of the main reef building corals, elkhorn (*A. palmata*) and staghorn (*A. cervicornis*), suffered mass mortality throughout the Caribbean (including Belize) due to white-band disease. The incidences of newly occurring diseases (e.g. black band, white plague, dark spot) have also increased, with subsequent infestation and death of numerous representatives of other species as well. Macroalgae, having a faster growth rate than corals, are often times able to colonize the available space before coral recruits can become established. In some instances, their proliferation on reefs has even resulted in smothering (overgrowing and shading) newly settled corals (recruits). However, where their density is sufficient enough, herbivores have functioned to limit substratum overgrowth by macroalgae thereby promoting the potential for coral recruitment. Major herbivores include sea urchins, parrotfish and surgeonfish. In 1983-84, the long-spined sea urchin (*D. antillarum*), a major herbivore on Caribbean reefs, experienced a mass mortality. Prior to the mass mortality, *Diadema* was probably the prime regulator of algal cover on shallow to intermediate depth reefs. The loss of these important herbivores, compounded with the over-fishing of herbivorous fish (i.e., parrot and surgeon), has been proposed by marine scientists as one of the main causes of current high algal abundance on Caribbean reefs (Hay, 1984; Hughes, 1994; McClanahan & Muthuga, 1998; Aronson & Precht, 2000; Jackson, Kirby, Berger, Bjorndal, Botsford, Bourque, et al., 2001).

Could the reefs of Belize be subjected to a similar fate? It is certainly a possibility if corals continue to decline in abundance and if the fishing of critical herbivorous fish (parrotfish) continues. Macroalgal proliferation on some reefs is also attributed to increased nutrient levels in the water. Whereas corals cannot, macroalgae are able to flourish in nutrient rich waters. However, when present in sufficient numbers, herbivores can help prevent the phase-shift from coral to macroalgae domination on reefs, even in the presence of some nutrient contamination.

The effect of hurricane disturbance on reef geomorphology and benthic (bottom-dwelling) communities is well documented and is an important environmental factor in Belize. Hurricanes have been recorded since 1787, including the 1961 catastrophic hurricane Hattie. Stoddart (1963, 1974) recorded the damages from Hurricane Hattie on Belize's reefs and cayes. He reported a swath of devastation in which most corals (80%) were removed and defined a hierarchy of coral resistance to mechanical damage from boulder star coral (*Montastraea annularis*)–most resistant, to staghorn coral (*A. cervicornis*)–least resistant. Stoddart (1963) predicts a full recovery period of 20-25 years but notes that in 1969 mobile debris, algal competition, and increased turbidity had limited the recovery in some areas (Stoddart, 1974).

Subsequent hurricanes have also been studied, with further evidence of their importance in shaping zonation of the barrier reef and atolls. Rützler and Macintyre (1982) highlight Hurricane Greta, which in 1978 caused significant lagoonward movement of staghorn (*A. cervicornis*), resulting in the expansion of its distribution. Hurricane Mitch (1998) caused 7-meter waves for several days. Mumby (1999) reports that approximately 90% of living elkhorn corals (*A. palmata*) was removed at some windward forereef sites on Glovers Atoll and coral recruit densities were reduced to 20% of levels recorded prior to the hurricane.

Reefs that are already stressed by human threat factors (pollution, over-fishing, etc.) have a difficult time rebounding from natural occurrences. In 1998, Belize's reefs were significantly impacted by two synergistic events: mass coral bleaching owed to increase sea surface temperature and Hurricane Mitch, a category 5 storm that brought torrential rain and catastrophic flooding. The combined effects of the bleaching and Hurricane Mitch plus chronic "background" stresses brought about dramatic reductions (50% and greater in some places) in live coral cover.

Management and conservation efforts to curb reef decline

Conservation of the reef ecosystem and sustainable management of marine resources have traditionally been supported by the general population, the many non-governmental organizations involved in resource management in Belize, and by most government departments. This broad-based approach is largely responsible for the successes to date. However, new conflicting views and a general impatience with the slow pace of "sustainable development" are fostering a shift in the business climate that now appears focused more on short-term economic goals involving large-scale development projects with corresponding large-scale environmental impacts.

Protection of Belize's marine resources is the shared responsibility of several governmental and non-governmental agencies. The Coastal Zone Management Authority and Institute (CZMAI) should be the focal point and coordinating body for marine conservation planning, monitoring, and research for the various sectoral or regulatory government departments (Fisheries, Environment, Geology, Forestry, and Lands Departments). Since its inception in 1998 it served successfully in this role and was used as a model of coastal zone management planning for other countries. The CZMAI hosted regular inter-sectoral meetings of the Coastal Zone Management Advisory Committee and local planning committees. These efforts came to a halt when the international funding ran out and the government of Belize did not implement the recommended national strategies for economic sustainability. Now the technical staff is gone, and no Advisory Committee meetings have been held since the summer of 2004. The decline of this once impressive Institution is almost as disturbing as the declines on the reef itself—and this one is completely within our nation's control.

The ever-increasing migration to coastal areas and the escalating coastal-marine tourism market have resulted in increased ad hoc economic, recreation, and development activities throughout Belize's coastal zone. This scenario has demonstrated an urgent need for sound planning and management of Belize's coastal resources. If implemented as intended, the Coastal Zone Management Plan will effectively define the policies, strategies and guidelines for the management and conservation of Belize's coastal resources for the long-term and for the balanced benefit of society.

In 2004 the Cabinet requested that CZMAI develop a coastal zone management plan for Belize, including the zoning of marine waters and development guidelines for the cayes and coastline. Since 1995 the Cayes Development Policy had been prepared and served as an overarching framework for the more detailed plans. Draft plans were developed for all nine planning regions, with varying degrees of local stakeholder input. However, no further actions have been taken to finalize and implement these plans because of the lack of political will and interest in the critical process of coastal zone planning.

Belize's relatively recent introduction to international tourism and commercial development markets offers an opportunity for managers to benefit from the experiences and mistakes of other countries, tailoring successful models into the Belizean context to promote sustainable development. However, the real world is rarely so thoughtful, and as development and financial pressures have increased so has the potential for serious environmental degradation.

Belize has adequate environmental legislation but lacks enforcement and monitoring capacity. For example, under the Environmental Impact Assessment (EIA) regulations of 1995, the Department of Environment enforces regulations and screens projects that may require EIAs. Similarly, the Land Utilisation Authority is responsible for Special Development Areas, which are also forms of strategic planning that provide zoning of land-use.

The Belize Tourism Board regulates the tourism industry, including the expanding cruise industry, which poses a major threat to the quality of the ecosystem and Belize's tourism product. Belize's traditional upscale ecotourism niche market is being overshadowed by the rapid expansion of cruise tourism creating the "K-mart of the Caribbean" image. Thus the high quality of Belize's tourism product is in jeopardy, as evidenced by the recent designation of the Belize Barrier Reef Reserve System World Heritage Site on the worst rated destinations list by National Geographic, due to skyrocketing cruise ship activity and coastal over-development and reef degradation (Tourtellot, 2006).

The Tourist Guide Regulations require that all tour guides meet standard levels of professional training and licenses can be revoked for non-compliance with environmental or other regulations. Many experienced dive guides are quite effective at "self-regulation" although new guides are in need of further conservation training. Dive operators have played a major role in the installation and maintenance of mooring buoys. However, these initiatives may be jeopardized by new pressure within the industry to accommodate the mass-tourism market rather than the traditionally small-scale ecotourism market.

The Fisheries Department manages the fisheries industry, which includes aquaculture. No fishing is allowed on SCUBA and there are other gear restrictions, size limits, and closed seasons. However, government resources are inadequate to patrol the waters of Belize or to fully enforce these regulations. Marine reserves have been established under the Fisheries Act to assist fisheries management by replenishing heavily exploited stocks, while also protecting essential habitats (coral reefs, seagrass beds, and mangroves).

The Environmental Protection Act of 1992 provides the framework through which the Department of Environment enforces regulations preventing pollution. Regulations for Environmental Impact Assessments and Industrial Effluents offer specific controls in industrial developments. Although enforcement personnel is severely limited, the small scale on Belize's industrial sector aids the identification and control of potential sources of industrial pollution. (See a fuller description of EPA and the EIA process in the Gonzalez' article in this volume.)

The important role of Marine Protected Areas

The establishment of marine and coastal protected areas has been an essential component of marine conservation efforts in Belize. Belize now has a total of 18 Marine Protected Areas (MPAs) covering about 22% of its continental shelf and atolls, but the vast majority of the MPA area (about 90%) is actually open to fishing, with less than 2% being fully closed to fishing (CZMAI database, 2004).

MPAs are a useful tool for addressing a number of threats to coral reefs, particularly those related to tourism, development, and over-exploitation of commercial species. They provide safe havens for depleted marine species to replenish outside fishing areas and maintain critical food web interactions and ecological processes that may be missing from fully exploited areas. Zoning schemes enable multiple uses in these areas, including recreational diving, sports-fishing, and traditional small-scale fishing and full protection (no-take zones) in key areas. However, with less than 2% of the continental shelf and atolls actually closed to fishing, the amount is clearly inadequate to sustain full benefits for the entire marine fishing area.

The value of protected areas in promoting sustainable fisheries and in regulating tourism and other activities is now well documented and the Hol Chan Marine Reserve has been cited as an international model. Research at Hol Chan and Half Moon Caye has illustrated that MPAs can result in fish populations with significantly greater abundance and larger-sized individuals (Polunin & Roberts, 1993; Carter & Sedberry, 1997). MPAs also support the potential ecological benefits of increasing herbivory on reefs, thereby reducing competition from macroalgal growth.

The role of NGOs and local community-based management is significant, as they assist or conduct the primary management functions in a number of the MPAs. The Fisheries Department also manages a number of marine reserves directly, but maintains links to the communities through local advisory committees for each MPA. Funding is greatly needed to develop adequate zoning plans, cover operational costs, securing necessary human resource for enforcement, implementation of monitoring/research programs to track the health of the ecosystems as well as for the "building up" of education and awareness of both visitors and local communities alike. The participation of local communities is also vital to the success of our coastal/marine MPAs.

A number of evaluations of MPA management effectiveness have been conducted since 2000. The overall results are approximately "moderately satisfactory"–indicating that there are minimal elements necessary for management. But the results indicate that Belize's MPAs have deficiencies that prevent effective management and reduce the probability that conservation objectives will be achieved. There are good policies, laws, knowledge, biogeographic characteristics, and management of legal and illegal uses. MPAs generally have good community support although a small but vocal group of fishermen has occasionally stated its opposition to MPAs. One of the main problems facing the effective management of MPAs is the lack of adequate resources for proper enforce management.

Looking to the future

It is not known whether our reef is on the path to recovery, holding steady (as it has for the last eight years since the major declines), or is facing further demise (which would render future recovery less plausible). McField (2002) quantified and documented declines to Belize's reef community structure from the combined impacts of the catastrophic Hurricane Mitch and mass coral bleaching event of 1998. These phenomena resulted in 48% reduction in the live coral cover among Belize's reefs. Research aimed at measuring reef recovery since such impacts was conducted in 2005. Bood (2006) found no sign of reef recovery based on the analysis of six reef sites. However, whether or not there has been recovery on a wider scale, there is a general belief among the global reef science community that maintaining critical functional groups, especially herbivores (i.e., parrot and surgeon fish, and sea urchins), can confer recovery benefits to reefs. No-take (i.e., no extractive activities) marine protected areas are important since they allow these critical functional groups to persist and reproduce.

The reefs are also dependent on a dynamic mosaic of associated habitats that provide critical biological and physiochemical services to the reef. Mangroves and seagrasses provide critical habitat for many reef species, including lobsters, many snappers and parrotfish, particularly during juvenile life stages. They also stabilize sediments and the shoreline, while taking up nutrients and cleansing the water so corals can thrive. The interdependence of these habitats can be broken by direct habitat destruction or by more subtle coastal degradation which renders them functionally impotent.

If we lose the ecological functionality of our reefs, mangroves, and seagrass beds, our fishing industry will certainly be lost; the value of our marine tourism product will be greatly reduced—relegated to visitors interested solely in fun and sun; and our environmental security, in a time of predicted rising seas and increasing strength and frequency of hurricanes, will be dramatically reduced or destroyed.

Without the vivid splendor of the living reef the Belizean people and those who care about marine life around the world will suffer a cultural, aesthetic, and spiritual loss. If we are to maintain the brilliant luster of the "jewel," for ourselves and the world, then we need to recognize the critical importance of each incremental management and development decision that impacts this irreplaceable national treasure.

One of the main challenges of marine conservation is finding a way to make the reef and other marine life real and personal to the average citizen. The unfortunate fact is that most Belizeans have never even seen their famous reef and have no experiential connection with marine life and marine ecosystems. Until we can personalize this relationship between human life and marine life, we will have a hard time garnering support for marine conservation efforts. Our country needs economic development. However, establishing a balance between short term profits for some and ecological benefits for all, will remain a continual challenge. Only when the people of Belize fully appreciate the value of maintaining a living reef and internalize the linkages between ecosystem health and their own health, including their culture and livelihood, will they be able to adequately assess the environmental and economic tradeoffs associated with alternate development options.

Unless the Government of Belize on behalf of the environment and the people (the human members of the ecosystem), make the right choices, our lives and our livelihood will be in peril. Our magnificent coral reefs, mangroves, and seagrasses will not have a future and will be unable to maintain a leading role in the sustainable development of our economy and the maintenance of the ecosystem's health and longevity.

References

ARONSON, R. B. & PRECHT, W.F. (2000). Herbivory and algal dynamics on the coral reef at Discovery Bay, Jamaica. *Limnology and oceanography 45*, 251-255.

ARONSON, R.B., PRECHT, W.F., MACINTYRE, I.G., MURDOCH, T.J. (2000). Coral bleach out in Belize. *Nature 405*, 36.

BOOD, N. D. (2006). *Recovery and resilience of coral assemblages on managed and unmanaged reefs in Belize: A long-term study*. Master's thesis. University of South Alabama.

BURKE, C. D. (1996). Coral mortality associated with the 1995 Western Caribbean bleaching event, Mexico Rocks patch reef complex, Belize. GSA *Abstracts with Programs 28*(7), A-274.

BURKE, L. & MAIDENS, J. (2004). *Reefs at risk in the Caribbean*. Washington, DC: World Resource Institute.

BURKE, R. B. (1979). *Morphology, benthic communities, and structure of the Belize barrier reef*. Masters thesis, Dept. of Marine Science, University of South Florida.

CARTER, J., & SEDBERRY, G. R. (1997). The design, function and use of marine fishery reserves as tools for the management and conservation of the Belize Barrier Reef. *Proceedings of the 8th international coral reef symposium 2*, 1911-1916.

CESAR, H., BURKE, L., & PET-SOEDE, C. (2003). *The economics of worldwide coral reef degradation*. Arnhem (Netherlands): Cesar Environmental Economics Consulting.

COASTAL ZONE MANAGEMENT AUTHORITY AND INSTITUTE (CZMAI) (2004). Raw data. GIS database. Belize City, Belize.

GIBSON, J. & HOARE, S. (2006). *Fisheries catch data collection–Glover's Reef.* Wildlife Conservation Society. August 2006.

HAY, M. E. (1984). Patterns of fish and urchin grazing on Caribbean coral reefs: Are previous results typical? *Ecology 65*, 446-454.

HUGHES, T. P. (1994). Catastrophes, phase shifts, and large-scale degradation of a Caribbean coral reef. *Science 265*, 1547- 1551.

JACKSON, J.B.C. (1997). Reefs since Columbus. *Proceedings of the 8th International Coral Reef Symposium 1*, 97-106.

JACKSON, B. C., KIRBY, M. X., BERGER, W. H., BJORNDAL, K.A., BOTSFORD, L. W., BOURQUE, B. J., BRADBURY, R. H., COOKE, R., ERLANDSON, J., ESTES, J. A., HUGHES, T. P., KIDWEL, S. L., LANGE, C. B., LENIHAN, H. S., PANDOLFI, J. M., PETERSON, C. H., STENECK, R. S., TEGNER, M. J., & WARNER, R. R. (2001). Historical overfishing and the recent collapse of coastal ecosystems. *Science 293*, 629-638.

JAMES, N.P. & GINSBURG, R.N. (1979). *The seaward margin of Belize barrier and atoll reefs. International Association of Sedimentologists.* Special publication, No. 3. London/Edinburgh/Melbourne: Blackwell Scientific Publications.

KOLTES, K. H., TSCHIRKY, J. J., and FELLER, I. C. (1998). Carrie Bow Caye, Belize. In B. KJERFVE (Ed.) *Caribbean coastal marine productivity.* (CARICOM): Coral reef, Seagrass and Mangrove Site Characteristics). Paris: UNESCO.

KRAMER, P. A. & KRAMER, P. R. (2000). *Ecological status of the Mesoamerican Barrier Reef: Impacts of Hurricane Mitch and 1998 coral bleaching.* Final report to the World Bank.

KRAMER, P., KRAMER, P. R., ARIAS-GONZALEZ, E., & MCFIELD, M. (2000). Status of coral reefs of Northern Central America: Mexico, Belize, Guatemala, Honduras, Nicaragua and El Salvador. In Clive Wilkinson (Ed.), *Status of coral reefs of the world: 2000* (pp. 287-313).

MINISTRY OF NATIONAL DEVELOPMENT, INVESTMENT, AND CULTURE. (2006, Sept.). *Belize external trade bulletin.* Belize: Central Statistical Office.

MARKS, K.W. a & LANG, J.C. (2006). *AGRRA Summary Products,* version (10/2006). Available online http:www.agrra.org/Release_2006-10.

MCCLANAHAN, T. R. (1997 March). Coral reef monitoring–The state of our art. *Reef Encounter 20.*

MCCLANAHAN, T. & MUTHUGA, N. (1998). An ecological shift in a remote coral atoll of Belize over 25 years. *Environmental Conservation* 25(2), 122-130.

MCCLANAHAN, T. R., MCFIELD, M., HUITRIC, M., BERGMAN, K., SALA, E., NYSTRÖM, M., NORDEMER, I., ELFWING, T., & MUTHIGA, N. A. (2001). Responses of algae, corals and fish to the reduction of macro algae in fished and unfished patch reefs of Glovers Reef Atoll, Belize. *Coral Reefs 19*, 367-379.

MCFIELD, M., WELLS, S., & GIBSON, J. (Eds.). (1996). *State of the coastal zone report, Belize, 1995.* Belize: Government of Belize, Coastal Zone Management Program and UNDP/GEF.

MCFIELD, M. (2002). Influence of disturbance on coral reef community structure in Belize. *Proceedings of the ninth international coral reef symposium, Bali*, Oct. 2000. Vol. 1, 63-68.

MUMBY, P. J. (1999). Bleaching and hurricane disturbances to populations of coral recruits in Belize. *Marine Ecology Progress Series 190*, 27-35.

POLUNIN, N. V. C. & ROBERTS, C. M. (1993). Greater biomass and value of target coral-reef fishes in two small Caribbean marine reserves. *Marine Ecology Progress Series 100*, 167-176.

PURDY, E. G., PUSEY, W. C., WANTLAND, K. F. (1975). Continental shelf of Belize–Regional shelf attributes. In K. F. Wantland & W. C. Pusey (Eds.), *Belize shelf-carbonate sediments, clastic sediments, and ecology: Studies in geology No. 2*. (pp. 1-52). Tulsa, OK: American Association of Petroleum Geologists.

RÜTZLER, K. & MACINTYRE, I. G. (1982). The habitat distribution and community structure of the barrier reef complex at Carrie Bow Cay, Belize. In K. Rützler and I. G. Macintyre (Eds.), *The Atlantic Barrier Reef ecosystem at Carrie Bow Cay, Belize I: Structure and communities. Washington*, DC: Smithsonian Contributions to the Marine Sciences 12.

STODDART, D. R. (1962). Three Caribbean atolls: Turneffe Islands, Lighthouse Reef, and Glover's Reef, British Honduras. *Atoll research bulletin 87*, 1-151.

STODDART, D. R. (1963). Effects of Hurricane Hattie on the British Honduras Reefs and Cayes, October 30-31, 1961. *Atoll Research Bulletin 95*, 1-142.

STODDART, D. R. (1974). Post-Hurricane changes on the British Honduras reefs: Re-survey of 1972. *Proceedings of the 2nd international coral reef symposium 2*, 473-483.

STODDART, D. R., THORPE, J. E., & BREGAZZI, P. K. (1962, June). Cambridge expedition to British Honduras. *The Geographical Journal 128*(2), 158-171.

TOURTELLOT, J. B. (2006, Nov./Dec.). Places rated: How do 94 World Heritage destinations stack up? *National Geographic Traveler*, 112-124.

VILLANUEVA, J. (2006). *Fisheries Statistical Report 2005*. Belize: Ministry of Agriculture and Fisheries.

WALLACE, R. J. (1974). *A reconnaissance of the sedimentology and ecology of Glovers Reef Atoll, Belize (British Honduras)*. Doctoral dissertation, Princeton (New Jersey) University.

YOUNG, E. R. (1994). Community descriptors for four sites along the barrier reef of Belize. *Fisheries Department Publication* TR-93-004, 1-23.

Part 3
Society

7. Understanding Our Coastal Communities at Age 25

Joseph O. Palacio

Introduction

Between the period 1981 and 2006 there is a dividing line in the social sciences of coastal communities of Belize. The line falls in 1996, the year that UNESCO declared the entire Belize Barrier Reef a World Heritage Site and further singled out seven sub-sites as being worthy of heightened attention. The UNESCO declaration symbolized a major shift in public thinking. Subsequently, the conservation ethic for Belize's coastal zone became more widely accepted by government, civil society, and the populace at large. Gradually, the spotlight on communities has changed from being exploiters to being stewards of coastal resources, making sure that these resources remain for future generations. Within a decade from 1996 fourteen additional Marine Protected Areas (MPAs) have been officially designated. To manage the MPAs, non-governmental organizations (NGOs) signed co-management agreements with the government of Belize (GOB), some on behalf of constituent communities. In this continuing evolution the role expectation of community members continues to be a topic deserving much understanding and study.[1]

This essay starts with an overview of the geography of the coast and the population in 22 communities, extending from Consejo in the north to Barranco in the south. Second, it traces episodes in the evolution of our current knowledge base

[1] I express gratitude to IDRC and COMPACT for funding the studies covered in this essay. The analysis and conclusions are mine and do not reflect those of the two funding agencies. I record my gratitude for the following persons who were most helpful during the fieldwork—Robert (Coppy) Mariano, Gene Hernandez, and Myrtle Palacio. Finally, thanks to members of the communities for their cooperation.

about coastal communities, where there has been convergence of influences from beyond the country with those originating locally. The convergence demonstrates that there is a dearth of ethnographic information, especially in the use of marine and coastal resources, the values associated with such use, the traditional knowledge available, and the belief systems that guide overall coastal behaviour.

The response to this need for ethnographic information forms the body of this essay, which is based on a review of three studies that I conducted from 2000 to 2005. Although the starting date of the studies comes after 1996, the year symbolizing the beginning of the marine conservation era, the first of these studies opened the door to analysing the social conduct in Belizean coastal communities in recent times. The antecedents are few. In 2000 Will Heyman and R. Graham had conducted a survey of fishers in southern Belize. Espeut (1994) and Brown (2000) had done surveys to mark the respective onset of the CARICOM Fisheries Unit and the Mesoamerican Barrier Reef System (MBRS). Craig (1966) and Gordon (1981) did some earlier ethnographic work. After 1981 no significant contribution to the ethnology of the coast of Belize was made until our work in 2001.

International Development Research Council (IDRC) of Canada[2] funded two of the studies that took place between 2000 and 2001 and the other between 2002 and 2004. The Community Based Coastal Resource Management (CBCRM) programme of the IDRC covered the entire Circum-Caribbean including the islands such as Cuba, Dominican Republic, and the CARICOM territories, as well as the mainland from Mexico to Colombia. The other study was project specific and focused on a survey in anticipation of a project [i.e., the Community Management of Protected Areas Conservation Project (COMPACT)]. From these studies I extracted five focal themes that could be isolated for comparative research within the field of social behaviour in coastal communities in Belize and the larger Circum-Caribbean.

Coastal communities

Definition

As part of initiating its programme of activities, the Coastal Zone Management Authority and Institute (CZMAI) presented a technical definition of a coastal zone of Belize. It is... "an area... of the coast of any land mass where land,

---

[2] The studies conformed to the long-term tradition of the IDRC to fund research by Third World scholars whose work in their own countries includes some in-depth theory of development as well as grounding through community-led fieldwork. The award of IDRC funds was offered on a competitive basis and the call for proposals encouraged scholars to select topics appropriate to their own interests within a broad range of possibilities.

water (seawater and freshwater) and air interact. Landward the coastal zone includes coastal sea influenced by natural or human-made processes on land or the continental shelf" (CZMAI, 1999, p. 3). Jolly and McRae (1998) have a more concise description, "coastal zone ecosystems are principally defined by the presence of some amount of salt in soils and water" (p. 82). A brief insight into cultural geography elaborates on the social significance of human use, which is the main topic of this essay.

Geographical spread

Moving toward the land from the immediate beach one comes across the part of the coastal zone that has been most subjected to human activity. Included in this segment is the beach itself and an area extending up to about ten kilometres into the mangrove wetlands and savannah covered coastal plain, two microenvironments where coastal towns and villages are located. Depending on the size of the community and the land demand, these areas expand along the coast as well as further inland, and in their wake have an unregulated and deleterious impact on the environment. To mitigate the degradation a law was passed against cutting down mangroves. The mangrove clear-cutting seen in residential areas, however, is dwarfed by the scale found in the industrial shrimp farms that are located adjoining Monkey River, Dangriga, and Belize City. Finally, a short distance away and further inland are located thousands of hectares of banana and citrus plantations.

While there is expansion going westward away from the beach, there is the opposite movement going toward the beach. One example is taking place in the village of Lucky Strike, located 8 kilometres in a straight line from the coast north of Belize City, where the Village Council has acquired land for lots. Their plan is to make them available to persons, including residents of Caye Caulker, who will want inland location, especially useful as refuge during hurricanes. All of these eastward-westward movements have not resulted from any master development plan for the coastline as a fragile ecosystem.

Going eastward from the coast one enters into the marine environment dominated by shoals, cayes, sandbars, reef patches, the Barrier Reef itself, and atolls. There are some differences in the configuration of these features south of Belize City from that northward. The dominating features north of Belize City that lie beyond the Barrier Reef are the two extensive atoll systems, Lighthouse Reef and the Turneffe Island. Between them and the coast are hundreds of cayes ranging in size from San Pedro Ambergris to little dots of mangrove patches. South of Belize City and lying especially between Dangriga and Monkey River are two distinct pathways, bordered by cayes and shoal patches. Closer to the beach is the Inner Channel and further away the Main or Victoria Channel.

Figure 1: Coastal communities

Population

The location of coastal communities, whose population in the last three cen-suses totalled more than fifty, is made up of seventeen villages, four towns, and one city (see Fig. 1). Stann Creek District has the largest number with six com-munities and Corozal District the fewest at three. Four of the villages are not im-mediately along the coast but have relied historically on the coast as primary means of transportation and livelihood (in Table 1 they are in italics).

As seen in Table 1, population figures have been most sensitive to in- and out-migration. At one extreme is the tiny village of Punta Negra (not included in Table 1) in the Toledo District, whose population stood at 55 in 1980 but shrank to 27 by 2000. At the other extreme is Riversdale in the Stann Creek Dis-

Table 1: Census figures for coastal communities
2000, 1991, and 1980

Community by District	2000	1991	1980	1980-2000 % Increase
Corozal District				
Consejo	217	136	60	261
Corozal Town	7,888	7,062	6,899	14
Chunox	1,058	741	439	144
Copper Bank	366	303	190	92
Sarteneja	1,640	1,365	1,005	63
Belize District				
San Pedro	4,499	1,365	1,005	348
Caye Caulker	630	688	435	45
Belize City	49,040	44,067	39,771	23
Bomba	81	66	51	30
Gales Point	247	344	365	-
Stann Creek District				
Mullins River	198	134	121	63
Dangriga	8,814	6,449	6,661	32
Hopkins	1,027	808	749	37
Riversdale	685	54	66	937
Seine Bight	830	544	465	78
Placencia	501	361	334	50
Independence	2,924	1,969	1,494	98
Sittee	312	308	278	12
Toledo District				
Monkey River	170	186	191	-
Cattle Landing	200	158	97	106
Punta Gorda	4,329	3,461	2,396	80
Barranco	183	184	229	-

Communities in italics are located slightly inland from the coast.
Source: CSO, Belize.

trict, whose population numbered 66 in 1980 but ballooned to 685 in 2000. Similarly, Independence went from 1,494 in 1980 to almost 2,924 by 2000. Job availability was the main cause for fluctuations in the three communities. Punta

Negra folk have migrated to Punta Gorda and other parts of Belize, while access to wage labour in banana plantations as well as tourism resorts along the Placencia Peninsula attracted large numbers to Riversdale and Independence. What has been taking place in these three communities has been repeated historically several times in other coastal towns and villages, including those not located immediately adjoining, such as Bomba, Gales Point, and Sittee.

The towns have also been affected by the push/pull of migration. The town showing the highest growth was San Pedro, almost quadrupling in population between 1980 and 2000. Coming next, but far below, was Punta Gorda with 80%. Corozal, Dangriga, and Belize City showed relatively small ranges of growth. The situation in Punta Gorda differs from other towns. The upswing in population comes from the heavy migration from rural Toledo District rather than from employment possibilities within the town itself. This type of speculation on why people are moving has not been answered by detailed demographic studies in Belize, notwithstanding the clear reasons for such scrutiny. Whereas we can guess that poverty is driving persons from rural to urban Toledo, and tourism and banana plantations are attracting people to the Placencia Peninsula, we cannot say who actually is coming, from where, in what numbers, and what kinds of jobs they are getting. In the absence of this type of sociological study I present my description of five coastal subregions showing differences in social stratification based on a socioeconomy of fishery and tourism. The information comes from my observations during extensive travels and discussions with residents.

Schema of subregions

The first subregion is the "Extreme South," which includes the town of Punta Gorda and four villages—Barranco, Cattle Landing, Punta Negra, and Monkey River. In this area are also some cayes that vary from being stop-over shelters for fishers to settlements with a few families. The people in this subregion are mainly Creole and Garifuna with some East Indians and Maya. In terms of fishing, the area is most adversely affected by over-fishing in the adjoining Gulf of Honduras by Guatemalan and Honduran fishers. Its tourism industry is still in its infancy relative to that in other parts of the coast. Finally, its mainland communities are the poorest with minimal job opportunities. As a result, large scale migration to other parts of the country and beyond is a main contributing factor to the demography and to the heavy reliance on remittances.

Next is the "Southern" subregion, which includes six villages—Placencia, Independence, Seine Bight, Riversdale, Sittee River, and Hopkins. The predominant livelihood derives from mainland sources, primarily fruit agriculture and shrimp farming. Within recent years the Placencia Peninsula, which is the marine resource heartland of this subregion, has experienced the heaviest growth in over-night tourism in the country.[3] Ethnically, this is one of the most heterogeneous subregions in the country with Creoles, Garifuna, East Indians, Maya, Ladinos, and recently settled North Americans.

Further north is the "Central" subregion characterized by two urban communities, Belize City and Dangriga, together with the villages of Gales Point and Bomba. Being hubs for commercial activities for their own surrounding communities is the hallmark of the urban communities in this subregion. Dangriga is the administrative and commercial district capital of the Stann Creek District, whose main economy consists of fruit and shrimp agriculture and tourism. Belize City is the administrative and commercial centre for the Belize District as well as for the whole country. Consequently, the exploitation of marine resources is a subsidiary cash earning source. The burgeoning cruise ship industry, however, is certainly increasing the rate of the use of marine resources as well as the economy of Belize City and surrounding communities (Claire & Seidl, 2005). The extent to which this income is percolating through the Belize City socioeconomy, as against remaining in the hands of major tour operators, needs deeper analysis beyond the scope of this document. Another feature of this subregion has been the spread of population from Belize City to its outskirts within the Belize River delta, best seen in the case of Ladyville together with its annex Vista del Mar, a new and steadily growing urban community. The population of Ladyville went from 1810 in 1980 to 3472 in 2000. As in the Southern subregion, ethnic heterogeneity is the rule in the Central subregion.

Slightly northeast of Belize City is the "Cayes" subregion dominated by San Pedro Ambergris and Caye Caulker. In both communities tourism has long supplanted fishing as primary wage earner (Auil & Kotch, 1993). While the Mestizos make up the predominant ethnic group, they have been joined by other Belizeans as well as a large North American population.

Finally, there is the "Northern" subregion, which includes Corozal Town together with three villages—Copper Bank, Chunox, and Sarteneja. Sarteneja is outstanding in this subregion for being fully dedicated to fishing, the only such community in the country. The remaining villages—Chunox and Copper Bank—are not fully on the coast, limiting their access to fishing. Unlike the case of other parts of the coast, much of the economic infusion into this subregion does not derive immediately from the coast. Corozal Town's economy relies almost exclusively on the sugar industry as well as the Free Zone area adjoining the Mexican boundary. The predominant ethnic group is Mestizo.

---

[3] Belize Tourism Board figures indicate that between 1988 and 2005 the destinations with the largest numbers of hotels in decreasing numbers were San Pedro, Cayo, and Placencia. During that period the numbers in Placencia increased sevenfold, while in San Pedro, the numbers increased almost threefold.

This brief overview of the users' profile shows that there have been noteworthy strides in economic opportunities impacting the livelihood of the common man and woman, more on the mainland than along the coastal inshore. The growth in fruit and shrimp farming has been noticeable, likewise the mushrooming of services, mainly in the Belize City area. While the mainland economy has attracted large numbers of men and women to the coastal plain, the diversification from fishing to tourism has done the same to some communities on the coastline, with Placencia showing the maximum impact. The public's perception of the coast is that it is affected mainly by tourism and fishery. On extending the geography of the entire coastal zone, we see a more diversified area, where the axis of the mainland has a far greater impact on the well being of the individual man and woman. Maintaining this integrated concept of the coastal plain and inshore sub-zones is both significant and necessary for regional planning.

Second, the profile displays a wide range of communities that can be compared, especially in terms of the dual livelihood of fishing and tourism. In the North is Sarteneja, which remains almost totally a fishing village; in the South and Cayes subregions are communities in which fishing has been almost fully displaced as the primary livelihood by tourism; and in the Extreme South is some transition from fishing to overnight tourism.

Third, this brief overview shows that along the coast of Belize the culture of ethnicity is no longer a primary index of social stratification. Rather social class has taken over, where access to capital combined with light skin pigmentation and foreign origin have become entrenched as the dominant features of those at the higher levels. In the South and Central regions the owners of the two ports, at Belize City and Independence, and of the shrimp and fruit farms occupy the highest strata followed by investors in resort hotels. The parallel in the Cayes includes investors of hotel resorts, which range in spectrum from the very high end to the least expensive. Again, these are light-skinned Belizeans and North Americans.

At the middle level there are light-skinned Belizeans, who have used their family fortunes to invest in smaller, modest hotels and are tour operators. These are followed at another level by those who own bed-and-breakfast operations and who may still engage in lobster fishing more in Caye Caulker than in San Pedro. At the lowest levels are the workers who are tour guides or are employed in lower end service jobs in, for example, restaurants and retail shops, or work as boat hands, and so on. At this lower level are Garifuna, darker-skinned Creole, Maya, and Ladino immigrants from Guatemala and Honduras. This stratification is more at a subjective level and awaits much data and analysis for refinement, which may push the topic of social stratification into the areas of access to financing, political affiliation, kinship networks, and skin colour–all topics about differences among themselves not normally spoken openly by Belizeans. The public and scholarly discourse on social stratification in Belize remains at the level of ethnicity, where ethnic stereotypic beliefs are still held.

Knowledge gaps

The limited information about the sociology of coastal communities in Belize is a major problem that Belize through its government and institutions of higher learning has to address with the greatest urgency. This lack contrasts with two streams of awareness, which are unfolding in the knowledge field within Belize. One stream comes from the trend to integrate the physical environment with the social well-being of inhabitants. The other comes from the overwhelming lead within the study of coastal resources that the natural sciences have over the social sciences in Belize and the larger Caribbean. It is necessary to demonstrate how both streams have an impact on our understanding of the community and its use of coastal resources.

Probably the most lasting result of the United Nations Conference on the Environment and Development (UNCED), which was held in Brazil in 1992, was to address the deliberate integration of people into environmental well-being, as a *sine qua non* of economic development. The instruments originating from UNCED have had lasting reverberations worldwide. Examples include the Convention of Biological Diversity, Agenda 21, and the Global Environment Fund (GEF). More directly at the level of Belize and neigbouring countries we can identify the Mesoamerican Biological Corridor, Mesoamerican Barrier Reef System, the setting up of the Coastal Zone Management Authority and Institute, the COMPACT Project, and the Small Grants Project (SGP) of the GEF— all of which have given substantial technical and financial assistance to Belize. More especially, the SGP has funded dozens of community-based projects designed around environmental conservation in all parts of the country. A decade and a half after UNCED, the social component in the link between environment and development has been felt in many coastal communities throughout Belize at a rate that had not existed before. The corollary is that the urge to know community structures and organization has never been as much as now.

On the other hand, the natural sciences have taken the lead by leaps and bounds in the study of Belizean and regional marine biota. The most outstanding example is the Caribbean Coral Reef Ecosystems (CCRE) Research Programme carried out at Carrie Bow Caye in the vicinity of South Water Caye, offshore from Dangriga, under the Department of Invertebrate Zoology of the National Museum of Natural History, Smithsonian Institution, Washington, D.C. The programme started in the 1970s and by 1998 about 700 research papers had been published by scores of scientists and their graduate students, who had spent time at the facility (National Museum of Natural History). There are hardly any topics in Belize that have received such detailed scholarly attention. Indeed, only a handful of studies on the social sciences of coastal communities have been done and even fewer have been published.

The MPAs are a meeting ground for the convergence of natural sciences with

183

the thrust on conservation originating from UNCED. They are spatial configurations where heightened biological diversity can take place with limited interference. In support, GOB has declared several of them protected areas and arranged co-management agreements with NGOs. As a result, MPAs have become major beneficiaries for financial and technical support from foreign conservation NGOs. However, not all community residents may want to participate in the co-management of MPAs. Furthermore, several fishers have not been informed about the benefits that could derive to them from such practices. I became aware of this lack of understanding from talking to fishers in Dangriga about the Glover's Reef and South Water Caye Marine Reserves, which are located in their traditional fishing grounds and together cover 60,000 hectares of sea (McField, 2000, p. 22). Many had heard about the reserves; and even if they wanted to become involved, they admitted that they did not know whom to approach. In short, MPAs do not provide adequate scope for coastal community involvement, notwithstanding their promotion as a forum for participation for the common man and woman. The reasons for the lack of participation were the topic of a study held with the support of the CZMAI (CZMAI 2001/2, pp. 58-65). Further community-based social science research could help to unravel this dilemma.

Notwithstanding an ignorance of the background social conditions, the promotion of more MPAs and their management formed a major component of the Belize Biodiversity Action Plan 1998-2003 as seen in the following suggested Action/Activity:

> Develop an appropriate management framework for Marine Reserves and other Protected Areas, both legally and institutionally, to ensure the production of management plans for all existing and proposed Protected Areas, frequent reviews of management needs, to evaluate the success of Protected Areas, and for the modification of management plans as necessary. (Jacobs & Castañeda, 1998, p. 4)

This brief overview on research efforts presents an appropriate context for this paper. It is an historical benchmark not only because of the significance of the twenty-fifth anniversary of our independence. It also demonstrates major gaps in the Belizean knowledge base in the combined fields of environmental integrity and community development, which should be overcome long before we celebrate the fiftieth anniversary of our independence. The gaps include demographic trends associated with large scale migration, social stratification resulting from transformations within the socio-economy, the role of MPAs in promoting community participation, and a typology of coastal communities within sub-groups. At this point, given the hundreds of papers already published on the natural sciences, there should be volumes of reviews on them to alert Belizeans about the topics that have been covered.

IDRC studies

Field instruments

As principal investigator (PI), I had considerable scope to define what the project would be and where it would fit within the needs of Belize, and more specifically the target communities. For the first IDRC study the questions that I sought to answer were: (a) how were the communities in southern Belize from Placencia to Barranco using their coastal resources in 2000; and (b) how had their predecessors used these resources, going as far back as the 1920s-1930s, the limit of recall through oral history.[4]

In formulating the project proposal I had been aware that I was emphasizing the use of resources, although the call for proposals specifically included the management of coastal resources by community members. In 1998 there were no examples of community managed coastal resources in Belize. One MPA was being managed under the auspices of the Belize Audubon Society (BAS). In 1969 the BAS entered into an agreement with GOB to manage Halfmoon Caye (Waight & Lumb, 1999, pp. 128-136). By the end of our study in 2001, there were plans for NGO co-management of MPAs, a procedure that effectively took place starting that same year with TIDE receiving permission to co-manage the Port Honduras Marine Reserve.

With coastal resource use as the principal focus of the study, I organized three sets of field instruments. One focused on current practices in fishing, tourism, the use of the beach for recreation by the local population, and the impact of development on the real estate of coastal property. The other instrument was on past practices of fishing, the location of fishing drops, coastal transportation, dory carving, folklore, and belief systems. The third was community meetings during which we had discussions on how men, women, and children as community members were reacting to the changes affecting them. These discussions were helpful in communities such as Placencia, which was going through much growth and development, as well as for those at the other extreme, such as Barranco, where the momentum was more the opposite—losing population, having greater difficulty to catch fish, and being far removed from tourism.

Building on what I had been able to achieve earlier, I was able to fine-tune objectives for the second IDRC project, which took place from 2002 to 2004. Although the geographic focus shifted from the subregion of southern Belize to

---

[4] Statistical data on the censuses and production figures for banana, citrus, and shrimp were available at Central Statistical Office, Belmopan. The Placencia Fishing Co-operative provided production figures for lobster and conch, and the fledgling Punta Gorda Rio Grande Fishing Co-operative did so for lobster for 2000-2001. Belize Tourism Board provided figures on hotel occupancy for destinations, including Punta Gorda and Placencia.

the town of Dangriga, my primary interest was still on the use of coastal resources. In this regard I found helpful Elizabeth Graham's archaeological survey (1994) of the Stann Creek District as a single compendium of resource use, albeit in prehistoric times. The comprehensive use by the ancient Maya of both marine and terrestrial resources is a model that is appropriate for scrutiny by ethnologists, if only to re-ascertain that coastal dwellers have always widened their exploitation to include both the land and the sea. For additional studies on coastal archaeology in southern Belize see McKillop (2002) and Guderjan (1993).

Inter-ethnic differentiation

The first phase of the IDRC study revealed some inter-ethnic differentiation in coastal resource use. While the Creoles of Placencia have remained highly dedicated marine folk, the Garifuna in the adjoining village of Seine Bight have maintained a dual orientation to the land and sea for subsistence and cash. In earlier times the specialization had led to barter with the Placencia residents exchanging fish for ground food from Seine Bight. After decades of mainly subsistence fishing receiving minimal financial rewards for painstaking work, the marine orientation of Placencia residents finally paid off in the 1960s, progressively moving forward from fishery to incorporate tourism. Simultaneously and with hardly any future from either the land or sea, the Seine Bight folk migrated in large numbers to take up careers and wage labour, leaving behind a skeletal population dependent on remittances. An out-migration from Placencia also occurred, but there remained at home a sufficiently large group to attend to their boats and do some fishing. In 2003 Garifuna men in the town of Dangriga were also not fully relying on the sea in contrast to the newly arrived Ladinos, who dominated fish production for the daily supply.

My field observations and interviews revealed that there were about 30 fishers in Dangriga, about half of whom were Garifuna. The method of harvesting for the Garifuna, however, remained at a small scale. They would leave at about 3:00 a.m. in small dories, paddle two to four kilometres from the beach, fish using hand-lines for a few hours, and return about 9:00 a.m. Fishing was not their primary means of livelihood; it was something they did when in need of ready cash or to keep company within a small group of friends and relatives. Another ethnic group catches larger quantities. They use gill nets and larger fibreglass boats and can time their return to the market to coincide with the hours of greater demand early in the morning. They may also sell in bulk to others who take the product out of town. These are mainly recent Ladino immigrants from the neighbouring countries of Guatemala and Honduras, who came earlier as migrant labourers to work in the banana fields in the southern part of the Stann Creek District.

If economically, marine resources no longer received high cash value from the Garifuna, the sea remained fully integrated into their belief system. Having identified during the first phase of the IDRC exercise some regard for folklore and sporadic ritual behaviour among them, during the second phase I was able to pursue further the extent of their traditional knowledge and spirituality within the marine realm. The results included detailed knowledge about the morphology of a one-kilometre stretch of broken reef (called *bajo* by the users), indicating which type of fish are to be found at certain segments and at what time of the year. Additional information came about the movements of fish, which ones are usually closer to the bottom of the sea and to the top. Informants discussed *adougahani* at length, a practice of ritual fishing by both men and women as part of the *dügü*[5] placation ceremony. The pattern forthcoming from the men in Dangriga and Seine Bight is that the sea is not a primary economic source for them; rather it is the locus of spiritual traditions well rooted in their culture. Not deriving cash income from the sea like others has led to the stereotypic image of Garifuna men as being lazy compared to their counterparts from neighbouring ethnic groups. For more information about topics on inter-ethnicity and fishery involving the Garifuna and Ladinos see Palacio, Coral, and Hidalgo (2006, pp.78-104).

Community development

The second phase of the IDRC-CBCRM provided opportunities to pursue my interest in community development, continuing from what had been community meetings in the first phase. This time the target was a community grassroots organization, the Buyei Juan Lambey (BJLI) Institute, which was planning a Garifuna tourism village project on the beach in Dangriga. I worked with them to conceptualize and initially implement the proposal, using funding from the project.

A community based organization in Dangriga, BJLI's main aim was to revive the Garifuna way of life in which spirituality overlapped with procuring fish and other resources from the sea. The participants consisted of women and youth suffering the depressed social conditions that were overtaking the town. BJLI's part in participating in the IDRC-CBCRM was to seek ways to revitalize two traditional fishing methods—*wamaredu*, a set net placed along the coast and *maciwa*, a crab catching weir. The possibility of a third method, namely cultivating seaweed, had to be scrapped for lack of time and resources. The *wamaredu* and *maciwa* are depicted in Figs. 2 and 3. The samples we built together with the BJLI were able to capture fish.[6]

---

[5] The *dügü* is a ceremony that the Garifuna hold to placate the spirits of their ancestors. It lasts up to three days featuring singing, dancing, and food offering. Essential to the ceremony is a fishing trip, called *adougahani*, held beforehand by men and women to the cayes to bring fish items for the offering. For additional information, see Foster 2005, pp. 159-175.

Figure 2: Wamaredu

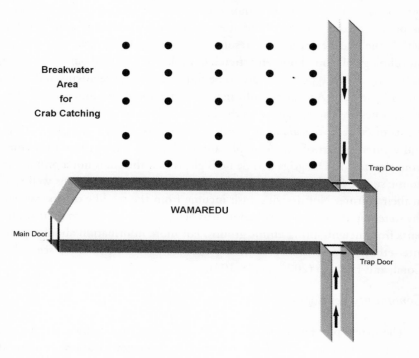

While the experiments needed time and resources to see them through their full completion, the BJLI, the host community group, was facing additional organizational problems. An analysis of the difficulties revealed a weakness. The leadership could not handle all the minutiae that necessarily accompany a complicated community development project, especially one built essentially on marine resource exploitation. While the leadership was comfortable in holding several types of healing ceremonies, which it had undertaken over several years, this project dealt with an area that was a novelty to the organization and needed another kind of leadership, one not available within BJLI. Here the contrast between BJLI and the Placencia Fishing Cooperative was clear. The latter had been in existence since 1962 and focused on the primary activity of marketing of fish products. It also retained membership in the Belize Fishermen's Co-operative Association, which afforded much support bolstered by an extended membership of 500 fishers from all over the country. Having started in 1998 and received its registration in 2001, the BJLI needed much organizational support that was seriously lacking, a fact that became more obvious as our project pro-

---

[6] Readers can obtain more information about the field experiment of these methods in Palacio (2004).

Figure 3: Maciwa

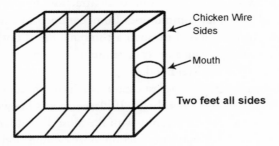

Chicken Wire Sides

Mouth

Two feet all sides

ceeded. This lesson in promoting community development around a coastal re-source needs further attention for any replication in the future.

Use of marine and terrestrial resources

Up to the 1950s and 1960s, the communities in southern Belize widened their use of both terrestrial and marine resources. Of course, agriculture and fishery were the two principal uses. Most communities had to rely on both for their food supply as well as the sale of surplus. The primacy of agriculture in communities now fully dedicated to the marine economy has also been observed in San Pedro (Gordon, 1981) and Sarteneja (from interviews to be discussed lat-er in the COMPACT review). Transportation was also significant. It included carving and repairing various kinds of dories as well as manning them all along the coast of Belize and extending to the neighbouring countries from Mexico to Nicaragua. While still doing agriculture, the concentration on fishery increased, especially in the sale of whole fish whose markets in Belize City as well as the port towns of Puerto Barrios in Guatemala and Puerto Cortes in Honduras, es-pecially during the Lenten season, were growing.[7]

Placencia especially benefited, with its fishers transforming their economy from whole fish as well as parts, such as shark oil, eventually to lobster, shrimp, and conch. Shark oil is an important folk cure for asthma and other respiratory illness in Belize as well as the neighbouring countries. Placencia fishers initiated tourism by taking guests to the same spots where they fished using the same boats but doing so during their off-fishing season. Initially, their cash capital

---

[7] During the forty days of lent the Roman Catholic Church prescribes that meat not be eaten so fish is eaten instead. Fish that have white flesh, such as snook, are especially en-couraged. This custom is prevalent throughout Central America.

outlay was minimal. Most significant for them was their cultural capital, namely knowlege of their marine micro-environments and their bountiful natural resources, while always looking for additional attractions for their visitors. On the other hand, all the other communities from Barranco to Monkey River were able to juggle their livelihood through a combination of both agriculture and fishery, with growing reliance on cash remittances from villagers, who had to leave for better economic livelihood.

During the earlier part of the last century, each community had its own characteristic based on its main livelihood. If Placencia was known as a fishing village, Seine Bight was the community with the most distant farmlands; Monkey River was known for its banana production, dory carving, and appetite for both sea and river fish; Punta Negra for its coconut oil and fish; Punta Gorda for its rice and ample supply of hardwoods; and Barranco for its banana and later its pineapple and rice. However, they all shared some values on fishing, the one activity that tied them together, notwithstanding their varying ethnic identities. These values were guided by an abundance of several species of fish. There are stories of persons going in their street shoes off the beach in Placencia to pick the conch that they wanted for dinner. In the final draft report of the first IDRC study (Palacio, 2001) there are other accounts on the abundance of fish. Concurrently there were several methods of exploitation, a deep awareness of the physical environment, and a wholistic belief system. Men, women, and children caught fish for the family pot. Although the small and barely profitable fish market was the greatest limitation on production, there were several practices geared to limiting what one would catch, which are detailed in Palacio (2001, pp. 39-43). Finally, there was a cosmology on interactions between the living and dead, which placed the control of the physical environment within the group's spirituality and beyond the realm of human behaviour. In this regard, the Garifuna have retained these rituals far more than their neighbours.

Community Management of Protected Areas Conservation Project (COMPACT)

While the IDRC studies were baseline on use practices, COMPACT added more information on use and included baseline information on attitudes and values of coast dwellers. There were other factors of complementarity in methods between the two studies. Whereas IDRC had been selective with limitations to the southern part of the country, COMPACT covered seven primary coastal communities, namely Punta Gorda, Punta Negra, Placencia, Dangriga, Belize City, San Pedro, and Sarteneja. COMPACT used a survey instrument with only a few open-ended questions. It also used focus groups with select community members. Some division of labour such as the fieldwork, analysis, and report

190

writing had to be done within the six weeks, from September 15 to October 30, 2001. Field persons from the local communities were hired to be assistants to the principal investigator (PI) and COMPACT provided a staff person as another PI assistant and understudy. The overall aim was to get a certain amount of information efficiently and within as short a time as possible. The objective of all of this preparation was to enable the selection of viable projects valued at up to US$50,000 each to community groups designed to lessen the human impact on the Barrier Reef (afterwards referred to as the Reef in this part of the essay on the review of COMPACT).

The following presents some of the findings of the survey.

Gender and age

Among the 35 respondents to the questionnaire instrument, seven were women represented especially in Placencia and San Pedro. The presence of the females in answering questionnaires and participating in the focus groups added much to our understanding of their roles. In both Placencia and San Pedro there was overwhelming support for women to take active roles in all aspects of the tourism industry, including acquiring all levels of diving qualifications. On the other hand, in Sarteneja where fishers predominate, a traditionally male occupation taking them away for weeks on end, there was diminished expectation for women's involvement. Again, this contrasts with conditions in Punta Gorda, where there is at least one active woman fisher.

With a decided shift toward tourism in almost all the communities, there will be an accompanying shift in more women and youth engaging in new domestic and extra-domestic economic activities. This evolving pattern in community social structure is already well established in Placencia and San Pedro. Fishing certainly does not offer such a scope for sustained participation for women and youth.

We specifically asked, "How do you see women and youth getting more cash income through activities related to the sea"? Notwithstanding the relatively higher profile women have in some communities, invariably the recommendations for women were to become tour guides and do traditional handicrafts and catering. For the youth, there was preference for internship with older persons and to branch into careers requiring further education for qualification. Most of the men at Sarteneja do fishing. However, diving with spear gun, one of their main methods of capturing lobster, is segregated by age. Older men dive closer to the surface, leaving the more strenuous work for younger men, who can go deeper.

Main livelihood

The results of the questionnaire showed that among the main sources of livelihood from the sea the following were listed most often: fishing, water-taxi operator, tour guide, and taking tourists fishing. We also collected information about less frequent occupations including fly-fishing, going on day trips for sightseeing and snorkeling, serving as captain and crew on tourist boats plying along the coast, bare-boating (tourists renting sailboats and traveling on their own), and game fishing. The larger proportion of possibilities for tourism indicates its potential to overtake fishing as primary marine activity. Indeed, except for Sarteneja all the communities showed higher frequencies in livelihood from tourism, confirming the declining role of fishery as principal livelihood throughout the country.

Part of the sea most used

There is a generalized pattern of distinguishing between in-shore and off-shore fishing. The former is now over-fished making it necessary for fishers in most communities to go further in the off-shore.

The Corozal Bay is in front of the village of Sarteneja; "further beyond" or *mas allá* (in Spanish) refers to the sea further east. The former is heavily over-fished and the latter is where people do their commercial fishing. In Placencia the Inner Channel stretches a few miles to the east and further out is the Main or Victoria Channel. In the former people fish for the household supply and in the latter they do commercial fishing at drops located nearer the Reef. They catch conch and lobster in both the Inner and Outer Channels.

In Dangriga and Belize City the fishers concentrate on cayes. Because of over-fishing, Belize City fishers now go mostly to the Turneffe Islands, a distance of 35 miles crossing the Reef.

In Punta Negra, fishers can still get good catches a short distance from the shore. This is also the case for Punta Gorda fishers. Because there are fewer cayes east and south of Punta Gorda, the fishers rely more on favourite drops as landmarks.

Generally fishers look for seagrass beds and rock outcrops for various species. They do recognize a wide variety of rock outcrops, starting from a few isolated patches to extended ranges nearer some cayes, to the atolls mainly around Glovers Reef, Turneffe Islands, Lighthouse Reef, and eventually the Barrier Reef. It is lobster fishers who most often use the reef, including the windward portions. Conch fishers, on the other hand, look for them in sand spots.

We were able to get the general range of fishers by communities. In Punta Gorda fishers cover a maximum radius of eight kilometres from the town, stretching from the Snake Cayes and swinging south a short distance from the town. In Punta Negra the furthest they go is a distance of 40 kilometres to the Sapodilla Range. Within this distance are several fishing drops that invariably yield within a few hours enough for a day's catch. In Placencia they travel northeast to South Water Caye, swing east to Gladden Spit, and proceed further southeast to Ranguana. In Dangriga they go north to Southern Long Caye and swing south to Tobacco and South Water Cayes. In Belize City they go in an easterly direction to the Turneffe Islands.

The use of these localized ranges has arisen more from familiarity and elimination due to over-fishing, and not from a sense of proprietary rights. The sense of exclusive territoriality among fishers is much less than one would expect, even against those coming across the border from Honduras and Guatemala. Indeed, during the spawning season traditionally men from different communities congregated at the same sites (see Craig, 1969, pp. 252-263). They murmured among themselves and complained about the aggressiveness of their colleagues from other communities. The biggest complaints were about MPAs and their wardens, who prevented fishing in certain zones.

Awareness of the reef

A segment of the questionnaire dealt with what respondents knew about the Reef and threats to it. The answers showed that respondents' knowledge was mixed—much user familiarity but minimal awareness of basic technical information. Almost all were familiar with the Reef and have visited or worked near it. Many knew the Reef's constituent parts, their fragility, and the sea depth before reaching it. However, very few knew about the Reef geomorphology—its age and its significance in the formation of Belizean land and waters. Their awareness straddles the area between technical expertise vs. folkloric information circulating within coastal communities. For example, in Placencia is the belief that touching the reef parts to pick up a lobster causes minimal damage, if any. On the other hand, they singled out sunscreen skin lotion as certainly causing damage.

The lack of technical skills certainly masks the passion that respondents had toward the Reef, especially parts that are nearby. There was strong possessiveness in Placencia toward Gladden Spit and the Silk Cayes. In Punta Negra and Punta Gorda it was toward the smaller reef systems in the Port Honduras Marine Reserve and the Sapodilla Cayes Marine Reserve. The same goes for parts near all the communities, except Sarteneja. The closest part of the Reef to them is Bacalar Chico. However, the villagers had not been integrated into its management plans. On the other hand, they pass by there frequently on the way to their fishing sites.

Attitudes

To find out the extent to which marine livelihood is embedded in the cognition of community members, we asked what immediately comes to the respondents' mind on hearing the term "maritime resource;" what fears they associated with the sea; and folklore that they might have heard associated with the sea. The patterns for each community were interesting.

The responses in Punta Gorda and Dangriga to what immediately comes to mind indicate a split between concepts related to economic value and those related to aesthetics, such as natural beauty and recreation. The fears mostly focused on bodily harm caused by fish, notably sharks.

In Placencia and San Pedro concepts related to controlling the maritime resources were the ones that immediately came to mind. In San Pedro especially, the greatest fear was not bodily harm but losing the natural resources that attract visitors and keep the economy going. As a respondent hotelier said, "What would I do if the coral reefs disappear"?

In Sarteneja concepts related to acquiring livelihood were most triggered by the term "maritime resource." As in San Pedro the loss of natural resource was the greatest fear in Sarteneja, but more specifically the loss of opportunities to fish. Actually, it was the scarcity of fish because of the proliferation of reserves. The impression is that Sarteneja respondents find themselves most at risk of losing their fishing livelihood more than their counterparts in the other communities.

On the topic of folklore, belief systems, and proverbs, in all seven communities only a few folklore were retained. Interestingly, versions of the Jackie Lantern legend were repeated in all communities, despite differences in ethnicity. It underlines the cultural crossover that marine folklore has undergone in coastal communities. The scarcity of folklore was an indication of the widespread slippage in community cultural memory of marine traditions. Insofar as they are necessary as backdrop for human behaviour, it may be necessary for COMPACT to include an income generation component to retrieve and enliven them within artistic expression for the welfare of the community as well as for tourism.

Two more questions were asked on cultural traditions. One was whether respondents perceived a greater reliance on marine resources at this time than twenty years ago. The answer was a resounding yes. The reasons given in Placencia, San Pedro, and Sarteneja underlined socioeconomic values that have already been indicated in the previous discussion. Placencia and San Pedro respondents argued that there was now greater reliance on tourism but not fishing. In Sarteneja it was that they do not have any alternative to meet the increasing cost of daily life.

Social values

Two questions were designed to gauge where fishing and tourism fit within the social value system in the communities; in other words, which livelihood is more prestigious and generates greater community adulation. One asked about the level of social acceptability for the following occupations: drop-line fishing, tour guiding, running water taxi, catching lobster, diving for conch, selling fish, and other. The other question asked which of the occupations the respondent would recommend to his/her child.

It did not take us too long to realize that ranking by prestige was not an important factor; rather it was ranking by the amount of cash one earns relative to the amount of work expended within a given occupation. Respondents were aware of the relatively high cash value that both fishing and tourism could fetch. Of course, tourism, even though it was not prevalent within a given community, was perceived as bringing more cash than fishing. This was the case in Sarteneja to a large extent because it was seen as taking less work for the amount of cash it could generate. In other communities where tourism had virtually taken over from fishing, such as San Pedro and Placencia, and increasingly so in Punta Gorda, Punta Negra, and Dangriga, the comparative advantage is plain to be seen.

In Punta Gorda, selling fish received the highest level of social value followed by the others, all of which received almost the same level. In Placencia it was tour guiding followed by fishing for lobster and conch.

In Sarteneja both lobster and conch got the highest score followed by selling fish; tour guiding, which is non-existent, came a distant last. If the Sarteneja respondents were reacting to their current conditions, they were quite specific on what they would recommend to their son as a preferred livelihood. They did not see a future in fishing. They argued that fishing is already overtaxed by the increasing numbers of fishers working within the increasingly limited space being made available to them from the MPAs. Tour guiding, therefore, became an attractive alternative, although they were not too certain what it would entail. They added that they had gotten away from farming because it was too much work for the returns; tourism they thought would give them correspondingly less work but more cash compared to fishing.

The expectation of respondents for their offsprings in the other communities echoes those of Sarteneja. Tour guiding and running water taxi ranked the highest.

Summary

In summary the COMPACT study elaborated on what the IDRC had done in terms of use and added new data on the attitudes and social values of community members. As in the case of any survey, the COMPACT study conclusions will need further refinement; for example, the emotive passion of possessiveness that communities have toward "their" portion of the Reef as well as their need to upgrade their technical knowledge about the Reef itself. There is also a need to explore the social values from two perspectives. One is the overlap between the perceived economic and aesthetic beliefs about the Reef, and the other is the extent of the social acceptability of occupations generated by the sea. Both of these are significant in promoting marine studies to our youth as well as generating a wider public appeal toward the welfare of our marine resources.

On the other hand, our knowledge of use practices is wider. We know about the gender expectations between Placencia and San Pedro, on the one hand, and Sarteneja, on the other. We also know about the wide range of occupations that accompany tourism, making clear why coastal residents are putting their hope on it for their economic upliftment. We know the range of fishing grounds for various communities. Finally, we know the general lack of folklore about the sea, placing the Garifuna cosmology in even higher profile relative to other Belizeans.

Focal themes

Five focal themes extracted from the previous three studies will help readers understand better Belize's coastal communities twenty five years after independence. Summarizing the main conclusions of these points will enable a comparison with other studies in Belize and the rest of the Circum-Caribbean. Highly significant is the concept of the community.

Community–the concept of ownership

Assumptions about the use of the term "community" are usually based on men, women, and children living and earning their livelihood within rural locations with set boundaries. To a large extent, these assumptions remained in all three of the previous studies, as seen in the use of term "community-based" coastal resources in the two IDRC studies. Caribbean rural communities can be anything but the fruition of these assumptions, an argument that Breton and others elaborate on introducing the results of the first phase IDRC studies (Breton, Davy, & Buckles, 2002, pp. 15-24). Men, women, and children may live partly in their "home" village, in another one or in a town or city in another part of the country. Besides, most villagers may acquire their cash sustenance primarily through remittances and not on income they generate locally. Finally, there is the case of the Sarteneja fishers, who live at home but spend large parts of the year along the whole of Belize's coastline, further demonstrating the distinction between place of residence and place of work.

Defining what is a community and where it is are dependent on the nature of the analysis that one is making. We have to admit, however, that a concept of the community closer to the assumption I raised, namely family groups residing within a locality, may be especially helpful in the study of coastal resources. This is true because it entails a socio-historical continuity that is so important in laying claim not only to the coastal resources but also to farmlands and/or houselots. As important as land ownership is to community membership and identity, I have not brought it up thus far in this review. Within a full-blown community study, it would have to be centred as an indicator of primary rights that one has within a given geographical location. In most places the deeper one's genealogical roots are, the greater the claim to one's community standing.

Livelihood–articulating within micro-environments

Earlier in this essay on "what is the coast," I described coastal micro-environments. Use practices in the IDRC studies included both marine and terrestrial resources as sources of livelihood. Unfortunately, there is an almost myopic exclusion of terrestrial resources under the current promotion of MPAs, as primary drivers of economic sustainability. All communities, including those fully marine dedicated ones, such as San Pedro and Sarteneja, had earlier and still make use of terrestrial resources. Efforts should be carried out to explore the revival of older and newer terrestrial practices. One result will be to enhance the concept of community ownership, mentioned earlier.

Traditional knowledge and cosmology–their role in community/cultural identity

Both topics have been discussed at length in this essay because of the tendency to overlook them and their importance in community/cultural identity. There is additional information about the importance of traditional knowledge and cosmology within the renewed discourse on intangible culture and cultural spaces, spearheaded by UNESCO (2001). Marine ecosystems would fit in the focus on cultural spaces, where oral and intangible cultural practices take place.

Community structures and organization

In Belize the formal community structure is the local government arm of the village council or town council. Neither one has any legal authority over coastal resources. That power lies only at the level of central government. Community leaders, however, have criticized this, arguing that local citizens know better about their own resources and should be empowered to control their use. The irony of this is that co-management agreements do allow NGOs to regulate behaviour within MPAs. Furthermore, the law enables co-operatives to function in these areas, such as the local marketing of fish products and extending cash advances to members. Traditionally, the co-operatives also received assistance from central government in the periodic checking of their accounts and methods of promoting group interaction.

Not to be overlooked as a primary foundation for community structure and organization are the informal systems of kinship, which remain as an intermediary for most exchanges within the rural community. Buyei Juan Lambey Institute in Dangriga used kinship effectively in recruiting members thereby giving a good example where a traditional system could be used for community mobilization. Finally, the various methods of exploiting natural resources are predicated on informal types of organization at the domestic and extra-domestic levels. There is a need to identify them and record how they are to be utilised.

Knowledge and community coastal research

As discussed earlier, after 1996 the United Nations and international NGOs were responsible to introduce the link between people's welfare and environmental integrity into the knowledge system of Belize. I have argued that the main contribution to this equation is to insert the community as a concept and a living reality. By its very experiential nature, the community demands much more research be done by Belizeans living and studying in Belize, even as they continue to share with others. We cannot repeat the relative academic exclusion of the Caribbean Coral Reef Ecosystems Research Programme, in which scores of natural scientists can come, do research, and leave taking with them the results of their work. As a social science the core of ethnology uses different techniques, methods, and patterns of articulation with the host society. Forging a strong base in ethnology is also a moral responsibility, where Belizeans can no longer shy away from the position of leadership that they should take.

References

AUIL, STEPHANIE & KOTCH, J. (1993). *Development of tourism on a fishery community: the role of the fisherman.* Paper presented at the Caribbean Conservation Association XXVII Annual General Meeting, Kingston, Jamaica.

BRETON, YVAN, DAVY, BRIAN, & BUCKLES, DANIEL. (2002). *In balancing people and resources: Interdisciplinary research and coastal areas management in the Caribbean.* Costa Rica: Editorial Fundacion UNA.

CENTRAL STATISTICAL OFFICE. (2006). *Abstract of Statistics: 1980, 1991, 2000.* Belmopan: Belize.

COASTAL ZONE MANAGEMENT AUTHORITY AND INSTITUTE. (2000). *State of the Coast Report 2000.*

COASTAL ZONE MANAGEMENT AUTHORITY AND INSTITUTE. (2000) *State of the Coast Report 2001/02.*

BROWN, DAVID N. (2000). *Social assessment of the Belize section of the Mesoamerican Barrier Reef System, Draft Report.*

CRAIG, ALAN K. (1966). *The Geography of fishing in British Honduras and the adjacent coastal areas.* Doctoral dissertation, Louisiana State University.

CRAIG, ALAN K. (1969). The grouper fishery of Cay Glory, British Honduras. *Annals of the Association of American Geographers,* 59, 252-263.

ESPEUT, PETER. (1994). *A socioeconomic baseline survey of thirty fishing communities in twelve CARICOM countries.* CARICOM Resource Assessment and Management Programme.

FOSTER, BYRON. (2005). Heart drum: spirit possession in the Garifuna communities of Belize. In J.O. Palacio (Ed.), *The Garifuna: A nation across borders: Essays in social anthropology.* (pp. 159-175). Benque Viejo del Carmen, Belize: Cubola Productions.

GORDON, EDMUND T. (1981). *Phases of development and underdevelopment in a Caribbean fishing village: San Pedro, Belize.* Doctoral dissertation, Stanford University.

GRAHAM, ELIZABETH. (1994). *The highlands of the lowlands: Environment and ar-*

chaeology in the Stann Creek District, Belize, Central America. Wisconsin: Prehistoric Press.

GUDERJAN, THOMAS H. (1993). *Ancient Maya traders of Ambergris Caye*. Benque Viejo del Carmen, Belize: Cubola Productions.

JACOBS, N.D. & CASTAÑEDA, A. (1998). *The Belize Biodiversity Action Plan 1998-2003*. Belize: BRC.

HEYMAN, WILL and R. GRAHAM. (2000). *The voice of the fisherman of southern Belize*. Belize: TIDE.

JOLLY, KIMO & MCRAE, ELLEN. (1998). *The environment of Belize: Our life support system*. Benque Viejo del Carmen, Belize: Cubola Productions.

MCFIELD, MELANIE. (2000). *Evaluation of management effectiveness, Belize MPA System Report*. Draft report to the CZMAI.

MCKILLOP, HEATHER. (2002). *Salt: White gold of the Ancient Maya*. Gainesville: University of Florida Press.

National Museum of Natural History/Smithsonian Institute. (2001). Research and Collections webpage. http://www.nmnh.si.edu/iz/ccre.htm.

NELSON, CLAIRE & SEIDL, A. (2005). In MARTHA HONEY & GERALDINE SLEAN (Eds.). *Belize cruise ship study*. Washington, D.C. and Palo Alto, California Center for Ecotourism and Sustainable Development.

PALACIO, JOSEPH O. (1993). Social and cultural implications of recent demographic changes in Belize. *Belizean Studies, 21*(3), 2-12.

PALACIO, JOSEPH O. (2000). *Past and current methods of community base coastal resources management in the southern coast of Belize*. Draft report submitted to IDRC-CBCRM.

PALACIO, JOSEPH O. (2002). *Community Management of Protected Areas Conservation Project (COMPACT) Community Assessment*: Draft report submitted to COMPACT.

PALACIO, JOSEPH O. (2004). *Exploring spirituality, income generation, and the use of coastal resources among the Garifuna in southern Belize*. Draft report submitted to IDRC-CBCRM.

PALACIO, JOSEPH O., CORAL, CAMILO, & HIDALGO, HUGO. (2005). Territoriality, technical revitalisation, and symbolism in indigenous communities, In Y. BRETON, D. BROWN, B. DAVY, M. HAUGHTON, and L. OVARES (Eds.). *Coastal resource management in the wider Caribbean: Resilience, adaptation, and community diversity*. (pp. 78-104). Ottawa: IDRC.

UNESCO. (2001). *First proclamation of masterpieces of oral and intangible heritage of humanity*.

WAIGHT, LYDIA & LUMB, JUDY. (1999). *Belize Audubon Society: The first thirty years*. Belize: Producciones de la Hamaca.

8. Twenty-five Years of Human Rights in Belize: From Theory to Practice, a Work in Progress

Antoinette Moore

Introduction

In the last half-century the understanding and appreciation of human rights have grown exponentially and taken root throughout the world, with human rights becoming the common denominator for judging how governments treat both citizens and non-citizens within their borders. Human rights are broadly defined as those guaranteed rights and freedoms to which all individuals, without distinction, are entitled by virtue of being human.[1] They include civil, political, economic, social, cultural, environment and development rights and have increasingly become both the philosophical and practical tools for individuals and groups to progress and improve their status in their respective countries.

Human rights are used as a domestic barometer to ascertain the availability and protection of basic freedoms such as freedom of expression, religion, assembly, and association and also the fair and equal access to education, employment, housing, health care, and other vital necessities of life. Historically, it has been the government's obligation to ensure that the rights of its citizens and others in its country are protected and, further, to provide appropriate remedies if these rights are violated.[2] Prior to the emergence and growth of international human rights law in the middle of the last century, countries generally did not interfere

---

[1] See generally Steiner and Alston, *International Human Rights in Context: Law, Politics, Morals* (2nd Ed.); Oxford University Press, 2000.
[2] Ibid. at pp. 56 *et seq.*

with what were considered the internal affairs of other sovereign nations so that if a country violated the rights of its own citizens or failed to protect their rights, the outside world would rarely assist those unfortunate individuals.[3] However, in the aftermath of World War II this principal of non-interference began to change requiring nations to cede some of their sovereignty in the interest of protecting human rights.

The United Nations Charter states that respect of human rights by governments is the basis for freedom, equality, and justice that should in turn lead to a more peaceful world.[4] It is now accepted in the new international order, which prominently features a human rights legal regime, that the protection of human rights is an international obligation of all members of the world community.[5] "Human rights is foreign to no country and native to all nations."[6] Consequently, human rights have begun to play a pivotal role in international relations, also becoming a factor in bilateral and multi-lateral trade, immigration, extradition and other agreements between countries.[7]

Since its independence from Great Britain in 1981, the nation of Belize has been part of this global trend to recognise and respect human rights. Belize, like many countries, has a mixed, and, some might say, complex human rights record. Relatively speaking, Belize is certainly not on par with the worst human rights offenders in its region or around the world. In fact, many consider Belize to have a good human rights record. However, this small Caribbean country situated in Central America has not escaped world scrutiny and judgment for persistently committing certain types of human rights violations over the years. Moreover, the human rights situation on the ground for many living in Belize is not good and reflects a very different picture of Belize than is often portrayed.

This article reviews some of the significant highlights related to human rights in Belize's 25 year history of independence and also begins the forward-looking exercise in this area of national discourse.

---

[3] Ibid.

[4] United Nations Charter, 1945, preamble, articles 1.2 and 1.3.

[5] Richard Bilder. (1999). "An Overview of International Human Rights Law." In Hurst Hannum *Guide to International Human Rights Practice* (3rd ed.); and Andrew Clapham, Hassiba Hadj-Saharoui & Lisa Oldring (Eds.), *"The promotion and protection of all human rights is a legitimate concern of the international community,"* Published with the permission of the Japanese Government for use in Courses at the Graduate Institute of International Studies, Geneva 1999.

[6] Kofi Annan, UN Secretary General, in 1998 on the fiftieth anniversary of the Universal Declaration of Human Rights.

[7] Supra at footnote 5.

Human rights in the laws of Belize

Domestic

When Belize became independent from Britain's colonial rule on the 21st of September 1981, the country adopted a written Constitution.[8] The preamble of the Belize Constitution states that Belize is "founded upon principles which acknowledge the supremacy of God, faith in human rights and fundamental freedoms...."[9] The preamble further says that the Belizean people require policies of state, which, among other things, "...protects the rights of the individual to life liberty and the pursuit of happiness..."[10]

In addition to these prefatory comments respecting human rights in the Belize Constitution, the Constitution contains an entire chapter devoted to the recognition and protection of human rights.[11] This part of the Constitution, entitled "Protection of Fundamental Rights and Freedoms," is similar to the human rights provisions in the written constitutions of most, if not all, Commonwealth Caribbean nations, including Jamaica, Trinidad and Tobago, Barbados, and Guyana.[12]

Chapter II of the Belize Constitution protects the civil and political rights of individuals in Belize, including freedom of movement,[13] conscience and religion,[14] expression,[15] and assembly and association.[16] The Constitution enshrines the fundamental right to life,[17] liberty,[18] the presumption of innocence,[19] a fair trial[20] and equality before the law.[21] It also protects certain economic rights, such as the right to property[22] and the right to work,[23] but excludes substantive provisions protecting the economic rights to health and education.[24]

---

[8] The Belize Constitution Act, Chapter 4 of the Substantive Laws of Belize, Revised Edition 2003.

[9] Ibid.

[10] Ibid.

[11] Ibid. at Part II.

[12] Sir Fred Phillips. (1985). *West Indian Constitutions: Post Independence Reform*, Oceana Publications, Inc., Supra at footnote 8, chapter II, section 10.

[13] Supra at footnote 8, chapter 2, sections 3(b) and 10.

[14] Ibid. at sections 3 (b) and 11.

[15] Ibid. at sections 3 (b) and 12.

[16] Ibid. at sections 3 (b) and 13.

[17] Ibid. at sections 3 (a) and 4.

[18] Ibid. at sections 3 (a) and 5.

[19] Ibid. at section 6 (3) (a).

[20] Ibid. at section 6 (2).

[21] Ibid. at sections 3 (a) and 6 (1).

[22] Ibid. at sections 3 (d) and 17.

[23] Ibid. at section 15.

The principle that rights and freedoms are limited so that the rights and freedoms of any person do not infringe on the rights of others or jeopardise the public interest is stated at the outset of the rights and freedoms chapter.

> 3. ...the provisions of this Part shall have effect for the purpose of affording protection to those rights and freedoms subject to such limitations of that protection as are contained in those provisions, being limitations designed to ensure that the enjoyment of the said rights and freedoms by any person does not prejudice the rights and freedoms of others or the public interest.[25]

The enforcement section of chapter II of the Belize Constitution provides that individuals who allege a breach of their fundamental rights and freedoms may apply to the Supreme Court of Belize for redress.[26] The Constitution gives the Supreme Court broad power to make declarations and orders and to issue writs and directions it deems appropriate to enforce and protect the individual's rights.[27]

The rights and freedoms codified in Belize's Constitution are many of the same rights that are universally recognised in the United Nation's 1948 Universal Declaration of Human Rights (UDHR).[28] Overall, the Belize Constitution, as the supreme law of the land, lays a solid legal foundation for the recognition and protection of human rights in Belize.

Since independence, in addition to the adoption of the Constitution, the National Assembly, Belize's legislative branch, has passed various domestic legislations that have enhanced the promotion and protection of human rights in the country. Among these laws is the Ombudsman Act of 1994.[29] Traditionally the role of an Ombudsman, adopted from the Scandinavian countries, has been that of a protector of rights by officially investigating citizen complaints of government abuse. In Belize, the act established the office of the Ombudsman who has the power to investigate and report to the National Assembly on malfunctioning of government functionaries and agencies. Although the Ombudsman Act became law in 1994, it was not until 1999 that the government appointed an individual to fill the post and perform the role of the Ombudsman. Belize's Ombudsman is not an Ombudsman for Human Rights as exists in some countries.

---

[24] Although the preamble of the Belize Constitution was amended in 2000 to include references to health and education arising from recommendations from the Political Reform Commission, the Constitution still does not enshrine these economic rights.

[25] Supra at footnote 8, chapter II at section 3.

[26] Ibid. at section 20 (1).

[27] Ibid. at section 20 (2).

[28] Universal Declaration of Human Rights, adopted 10 December 1948, G. A. Res. 217A (III), U.N. Doc. A/810, at 71 (1948).

[29] Chapter 5 of the Substantive Laws of Belize, R.E. 2003.

In 1998 the Families and Children Act became law in Belize.[30] It was an attempt to modernise and consolidate the numerous laws relating to families and children, including paternity, maintenance, custody, adoption, and child welfare. A unique feature of this law is that it imports into it the United Nations Convention on the Rights of the Child (CRC),[31] an international human rights treaty dealing with children's rights that Belize had ratified earlier in the decade. Included in the "Guiding Principles in the Implementation of the Act," in schedule one of the Families and Children Act, is the following,

> 4. A child shall have the right…(c) to exercise, in addition to all the rights stated in this Schedule and the Act, all the rights set out in the U.N. Convention on the Rights of the Child with appropriate modifications to suit the circumstances in Belize, that are not specifically mentioned in the Act, or in this Schedule.[32]

The 1992 Domestic Violence Act (DVA)[33] and the 1996 Protection Against Sexual Harassment Act[34] are two other laws passed in the last 25 years in Belize that have human rights implications. These laws were a starting point in implementing at the national level the rights contained in the Convention on the Elimination of All Forms of Discrimination against Women (CEDAW).[35] Belize had ratified CEDAW in 1990. The Domestic Violence Act is used routinely in every district throughout the country. This, of course, reflects the pervasiveness of domestic violence in the country. While it is disturbing that domestic violence is endemic in Belize, it was a progressive move to enact a law to protect individuals against violence from an abusive spouse or other family member.

The Protection against Sexual Harassment Act, on the other hand, has hardly, if ever, been used since it became law in 1996. It is not that sexual harassment on the job, at school, and in other institutions does not exist in Belize, but the law does not seem to be the vehicle used by victims to cope with this particular problem. Currently, Belize is the only Commonwealth Caribbean country with a sexual harassment law and other countries in the region have ex-

---

[30] Chapter 173 of the Substantive Laws of Belize, R.E. 2003.

[31] Convention on the Rights of the Child, adopted 20 November 1989, entered into force 2 September 1990, G. A. Res. 44/25, 44 UN GAOR, Supp. (No. 49), U.N. Doc. A/44/49, at 166 (1989).

[32] Supra at footnote 29.

[33] Chapter 178 of the Substantive Laws of Belize, R.E. 2003.

[34] Chapter 107 of the Substantive Laws of Belize, R.E. 2003.

[35] Convention on the Elimination of All Forms of Discrimination against Women, adopted 18 December 1979, entered into force 3 September 1981, G.A. Res. 34/180, 34 UN GAOR, Supp. (No. 46), UN Doc. A/34/46 at 193 (1979).

[36] Access to Justice for Women in the English-Speaking Caribbean Countries, Experts Meeting in Kingston, Jamaica, September 2005.

pressed their interest in using Belize's law as a model to draft their own legislation in this area.[36]

The Freedom of Information Act[37] is another law passed in Belize that helps to advance the protection of human rights in the country. "Freedom of information is a fundamental human right and is the touchstone for all freedoms to which the United Nations is consecrated."[38] Belize's freedom of information law implements the constitutional right to information. This right is articulated at section 12 (1) of the Belize Constitution saying that freedom of expression includes receiving and communicating ideas and information without interference.[39] The provisions of Belize's act allow citizens to seek and obtain information, within a specified time frame, from any agency of government so long as that information is not classified as exempt under the law. Where the government authority denies a specific request for information claiming, for example, that a document is exempt, the Ombudsman is empowered to review the decision and inspect the requested document.[40]

The Freedom of Information Act was enacted in 1994 but only first received a high profile among the general public in Belize in 2005 when the Belize Printers Association used the law in an attempt to uncover the terms of the government's sale of the Government Printery to private parties in an undisclosed contract. Belizeans have begun to consider employing the Freedom of Information Act as a tool to gain access to suspected corrupt activities of their government and to other vital information to assist them in fully participating in their democracy.[41]

The laws mentioned here are a few examples, not a comprehensive list, of domestic laws in Belize that concern different aspects of human rights.

Regional

At the regional level, Belize is one of 34 member countries of the world's oldest regional organisation, the organisation of American States (OAS).[42] The OAS Charter includes references, though not expansive, to human rights and equality, economic rights and the right to education. Some argue that these references

---

[37] Chapter 13 of the Substantive Laws of Belize, R. E. 2003.
[38] United Nations General Assembly, 1946 quoted in *Open Sesame: Looking for the right to information in the Commonwealth,* Commonwealth Human Rights Initiative, 2003.
[39] Supra at footnote 8.
[40] Supra at footnote 28, sections 35-40.
[41] Op cit. at footnote 38, p. 20. Transparency International's *Annual corruption perceptions index* for 2003 indicates that Belize had a CPI score of 4.5 with the score of 10 being "very clean" and 0, highly corrupt.
[42] *Basic documents pertaining to human rights in the Inter-American system,* General Secretariat, OAS, updated May 2001 and op cit at footnote 5 (Hannum).

to human rights in the OAS Charter obligate all OAS members to generally respect human rights in their territories.[43]

The OAS adopted the American Declaration of the Rights and Duties of Man (the American Declaration) in Bogotá, Colombia in 1948.[44] The American Declaration pre-dates the renowned United Nation's Universal Declaration of Human Rights by a half a year. The American Declaration is an innovative human rights instrument, partly because it includes duties or responsibilities, along with rights, as one of its prominent features.[45] Belize is bound by the provisions of the American Declaration by virtue of its membership in the OAS. The American Declaration along with the OAS Charter and other regional declarations and conventions and oversight institutions form a comprehensive system to promote and protect human rights in the Western Hemisphere.[46]

In 1969 the OAS opened for signature the American Convention on Human Rights (the American Convention) and in 1978 the American Convention entered into force, having received the requisite number of ratifications from OAS member countries.[47] Belize has not ratified the American Convention and thus is not a party to it. In this regard, Belize is like many other Commonwealth Caribbean countries that have failed to ratify their region's human rights convention. Interestingly, on the other hand, most of Belize's Central American neighbours have ratified the American Convention. The American Convention is the definitive interpretation of the American Declaration's meaning; hence, Belize and its Commonwealth Caribbean neighbours are arguably bound by the norms in the Convention notwithstanding their failure to ratify it.[48]

The OAS Charter created the Inter-American Commission on Human Rights as its principle organ to promote the observance and protection of human rights in the region.[49]

Subsequently, the American Convention established the Inter-American Court of Human Rights.[50] The Court has jurisdiction only over OAS member countries that are party to the American Convention; thus, Belize does not come

---

[43] Dinah Shelton. (1999). "The Inter-American Human Rights System." In Hurst Hannum (Ed), *Guide to international human rights practice* (3rd ed.). Transnational Publishers, Inc.

[44] American Declaration of Rights and Duties of Man, signed 2 May 1948, O.A.S. Off. Rec. OEA/Ser.L/V/II.23, doc.21, rev.6.

[45] Op cit at footnote 1, pp. 869 and 870.

[46] Supra at footnote 44.

[47] American Convention of Human Rights, signed 22 November 1969, entered into force 18 July 1978, O.A.S.T.S. No. 36, O.A.S. Off. Rec. OEA/Ser.L/V/II.23, doc.21, rev.6.

[48] Supra at footnote 44.

[49] Supra at footnote 44, p. 122.

[50] Ibid.

under the jurisdiction of the Inter-American Court. However, all countries belonging to the regional organisation, including Belize, are subject to the provisions of the American Declaration and fall within the jurisdiction of the Inter-American Commission. Belize has been the subject of the Inter-American Commission inquiries twice in the last 25 years. These two instances are discussed in the section on Human Rights reality on the ground (see p. 215).

Belize is a party to other regional human rights treaties, including the 1994 Inter-American Convention on the Prevention, Punishment, and Eradication of Violence against Women (Convention of Belem Do Para).[51] This treaty states that "every woman has the right to be free from violence in both the public and private sphere," and further that "the right of every woman to be free from violence includes, among others: the right of women to be free from all forms of discrimination; and the right of women to be valued and educated free of stereotyped patterns of behaviour and social and cultural practices based on concepts of inferiority or subordination."[52] In the area of human trafficking and child protection, in 1997 Belize ratified the Inter-American Convention on the International Traffic in Children.

Belize is not a party to other OAS human rights instruments, including the 1985 Inter-American Convention to Prevent and Punish Torture; the 1994 Inter-American Convention on Forced Disappearance of Persons; and the 1999 Inter-American Convention on the Elimination of all Forms of Discrimination against Persons with Disabilities, and the two protocols to the American Convention, one dealing with death penalty abolition and the other with economic, social and cultural rights.

International

The notion that all persons are entitled to certain rights has been with us in different forms for centuries; however, the language of human rights and the idea that human rights should be monitored and regulated by international law emerged in the modern era.[53] The development of international human rights law is mainly a product of post World War II. It was part of the world's response to the gross human rights violations and atrocities that occurred during that war.[54]

---

[51] Belize deposited its instrument of ratification of this treaty with the General Secretariat of the OAS on the 15th of November 1996.

[52] Convention of Belem do Para, articles 3 and 6.

[53] See, for example, the Magna Carta, 15th June 1215, the Bill of Rights in the US Constitution; Op cit at footnote 1, p. 324 et seq.

[54] Ibid. These atrocities included, of course, the concentration camps in Germany and in occupied Poland (Auschitz-Birkenau, Treblinka, Warschau, and Kraków-Plaszów, among others).

The primary source of international human rights law is numerous multilateral human rights treaties that establish international norms and standards and create binding obligations for the states that have ratified them.[55] Another source of international human rights law is customary law. These are standards and norms that, through usage and global course of conduct, have become universally accepted as law over an extended period of time.[56] In these instances, regardless of whether a country is a state party to the pertinent treaty or not, the country is bound, like all countries, by customary human rights standards and norms.

Belize was admitted to the United Nations on the 25th of September 1981. Over the past 25 years, Belize has ratified almost all the major international human rights treaties, and as a result, is considered to have a very good treaty ratification record. Belize was still under British colonial rule in 1948 when the United Nations adopted the Universal Declaration of Human Rights. By virtue of Belize's membership in the United Nations and because of the customary law status of the UDHR, Belize is bound by the Universal Declaration. Furthermore, as stated previously, Belize has adopted substantial portions of the UDHR in its national constitution.

The Convention on the Rights of the Child (CRC) is the most widely adopted of all human rights treaties, having been ratified by the governments of almost every country in the world. Belize boasts being the fifth nation in the world to ratify the CRC in 1990 and thereafter in 1998, Belize imported the CRC into its domestic law. Then in 2000, demonstrating its intention to ratify, Belize signed the two optional protocols to the Children's Convention: one prohibiting the sale of children, child prostitution, and child pornography; and the other Optional Protocol on the involvement of children in armed conflict.[57]

Belize later ratified both of these CRC protocols in 2003.[58] Belize ratified the International Covenant on Civil and Political Rights (ICCPR),[59] but has

---

[55] Op cit. at footnote 5 (Bilder).

[56] Op cit. at footnote 1, p. 324 et seq.

[57] When Belize ratified the CRC Optional Protocol on the involvement of children in armed conflict, it declared that Belize, in accordance with the article 3 of the Protocol., could voluntarily recruit persons who had attained sixteen years of age but were less than eighteen years old. The declaration further stated that when Belize recruited persons in this age range that it would observe certain principles, including obtaining reliable proof of age; parental consent; informing the minor recruit of the duties entailed in service; and giving the minor recruit the ability to withdraw from military service within the first month after enlisting.

[58] Belize has also committed itself to other international instruments dealing with children, including the World Summit Goals for Children, the Dakar Education for All Goals, the Millennium Development Goals, and the Protocol to the Convention against Transnational Organized Crime to Prevent, Suppress and Punish Trafficking in Persons, Especially Women and Children.

not ratified the First Optional Protocol to the ICCPR giving individuals in the country the right to petition to the UN's Human Rights Committee created by the Covenant. Belize has also not ratified the Second Optional Protocol to the ICCPR, which aims at the worldwide abolition of the death penalty. The Constitution of Belize protects most of the civil and political rights found in the ICCPR.

Belize acceded to the Convention against Torture and Other Cruel, Inhuman or Degrading Treatment or Punishment (CAT),[60] and ratified the Convention on the Elimination of All Forms of Discrimination against Women (CEDAW).[61] Belize has also ratified the Optional Protocol to the CEDAW, recognising the competence of the Committee on the Elimination of Discrimination against Women to receive and consider communications by individuals or groups who claim that the state party has violated their rights under CEDAW.[62]

Belize ratified the 1951 Convention Relating to the Status of Refugees and its 1967 Protocol[63] and thereafter domesticized its obligation to protect the rights of refugees by its passage of the Refugees Act.[64] Against the lobbying of the United States, Belize was among the first of many countries to ratify the Rome Statute of the International Criminal Court,[65] helping to create the first international tribunal with jurisdiction over crimes against humanity, war crimes, and other gross violations of human rights.

In 2000, when the government of Belize ratified the CRC protocols, it also signed the Convention on the Elimination of All Forms of Racial Discrimination (CERD) demonstrating its intention to ratify this important convention, which it later did.[66] In that same year, Belize signed the International Covenant

---

[59] International Covenant on Civil and Political Rights, adopted 16 December 1966, entered into force 23 March 1976, 999 U.N.T.S. 171. Belize acceded to the ICCPR on the 10th of June 1996.
[60] Belize acceded to the CAT on the 17th of March 1986.
[61] Belize signed CEDAW on the 7th of March 1990 and ratified CEDAW on the 16th May 1990.
[62] Optional Protocol to CEDAW, adopted by the United Nations General Assembly, Oct. 6, 1999, entered into force Dec. 21, 2000. See articles 1 and 2. Belize ratified the Optional Protocol to CEDAW on the 9th of December 2002.
[63] Convention Relating to the Status of Refugees, signed 28 July 1951, entered into force 22 April 1954, 189 U.N.T.S.137. Belize acceded to the Refugee Convention on the 27th of June 1990.
[64] Chapter 165 of the Substantive Laws of Belize, R.E. 2003.
[65] Rome Statute of the International Criminal Court, 1998. Belize signed and ratified on the 5th of April 2000.
[66] Convention on the Elimination of all Forms of Racial Discrimination, Adopted 21 December 1965, entered into force 4 January 1969, 660 U.N.T.S. 195. Belize signed CERD in September 2000 and ratified this convention on the 14th of November 2001.

on Economic, Social and Cultural Rights (ICESCR)[67] but has yet to formally ratify it. The ICESCR, which includes such rights as health care, education, and an adequate standard of living, call for the progressive realisation of the rights contained in it based on the state's available resources.[68] Many developing countries assert that they are at a disadvantage in implementing the economic rights contained in this covenant because of severe resource constraints. The ICESCR however takes into account the differing abilities of countries to implement the covenant's mandates and calls for implementation of the covenant by state parties individually and "...through international assistance and co-operation, especially economic and technical..."[69]

Also, in 2001, Belize ratified the International Convention on the Protection of the Rights of All Migrant Workers and Members of Their Families.[70] The ratification of this treaty is especially significant in a country with a steady flow of migrants from surrounding Central American countries, other parts of the Caribbean, Asia, North America, and Africa entering into and working in Belize. Unfortunately, as with many of the international and regional human rights treaties that Belize has ratified, except notably the CRC and, to a lesser extent CEDAW, the general population in Belize has little, if any information on what is contained in this document on migrants' rights and how to use it for their protection.

In the area of labour rights, again Belize's ratification track record is very good. Belize is one of 179 member countries of the International Labour organisation (ILO) and has been a member of the organisation since its independence in 1981. Established in 1919 by the Treaty of Versailles along with the League of Nations, the UN's predecessor, the ILO is not strictly speaking a human rights organ. The ILO was the only component of the League to survive the Second World War. The ILO stated its concern for the fair treatment of working men women and children at its creation and has since been a strong "...defender and promoter of human rights on a daily, working level."[71]

Belize has ratified 49 ILO conventions, including the fundamental human rights ILO conventions dealing with freedom of association, collective bargaining, the elimination of forced and compulsory labour, the elimination of dis-

---

[67] *International covenant on economic social and cultural rights*, adopted 16 December 1966, entered into force 3 January 1976, 993 U.N.T.S. 3.
[68] Ibid. at article 2.
[69] Ibid.
[70] *International convention on the protection of the rights of all migrant workers and members of their families*, adopted 18 December 1990, G.A. Res. 45/158. Belize ratified this convention on the 14th of November 2001.
[71] Lee Swepston. (1999). "Human Rights Complaint Procedure of the ILO. In Hurst Hannum (Ed.), *Guide to international human rights practice* (3rd ed.). Transnational Publishers, Inc.

crimination in employment and the abolition of child labour.[72] Belize has denounced five of the 49 ILO conventions it had ratified, so that Belize is currently subject to 44 ILO conventions. ILO conventions ratified by Belize have the force of law in Belize pursuant to the International Labour Organisations Conventions Act.[73]

Belize has not ratified ILO Convention number 169 Concerning Indigenous and Tribal Peoples in Independent Countries.[74] ILO Convention number 169 updated the older ILO Convention number 107 regarding indigenous peoples. ILO Convention 107 advocated the old philosophy of assimilation of indigenous peoples into the dominant societies in which they live, while the newer ILO convention promotes self-determination of indigenous peoples around the world, acknowledging the development of indigenous rights in international law. Considering the longstanding concerns of the indigenous peoples of Belize and Belize's otherwise good ILO ratification record, it appears, at least curious and at worst purposeful, that the government has failed to ratify this particular convention.

Most international human rights instruments require that state parties regularly report on their progress in implementing the rights contained in the treaty to a committee generally created by the treaty and comprised of independent experts. After reviewing each country's report, the committee's issue concluding observations stating their concerns and recommendations for future conduct by the state in the relevant human rights area. Although Belize has a relatively good ratification record, it falls down substantially in its obligation to consistently report its implementation progress to the human rights treaty committees after ratifying the various treaties.

With the exception of reporting to the Committees for the CRC and CEDAW, Belize has generally failed to report on time or at all to the respective treaty committees. This prevents the established international monitoring mechanism from assessing whether Belize is adhering to the rights covered in the treaties or not. For example, in the 20 years that Belize has been a state party to the Convention against Torture, it has appeared before that treaty's Committee only once even though the Convention requires that reports be submitted every four years after the state party gives its initial report.

Even the Committee on the Rights of the Child noted the "importance of a reporting practice that is in full compliance with the provisions of...the Convention. An important aspect of State parties' responsibilities to children under the

---

[72] Chapter 304:01 of the Substantive Laws of Belize, R.E. 2003.
[73] Ibid. at section 3.
[74] ILO Convention number 169 Concerning Indigenous and Tribal Peoples in Independent Countries, adopted 27 June 1989, entered into force 5 September 1991 by the General Conference of the International Labour Organization, Geneva.

Convention is ensuring that the Committee has regular opportunities to examine the progress made in the implementation of the Convention....As an exceptional measure, in order to help the State party catch up with reporting obligations so as to be in full compliance with the Convention, the Committee invites the State party (Belize) to submit its third and fourth periodic report in one consolidated report..."[75]

Dissemination of both the country's written report to the committee and the Committee's concluding observations is another crucial aspect of implementation of the rights in the treaty. The Committee on the Rights of the Child commented and recommended that Belize make its report and the Committee's observations "widely available in the languages of the country... to the public at large, civil society Organisations, youth groups, professional groups, and children in order to generate debate and awareness of the Convention, its implementation and monitoring."[76]

Here again, Belize has consistently failed to broadly disseminate to the Belizean population its human rights treaty reports and the Committee's concluding observations. Belize is not complying with two essential components of the international human rights system by not regularly reporting and not informing the public when its does report.

Human rights organisations in Belize

Besides the national laws and treaty ratifications in any country, the existence and strength of human rights nongovernmental Organisations (NGOs) in the country is another way to examine the human rights situation and to judge the capacity of citizens to effectively challenge the government's infringement of their rights. Since independence, there has been a steady growth of NGOs devoted to the promotion and protection of human rights in Belize.

The Human Rights Commission of Belize (HRCB), an NGO, was founded in 1987 and carried the human rights banner in Belize for the last 19 years, sensitising and educating the Belizean public about human rights, encouraging individuals to assert and stand up for their rights, and denouncing the government for violations. HRCB routinely conducted nationwide workshops in the mid to late 1990s covering every corner of the country teaching and preaching human rights. For many years, HRCB confronted negative reactions to their human rights message because of mistaken beliefs by many ordinary Belizeans about human rights. The organisation painstakingly began to break down these erro-

---

[75] CRC/C/15/Add. 252, 31st March 2005, p. 18, paragraph 78 (UN Committee on the Rights of the Child Report, 2005).
[76] Ibid. at paragraph 77.

neous ideas, particularly the myth that human rights were only concerned with the rights of criminals and "aliens" (the term used for migrants from other Central American countries into Belize).

The HRCB secretariat, first in Belize City and then in Belmopan, operated as the advocacy arm of the organisation, assisting the ordinary men and women whose rights had been violated and who believed they had nowhere else to go and no one else who would listen to and help them. The organisation helped identify routinely abusive police officers and was instrumental in the dismissal of one of the most notoriously brutal officers in the country. HRCB's national coordinator served on the Commission of Inquiry investigating the "riot" that occurred in 2001 in the Orange Walk District. The organisation's Board members participated as human rights observers when Belize's Ministry of Foreign Affairs and Belize Defence Force embarked on the agreed upon removal of non-Belizeans from the adjacency zone with Guatemala.

Although the organisation continues to have active and committed volunteers in the six districts of Belize, the secretariat closed in 2005 as a result of a lack of financial and other resources. HRCB served a critical role in the recognition and development of human rights in Belize in the last 20 years.

The National Organisation for the Prevention of Child Abuse and Neglect (NOPCAN) founded in 1992 was a needed addition to the human rights Organisations in Belize. The organisation bases its work on the CRC and is aimed, as its name suggests, at preventing the neglect and abuse of children. Because of the steadily increasing abuse of young people in Belizean society, the need for this type of organisation became apparent and critical. Over the years, it has gained broad based respect and support. NOPCAN works with government, other NGOs, and international Organisations to accomplish its goals. In 2004 NOPCAN coordinated the drafting and presentation of the NGO report to the UN Committee on the Rights of the Child. It is currently engaged in a campaign to abolish corporal punishment of children in schools and throughout society.

Founded in 1969 the Society for the Promotion of Education and Research (SPEAR) pre-dates Belize's independence and is not considered a human rights organisation per se, but its aim to educate the public to increase public participation in decision-making and democratic change in Belize essentially constitutes human rights work. SPEAR's mission, is, in part, "...to empower people to struggle for justice, democracy and sustainable development."[77] About a decade ago, SPEAR published an illustrated reader-friendly book on constitutional rights, written in Creole.[78] SPEAR has most recently aired a series of videos on national television educating the public about different components of civil so-

---

[77] SPEAR Mission Statement.
[78] *Individual rights: A manual on the constitution and your individual rights.*

ciety, including children's rights and the fundamental rights in the Belize Constitution. These television programmes expose the nation to an increased understanding of human rights.

The Women's Issues Network (WIN) is an umbrella organisation comprised of groups that are concerned with women's rights and other issues affecting women such as HIV and AIDS. WIN currently has 13 member agencies, including the Women's Department, a government office that falls under the Ministry of Human Development. The Women's Department, along with concerned NGOs, spearheaded the passage of a National Gender Policy, aimed at empowering women and tackling gender discrimination, including the areas of wages, credit, and equal protection under the law.[79]

Belize's women's rights movement has been one of the most visible and successful components of the larger human rights movement in Belize since independence. It is largely in part because of the advocacy of the women's movement that the government ratified CEDAW and the regional Convention of Belem Do Para. It is also the power of the women's lobby that ensures that the government of Belize reports to the UN Committee responsible for the oversight of the implementation of CEDAW.[80] This is especially significant since, as noted, Belize has failed to regularly report to the other UN committees created by human rights treaties it has ratified.

The Belize organisation for Women and Development (BOWAND), Belize Rural Women, and Belize Women against Violence (WAV) were women's rights Organisations that grew and withered away in the 1980s and early 1990s. These groups were key participants in the early recognition of gender inequality as an issue in Belize.[81]

Belize's Alliance against AIDS (AAA) was founded in response to the AIDS pandemic engulfing Belize along with other parts of the world since the discovery of the disease. Belize, with its small population, has rapidly become the country with the second highest rate of AIDS in the seven Central American countries and among the highest rate of infection in the Caribbean. In 2002 the government created the National AIDS Commission of Belize to deal with the growing health and social crisis. AAA is an NGO that actively works with the Commission and other NGOs to educate in order to prevent and control the spread of the disease in Belize and to advocate for the rights of persons with HIV/AIDS. The organisation has put the fight against discrimination towards those living with HIV/AIDS squarely in the forefront of its advocacy campaigns.

The creation in March 2004 of the Belize Centre for Human Rights Studies

---

[79] National Assessment Report for Barbados + 10, GOB, September 2003.
[80] Belize Report to Committee on the Elimination of Discrimination against Women.
[81] Irma McClaurin. (1996). *Women of Belize: Gender and change in Central America*. NJ: Rutgers UP, p. 3.

(the Centre or BCHRS) is among the newer developments in Belize's human rights NGO scene. The Centre was launched in the last year of the UN's Decade for Human Rights Education (1995-2004). Despite having an international obligation to do so, Belize had done nothing during this decade or, for that matter, at any earlier period to promote formal human rights education. What human rights education had been occurring in Belize was done almost exclusively through the country's NGOs.

The Centre's mission is to provide formal human rights education to tertiary level students as well as to other targeted sectors of Belizean society. The Centre's vision is to inculcate future leaders of Belize with human rights education and sensibilities so that when they assume leadership positions they may be inclined to use a human rights approach to their decision-making and overall work. In August 2004, the Centre began offering an introductory human rights class to students at the University of Belize, a first of its kind in Belize. One of the long-term objectives of the Centre is to mainstream human rights into the university curriculum and to have the introductory human rights class be a core course within the University. The Centre is building on HRCB's years of educational work throughout Belize, but utilising academia rather than informal workshop settings used in the past.

It is remarkable that individuals and groups who had for many years worked on behalf of women, children, disabled, the elderly, migrants and other vulnerable populations in Belize never classified what they did as human rights work. In fact, some of the NGOs assisting those most at risk in Belize had even shunned the term "human rights," not fully understanding the concept and accepting the myth that human rights were only concerned with the rights of criminals. A visible shift began in the last six or more years with greater cohesion within civil society, an appreciation for the overlap of human rights issues, and an embracing of the power of human rights. The language of human rights is increasingly being used to describe the work of NGOs who serve vulnerable populations in Belize; at long last, the efforts of much of the NGO community are appropriately being placed in the human rights framework. Human rights are no longer the tangential and isolated concept it once was in Belize's NGO community.

The human rights reality on the ground

Through NGOs, the media, the law, and the broader global landscape, human rights have slowly entered the consciousness of Belizeans. As a result, throughout Belizean society, people have begun to speak about their "rights" as a matter of course. What this has meant for the human rights situation on the ground is that more ordinary people have challenged government action in the country's courts; there exists the nascent use of the regional and international human rights machinery by Belizeans; and there is an expectation that Belizeans, at all levels, deserve and should fight for justice and equality.

To further scrutinise human rights in Belize over the last quarter of a century, it is instructive to assess the status and well being of selective vulnerable groups and also to analyse certain thematic areas of human rights in the country.

Vulnerable groups in Belize

Women

Women in Belize suffer from the same endemic and systematic discrimination as do women in most countries around the world. Although concrete efforts have been made to address this social and cultural phenomenon in Belize in the last two and a half decades, there remains substantial attitudinal and other terrain to traverse before Belizean society achieves anything approaching gender equality.

The laws of Belize have developed to eliminate the discrimination that previously existed against unmarried women, particularly in the area of inheritance laws and at separation from long term common law relationships.[82] Also, as mentioned, the Domestic Violence Act provides a veneer of legal protection against spousal and family abuse. The number of protection orders sought have been increased each year,[83] a statistic that demonstrates either increases in domestic violence cases or women's increased awareness of their legal options when abused, or both. The Women's Issues Network describes the number of actual domestic violence cases in Belize as a "pandemic."[84]

Despite the various laws in place to improve the lives of women, the strength of the women's movement, and the larger numbers of women attending higher education, for the most part, "...economic uncertainty, domestic violence, and lack of self-esteem characterise the lives of many Belizean women."[85]

In 2004, a primary schoolteacher was successful in challenging the policy of the Catholic school management to fire unmarried teachers who became pregnant. The management's policy had long been criticised but until this individual woman brought her constitutional claim, the policy remained intact because no one had legally contested it. In the Chief Justice's decision in favour of the

---

[82] See sections 148:01 et seq. of the Supreme Court of Judicature Act, Chapter 91 of the Substantive Laws of Belize, R. E. 2003.

[83] Chief Justice's Annual Report on the Judiciary 2005-2006 delivered on 16th January 2006.

[84] Winning Women, *WIN Newsletter*, vol. 4, no. 4, Nov.-Jan. 2004/05.

[85] Op cit at footnote 81, at p. 3.

teacher, striking down the policy as unconstitutional, he pointed to Belize's international obligation as a party to CEDAW not to permit policies that discriminate against women.[86]

In the years since independence, at any one time no more than two women have been in the National Assembly's House of Representatives, the legislative branch of government. The number of women ministers serving in the powerful Cabinet has also been unrepresentative of Belize's 50% female population. Typically, there has been one woman in the Cabinet and that woman is assigned the portfolio of the Ministry of Human Services, the ministry with the largest number of departments and the smallest budget. This rigid role confinement changed for a brief period when a female Minister had the Belize Defence Force (BDF) portfolio assigned to her. This did not however last long as Cabinet reshuffling occurred, the BDF portfolio was taken from her and the Ministry of Human Services was reassigned to her, in keeping with the practice.

The titular head of state, representing the Crown in Belize, is the Governor General. Since independence one woman has served in this constitutional post. There are several female magistrates in Belize but it was only in 2006, that the first woman was named as a justice of the Supreme Court of Belize. In Belize's 25 years of independence the powerful positions of Director of Public Prosecutions, the Attorney General, and Solicitor General have never been filled by a female.

Children

Belize is a young country. It has just celebrated its 25th anniversary of independence. The country is also young because more than 60% of its population of 301,000 is under 25 years of age.[87] This makes issues affecting young people, children, and children's rights ever topical in Belize. Child labour, access to education for all, including those with special needs, neglect and abuse, juvenile justice issues, and economic support for poor families are all issues that consume significant attention from the public and the government of Belize.

The human rights of children in Belize were often thought to be limited to restricting parents from employing corporal punishment in disciplining their children and many misconstrued children's rights thinking it meant that children were allowed to do whatever they wanted without parental discipline. Children's rights were therefore considered incompatible with traditional parenting methods in Belize. This caused strident resistance to the idea of children's rights. With increasing rates of crimes against children, the public has become keenly aware of the need to protect children in different ways than in the past. This realisation has begun to soften many people to children's rights.

---

[86] *Roches v Wade*, Supreme Court Action number 132 of 2004.
[87] Central Statistical Office website at www.cso.gov.bz/statistics.html.

Belize's poverty rate is 33.5% but 39% of all children in Belize are living in poverty.[88] The numbers of impoverished children are even higher in the Toledo District, especially among Maya children.[89] Poverty puts children in an even more vulnerable position by virtue of being merely children. About 14,000 children or 10% of the country's children are considered vulnerable because of HIV/AIDS.[90] This includes children orphaned by AIDS, living themselves with HIV/AIDS, or in homes with adults who are HIV positive or have AIDS.[91] This vulnerability places Belizean children at greater risk than ever before to illness, sexual exploitation, and poverty.

The right for children to participate in decisions affecting them is not easily accepted in Belize, but strides forward have nonetheless been made. Among these advancements was the first ever Children's Election held in May of 1998. In this children's election 41,567 children and adolescents voted that their right to an education was the right they considered most important.[92] Next in order of importance to the children who voted was their right not to be neglected or abused. UNICEF and the Children's Advisory Committee had helped organise this innovative event to promote children's participation. The election results greatly informed adults and are routinely cited when people discuss children's rights in Belize.

Another important aspect of children's rights is juvenile justice. In Belize there is no comprehensive legal aid programme, nor is there a juvenile legal aid programme.[93] One consequence of this is that juveniles more often than not appear before magistrates and judges without the benefit of legal counsel, sometimes for very serious offenses.[94] Parents or guardians, or the juvenile officer from the Department of Human Services, where parents and guardians are not available, are mandated to appear in court with juveniles.[95] By law, when the accused is a juvenile, the judge should hear the case in chambers.[96] It has been noted that when a juvenile is co-accused with an adult, the rights afforded the juvenile are sometimes overlooked.

---

[88] The Impact of HIV/AIDS on Children in Belize, p. 25 quoting the 2002 Poverty Assessment Report.

[89] Ibid.

[90] Ibid.

[91] Ibid. at p. 8.

[92] Starla Bradley-Acosta. (2004). *Children should be seen and heard: A snapshot of children and adolescent participation in Belize.* For UNICEF and NCFC.

[93] Legal Aid in the CaribbeanATN/CT-8499-RS, Country Report: Legal Aid in Belize, prepared for the Inter-American Development Bank by Ian Morrison of the Canadian Bar Association.

[94] Legal Aid provides a lawyer where a person is accused of murder and cannot afford to hire a lawyer.

[95] Juvenile Offenders Act, Chapter 119 of the Substantive Laws of Belize, R.E. 2003.

Cases involving juveniles are heard throughout the country in the six district courts cloaked in their juvenile court jurisdiction. It has been observed that the array of rights to which juveniles are entitled are at times overlooked when the juvenile is co-accused with an adult and the overburdened district court attempts to quickly convert from a court dealing with adults to a specialised juvenile court.

Unless charged with murder, the criminal justice system in Belize fails to provide young people accused of crimes with lawyers; it also fails to provide a support system to guide these often troubled youth through what is and/or can be an intimidating and confusing process.

One of the yet unchallenged issues in children's rights and juvenile justice is the mandatory life sentence imposed on minors convicted of murder.[97] As the law currently stands, minors who commit murder are not subject to the death penalty; however, judges have no discretion in sentencing them and are legally mandated to sentence these minors to life imprisonment. This means that to reduce the sentence, judges may not consider the background of the convicted minor nor can they take into account the surrounding circumstances of the murder. Under Belize law, a life sentence means that convicted persons will spend the remainder of their natural life in prison. After a set number of years no review is done of the sentence of these minors.

The mandatory life sentence imposed on juveniles in Belize violates article 37 of the Convention on the Rights of the Child. The UN Committee on the Rights of the Child has recommended that Belize change its law as it relates to sentencing of juveniles convicted of murder.[98] In the past, Belize accepted a recommendation from the Committee in relation to children accused of criminal offenses by changing the age of criminal responsibility from 7 to 9 years old.[99] The National Assembly could pass a legislative amendment to bring Belize into compliance with its obligations under the CRC.

Reports of both physical and sexual abuse of children are increasing. In the last several years, the Supreme Court criminal docket has been filled with cases of rape, incest, and carnal knowledge, the offense of engaging in sexual intercourse with females under the age of 16 years old.[100]

---

[96] Ibid.

[97] See section 146 (2) of the Indictable Procedure Act, Chapter 96 of the Substantive Laws of Belize, R.E. 2003.

[98] CRC/C/15/Add. 252, 31st March 2005, p. 17, paragraph 71 (c) (UN Committee on the Rights of the Child Report, 2005).

[99] Number 36 of 1999; see section 25 in the Criminal Code, chapter 101 of the Substantive Laws of Belize, R.E. 2003.

[100] Chief Justice's Annual Report on the Judiciary 2005-2006 delivered on 16th January 2006.

The overall consensus of the NGOs submitting this report is that, while some progress has been apparent in this reporting period, particularly in the area of child sexual abuse, it has been slow and insufficient. More progress has been made in developing policies...than in implementing them. Although pieces of services are provided, they do not effectively fit together to bring about a real and practical implementation of the CRC.[101]

Endorsed in September 2004 by both Belize's Prime Minister and Leader of the Opposition, the National Plan of Action for Children and Adolescents is an example of progress in the area of policy.[102] The National Plan is an in-depth plan for the time period of 2004 to 2015 to improve all aspects of the lives of children and youth in Belize. NGOs, the government of Belize, and the United Nations are all partners in this plan.

A great deal of work has been done to teach Belizeans about children's rights, laws to protect children are in place, and the CRC was ratified and written into the law of Belize almost a decade ago. Yet, children are the poorest of Belizeans. Children are vulnerable because of HIV/AIDS. Children are routinely neglected, abused, raped, exploited, and killed, sometimes by their own family members. Children do not have the things that they need to access education and consequently many go under- or uneducated. With increased frequency, children are becoming convicted criminals, are imprisoned for years, and emerge from behind the walls as hardened individuals with no hope for the future. The situation on the ground for children in Belize is grave, socially, emotionally, psychologically, and physically.

Migrants and refugees

Throughout the 1980s and into the early part of the next decade, during the various civil wars in neighbouring Central American countries of Nicaragua, El Salvador, Guatemala, and Honduras, Belize became the home to over 40,000 people seeking better economic opportunities or seeking refuge from persecution in their home countries.[103]

As previously mentioned in this article, Belize is a state party to the International Refugee Convention and in 1991 enacted a domestic Refugee Act.[104] The local law created a Refugee Office and called for the appointment of a Director of Refugees. Under the law, when a person entered Belize seeking asylum, the Refugee Office convened the statutory eligibility committee that then deter-

---

[101] NGO Report from Belize to the UN Committee on the Rights of the Child, June 2004.
[102] *The Reporter* newspaper article by Renee Trujillo, dated 26th June 2005, p. 9.
[103] Help for Progress statistics.
[104] Refugee Act, Chapter 165 of the Substantive Laws of Belize, R.E., 2003.

mined if the person met the refugee criteria as outlined in Belize's Refugee Act as adopted from the Refugee Convention.[105] If the person was granted refugee status in Belize, he or she was provided a refugee card and given assistance from the UNHCR, which had an office and presence in Belize until 1999.

According to the UNHCR, 8,578 refugees were recognised in Belize between the years 1981 and 1993.[106] Belize has not recognised any refugees since 1994.[107] Help for Progress, a local NGO, has been the implementing agent for UNHCR, assisting refugees and migrants in Belize, and also acting as the liaison with the UNHCR regional office in Mexico since the UNHCR closed its Belize office.

In 1999, the government of Belize instituted an amnesty programme offering undocumented migrants the opportunity to regularise their immigration status in Belize. Approximately 4,709 migrants benefited from the programme.[108] While this was a positive step in recognising the rights of migrants and refugees, the government's dismantling of its Refugee Office and eligibility committee in 2000 was a retrograde step. In the years after the elimination of the Refugee Office and eligibility committee, asylum seekers in Belize are without the international human rights protection guaranteed by law. There is no longer any system in Belize to determine their lawful eligibility as refugees. Under the current situation, Belize is not adhering to its international, or, for that matter, domestic obligations with respect to refugees.

Another remarkable breach of human rights involving the migrant community is when persons convicted of immigration offenses are sentenced to pay a fine of $1000 or serve a prison term of six months and are unable to pay the fine; they may serve indefinite periods of time past the six months in the Belize Central Prison. This is because Belize cannot afford to deport them back to their country of origin or for some other reason, as in the case of Cubans. It is unacceptable that Belize violates the rights of undocumented persons in this manner.

Indigenous peoples

The struggle for land and other rights by the Maya of Belize has mirrored other struggles in the region by indigenous peoples.[109] The following statement accurately describes the condition of the Maya of Belize.

---

[105] Ibid.
[106] Interview with Enrique August, HFP Project Coordinator responsible for implementing UNHCR Refugee and Asylum Protection Project, Belize.
[107] Ibid.
[108] Ibid.
[109] See, for example, the *Case of the Mayagna (Sumo) Awas Tingni Community v Nicaragua*, Inter-Am. Ct. H. R. (Ser. C) No. 79, 31st of August 2001.

In the contemporary world, indigenous peoples characteristically exist under conditions of severe disadvantage relative to others within the states constructed around them. Historical phenomena grounded on racially discriminatory attitudes are not just blemishes of the past but rather translate into current inequities. Indigenous peoples have been deprived of vast landholdings and access to life-sustaining resources, and they have suffered historical forces that have actively suppressed their political and cultural institutions. As a result, indigenous peoples have been crippled economically and socially, their cohesiveness as communities has been damaged or threatened and the integrity of their cultures has been undermined.[110]

In 1996, in the ongoing effort to preserve their culture and protect their rights, an organisation and a few individuals, on behalf of the Maya communities, instituted a Supreme Court lawsuit against the government of Belize after the government granted a logging concession to a Malaysian logging company in the Toledo District on lands traditionally used and occupied by the Maya.[111] Settlement discussions with the government of Belize began as a consequence of the domestic case and also a subsequent human rights petition filed by the Maya people in the Inter-American Commission on Human Rights in 1998.[112]

In October 2000, the discussions between the government and the Maya representatives resulted in the leaders of five Maya Organisations and the Prime Minister of Belize signing a document called the Ten Points of Agreement (TPA).[113] It is most significant that point 6 of the TPA states, "That the government of Belize recognises that the Maya people have rights to lands and resources in Southern Belize based on their outstanding use and occupancy."[114] Despite this agreement, little progress has been made in the recognition of land and other rights of the indigenous peoples of Belize.

As mentioned, in 1998 the Toledo Maya Cultural Council (TMCC) on behalf of the Maya people lodged a petition against the government of Belize with the Inter-American Commission on Human Rights saying that Belize was violating the rights of the Maya by, among other things, granting logging and oil concessions to companies on land traditionally used and occupied by the indigenous peoples of the area. In October 2004, the Commission issued their report finding that the government of Belize had and continues to violate the

---

[110] S. James Anaya, *Indigenous Peoples in International Law*, Oxford University Press, 2000.

[111] *TMCC, et al. v The Attorney General of Belize*, Supreme Court of Belize Action no. 510 of 1996.

[112] *The case of Maya indigenous communities of Toledo v Belize*, Case 12.053, Inter-Am. C.H.R. Report No. 40/04 197 (2004).

[113] Ten Points of Agreement between the Government of Belize and the Maya Peoples of Southern Belize, signed on the 12th of October 2000.

[114] Ibid. at point 6.

rights of the Maya people of southern Belize by its land policies and denying the Maya the right to land tenure security in accordance with their cultural practices.[115]

The human rights concerns of the Maya were again expressed in a more recent domestic lawsuit.[116] In this case, the Sarstoon-Temash Institute for Indigenous Management (SATIIM) challenged a decision by the government of Belize to permit an American oil company to conduct seismic testing in a national park that was co-managed by SATIIM and surrounded by Maya and Garifuna communities. Although the case centred on environmental issues, it clearly re-raised the spectre of indigenous land rights. Ultimately, the court quashed the government's authorisation for the oil company to conduct seismic testing in the Park but the decision was based only on the company's failure to conduct a lawfully required environmental impact assessment. The decision did not reach the question of indigenous land rights, but the judge noted twice in his ruling that he did not address the issue because no land claim had been made in the case.[117]

Until a sustainable resolution of the land issue is reached and indigenous rights recognised and respected, the Maya people of Belize continue to be on the lowest rung of the economic, political, and social ladder in the country. This human rights problem, like others, persists and festers in Belize. It is seen as especially hypocritical for the government to exploit and tout the cultural heritage of the Maya as a tourist attraction, giving lip service to the Maya's contribution to Belize's cultural diversity on one hand, while on the other hand, saying that those Maya who wish to retain their culture and do not integrate into Belize's mainstream are unenlightened and backward.[118]

The elderly and disabled[119]

The treatment of these two vulnerable groups within any society speaks directly to the issue of discrimination and reflects on the society's overall commitment to human rights. The international definition of "older persons" are those who are 60 years or older. In Belize this is approximately 6% of the overall pop-

---

[115] Supra at footnote 111.

[116] *SATIIM v Forest Department/Ministry of Natural Resources,* Supreme Court of Belize Claim number 212 of 2006.

[117] Ruling in *SATIIM v Forest Department/Ministry of Natural Resources*, 27th September 2006.

[118] Comments made by a Government of Belize representative on behalf of the government.

[119] Interview with Lindy Jeffery, Director of the National Council on Aging and a Board member of the Mental Health Association.

ulation. As people live longer, older persons will comprise a greater portion of the Belizean population. For older persons in Belize, issues such as financial security, accessible medication and health care, and recognition and respect are key to achieving equality and improved lives.

Although Belize is a party to the 2002 Madrid International Plan of Action for Older Persons, there is no domestic law that protects the rights of older persons in Belize, as there are for other vulnerable groups. The Cabinet adopted a National Policy for Older Persons in 2002 but this has not yet translated into legislation. The National Council on Aging, formed in February 2003, is the quasi-governmental organ coming under the Ministry of Human Services that works with service providers such as Helpage to assist older persons in Belize.

There is no governmental department or unit governing those with disabilities nor is there a national policy dealing with persons with disabilities. On Mental Health Day and other occasions attempts are made by service providers to sensitive the public to the plight of the mentally ill. The Mental Health Association is a nongovernmental organisation working as a service provider for the mentally ill under the government's Ministry of Health. Another service provider for the disabled in the forefront of the rights of the disabled is the Belize Council for the Visually Impaired.

The worth and dignity of the human person is at the core of human rights. Discriminating against any persons because of their status, immutable characteristics or situation in life is anathema to human rights. Discrimination against the elderly and those with disabilities is a reality in Belize, but the increased pressure for respect of all human rights and in particular for the rights of those most vulnerable will help change this reality in the coming years.

Thematic human rights topics in Belize

Labour and freedom of association

The trade union movement in Belize has an extensive pre-independence history, going back to the early twentieth century. Trade unionists throughout Belize were part of the anti-colonial struggle and have played a significant role in Belize's human rights movement post independence.

The Women's Workers Union (WWW), formed in 1991, was short lived but was "unprecedented" in its efforts to organise women workers. Despite the WWW phasing out, it inspired BOWAND's successful 1992 campaign to have the minimum wage increased for jobs dominated by women, such as shop assistants and domestics.[120]

The passage of the Trade Unions and Employers' Organisations (Registration, Recognition and Status) Act of 2000[121] was a step forward in labour rights in Belize. Although unions were an active part of Belizean society from prior to independence, there was no law that required the recognition of unions. The new law changed that and also included the protection of the basic right of association. However, here again the protections provided by the written law do not always give the actual coverage for individuals on the ground as shown in the first case under the union recognition law.

When six banana workers engaged in union organising at the banana plantation they worked at were fired, apparently because of their union activities, it was not unusual since the banana industry in Belize had been notoriously antiunion. These workers challenged their terminations by lodging a lawsuit in the Supreme Court against the banana grower under the then new law, protecting their rights to associate and organise.[122] But five years after the firings and two years after the banana workers trial, the lawsuit is still pending in the court and the Trade Unions Recognition Act has not been used again to this writer's knowledge.

An extended teacher strike in 2005 was part of the countrywide anti-corruption fervour and demonstrated the power of the contemporary union movement in Belize and again showed how trade unionism intersected with the struggle for human rights and the fight for general societal improvements. Towards the end of the union action, government negotiators, one of whom had been a former union advocate, caused dissention among the union ranks evidencing weakness and division in the movement.[123]

Freedom of expression and assembly

The critique has been made that there is a lack of people's participation in the legislative process and in other areas of public life in Belize to such an extent that this lack of participation is "a feature of Belize's political culture."[124] A "fear of victimisation and reluctance to speak out" are cited as a significant part of the reason for this aspect of Belize's political culture.[125] As the examples discussed below reflect, there is the growing potential for change in this part of Belize's political culture.

Post independence and prior to 2005, two incidents stood out on the issue of

[120] Supra at footnote 81, at p.105.
[121] Chapter 304 of the Substantive Laws of Belize, R.E. 2003.
[122] Reyes et al v Mayan King, Supreme Court of Belize Action number 309 of 2001.
[123] *Amandala* newspaper 2005.
[124] Brown-Johnson, Vernon, & Finnetty. (20021). "Democratic Governance and Citizen Security in Central America: The Case of Belize" *CRIES*, p. 53.
[125] Ibid.

freedom of expression in Belize, namely, the protests at Benque Viejo del Carmen and Tower Hill. In both instances, protesters were demonstrating against increases in transportation costs, specifically, bus fares and also the non-availability of buses.[126]

On the 30th of July 2001, during the incident at Tower Hill Bridge in the Orange Walk District, protestors blocked the toll bridge, burned tires in the middle of the bridge, and stoned the police and Belize Defence Force soldiers as these armed forces advanced on the crowd. The Riot Act was read before the subsequently two persons had been shot, non-fatally, by the police. The Commission of Inquiry appointed by the Prime Minister to investigate the incident, determined that the reading of the "Riot Act" had been done unlawfully.

Then on the 22nd of April 2002, in Benque in the Cayo District, a number of students demonstrated because the price hikes were going to affect their ability to get to and from school. The police yielding M16 rifles shot into the crowd and seriously injured two young men who were among the protestors. The police used tear gas indiscriminately, so that young school children and persons in their homes were affected. Eleven young men who had participated in the demonstration were charged with illegal assembly as a result of this incident. Their cases were never prosecuted in court but were pending for several years after the protest. The Human Rights Commission of Belize investigated the Benque protest and the police response to it, finding that the police had used systematic police brutality against teenage boys and young men who demonstrated.

In 2005, in the wake of growing public discontent about the high cost of living, unkept promises, alleged government corruption, lack of accountability, and general mismanagement, massive protests of unprecedented size and intensity began in Belize. Leading up to this year of rebellion, a peaceful march of approximately 10,000 people dubbed the "March for Belize" took place in August 2004.[127]

In the nation's capital in January 2005 thousands of people came to demonstrate as the lawmakers in the House of Representatives debated the annual budget, which included a government proposed tax increase.[128] While it could be argued that these public exercises demonstrated that the enjoyment of freedom of expression and assembly were alive and well in Belize,[129] others have remarked that as the people increasingly voiced their dissatisfaction with government and demanded accountability, the government increasingly responded

---

[126] Channel 5 News archives, July 2001 and April 2002.

[127] *Amandala* newspaper, August 2004.

[128] Channel 5 News archives, January 2005.

[129] "...a mark of maturity attesting that at the end of the day, Belize is a country governed by the rule of law concomitant with the constitutional right of free speech, including the right to protest, but respect for the rule of law." Chief Justice Annual Report, January 2006.

with repression. Teachers and other persons who were peacefully protesting said they were brutally handled by the police during the demonstration.[130] Throughout 2005 other demonstrations and labour actions took place at a sustained rate never experienced previously in Belize.

Police brutality/freedom from torture inhuman or degrading treatment and punishment

HRCB and the Ombudsman's office have routinely commented that the most frequently heard type of complaint they receive in their respective roles relates to police brutality or the excessive use of force by law enforcement officers.[131] Police brutality is so commonplace in Belize that learning that a police "roughed up" someone, whether the person was arrested for an offense or not, rarely turns a head. In 2006, three men, a father and his two sons, sued the government of Belize claiming that their Constitutional right not to be subjected to torture, cruel or degrading treatment had been violated when police beat each mercilessly and used electric shock on two of them in an effort to extract information.[132] The government, unable to defend the case, has offered to settle this case.

Just as US soldiers in the Vietnam War said they "destroyed the village to save it," police officers in today's Belize claim that they must break the law to uphold it. Over the years, police officers have been arrested for breaking the law they are sworn to uphold. On Belize's Independence Day in 1999 in the nation's capital, Belmopan, a popular businessman was detained for a minor squabble he was involved in during an independence celebration. Within a couple of hours in police custody, he was dead.[133] The police originally said that he had strangled on his own vomit since he was intoxicated. It was however later revealed in the post mortem examination that he died from a ruptured liver and sustained other injuries consistent with having been beaten. A police constable was arrested and charged with the murder. He was ultimately acquitted in the Supreme Court because of insufficient evidence.

Three men were fatally shot by police in 2003 under suspicious circumstances. Two of the police officers involved in these shootings have faced criminal charges. In one case, the policeman was convicted of manslaughter and is serving a 13 year sentence for causing the death of a man who came unarmed to the police station to bail a friend out of the lock out. In 2005 nine police officers were convicted of criminal offenses from theft to rape to manslaughter. Besides those convicted, another 10% of the police department were on interdiction,

---

[130] Channel 7 News archives, January 2005.
[131] Ombudsman Annual Reports.
[132] *Faux v Attorney General*, Supreme Court of Belize Action number 212 of 2006.
[133] Channel 7 News Archives, September 1999.

suspended while pending the outcome of criminal trials or internal police tribunals. In a police department with a little less than 800 police officers, these numbers are staggering. The Police Department's "zero tolerance" policy for police misconduct, corruption, and brutality is apparently not an adequate disincentive for many police officers.

After the expansion of the Prison Rules to allow corporal punishment for an increased number of offenses,[134] in 2000 at least five inmates were "flogged" at the Belize Central Prison in Belize. Flogging of prisoners became an issue of great controversy. It was hotly debated on radio and in newspapers by the public at large, the legal community and NGOs in Belize. The constitutionality of flogging prisoners in Belize was discussed at a human rights seminar hosted by Penal Reform International, the Attorney General's Ministry of Belize, and Simons Muirhead & Burton, a British law firm that has been involved in death penalty abolition and prison reform work in the Caribbean.[135]

In September 2000 this writer interviewed three of the five men flogged under the new rules. Each explained the procedure used in carrying out the prison flogging. Each men was individually taken into a small dark room where his feet and hands were tied. He was blindfolded and a hood placed over his head so he could not see and therefore could not identify the instrument used to inflict the beating or who carried it out. Each said that someone came in during the process and felt or examined his body, and the men assumed that this was a doctor but he was unable to speak with or see this person. As each man recounted his experience, it was evident that each believed the prison authority had taken advantage of all of them because they were isolated and had no recourse to the injustice. "They chance we, what can we do, we are here already."[136] This statement by one of the men recognised that it was their status as prisoners, their vulnerability, that permitted the violation of their rights.

This is one stark example in which a law in Belize was used to violate the human rights of vulnerable individuals.

Prison conditions

Currently, Belize is statistically among the top ten nations in the world for its high ratio of prisoners to its overall population. Belize has 487 prisoners per 100,000 people in its population, ranking seventh in the world and tying with Cuba for its high prison population.[137] The other countries in this undesirable top

---

[134] Prison Rules, Subsidiary Laws of Belize.
[135] Kirk Anderson. (2000). *The flogging of prisoners in Belize–Is this practice constitutionally valid?* Commonwealth Caribbean Human Rights Seminar.
[136] Course Paper by Antoinette Moore, International Human Rights Law, Masters of Studies Programmeme, Oxford University, 2002.

ten category with Belize are the United States, Russia, Cayman Islands, Belarus, Kazakhstan, Bahamas, US Virgin Islands, Bermuda and Kyrgyzstan.[138] Others in this unenviable category include Turkmenistan, Cuba, Kazakhstan, Suriname, Ukraine, and Dominica. Second place United States has only 5% of the world's population, yet has 25% of the world's jail and prison population. Belize has 460 prisoners per every 100,000 people in its population, ranking sixth in the world, compared with, for example, Western Europe, which has 85 prisoners per 100,000, Nigeria with 30 per 100,000, and India with 31 per 100,000.[139]

Does having one of the highest imprisonment rates in the world in comparison to its population mean that Belize has a very high rate of crime, and/or that alternative means of non-custodial punishment are not available, or they are not being employed by the courts in Belize? Or does it mean that Belize is an especially punitive society? There is no doubt—the crime rate in tiny Belize is very high. The murder rate in Belize is one of the highest in the region compared with the population, but most prisoners are not incarcerated for murder or, for that matter, any other violent crime.[140] It does not appear that the courts in Belize are extensively using the alternative sentencing scheme that became law in the 1999 Criminal Justice Act.[141] The punitive rather than the rehabilitative aspect of sentencing seem to remain the guidepost for sentencing in Belize.

In 2002 the Belizean government privatized the Belize Central Prison. The crimes occurring within the prison, the escapes from the prison, and the overall intolerable living conditions at the prison led to government's decision to privatize. Members of the Rotary Club of Belize formed the Kolbe Foundation, named after the patron saint of prisoners, Maximilian Kolbe, and assumed management of the prison. Although none of the new leadership had prison management training, criminology, or any experience as prison wardens, there is little doubt that the prison conditions have greatly improved under the management of the Kolbe Foundation.

The chairman of the Kolbe Foundation Board of Directors says that the Foundation's goal is that the prison be a "secure, humane facility." He said when the Foundation took over, "The first change was treating inmates as individuals

---

[137] Prison International website.

[138] Ibid.

[139] Retrieved Nov. 2006, from http://www.prisonstudies.org (2003). For another comparison, see also 2005 figures from the Sentencing Project webpage: http://www.sentencingproject.org/pdfs/1044.pdf. Belize is ninth with 470 prisoners/100,000; others are US (738), Russia (594), St, Kitts/Nevis (536), Bermuda (532), Virgin Island-US (501) & UK (464), Turkmenistan (489), Cuba (487), and Palau (478).

[140] Statistics from the Belize Central Prison. "Most of the inmates committed theft or drug-related crimes, and their average sentence length is five years," John C. Woods, chairman of the Kolbe Foundation Board of Directors.

[141] Chapter 101 of the Substantive Laws of Belize, R.E. 2003.

with dignity instead of as numbers."[142] According to the prison, the recidivism rate has gone from 60% to 25% and this is, in part, attributed to their rehabilitation programme. The Kolbe Foundation rehabilitates the inmates through a Christian-based programme. Some prisoners and others complain that freedom of diversity of religion and choice of faith for inmates is a human rights issue still to be addressed at the prison.

Belize has not ratified the Optional Protocol of the Convention against Torture allowing for spot checks at all institutions of confinement, including the prison and the district police lock ups. This would certainly assist in monitoring Belize's compliance with human rights standards in these facilities.

Death penalty

The retention or abolition of the death penalty is one of the hot button topics people have traditionally associated with human rights. Indeed, the death penalty is a singularly important human right since it involves both the right to life and the prohibition against inhumane treatment. It is an issue that polarises and has regrettably alienated portions of the public from human rights because of a misunderstanding that death penalty abolition does not comprise the totality of human rights.

In Belize, the death penalty had been the mandatory punishment for anyone over 18 years of age convicted of murder.[143] Hanging is the method of execution. The last execution in Belize was in 1985.[144] After 1985 although individuals were sentenced to death, none was executed for a variety of reasons. Belizeans believed this was because the final and highest court of appeal for Belize to which convicted murderers could appeal was the Judicial Committee of the Privy Council (the Privy Council).[145] The Privy Council was located in England and their judges were too distant and lacked the local sensibility and understanding to implement the death penalty in Caribbean countries like Belize.

In 2002, using the public cry that hangings should resume to deal with the increased murder rate in Belize, the government of Belize proposed a constitutional amendment eliminating the third tier of appeals to the Privy Council for

---

[142] John C. Woods, chairman of Kolbe Foundation Board of Directors.

[143] Criminal Code, Chapter 84 of the Substantive Laws of Belize, R.E. 1980.

[144] Kent Bowers was executed after being convicted of murdering a member of a wealthy Belizean family.

[145] Belize Constitution, chapter 7, section 94.

[146] Belize Constitution (Fifth Amendment) Bill, 2002. To read Chief Justice Dr. Abdulai O. Conteh's presentation (1 March 2003) at the Working Session of the Implementation of International Human Rights Protections, see: http://www.internationaljusticeproject.org/pdfs/Conteh-speech.pdf.

convicted murderers.[146] Because of pressure from the Human Rights Commission of Belize and others, district meetings were held throughout the country about this proposed law. Opponents of the proposed amendment testified before the committee and district wide hearings were held amounting to a referendum of sorts on the death penalty. Although there was clear support for capital punishment, there was also an understanding that it was dangerous to allow the government to start eroding the rights of any portion of the population. The bill was defeated. The bill, along with a similar bill from Barbados, was the subject of an Inter-American Commission of Human Rights inquiry and advisory opinion.[147]

Then in the case of *Reyes v The Queen*, the Privy Council struck down the mandatory death sentence in Belize ruling that it was unconstitutional.[148] For the first time, high court justices in Belize could use their discretion to impose a sentence other than death on a person convicted of murder. This historic case has reduced the use of the death penalty in Belize, as have similar cases throughout the Commonwealth Caribbean in recent years.[149] Since Reyes, trial judges in Belize must consider any possible mitigating or aggravating circumstances of the killing as well as the background and possibility of reform of the offender in determining whether life or death is the appropriate sentence to impose on a convicted murderer.

General human rights situation

In the first ever full research mission of Amnesty International to Belize in December 2002, the organisation's parting observations were that, "Belize's possible expansion of the use of the death penalty, its denial of meaningful review to potential applicants for asylum and its inconsistent access to justice for victims of alleged violations put its human rights reputation in the region at risk."[150]

A couple of years before its visit, Amnesty International, perhaps the most renown of all international human rights NGOs, published a report on Belize.[151] In its report, the organisation cited fatal shootings by police, torture, ill treatment by security forces, and prison conditions as the primary human rights concerns in Belize, other than the death penalty.[152] The report also noted that the or-

---

[147] Inter-American Commission on Human Rights, 1998.
[148] *Reyes v The Queen*, 2 AC 235 (2002).
[149] *Hughes* (St. Lucia) at (2002) 2 AC 259; *Fox* (St. Kitts) at (2002) 2 AC 284.
[150] Press Release, AI Index: AMR 16/004/2002, 4th of December 2002.
[151] Amnesty International, Government Commitments and Human Rights, 4th of July 2000.
[152] Ibid.

ganisation welcomed the government's response that they investigated any wrong doing and would sanction those found responsible but was concerned about the independence and impartiality of the police investigations and the lack of judicial prosecutions.[153]

On a daily basis, a variety of human rights violations occur in Belize. Despite the heightened sensitivity of rights on the ground, there remain major constraints for men and women on the streets to assert and defend their human rights in Belize. Included among these are ignorance about specific strategies to enforce one's rights; the high cost of bringing lawsuits to defend one's rights, in particular the costs of lawyers; the lack of legal aid for constitutional cases; the fear of challenging the seemingly all powerful state; the fear of being victimised by the omnipresent partisan politics; and the attitude of acceptance or "passivity" that characterises the Belizean personality.

Over the last 25 years, and especially in the last decade, the idea of human rights has started to become imbedded in the conscience and culture of Belizeans. Human rights activists in the country, along with others, have helped to create an environment in which people recognise that they have rights and are insisting that the government respect those rights.

Conclusion

As a nation, Belize understands and accepts the theory and premise upon which universally recognised human rights are based. The Belize Constitution, the national laws, and Belize's regional and international human rights treaty ratifications are all a testament to this fact. Primarily because of the work of human rights Organisations and other members of civil society, the continuing process of dispelling the myths and misconceptions about human rights has been largely successful over the years. Many in Belize have been inspired by a world movement to fight for their rights and have become increasingly energised and emboldened in their attempt to hold the government accountable for its violations of human rights.

In the final analysis, however, the question for this growing nation to answer in the next 25 years is whether the people and the government of Belize have the will and the courage and are truly prepared to do what is required to translate the theory of human rights into everyday practice that will improve and fundamentally transform the lives of people so that the dignity of all in Belize is respected.

---

[153] Ibid.

Acronyms

- AAA — Alliance against AIDS
- AI — Amnesty International
- BOWAND — Belize Organization of Women and Development
- BCHRS — Belize Centre for Human Rights Studies
- CAT — Convention against Torture and Other Cruel, Inhuman or Degrading Treatment or Punishment
- CEDAW — Convention for the Elimination of all forms of Dis crimination against Women
- CERD — Convention for the Elimination of all forms of Racial Discrimination
- CRC — Convention on of the Rights of the Child
- DVA — Domestic Violence Act
- HFP — Help for Progress
- HRCB — Human Rights Commission of Belize
- ICCPR — International Covenant of Civil and Political Rights
- ILO — International Labour Organization
- NGO — Nongovernmental Organization
- NOPCAN — National Organization for the Prevention of Child Abuse and Neglect
- OAS — Organization of American States
- SATIIM — Sarstoon-Temash Institute of Indigenous Management
- SPEAR — Society for the Promotion of Education and Research
- TMCC — Toledo Maya Cultural Council
- TPA — Ten Points of Agreement
- UDHR — Universal Declaration of Human Rights
- UN — United Nations
- UNHCR — United Nations High Commission for Refugees
- WAV — Women Against Violence
- WIN — Women's Issues Network
- WWW — Women's Workers Union

9. State Crime and Punitive Discipline: Rocks on the Lid of a Boiling Pot?[1]

Michael Rosberg

Introduction

gOne often hears Belizeans describing Belizeans in critical, moralizing terms. They say Belizeans these days have become too egoistic and lazy, too impatient for success, and greatly lacking in moral fiber. Belizeans are not trying hard enough; they want the will to change. Belizeans, in short, have become backsliders; paradise is being lost. With crime and violence rising-and with young people so often involved as the perpetrators–there's much interest in punishing wrong doers to regain it.

One Belizean poet of the streets offers this punitive solution: "Hang dem high!" The popularity of the poet attests to the popularity of the sentiment with the person in the streets. His unquestioned assumption: *society needs protection from its citizens*. He assumes that punitive measures work.

A second poet has become equally popular by lamenting from the same streets, "Life haad out ya!" This poet decries the rising cost of living and the apparent indifference of a system that neither knows nor cares about the pain of the poor. This poet is commenting on the other face of the coin: *citizens need protection from this society*.

A striking paradox exists: life is so painful one cries out, demanding greater pain. So it is worth asking how this self-contradictory mentality evolved, why it persists, and whether the punitive solutions proposed, however popular, are likely to prove very effective.

[1] Thanks is extended to UNICEF in Belize which permitted use of data from the study on the Impact of Crime and Violence on Children and Adolescents, 2005. The study was coordinated by the Community Rehabilitation Department (CRD) of the Ministry of Human Development.

Amandala newspaper ran an opinion piece, "Social order," in which the author comments disapprovingly on the smirks and public postures of defiance by two youths charged with murder and is certain of the solution:

I don't think that these young men would be amused if they thought that after due judicial process, there might be a black bag and a rope waiting for them...The thought of a black bag and a hangman's rope is a very gruesome thing. It is very fearful and there can be no doubt that it deters. (Feb. 5, 2006)

In like manner, and before recommending "punishing criminals so severely, they will never be tempted to repeat their offenses," a 2002 opinion piece from *The Reporter* newspaper refers to sociologist Jack Katz for one explanation for criminal behaviour—there are in fact immediate benefits to criminality, which he labels the "seduction of crime." According to Katz, choosing crime can help satisfy personal needs (in Flores, p. 13). Some of us are apparently good and do not commit crimes. Katz argues that those who do are probably bad: "People who consider themselves "bad" or "criminal" may simply need fewer situational inducements to commit crime than those who see themselves as "good" or "law-abiding" (quoted in Flores, p. 13).

This kind of argument is what the Marxists used to call "ahistorical"—it tries to explain behaviour without reference to context. People may either consider themselves "bad" or "good." The self-categorization apparently proceeds from nowhere. But the ultimate source and form of correction is certain; it is administered by the state and it is the death penalty.

Émile Durkheim, the father of modern sociology, demonstrated a strong connection between individual behaviour and what is occurring in society. In *Suicide* (1897/1997), Durkheim introduced the use of statistics into sociology and discovered an inverse relationship between suicide rates and the status of the Parisian stock market (or bourse). Durkheim predicted that market implosions would more frequently do damage to unmarried, non-commissioned soldiers than to those with many social ties. Unmarried, non-commissioned soldiers tended to be poor males with fewer links to society than officers, and therefore, men less buffered from confusion and despair by the support of family, wives and friends. The word he used for the sense of being confused and adrift in society was "anomie," a kind of anonymous state.

Astoundingly, the statistics Durkheim presented showed that whenever the economy collapsed and prices at the bourse plummeted, more bachelor soldiers killed themselves. The relationship was remarkable because most of the non-commissioned soldiers would have been too poor to be investing in the market and affected by its set-backs. Durkheim was able to add credence to his argument that "society" was no mere abstraction. It generates and perpetuates powerful 'norms' that shape a population's behaviour. It apparently has the power to kill. So, when white collar embezzlement and corruption at the national level

Table 1: Total crimes by age range for 2004 and 2005*

Age Range							
	Total	Under 12	13 to 14	15 to 17	18 to 25	26 to 45	Over 45
Total 2004	1,677	93	101	91	427	877	88
Total 2005	1,409	114	102	108	335	646	104

send the economy into a tailspin, we should not be surprised to discover that it also has the power to increase crime.

The opinion piece writer quoted above rejects non-punitive corrective action, saying "...these (formative) factors are not easily subject to treatment or change: it is not realistic to expect society to heal broken families..." (p. 13). But because social forces generate anti-social behaviours, the punitive measures recommended and attempted by Belizeans cannot reverse rising crime rates. They are stopgap measures that fail to deal with the source of the nation's problems. As will be shown below, the stopgap measures may even contribute to the problems.

The impact of crime and violence on children and adolescents

For the years 2004-2005, violent acts committed against persons of all ages (including children and adolescents) are shown in Tables 1 through 5 respectively. Some of the findings relevant for this discussion on authoritarianism and punitive discipline are included in the following observations:

Violence Levels: Decreased from 1,677 (2004) to 1,409 (2005).

Violence by Age (see Table 1): Such gender-based violent acts as unlawful carnal knowledge and indecent assault tend to be directed at younger women (12-17 years) and taper off with age (18 through 'over 45'). In contrast, violent acts such as insulting words, harm, wounding, common assault, damage to property, threatening words, threat, harassment and breach of protection order tend to be increasingly directed to women as they become more mature (18 through "over 45"). Violence by age increased for youth between the ages of 12 through 17 years, reduced for those between the ages of 18-45 and increased for those over 45.

Violence by Sex (see Table 2): Disaggregated by gender, violent acts recorded for 2004, such as unlawful carnal knowledge, rape, indecent assault, common

---

* The statistics for Tables 1, 2, 3, 4, and 5 were generated by the Joint Intelligence Coordinating Center (JICC), Belmopan, Belize (2003).

Table 2: Total crimes by sex for 2004

Sex			
	Total	Male	Female
Total 2004	132	25	107

and aggravated assault, psychological abuse, threatening words, abusive words and breach of protection order are overwhelmingly targeted at women (81.1% of cases in 2004).

Violence by Area of Occurrence (see Table 3): Gender-based violence is far more likely to occur in the victim's residence, a relative of the victim's residence, or in both the residences of the victim and the accused than it does in public. For example, in 2004, 17% of gender-based violence occurred in public; 66% in residences. The figures for 2005 were 20% and 58.8% respectively.

The location of violent crimes is important for a discussion of severe punitive discipline of children. As the Alabama Coalition Against Domestic Violence webpage indicates:

Domestic violence affects every member of the family, including the children. Family violence creates a home environment where children live in constant fear. Children who witness family violence are affected in ways similar to children who are physically abused. They are often unable to establish nurturing bonds with either parent. Children are at greater risk for abuse and neglect if they live in a violent home.

Statistics show that over 3 million children witness violence in their home each year. Those who see and hear violence in the home suffer physically and emotionally.

Ackerman and Pickering (1989) specify the effects on children, "Families under stress produce children under stress. If a spouse is being abused and there are children in the home, the children are affected by the abuse."

Table 3: Total crimes by area of occurrence for 2004 and 2005

Area of Occurrence							
	Total	Public	Victim's residence	Relative's residence	Both victim/ accused's res.	Accused's residence	Unknown
Total 2004	1,677	284	291	7	718	91	286
Total 2005	1,409	285	262	36	447	84	295

Table 4: Total crimes by district for 2004 and 2005

District							
	Total	Corozal	Orange Walk	Belize	Cayo	Stann Creek	Toledo
Total 2004	1,677	86	136	934	281	171	60
Total 2005	1,409	53	164	731	283	130	48

Table 5: Total crimes by motive for 2004 and 2005

Motive					
	Total	Alcohol	Jealousy	Drugs	Missunderstanding	Other
Total 2004	1,677	199	213	20	625	620
Total 2005	1,409	150	96	20	586	557

In other words, where adults are victims of domestic violence, children are too.

Violence By District (see Table 4): Most violence was reported in Belize followed by Cayo. The least was reported in Toledo District. Reported violence levels decreased between 2004 and 2005 in Corozal, Belize, Stann Creek, and Toledo, and increased in Orange Walk.

Violence By Motive (see Table 5): Except for "Other", the most common reported motive for violence was "Misunderstanding" followed by "Jealousy" in 2004 and "Alcohol" in 2005. The least frequent reason given for violent behaviour was "Drugs".

Types of youth crime

Some of the crimes in the preceding list include illegal acts against children and adolescents committed by caretakers, but may exclude ones not reported. These acts would reduce their sense of security just as crimes committed against adults do.

Belize was one of the earliest signers of the United Nations Convention on the Rights of the Child (CRC, 20 November, 1989) and has much protective legislation complying with that accord (See Legislative Amendments in Belize since initial CRC Report).[2] Information presented below on the Crime and Vi-

---

[2] Thanks to the National Committee for Families and Children (NCFC) for contributing this information.

olence study suggests a sizeable gap between official ideals about children's rights and legal expectations regarding the treatment of children, and acts of violence actually committed against them. Because such acts are inflicted by many caretakers, one must also conclude that there is a sizeable gap between what Belize officially believes to be unacceptable forms of child correction and what is broadly believed by Belizeans. The origin and implications of this gap are discussed below.

Severe discipline: Origins and justification

Belizeans who support severe forms of discipline say they do so for some of the following reasons:

- I was raised this way and it did me no harm; in fact, it taught me right from wrong and I'm glad it was done.
- You have to "bend the tree whilst it's young;" correction offered later won't take.
- The more severely you lash a child the better adult it will become.
- The child who is lashed knows it is loved.
- This is my child and nobody has the right to tell me how to raise it—certainly not government.
- Not lashing the child lets it become willful and spoiled.
- I lash my child when my child shows me disrespect.

Curiously, the word "lash" is often chosen to justify the form of discipline that comes to the speaker's mind. Of the many words that could be used when talking about child-correction (e.g. correct, beat, hit, knock, lecture, remove, scold, slap, spank, strap, strike, thrash, withhold rewards, whack), "lash" is chosen. In other English-speaking countries, "lash" is used as a term to describe the punishment of prisoners, sailors, or slaves. But, it is seldom used because most of the population in such countries have limited connection to slavery, and because in most of them, lashing prisoners and sailors went out of favour with pirates and capital punishment. It is ironic that in Caribbean Anglo-phone countries including Belize, "lash" is the term used to describe the form of correction meted out to children and often chosen by the descendents of the very people forced to endure slavery and lashing by colonial masters.

It is also interesting that "disrespect" is offered as one of the justifications for severe punishment of children. Lashing to ensure "respect" implies a hierarchical order between adults and children that is to be preserved through force. The human relations model upon which those who recommend severe disciplinary measures are acting is, in other words, one of power between superiors and inferiors. Children must be disciplined to maintain the social order. In colonial times of slavery and the one hundred years of debt peonage that followed it,[3] power-holders lived under the continual threat of slave rebellions or worker strikes and force was one of several tactics resorted to for the preservation of social disequilibria and the maintenance of economic privileges (Bolland, 1977, p. 160). With the colonials gone, it is startling to realize that the descendants of their former victims have found sufficient utility in those tactics to preserve them voluntarily when relating to their own children. It is probably safe to conclude that severe measures of child correction are a colonial vestige and one useful in preserving power-based social relations. With many other methods of child correction possible, it is interesting to investigate the evident utility of this strategy to many Belizean parents and caretakers.

Lashing and morality

While there may be an apparent contradiction between mocking children or thrashing them to within an inch of their lives on one hand, and attempting to promote a good Christian society on the other, the inconsistency has been honored and upheld for a very long time. If the world is seen in terms of opposing camps of good and evil, then when evil begins to infiltrate good, it must be driven back. Extreme measures seem to become justified. With such logic and moral intent did the Medieval Church scourge and torture non-believers and burn heretics at the stake. The same logic justifies the jihad of extremist Muslims or the invasion of oil-rich Middle Eastern countries by fundamentalist rulers in the oil-dependent West.

Should lashing prove an effective means of driving out evil, the stratagem could at least be defended. But where such measures fail to achieve desired effects, or worse, where they appear to achieve opposite results from those intended, then the logic of defending punitive measures becomes questionable. Indeed, the entire moral world view becomes somewhat shaky. Then another way of conceptualizing reality becomes necessary, and along with it, other ways are required for dealing with the behaviour of those who threaten our security and our advantages.

For this reason, the results of a recent Belizean study on the impact of crime and violence on children and adolescents have particular value.

---

[3] Belizean slavery ended in 1836. Until 1934 when the successful labour strikes led by Antonio Soberanis forced a change in the laws, breach of a labour contract was a criminal act punishable by imprisonment (Bolland, 1977, p. 160).

Crime and violence: findings and implications of study

In 2005, this writer coordinated a national, clustered, stratified, random sample survey of children and adolescents (ages 3-17 years), tracking them by age, gender, district and ethnicity (Rosberg, 2005). The study was to detect the impact upon them of crime and violence.[4] Qualitative measures were also used for two purposes. First, what the respondents reported would help us understand the statistics derived from questionnaires (older respondents) and from observing and measuring their performance during games (all respondents). Their explanations helped make sense of the measurements. Second, by asking respondents about the impact of crime and violence on children and adolescents, we were able to understand their predictions. Usually, it is grown-ups who tell the rest of us why children behave as they do and find the statistics to support the explanations. Sometimes, the explanations have more to do with morality than logic. For example, much has been made of the fact that many anti-social acts are the work of young people from single-parent (usually female-headed) households. The conclusion drawn from this approach is that single mothers make "inadequate" parents and produce "delinquent" children. Alternatively, we are assured that adolescents are by nature delinquent. The first explanation promotes accusations against single mothers; the second, against adolescents for violence perpetrated against society. Neither explanation considers the impact of state violence (Bessant, Hil, Watts, & Webber, 1993, p. 3) constantly worked against the poor in the form of inadequate provision of services or employment opportunities, or of the survival and life inequalities that result when special favours are granted to wealthy supporters of the politicians. When such inequalities are factored in, the logic of the "inadequate" behaviour of single parents and the logic of the behaviour of their "delinquent" children becomes evident.

For this study, ten Youth Data Collectors were selected from among unemployed high school graduates with computer skills. They were trained to collect qualitative and quantitative information and to enter the latter into spreadsheets. Through discussions, qualitative data were gathered. These data were analyzed to reflect respondents' opinions regarding the relationships between crime and violence, on one hand, and anti-social behaviours, on the other. Quantitative data gathered through games and a survey questionnaire measured exposure to various sorts of behaviours and various sorts of experiences in homes, schools, and public places.

---

[4] Thanks to UNICEF who provided funds and gave permission to use the results of the study in this chapter. The Community Rehabilitation Department of the Ministry of Human Development was responsible for the overall coordination of the study and for organizing the data sample of children and adolescents; the Central Statistical Office drew the survey sample.

From the qualitative information, hypotheses were tested using the quantitative information provided through games and a survey questionnaire. Through the discussions with the young people we were being told that restricted employment opportunities were resulting in low skills, poor jobs, and low incomes. This in turn was affecting nutrition, health, and child-rearing techniques. As a result and in anger, the respondents were saying that a portion of Belize's young people were turning to anti-social behaviours to get for themselves what they felt their society was denying them and what they felt they were owed. Stated as a prediction or hypothesis, the young people were saying that there would be a relationship between "security deficits" and "security-seeking behaviours." In the statistical part of the study, "security deficits" included experiences depriving respondents of emotional/mental, financial, or physical security. Respondents reporting frequent teasing or mocking in their homes, being left home alone, and/or feeling unloved by either parent were considered deprived of emotional and/or mental security. Respondents consistently going without lunch, for example, or frequently being kept home to care for younger siblings were classified as experiencing financial insecurity. Respondents reporting being frequently shouted at, lashed, caned, beaten, burned, stabbed, or reporting being shot at home, were considered lacking in physical security. These were self-reported data, either true or false; it was not possible to determine. Nevertheless, if true and frequently reported, homes where young people are treated violently must be considered plentiful. If false and frequent, young people in Belize would be seen to have complex psychological problems.

The second part of the statistical study asked about the behaviour of respondents outside the home including being sent to the corner by the teacher, sent to the principal, failing one or more grades at school, expelled from school, wanting to join a gang, or joining one, carrying/selling drugs, participating in a break-in, being arrested or jailed. Such experiences were considered security-seeking behaviours, that is, efforts to garner attention, to feel greater safety (e.g., joining a gang), or to take care of financial needs. We even asked about being robbed in public, about being beaten by the police, about being raped away from home.

Suppose a child was consistently going to school with no lunch. Suppose a child was being mocked at home or being left home alone. Suppose a child was being hit frequently at home. Would such children exhibit anti-social behaviours more than children not experiencing such things? To find out, cross-tabulations were run as percentages to compare security-seeking behaviours reported by young people to security deficits experienced at home and reported. Is it possible that patterns of security deficits and security-seeking behaviours would differ from one sex to the other, from one district to another, or from one ethnic group to another? To find out, we compared security deficits against security-seeking behaviours for young males. We did the same comparisons for young females, and we did it for young people from each district and from the major ethnic groups of Belize (i.e., Creole, Garifuna, Mestizo, Maya, Chinese/Taiwanese, East Indian, and Syrian-Lebanese).

The researchers also wanted to be sure that the relationships appearing between security deficits experienced in homes and security-seeking behaviours exhibited outside them were not occurring by chance. Maybe we just happened to be given a sample of young people by Central Statistical Office (CSO) and Community Rehabilitation Department (CRD) who failed to represent young males, young females, and youngsters from each of the districts or who failed to be faithful representatives of their ethnic groups. Maybe the experiences and the behaviours of the young people in our sample were somehow different. Therefore, we ran a simple statistical test called the chi-square (X^2) each time we found a strong relationship between home violence and an anti-social behaviour. Unless the X^2 score was very low (i.e., the connection would show up accidentally only one time—or even less often—in a hundred samples CSO drew for us), we would not believe that the connection found between a reported security-deficit and reported anti-social behaviour was anything more than a lucky co-incidence. This proved, most unfortunately, to be the major disappointment of this study. The data collectors were not provided with enough young people to ensure that the relationships reported could be considered statistically valid. Where we needed to be provided with 1,850 respondents, only 587 were provided (32% of what we needed). The results, therefore, have to be considered anecdotal. Nevertheless, patterns were consistent and clear. And results held a number of surprises.

The first surprise was how frequently respondents reported harsh treatment at home.[5] They were most afraid of being hit hard at home (57.1% in Belize District, 44.7% in Cayo). In Stann Creek and Cayo District, emotional/mental abuse was reported among 24.2% and 21.7% respectively. About 20% of girls reported mental/emotional abuse (8.9% of the boys). Sexual abuse was reported by 6.1% of respondents in Stann Creek and 4.8% of them in Belize District.

Almost 80% of school-aged boys and 83% of girls reported feeling unloved by their mothers while growing up. Nearly 37% of boys and 43% of girls felt unsafe on the streets of Belize. About 38% of boys and 53% of girls reported having been caned. Another 8% of boys and 2% of girls reported having been stabbed. Overall, 25% of the boys and 30% of the girls reported exposure to some form of crime or violence.

And self-reported participation in criminal activities was high too. Nearly 12% of the boys and 5% of the girls had carried drugs for somebody. About 10% of the boys and 7% of the girls reported having been involved in a break-in.

---

[5] This finding corresponds with the high incidence of assaults in the home collected by the police and reported above.

The emerging behavioural patterns from the statistical comparison of security deficits experienced to security-seeking behaviours was remarkable too:[6]

• **Repeating a year of school**: Children and adolescents in Belize whose mothers do not live at home with them are more likely to fail a year of school than others. Wanting to Join a Gang: Children and adolescents whose mothers do not live at home—most especially boys—are most likely to consider joining a gang. Being kept home from school to work and being left home alone are also statistically significant predictors.

• **Carrying drugs**: Children and adolescents who have been left home alone are also more likely to carry drugs than those not left home alone. The connection is especially strong for girls and for children and adolescents who report having been caned as a form of discipline. Also, boys who report having been kicked as a form of discipline are more likely to have carried drugs than boys who do not report kicking.

• **Selling drugs**: Girls who report having been lashed are more likely to report having sold drugs than girls who have not been lashed.

• Getting arrested: Girls whose fathers are dead are more likely to have been arrested than girls whose fathers are not dead.

• **Seeing a gun**: Girls who report having had their feelings hurt (i.e., emotional/mental abuse) are most likely to report having seen a real gun. The same relationship appears for girls who report having been lashed and for those who were caned.

• **Knowing a gang member**: Boys who report having had their feelings hurt (i.e., emotional/mental abuse) are most likely to report knowing a gang member.
Knowing a Criminal: Girls who have been exposed to people in their homes who smashed objects in anger are more likely to report knowing a criminal than girls who have not. The same relationship holds for girls who report having been kicked.

• **Hearing gunshots**: Girls who have been slapped are more likely than those who have not to have heard gunshots.

• **Seeing a shooter**: Girls who report having been left home alone are more likely than those who have not to have seen a person shooting at another person. The same relationship holds for girls who have been hurt so badly that they had to be taken to the doctor.

• **Being robbed**: Girls who report having been exposed in the home to a person who smashed objects in anger are more likely than those who have not to have been robbed.

• **Seeing bodies in the papers**: Girls who report having had their feelings hurt (i.e., mental/emotional abuse) are more likely than those who have not to remember having seen pictures of dead bodies in the newspapers.

• **Seeing bodies on TV**: Girls who report having been caned are more likely than those who have not to remember having seen dead bodies on TV.

---

[6] Percentages and chi-squares are contained in the report to UNICEF.

• **Knowing a person who died of AIDS**: Girls who report having been exposed in the home to a person who smashed objects in anger are more likely than those who have not to have known a person who died of AIDS. They are also more likely if they have been deliberately burned.

• **Engaged in sex for a gift**: Boys who have been cut with a knife as a form of discipline are more likely than those who have not to have engaged in sexual intercourse to receive a gift in return. Similarly, they are more likely to have engaged in sex for a gift if they have been disciplined so severely that they had to be taken to hospital. Girls who have been deliberately knocked out because of disciplining report being more likely than those who have not to have engaged in sex to receive a gift in exchange.

• **Posing nude for pictures**: Both boys and girls who report feeling that their fathers did not love them are more likely to have posed nude for pictures than boys and girls who believed their fathers did love them.

• **Having somebody attempt sexual touching**: In Belize, Creole children and adolescents who report having had their feelings hurt (i.e., mental/emotional abuse) are more likely to have been touched sexually by another person than Creole children who did not report the mental/emotional abuse. The relationship also applies to Creole children and adolescents who report having been kicked. These relationships do not appear for children and adolescents of other ethnicities.

• **Having been touched sexually by somebody**: Urban children and adolescents who report having been exposed in the home to a person who hurt their feelings, who smashed objects when disciplining them, who had people throw objects at them, or who had been lashed are more likely to have had a person touch them sexually than those who were not so exposed. Creole children and adolescents who reported having been burned as a form of discipline, or to have been lashed, or to have been kicked were more likely to have been touched sexually than those Creole children and adolescents who had not. Garifuna children and adolescents who reported having been slapped as a form of punishment were more likely to have been touched sexually than those Garifuna children and adolescents who had not.

• **Having somebody try to rape you**: Creole children and adolescents whose fathers are not alive and those whose fathers do not live at home report having been victimized by an attempted rape more than other Creole children and adolescents.

• **Having been hurt by the police**: Creole children and adolescents whose fathers are not alive report having been hurt by the police more than other Creole children and adolescents.

Discussion

Again and again, the preceding relationships reinforce the prediction made to us by the young people interviewed for the study. Children who are deprived of adequate mental/emotional, financial and/or physical security, that is, who are exposed to a strategy of punitive rather than supportive nurturing, are those most likely to take matters into their own hands. They seek the sort of security they desire. They engage in anti-social acts; and sometimes they expose themselves to dangerous situations, or are exposed to them by virtue of their poverty.

The implications of the study therefore suggest that attempting to reduce crime and violence by punishing apparent moral deficiencies of behaviour with harsh measures is counter-productive. Young people acting out in anti-social ways are already reacting to security deficits. Harsh punitive measures that attempt to contain inappropriate security-seeking behaviours fail to deal with the problem already created by earlier harsh punitive measures. While they may temporarily halt socially undesirable activity, they do so by increasing the offender's need to intensify anti-social behaviours. Over time, they worsen rather than reduce the problem.

In this regard, capital punishment too must have limited effect. It may succeed in ridding society of individual offenders, but it fails to teach the lesson desired to others who have yet to commit capital offences. For example, the author of the opinion piece cited earlier in the chapter said, "I don't think that these young men would be amused if they thought that after due judicial process, there might be a black bag and a rope waiting for them" (Flores, 2002). But the author was provoked into writing the article because the young men were amused—or attempting rather convincingly—to project that impression, and were surely Belizean enough to know that they potentially faced the death penalty. While the article's author was promoting a strategy of protecting society and the State's authority by crushing rebellion through intimidation, the young men were doing their best to reject that authority and achieve objectives that they felt the State had denied them. They were doing that because the intimidation measures were provoking a defensive reaction. Where the writer asserts that "there can be no doubt that it (intimidation) deters," these young men were demonstrating that it can also have the opposite effect. The more insecure they are made to feel, the greater their need to take measures to increase their sense of security, in this case to pretend they were not intimidated.[7]

Why then are the parents of some Belizean youngsters engaged in employing such severe disciplinary measures to manage their children's behaviour? Perhaps part of the answer lies in the fact that about the only known management method practiced in Belize is authoritarianism. Parents do what they think they're supposed to do. Miller (1991) refers to the Caribbean's:

> ...existing over-centralized, authoritarian style of governance. In fact, this style has the effect of causing these qualities to manifest themselves in the form of anti-

---

[7] In the 1970s, African-Americans used to refer to such a performance as "selling wolf tickets.

social/deviant attitudes/behaviours which undermine the social order, and which hinder rather than contribute toward local/nation development. (p. 2)

Assad Shoman (1987) says Belize is an economic satellite of the industrialized countries, feeding them what raw products it has (i.e., hardwoods, and more recently, shellfish, citrus, sugar, bananas and tourism), and purchasing manufactured goods from them. Those inheriting the reins of government from the British were not encouraged to make changes in the authoritarian system, because the foreign industrialists benefited from having things remain essentially unchanged. The Belizean leadership assuming power from the colonials, needed to maintain socio-economic disequilibrium (pp. 88-89). There were also advantages for the Belizean import-export bourgeoisie if class relations remained unchanged, and concomitant privileges and opportunities for the politicians and managers replacing the British, and accommodating themselves to the local moneyed class. Disadvantaged Belizeans, by virtue of their supplications for assistance and special favours, helped to ensure the continuation of the economic and power systems. Their only alternatives have been to engage in brief acts of rebellion or to flee (Bolland, 1977, p. 160; Barnett, 1991, p. 73). As seen in the newspaper article mentioned earlier, the nearly inevitable reaction to rebellion is repression.

For most Belizeans, including many parents, the result is heightened insecurity. Authoritarianism prompts those who need favours from above to "kiss up." But it also makes it necessary to "kick down," that is, to suppress rebellion from below. Thus, the more insecure a Belizean parent's situation in life, the more intolerable disrespect from below becomes. Imagine a single mother, poorly nourished and housed in deplorable conditions, perhaps in questionable health, having low skills, facing high expenses, lacking any support system or any assurance that she can resolve the challenges and indignities heaped upon her. Such a parent is not in the best position to practice sophisticated child-rearing methods. She is simply too intimidated, too exasperated to do much beyond ignoring her child's unbridled behaviour for as long as possible, and then, in a rage, needing to turn upon that child with a stick or sash cord. In short, her security deficits are easily as intense as those of her child. Notwithstanding Belize's professed intentions to honour the CRC and to enforce its child-protection legislation, this woman is hardly in a position to readjust her relationship with her child. TV ads from the human development organizations in Belize may decry the inhumane treatment of her child. Social workers may consider that mother ignorant and offer workshops and home visits to raise her consciousness and get her to change her ways. For the most part, however, these morally based strategies will fail because she, and most parents facing her level of insecurity, cannot afford to adjust. Given her circumstances, her behaviour is rational even if it portends negative consequences for her child. She, like many Belizeans advocating severe punishment, has less space to be concerned with child correction than with nurturing her own security deficits. Parents who shout, throw objects and who wield sticks, belts, knives, and guns may be as busy making themselves feel better in the face of their anxieties as they are correcting the misbehaviour of their children.

Unwittingly, such behaviours become reified in the behaviour of children—society does not move away from anti-social behaviour because the insecurity of children being teased and beaten and denied material essentials is being increased. Elsewhere, I have suggested that the impact of colonialism has been nefarious and more enduring than we may have realized (Rosberg, 2005). Twenty-five years after the British were forced by Belizeans to cede control of their colony, many of the people of that colony remain victimized by what the British had done over the previous two hundred years. Some of the older generations continue to beat the indignity into the younger ones.

Conclusion

The UNICEF/CRD study suggests that a more effective alternative to social order through intimidation and preaching may be found in ensuring that security deficits among Belizean children are met. Because the insecurity of parents is part of the source of anti-social security-seeking in the children, part of reducing their deficits must include actions to reduce the plight of their parents. And because insecure parents of insecure children are responding to the imperatives of their own security deficits, one must look elsewhere for solutions. Human development service organizations of the state and non-governmental organizations are positioned to respond in innovative ways.

The report on reducing the impact of crime and violence prepared for the Community Rehabilitation Department of Belize and UNICEF divided recommendations into those designed for immediate action and longer term ones calling for systemic responses. The immediate responses are subdivided into ones directed at child and adolescent interest groups, physical and emotional violence in children's environments, sexual violence, violence specifically directed against children in special interest groups (e.g., minorities, disabled, out-of-school), juvenile offenders, and, social/criminal violence affecting children and adolescents). Recommendations for immediate response include a range of tactics including training, public sensitization, advocacy, mediation, improved procedures and check-lists, improvements in data collection and reporting, counseling, improved legal protection and prosecution procedures, raising the age of criminal responsibility, decriminalization of loitering and supervised sports and other activities for children and adolescents, half-way house opportunities, and training for police, nurses, social workers and other front-line personnel. These are useful measures and can, if implemented, do much to ameliorate the impact of criminal and violent acts worked upon children and adolescents.

However, eight recommendations for systemic change contend more fundamentally with institutionalized authoritarianism. The technique was possibly used by caregivers to help them cope with their own insecurities. The study points to a strong relationship between security deficits experienced by children and their parents or other caregivers and (frequently anti-social) security-seeking behaviours. It follows that helping children and caretakers compensate for their security deficits will result in measurable reductions in anti-social, security-seeking behaviours. Security deficits include ones which are emotional/mental, economic and/or physical in origin and there is good information available about how to help children, adolescents and adults overcome such personal deficiencies. There are also effective models operating around the world. These can be researched, adapted and developed in Belize.

However, service organizations in Belize have a series of functional deficiencies to overcome, many unfortunately, the byproduct of the fact that they exist, and operate in, an authoritarian context and are themselves staffed by employees produced by authoritarianism. Some of the problems include:

- **Silo operations**: Many Belizean service delivery organizations (SDOs) tend to operate in isolated fashion or to maintain a competitive relationship with other SDOs. It is as though each SDO is located at the bottom of a barn silo and out of communication with all the others. They tend not to be aware of opportunities being extended to target populations by other organizations which might be useful to their own clientele. Sometimes, they find themselves offering very similar opportunities to the same target group, and the requirements for benefiting from different SDOs may differ. Meantime, there are insufficient extension workers from these SDOs to offer appropriate service to very many low income communities. And sometimes, the SDOs compete among themselves for the favour of political parties, ministers or donor agencies. While SDOs are concerned with 'duplication of services', there is actually a need for greater duplication, coupled with greater coordination of service provision.

- **Top-down operations**: Belizean service delivery SDOs are sometimes the recipients of grants from foreign donor agencies or invited to participate as implementers for UN Agencies. In some cases, projects are designed before the SDOs become involved. And some of the projects have even been designed by non-residents of Belize with limited understanding of local forces affecting development. Such projects reduce the ability of SDO extension officers to relate responsively to communities. Instead, they have a need to deliver activities on schedule and within the constraints of the budget. Merely completing activities becomes more important than achieving improvements. Also, given existing patron/client dependencies in Belize, some SDOs and their field officers are accustomed to relating to target groups as the recipients of welfare; they hand down opportunities and advice. Therefore, it can be said that service delivery for development in Belize is largely 'supply-based' rather than 'demand-based' (i.e., responding to the set of services individual low income Belizeans actually need to escape poverty and dependency).

- **Community misunderstood**: "The community" is sometimes considered a utopian monolith by SDOs. The interests, needs and concerns of individual community residents are poorly understood. There is often division of "the community" into dynamic and shifting alliances and competing factions with individuals joining and leaving as opportunities and their own needs change. Many projects are designed to depend on community volunteers. But equal effort to bring benefits to all will not be forthcoming–especially because of the internal tensions and also because people are too poor to remain volunteers for very long. Local participants become discouraged quickly and projects quietly die.
- **Entrepreneurship ignored**: One of the greatest weaknesses observed is that Belizean projects seldom consider the central role in development of entrepreneurship. Where low income residents of urban neighbourhoods or rural villages depend on the largesse of government representatives and the bureaucrats they appoint to the civil service, there will be few fundamental and sustainable improvements achieved from projects that pay no attention to dismantling such dependencies by promoting economic self-sufficiency. Even where local infrastructure is improved (sometimes thanks to foreign grants or loans), it cannot be maintained without local investments either directly or through taxation. That will require improving the ability of low income individuals to generate income. Development work in Belize, therefore, has to find ways of coupling income generation with the provision of health, education, infrastructure, and other social services. And the income generation needs to be coupled with savings and loans opportunities which focus on increasing productivity. Entrepreneurship does not need to be integral to all projects (e.g., vaccination of babies, school books for all students, installation of water and sewerage systems). But by improving lateral coordination among service delivery agencies, necessary, non-income generating services can be linked to entrepreneurship.

The systemic recommendations of the UNICEF/CRD study on the impact of crime and violence on children and academics attempt to respond to the challenges just mentioned. They propose establishing responsive outreach initiatives to individuals living in low income neighbourhoods or villages. Rather than asking people "what do you need or want?" as some of the politicians do, these initiatives would train SDO representatives to begin asking, "what are you trying to achieve with your life?" a question that may be hard for many to answer, often, they have been busy giving over votes and labour in exchange for subsistence. More powerful Belizeans have benefited at their expense.

SDO representatives and the low income individuals with whom they work can then develop a personalized action plan for each individual intending to achieve change. It will soon become apparent that particular services needed by one person are needed by many, though the set of services needed may vary among individuals. Therefore, a single SDO can offer an appropriate (i.e., demanded) service to many individuals. Another SDO can offer another demanded service in the same location (though participants might differ slightly). In fact, a set of SDOs would be required to respond to the range of needs in a given community without needing to duplicate the service of other SDOs.

If SDOs are to cooperate, but are presently operating within separate silos, how is this change to come about? Presently in Belize, there is a project that functions this way. It is coordinated by Ministry of Health and involves ten Belizean NGOs and SDOs. UNFPA obtained funds from the Organization for Petroleum Exporting Countries (OPEC) for this effort to achieve HIV/AIDS reduction among Youth in Especially Difficult Circumstances. Before funds were ever discussed, the NGOs, the Ministry of Health, and UNFPA worked together to identify target communities, expected outputs and related activities for the NGOs. They now work on separate activities, each of which has been costed. Thus, there is no need to compete for the attention of UNFPA, OPEC, or of participating youth. On the contrary, the NGO representatives to the Project Steering Committee find themselves sharing information and advice and resources, and are scheduling joint visits to target groups.

The approach recommended here helps link development service provision to activities that promote individual entrepreneurship and savings and loans opportunities among low income individuals. One other element, at least, is necessary and that is advocacy. Advocacy often dies the same quiet death as community projects built on volunteerism and cooperation where trust is low and pockets are empty. The greater one's dependency upon government bureaucrats and representatives, the less sense it makes to advocate for change. And the greater the mistrust of peers who compete for the attention of the same bureaucrats and elected officials, the less sense it makes to abandon those with power for unity with those whose loyalty is questionable (i.e., with peers).

Therefore, advocacy must be built on enduring alliances of low income individuals who lobby for change because they must, not because somebody is trying to convince them that change is morally right. There are examples of individuals who stick with alliances because they are needed. For example, milk producers will opt into a dairy co-operative when they lack other ways to pasteurize their milk and produce other milk products. Otherwise, they cannot put their milk into the market. Because a certain amount of milk is needed to keep the co-operative dairy in operation, milk producers will encourage other dairy farmers to join. Similarly, if dairy farmers require a legislative change for the sake of their business, they will encourage their collective action organization to advocate for the change, and will persist until the change is achieved. Because of the existence of the collective action organization, the dairy farmers will cooperate with other dairy farmers instead of competing; and for the same reason, they will not fall away from advocacy.

These principles need to be applied to the formula for developing a systematic response to the problem of authoritarianism and punitive measures of correction. To help break the bonds of dependency which intensify competitive and anti-social security-deficits among security-seeking caretakers, collective action organizations will be required by those engaged in personal entrepreneurship strategies. Where a number of such entrepreneurs are receiving assistance from SDOs, there is value in making purchase of shares in a collective action organization (CAO) as one of the conditions required of the emerging entrepreneurs. The CAO can then sell needed goods and services to the entrepreneurs at competitive prices. It is the CAO that can carry out the advocacy work desired by its members. In fact, where a number of such CAOs work together, more effective advocacy work becomes possible. Where their members used to beg civil servants and elected officials for favours, they now can negotiate as entrepreneurs—in fact, as entrepreneurs with votes.

Present authoritarian efforts to stifle chaos can be compared to loading rocks onto a boiling pot. In this case, the pot is Belize; its boiling contents, security-seeking citizens; and the rocks, repressive social containment measures. More rocks on the lid—that is, increased repressive measures—will fail to quiet the Belizean pot. On the contrary, they will ensure it boils over. In contrast, the recommendations for systemic change in the UNICEF/CRD report summarised above make several changes: assistance is responsive rather than top-down and its provision is coordinated across agencies. It is designed to facilitate the emergence of sustainable advocacy organizations. And perhaps most importantly, it operates, not on the basis of moral disapprobation of behaviours to which desperate people resort, but rather, to encourage and assist such people's efforts to free themselves from humiliating dependencies, to create a better life for themselves and to allow them to participate in the sustainable development of Belize.

References

ACKERMAN, ROBERT J. & PICKERING, SUSAN E. (1989). From the Alabama Coalition against Domestic Violence. See http://www.acadv.org/children.html.
ALABAMA COALITION AGAINST DOMESTIC VIOLENCE. Retrieved March 2006. See http://www.acadv.org/children.html.
SOCIAL ORDER. (5 February, 2006). *Amandala*, Belize City, Belize.

BARNETT, CARLA. (1991). Aspects of state policy on land distribution and use in the crown colonial period and after. Fourth Annual Studies on Belize Conference. *SPEAReports 7*. Belize City: Society for the Promotion of Education and Research.

BESSANT, JUDITH, HIL, RICHARD, WATTS, ROB, & WEBBER, RUTH. (1999, 17-18 June). *Thinking the problem of youth violence and families*. Paper presented at the Children and Crime: Victims and Offenders Conference convened by the Australian Institute of Criminology and held in Brisbane.

BOLLAND, O. NIGEL. (1977). *The formation of a colonial society: Belize, from conquest to crown colony*. Baltimore, MD: Johns Hopkins University Press.

DURKHEIM, ÉMILE. (1997). *Suicide*. (George Simpson, Trans.). New York: Simon & Schuster. (Original work published in 1897)

FLORES, ALLEN. (March 17, 2002). Is crime rational? *The Reporter*.

MILLER, ERROL. (1991). *Men at Risk*. Kingston: Jamaica Publishing House.

ROSBERG, MICHAEL & JOHNSON, MELVA. (2000). *Preparing for the new millennium: National Human Development Report 1999*. Belize: National Human Development Advisory Committee/UNDP/UNICEF. 2000.

ROSBERG, MICHAEL. (2005a). *Impact of crime & violence on children & adolescents: Responding to the emotional, physical and financial security needs of children and adolescents*. Belize: Community Rehabilitation Department/UNICEF.

ROSBERG, MICHAEL. (2005b). *National poverty elimination strategy & action plan: Outcome of existing poverty reduction measures*. Belize: National Human Development Advisory Committee/Ministry of National Development.

ROSBERG, MICHAEL. (2005c). *The Power of greed: Collective action in international development*. Edmonton: University of Alberta Press.

SHOMAN, ASSAD. (1987). *Party politics in Belize, 1950-1986*. Benque Viejo del Carmen, Belize: Cubola Productions.

UNICEF/CRD (2005). *The impact of crime and violence on children and adolescents*. Belmopan, Belize: Ministry of Human Development/Community Rehabilitation Department.

10. Emigration from Belize since 1981

Jerome Straughan

By September 21st 1981, the day Belize gained its independence from Britain, thousands of Belizeans had already left the country for the United States and to a lesser extent other countries. With hundreds of Belizean men having first emigrated to Panama (where they worked in the Canal Zone) in the early 1940s, Vernon (1990, p. 7) notes that the flow of large numbers of Belizeans to the United States continued during this same time period. During World War II several hundred Belizean men were recruited to work in the United States (to meet labor shortages caused by the war), first in the southern US and later in northern states such as Massachusetts (Ashcraft, 1973, p. 56; Wade, 1986-87; Babcock, 2003).[1] This flow continued throughout the 1950s spurred by unfavorable economic conditions in Belize, which started early in the decade after the 1949 devaluation of the Belizean dollar (Setzekorn, 1981, p. 212) and the pull of a booming American economy.

In the early 1960s there was every indication that sustained emigration would continue, especially because of one event in the history of Belize. In 1961 US emigration picked up pace when Hurricane Hattie devastated the then called British Honduras (namely Belize City) and in its offer of assistance, the US granted refugee status to many Belizeans. Hyde (1995, p. 224) writes that the trickle of Belizeans migrating to the United States in the 1950s broadened

---

[1] Belizeans had been migrating to the United States since the early 20th century, settling mainly in New York and other cities such as Chicago. As a result, even in the early 1920s in New York City, the Honduran Society was formed by a group of Belizeans and their descendants. Led by Austin Panting and Archibald Arnold, they kept alive interest in Belize and its problems (Cited in Donohoe, 1946, p. 56). When Belizean nationalist Antonio Soberanis Gomez visited New York in the 1930s he was hosted by an organized group of Belizeans living in New York/New Jersey. From the early days what characterized the Belizean population in New York/New Jersey was a significant number of middle class, Protestant Creoles from Belize City.

into a movement after the hurricane. Perhaps, the colonial government did not make such an offer of refugee assistance because at that time Britain was in the process of enacting immigration laws to restrict immigration from its colonies.[2] It is also important to note that while Belizean women were emigrating from the 1950s, this gendered emigration picked up pace in the 1960s (into the 1970s) lured by greater employment opportunities for women.[3] And by the 1970s several waves of Belizeans emigrated to the US[4] While a relatively small number migrated to the United States legally, the majority entered the US surreptitiously "tru the back" or overstayed their visitor's visa. Indeed, the country was in the midst of the last significant wave of US emigration when Belize became independent.

The United States was the destination of choice for various reasons. First is the proximity of Belize to the US. Most Belizeans first traveled by sea to the United States on ships that docked at ports such as New Orleans on the Gulf of Mexico. When commercial air travel was inaugurated in the early 1950s, Belizeans, rather than traveling a week by sea, chose to fly, reaching the US in three hours. Of course, air travel was not affordable for many Belizeans and was initially used only by the affluent. More important, by the 1950s more Belizeans were traveling to the US through Mexico; by the end of the 1960s knowledge of Mexican road links greatly helped to increase emigration. Although Belize was a British colony, the country has had long-standing ties—perhaps because of proximity—with the US. Being an English speaking country strengthened such ties. Correspondingly, the US has had a long involvement in the economy of Belize. Indeed by the early 20th century the Belizean economy was increasingly dependent on the United States rather than on Britain (Bolland, 1986, p. 30), and US companies enjoyed considerable influence in local business circles (Grant, 1976). Correspondingly, there has been greater trade between Belize and the US than between Belize and Britain (Moberg, 1996, p. 19; Shoman, 1995, p. 100).

Historical ties between countries tend to reduce cultural barriers and increase the propensity to migrate (Fawcett & Arnold, 1987, p. 462-3). In the case of Belize, by the early 20th century the propensity to emigrate started with US cultural influences largely replacing that of Britain, especially in urban areas (Bolland,

---

[2] The 1962 Commonwealth Immigration Act restricted entrance of Caribbean immigrants into Britain with the exception of dependents of those colonials already in the United Kingdom.

[3] Creole and Garifuna women were far more likely to migrate on their own than Mestizo-Maya women. This had a lot to do with cultural differences. In turn, many of these Black Belizean women facilitated the emigration of relatives and friends.

[4] By the mid-1970s, according to the US State Department, the number of Belizean migrants in the United States was approximately equal to the remaining working population in Belize (Pastor, 1985, p. 19).

1986).[5] This initially occurred through religious institutions whose influence (via Belize's church-state system of education) extended to Belizean educational institutions through textbooks and teachers. Correspondingly, there has been an expansion of information about North America, specifically the USA. Since the 1960s, this has occurred particularly through the US mass media—in the form of television, radio, movies, music, magazines, and newspapers—and the dissemination of commercial products. In the case of TV, 1981 was the year when Belize gained access to American programming. Belizeans also learned more about the United States through Belizeans living there. Most received a favorable impression of the country when they received letters that often contained money or packages (or barrels) filled with an array of consumer goods ranging from clothes to electronic products.[6] The stories returning Belizeans told added to the lure of America. Thus, English-speaking Belizeans have been significantly influenced culturally by the United States, and this has resulted in many becoming more Americanized. These factors increased the propensity for Belizeans to migrate, especially those from urban areas (Belize City and district towns) where US influences were greatest.

Most important, Belizeans were migrating in search of a better life. By the late 1960s, Belize recovered from Hurricane Hattie and the economy of Belize had improved. But economically macro-level push and pull factors still spurred the emigration of Belizeans, namely to the United States. By the early 1970s the export of agricultural and marine products was playing a greater role in the economy. But in terms of push factors Belizeans emigrated because economic conditions in the country still resulted in high unemployment, underemployment, and low wages (Shoman, 1995, p. 295). In turn, there has been a general lack of reasonable prospects for mobility, even for many with jobs.[7] This was es-

---

[5] Everitt (1984, p. 319) states that in addition to the migration for better employment opportunities, the massive movement of Belizeans to the United States was as a result of a long distance acculturation process that drew Belizeans to the "promised land" of North America. Furthermore, where cultural factors and the emigration of Belizeans to the United States are concerned, while Shoman (1995, p. 120) refers to the cultural penetration of Belize by the United States, Vernon (1990) goes a step further in noting that cultural (and psychological) dependency were non-economic factors in the emigration of Belizeans.

[6] Vernon (1992, p. 46) notes that the emigration of so many Belizeans increased contact with US culture and society and consequently created greater preferences locally for US fashion, music, and consumer products.

[7] In his study of the Garifuna in Los Angeles, J. Palacio (1992) discovered that the catalyst for emigration was "self-improvement." Similarly, M. Palacio (2002) found in a study of the Garifuna in Dangriga that respondents saw the US as providing better opportunities for five reasons: improvement of living standards, the expansion of one's horizons, opportunities for self-improvement, ease of acceptance, and jobs that were readily available.

pecially true for urban areas, where emigration originated.[8] Correspondingly, they migrated to the US because of better employment (and business) opportunities, higher wages, and a chance to advance occupationally. Belizeans also saw the United States as a place where they could not only broaden their horizons, but further their education and/or learn new skills.[9] Lastly, the information Belizeans received from the US media and Belizeans in the United States portrayed an attractive lifestyle, with a consumer culture based on a higher living standard. Thus when Belizeans in the US sent money, packages, or returned to Belize with glowing stories of life "dah states" and seemed materially successful, these stories and images provided ample "evidence" about the US living standard and comparative opportunities. But it is important to note that Belizeans were not emigrating solely for economic reasons. Economic motives often coalesced with other motives. Over time Belizeans' decision to migrate tended to become somewhat disconnected from economic conditions in Belize and determined more by other factors.[10]

So many Belizeans were in the United States before the 1980s that in the post-independence emigration of Belizeans, social factors were just as important as economic factors. Push and pull factors might have helped to set the stage for US-bound migration. But by the early 1980s Belizeans were to a greater extent emigrating within a social context. Even before the 1980s many Belizeans, especially from urban areas, had relatives, friends, or acquaintances in the United States. Indeed, many Belizeans had close relatives in the United States, especially middle class Belizeans. This was especially true for urban Creoles (and Garifuna) who had a longer history of labor migration (Brockmann, 1985, p. 201).[11] As a result, some Belizeans emigrated to the US to join family members. Others who wished to migrate could rely on relatives or friends in the US to facilitate their travel and settlement. This resulted in the self-perpetuating process of

---

[8] Of the few jobs that were available in the urban areas, especially until the early 1970s, government was the chief employer (in the civil service, teaching, nursing, etc.) followed by a few commercial establishments. Others created their own jobs or worked at odd or irregular jobs.

[9] In his review of the educational system in Belize during the 1980s Bolland (1986, p. 50) wrote that there was a paucity of opportunity for training in professional and technical skills in the country, which bodes ill for the development of the country.

[10] Barry (1995, p. 125) notes that Belize's alarmingly high rate of emigration cannot be explained entirely by economic factors. And for Vernon (1990, p. 12) economic considerations were fundamentally necessary but not sufficient for a comprehensive understanding of the forces that induced the Belizean exodus to the United States.

[11] Writing about Garifuna emigration, Palacio (2002, p. 14) is critical of the literature on Belizeans emigrating to the US. She notes that scholars such as Young (1990) focus mainly on the involvement of Creoles in this emigration, which they see as commencing around the early 1960s. She claims that Garifuna emigration was earlier and documents this emigration from the mid-1940s, through the 1950s, and into the 1960s.

chain migration, based on social networks, which made emigration more pervasive.[12] Also this social aspect of migration helped to determine which Belizeans migrated (especially in terms of ethnicity and residence in Belize) and when.

Thus US bound migration was institutionalized long before independence, and a culture of emigration had developed with a "migration ethos." Correspondingly, Belizeans still had "states feva," in terms of their desire to migrate and be part of the American experience.[13] Migration became normative for many to the point that going to "States" ceased to be an exceptional affair and became the "proper thing to do." Emigration became a rite of passage, especially for youths. Furthermore, although some Belizeans were more likely to migrate over others, migratory behavior spread outward to encompass broader segments of Belizean society. The teacher, civil servant, policeman, nurse, and secretary were just as likely to migrate as school-leaving youths, the unemployed, and laborers. By this time when Belizeans became more savvy about traveling to the US, working class Belizeans were as likely to migrate as middle class Belizeans.[14] Hence, one of the first significant waves of Belizeans migrating to the US occurred before Belize gained its independence.

When Belize became independent, many Belizeans in the United States were undocumented. Some left Belize when the country was still British Honduras, and for those who were granted a nonimmigrant visa to travel to the United States, they traveled with colonial passports indicating that they were British subjects. Many had obtained a visa because with migration at a fever pitch they became savvy about how to obtain a visa. Visa in hand, most bought a plane ticket to travel on TACA, TAN, SASHA, or BAL airlines and entered the US through New Orleans or Miami. They then flew to destinations such as New York, Chicago, and Los Angeles, and many overstayed their visa and became undocumented. For Belizeans who didn't have that option, emigrating "tru di back" was an easier and affordable way of reaching the United States. By road they traveled to Tijuana and other Mexican border cities and surreptitiously entered the United States. Some Creole and Garifuna Belizeans might have had a

---

[12] Chain migration can be defined as that movement in which prospective migrants learn of opportunities, are provided with transportation, and have initial accommodation and employment arrangements by means of primary social relationships with previous migrants (MacDonald & MacDonald, 1964). Correspondingly, Portes and Rumbaut (1996, p. 276) note that very often social networks have a tendency to acquire sufficient strength to induce migration for motives other than those that initiated the flow.

[13] Some Belizeans emigrated out of curiosity and with a sense of adventure. The big cities' bright lights beckoned and they wanted to see what it was like in America.

[14] It was middle-class Belizeans and Belizeans experiencing upward economic mobility who initially dominated in the US movement. This was especially true for Belizeans who emigrated legally to the United States. As stated, the middle class status of many Belizeans also made it possible for them to obtain US visas.

more difficult time traveling through Mexico than Mestizos (because of their physical features), but once at the border it was easier for them to enter the United States than Mestizos because of the association of "looking Latino" with illegality and the resemblance of Creoles and Garifuna to Afro-Americans.

Family reunification and labor certification provision of the 1965 Immigration Act made it possible for some undocumented Belizeans to adjust their status (become permanent residents). One "green card" route was marriage or being sponsored by a family member who was a US resident or citizen. By being employed as domestics, nurses or in other occupations certified for legal entry, few Belizeans (but many Caribbean folk) were able to take advantage of the occupational preference quota.[15] Lastly, through service in the US military, especially during the period of the Vietnam War, some Belizeans were also able to regularize their status (an expedited route to US citizenship). But for some of the undocumented wanting to adjust their status through the preference system, the fact that Belize was a colony meant that only a limited number of Belizeans were granted these visas because the Belizean quota for US immigrant visas was tied to a British quota. Nevertheless, even before 1982 legal migration to the US was increasing as the greater number of Belizean permanent residents (or US citizens) filed for family members. As for naturalization, when Belize gained its independence a limited number of Belizeans had become US citizens. (Belizean citizenship was not automatically granted to these Belizeans and politics was a factor in this decision).

By independence there were also Belizeans in Britain, and to a lesser extent in Canada. The case of Belizeans migrating to Britain is unlike that of other English speaking Caribbean countries. Before the first wave of Caribbean folks arrived in that country, a significant number of Belizeans were already in Britain. Like other Caribbeans, most went to Britain to support the war effort (World War II). Most were recruited by the colonial administration to do forestry related work in Scotland; and while some joined the British armed forces (or served in a Women's Auxiliary Corps), others worked in other aspects of the war such as Home Defense in different parts of the country (Donohoe, 1946, p. 16; Setzekorn, 1981, p. 211; Ford, 1985; Moberg, 1992, p. 149). After the war many chose to demobilize in Britain. But this did not mark the beginning of significant Belizean emigration to Britain, as several scholars note about Caribbean migration to Britain (Davidson, 1962; Peach, 1968). With most of these men marrying local women and starting families in the UK, it seems that many severed or had limited ties with Belize. As a result, there was hardly a process of

---

[15] Because of a combination of these routes, by 1968 females accounted for 58% of legal immigration from Belize, and they have consistently represented more than 50% of the legal flow until the early 1990s (Immigration and Naturalization Service statistics as documented by Vernon, 1990).

chain migration, whereby these men would have facilitated the migration of other Belizeans. Along with social factors, the failure of significant emigration to Britain can also be attributed to (1) a lack of information about employment opportunities in that country, (2) how Caribbean labor was recruited (and assisted) to work in British public services and industries (Davidson, 1962, 1966; Brooks, 1975; Foner 1978, Thompson, 1990; Gmelch, 1992; Western, 1992; James & Harris, 1993; Byron, 1994), and (3) overall how accessible and affordable this trans-Atlantic travel by ship was for Belizeans (see Davidson, 1962; LePage & Tabouret-Keller, 1985; Western, 1992).

In the 1950s when British immigration laws were less restrictive, Belizeans did not migrate to that country at the same rate as did Jamaicans and other Caribbeans. But some Belizeans (most educated and/or middle class) did go to Britain, many via other Caribbean countries. This resulted in a steady trickle of Belizeans emigrating to Britain, even after Britain enacted restrictive immigration laws. (Some were once students in Britain, others dependents, and a few were families). The British military presence in Belize was a significant factor in some Belizeans emigrating to Britain. With Guatemala pressing its territorial claim to Belize (and threatening invasion in the 1970s), Britain provided for the defense of Belize by stationing troops in the country. This led to unions between Belizean women and British soldiers, and many of these women (and their children) eventually went to Britain. A trickle of Belizeans, unrelated to British armed forces, continued to migrate to the UK as well.

In the case of Canada, few Belizeans took advantage of liberal Canadian immigration laws (and Commonwealth connections) enacted in the 1960s to migrate to that country. This contrasted with Caribbean migration to Canada. But some Belizeans did migrate to Canada, and again education and class were factors, especially when immigration legislation (based on a point system) gave preference to immigrants according to their human capital and based on the labor demands of Canada. Consequently, while few Belizeans went earlier to Canada to do domestic work, a greater number who emigrated were professionals (namely teachers and nurses), many having been students in that country.[16] Regionally, Belizeans were also in Mexico, Central America, and the Caribbean (namely Cayman and to a lesser extent in Jamaica). This regional emigration started around World War II. When news of job opportunities in the Panama Canal zone began to surface, hundreds of Belizean men migrated to that country to seek employment (Donohoe, 1946, p. 15, 53; Setzekorn, 1975, p. 211). On their return to Belize, some went on to the US. In the 1950s

---

[16] Between 1956 and 1966 there seem to have been some movement of domestics from British Honduras to Canada (Records on the Immigration of Domestics Canada archives RG 76, Vol. 838, file 553-36-563). Caribbean women who were willing to do domestic work were offered some of the few jobs available to landed immigrant status in Canada.

Belizeans also found work in Guatemala and Honduras, especially in port towns of costal areas, where US companies had their shipping operations, for bananas (See Palacio 1992, p. 12).[17] Belizeans had a most favorable reception in Guatemala, which claimed Belize as its 23rd department. (Several stories on this period ran in the *Amandala* newspaper). But by the late 1960s, fewer Belizeans were migrating to these countries, which differed from the pattern of interregional migration (Hamilton & Chinchilla, 1991; Repak, 1995; Mahler, 2006).

Migration at independence

Politics and political discontent have never been the most significant or direct factors in the emigration of Belizeans, but some Belizeans did experience anxieties over independence and chose to leave the country.[18] Independence came with the People's United Party (PUP), who had governed the country for 27 years. It could be argued that even before independence, when the opposition parties–the National Independence Party (NIP) followed by the United Democratic Party (UDP)–were unable to win national elections, some Belizeans emigrated disillusioned over the political fortunes of the opposition, as well as uncertainty over the future.[19] It is the view of Young (1994) that the exodus of Belizeans to the US was also for political reasons, in particular Creoles refused to participate in the perceived Mayanization/Latinization in Belize's nation-build-

---

[17] Their employment for US companies reflected the tendency of these companies to employ a largely West Indian workforce (Purcell, 1993). In the 1940s Central American countries imposed restrictions on West Indian immigration and curtailed the civil rights and movements of existing Afro-Caribbean populations within their borders (Echeverri-Gent, 1992). And after the 1950s West Indian workers were replaced in many jobs by Ladinos, many of whom were newcomers to the once inaccessible eastern coast of Central America (Purcell, 1993).

[18] The migration of many Belizeans in the 1960s, 1970s, and 1980s may have even been in part prompted by political factors; many Belizeans may simply have "voted with their feet." In combination with other factors, many supporters of the then-opposition UDP migrated after being disillusioned because the opposition was unable to win general elections in 1969, 1974, and 1979. Also as it relates to political factors, many Belizeans thought the government of the day was not enacting economic (and educational) policies that would significantly raise the living standards of Belizeans and fulfill their expectations and aspirations. Instead many accused the government of being so focused on independence that they neglected to develop the country.

[19] Ueda (1994) states that in terms of the globalization of migration uncertainty over the future determined in many countries how people reacted to push and pull forces. "Often it was the prospect of economic decline–the perception of a future gap between possibility and capability–that precipitated a decision to move" (p. 53).

261

ing by the PUP government. (This resulted in a greater number of Belizeans in the US being NIP and then UDP supporters).

The country's independence coincided with a mass exodus of Belizeans to the United States in at least two waves.[20] These migration waves of the late 1970 and mid-1980s represented the last significant wave of Belizeans emigrating to the US By this time more Belizeans had relatives and friends there, and an expansion in social networks facilitated this migration. As a result, US-bound migration came from more diverse points of origin in Belize and coincided with these migration waves. Not only were immigrants coming from Belize City and Dangriga, but also from other areas. And along with Creoles and Garifuna, US emigration from the late 1970s and continuing through the 1980s saw Belizeans from other ethnic groups, namely Mestizos, migrating in significant numbers. By the 1980s Belizean women also outnumbered male immigrants (Barry, 1995, p. 126). Vernon (1992) notes that "the 20,000-30,000 Belizeans who emigrated to the US during the 1980s did so not only to pursue better employment opportunities, higher wages, and the greater availability of housing, health care and education, but also to send money back home for dependents" (p. 46).

Belize became an independent country in less than prosperous times. Almost immediately after independence, Belize experienced an economic crisis as a result of global economic forces and certain policies of the Belizean government that increased the country's debt. This further propelled Belizean migration to the United States, which was already a constant migration stream. Barry (1995, p. 39) notes that economically, independence came at a bad time for Belize as high oil prices, low sugar prices, and a recessionary world market pushed the country to the edge of bankruptcy as foreign exchange reserves dried up and the government's budget deficit widened. The areas hardest hit by this economic crisis were the districts of Corozal and Orange Walk where the sugar industry is located. Low world prices pushed the industry into a slump in the early 1980s, which then led to layoffs and economically had a spiraling effect. As a result, many Belizeans from the northern districts migrated to the United States in the wake of a slumping economy, and the number of Mestizos migrating to the US significantly increased.[21]

---

[20] Almost 50% of Belizeans in the United States entered after 1980. In the early 80s Bolland (1986, p. 95) notes that one percent of the population of Belize per year migrated to the United States. And by 1985 Vernon (1990, pp. 8-9, 12) calculates that Belizean immigrants in the US represented 35 to 40% of Belize's population. Woods, Perry, and Steagall (1994, p. 17) calculate that during the 1980-1991 period alone, some 41,400 Belizeans appear to have emigrated and that about 34,000-35,000 went to the United States.

[21] See Crucita Ken's essay in this volume for a full description of the two northern districts.

This economic crisis helped usher in a new government in 1984, when for the first time the UDP was victorious in general elections. This was also three years after the PUP triumphantly led Belize to independence. However, even a change of government and a subsequent improvement in the Belizean economy could not stem the tide of Belizeans migrating to the United States. Emigration continued into the late 1980s because even though the economy improved with the UDP administration, much of the steady economic growth, which was a result of foreign investments, benefited investors more than a large number of Belizeans (Barry, 1995, p. 40).[22] Correspondingly, there were continued high unemployment rates, declining government services, and frustration with high indirect taxes. Many felt that these factors contributed in 1989 to a narrow PUP election victory over the one term UDP.

Independence also marked an increase in US influences in Belize.[23] Perhaps the most significant of US influences was television. The early 1980s saw the arrival of American TV in Belize via satellite technology.[24] With the arrival of TV, Belize became saturated with US TV programming. As a result, watching TV quickly became the favorite national pastime (Barry, 1995). For Snyder, Roser, and Chaffee (1991), apart from changing consumer preference, the US media also contributed to Belizeans' desire to emigrate.

Accompanying the arrival of US television was an even greater US presence and involvement in Belize (Bolland, 1986, p. 60; Barry, 1995, p. 125).[25] This

---

[22] Barry (1995, p. 97) also notes that that despite steady economic growth since the mid-1980s, unemployment and underemployment persist in Belize.

[23] Vernon (1992, p. 40) writes, "As much as independence was symbolic of the waning of British influence, it marked the intensification of US influence in economic and political decision making and made a mockery of the greater degrees of self-determination that independence was promised to bring." He went on to note that since independence the US influence grew tremendously, and it made its mark felt on all aspects of Belizean society. Indeed, most foreign investors and most land speculators have been US citizens (Vernon, 1992, p. 46).

[24] No one had earlier invested in a TV station because Belize was considered too small an audience to warrant it (Lent, 1989, p. 19). So prior to this time, Belizeans in the northern and Western part of the country were able to get TV reception from Mexico, and Guatemala (Oliveria, 1985 & 1986). Perhaps because TV reception was so poor in Belize City, few Belizeans in the city had television sets. However, by the late 1970s the affordability of VCRs made it possible for many Belizeans to watch delayed American programming. Eventually, the setting up of a television earth station in 1981, made it possible to receive US programming through the pirating of satellite signals.

[25] The growing US influences on Belize were increasingly visible, particularly in the number of religious groups, the increase in consumer goods, and the proliferation of media products (Bolland, 1986, p. 60). In turn, a study of 342 young Belizeans indicated that those who had information about the US were more likely to want to emigrate (Roser, Synder, & Chaffee, 1986).

presence came in the form of growing US economic influence with the further expansion of trade and investment in Belize. It was also during the 1980s that the US government targeted the Caribbean and Central America as areas for major investment and political concern (the threat of socialism/communism in the region). As a result, Belize was a recipient of this concern and US business interests were promoted in the country. In addition to being Belize's principal trading partner and the main source of investment, the US became the largest provider of economic assistance to the country through the USAID program, which poured money into the economy and infrastructure (Sutherland, 1998, p. 61). Lastly, an expansion in tourism brought an increase in US influences with more Americans visiting the country.

By the mid-1980s it was estimated that one-fourth of all persons born in Belize resided in the United States (Pastor, 1985, p. 19). In terms of the legal status of Belizeans in the US, the 1980s were significant in two ways. For Belizeans wishing to migrate legally and undocumented Belizeans hoping to adjust their status, independence meant a larger country quota, as the Belizean quota was no longer tied to the British quota. Starting in 1982 statistics from the US Immigration and Naturalization Service (INS) showed an increase in the numbers of Belizeans legally admitted to the United States for permanent residency. But without family members who were legal residents or US citizens, which meant having greater preference in the family reunification provision of the US law, many Belizeans did not immediately benefit from an increase in the quota. Belizeans also had a low naturalization rate, which would have made non-quota immigration possible. Consequently, in 1984 the United States Embassy in Belize estimated that two out of three Belizeans in the US were living in the US illegally.

The mid-1980s also marked the passage (in 1986) of the Immigration Reform and Control Act (IRCA) by the US Congress. In her research on Mexican undocumented migration, Hondagneu-Sotelo (1994) indicates that the IRCA "had a more profound impact on undocumented immigrants than any other piece of legislation ever passed in the United States" (p. xiv).[26] Many undocumented Belizeans were able to legalize their status through the legalization provisions of the act often known as "Amnesty."[27] In turn, IRCA reduced the number of undocumented Belizeans in the US. But despite the increasing number of

---

[26] IRCA legalized a large portion of undocumented immigrants already established in the United States, and a portion of the undocumented who had worked in US agriculture. There were two legalization programs: the Special Agricultural Worker (SAW) plan and a more general amnesty. Amnesty required continuous "illegal" residence in the US prior to January 1982 as the major eligibility criterion, and SAW required applicants to have worked a minimum of ninety days in US agriculture between May 1985 and May 1986.

Belizeans who were able to become legal US residents, a significant number of Belizeans remained undocumented by the end of the 1980s.[28] This varied by ethnicity.[29]

During the 1980s Belizeans also migrated to other countries, but not in the volume as US-bound emigration. In 1975, when the Netherlands granted independence to Suriname, similar to other colonial countries, it granted Dutch citizenship to Surinamese who resided in the Netherlands at independence. Prior to independence, Belizeans carried British passports and as "colonial subjects" had the right to reside in their "mother country." But after the massive immigration in the late 1950s and early 1960s from former colonies such as the West Indies, Britain tightened its migration laws, thus affecting Belizeans' ability to easily re-locate there.[30] Some Belizeans did go to Britain in the 1980s. When Belize became independent, a pre-independence defense arrangement with Britain remained in place. This led to more unions between British servicemen and local women. These women were often from other areas of Belize such as Cayo and Toledo where British troops were stationed. This meant that some of the women were of Mestizo descent.

Because of Commonwealth connections, Canada had a greater presence in Belize, largely in terms of governmental assistance and tourism. This presence

---

[27] From 1988 until around 1992, much of the significant increases in the number of Belizeans granted US permanent residency came as a result of IRCA legalization. The data shows that of the 6,252 applicants to the IRCA program (not counting 450 Belizeans from the 1972 registry provisions of the program), 2,630 were Belizeans who overstayed their visas and 3,490 were Belizeans who entered the US prior to 1/1/82. 132 Belizeans applied under provisions of the agricultural worker program (SAW). But some undocumented Belizeans didn't take advantage of amnesty.

[28] Many of the undocumented arrived after the cut off date for legalization (Jan. 1, 1982). Incidentally, data from the Amnesty program indicated that until 1982 for every Belizean visa overstayer, two Belizeans entered the United States surreptitiously by crossing the US border. In 1990 Vernon stated that two-thirds of Belizean immigrants were in the United States illegally, but this estimate was too high for that time, considering the various routes that Belizeans took since the early 1980s to adjust their status.

[29] Anecdotal information suggests that based on time of arrival, access to information and legal assistance, class background, and rates of citizenship undocumented Belizeans vary according to ethnicity. As a result, Mestizos are more likely to be undocumented than Garifunas, with Creoles somewhere between the two groups. This reflects the higher naturalization rate of the Garifuna, partially as a result of military service, and for Matthei and Smith (1996) how visa savvy this group is in terms of "getting straight" (becoming legal).

[30] With passage of the last restrictive British immigration law under the Thatcher government Belizeans had even less of a right to reside in Britain. Belize was the largest of the remaining British possessions, but the smaller colonies such as Montserrat, Cayman Islands, and Bermuda had that right. After the volcano erupted in Montserrat is a good example.

led to the migration of more Belizeans to Canada, in particular the Toronto area. Commonwealth connections also led some Belizeans to emigrate to the Cayman Islands. Like Belizean immigrants before them, starting in the 1970s, many were recruited for government jobs. Lastly, as tourism grew in Cancun (and other areas in southern Mexico), a few Belizeans, especially from the northern districts, went there and were able to put their bilingual skills to good use in the tourist industry. In the early 1980s migration to Cancun was exacerbated in the northern districts by their economic crisis, which was caused by falling sugar prices. In the 1980s this was one of several places Belizean were seeking jobs. But the numbers were not large.

Migration in the 1990s

During the 1990s Belizeans continued to migrate to the United States. But by the mid-1990s there was statistical and anecdotal evidence that legal and illegal emigration had declined.[31] Several factors accounted for this decline. Socially, it would seem that by the mid-1990s Belizeans who wished to migrate had already done so. Consequently, some Belizean families were reconstituted in the US. Others who could migrate opted to stay in Belize for various reasons. As the number of Belizean families that emigrated increased and the length of the time that they resided in the US also increased, the ties between Belizeans in the US and in Belize weakened, and in some cases were even severed. Also fewer new networks were formed that could facilitate migration. Overall, for some Belizeans contemplating the move, there were fewer compelling reasons to emigrate (education still being an exception).

Economic factors also weighed in and contributed to a decline in Belizean migration. Many perceived that they might experience greater difficulty in finding employment or employment commensurate with their education and skills. In the last two decades wages in Belize also improved, and many Belizeans experienced some degree of economic mobility.[32] As a result, emigration became less attractive; some Belizeans became concerned that they might experience downward mobility and a demotion in social status (status inconsistency) if they emigrated. Many were concerned that they would never be able to

---

[31] Mahler and Ugrina (2006, p. 4) note that since the early 1990s, 84% of Belizean who emigrated left for the United States. But during the 1990s the yearly rate of Belizean emigration fell by nearly a third to a total of 2,181 per year, down from an average of 3,050 in the 1980s. Correspondingly, statistics of US legal immigration rates from Belize indicate a significant decline from the 1980s to the 1990 in the number of Belizeans granted legal permanent residency (see Yearbook of Immigration Statistics, Department of Homeland Security).

recapture the standard of living they had in Belize, especially since many were able to replicate US consumption patterns and living standards in Belize. Changes in US immigration laws and tighter immigration controls (including enforcement) also dissuaded some Belizeans from migrating, or made it more difficult for many to migrate. Thus, some potential migrants chose to not risk an uncertain future in America. Lastly, there was a reduction in the migration ethos that took hold of Belize. As a result, migration was not at the fever pitch that it once was.

However, other Belizeans continued to emigrate to the United States to seek work, to further their education, and to reunite with family. They also went to the US for the American experience. Indeed, in response to Emory King's rosy portrayal of Belize in his book *I Spent It All in Belize*, the author of *Inside Belize* stated in the mid 90s:

> For some, Belize does have all the lure of a tropical island, but life is not all paradise for all Belizeans, and the King vision is not shared by all. Large numbers of them in fact leave for the United States to escape high unemployment, dead-end jobs, and empty futures. (Barry 1995, p. xvi)

As a result the United States was still attractive to some educated Belizeans (without good stable jobs) and to poorer and less privileged Belizeans.[33] But supporting systems in the US did not exist as they once did. Nevertheless, by the late 1990s there was some indication that emigration had picked up. This emigration was not very noticeable because it didn't occur in waves, and because Belizeans had become more dispersed through the United States and less concentrated in some areas.

Through the 1990s, many Belizeans in the United States remained undocumented. Life got a little harder for these immigrants with the passage in 1990 of stricter immigration laws and in 1996 more restrictive laws (after the Republican takeover in 1994 of the US Congress). For instance, changes in the rules

---

[32] From the mid-1970s to early 1980s, teachers and government workers made up a significant portion of Belizeans emigrating to the United States. But as wages for these workers improved and there were greater avenues for mobility, many chose to stay in Belize. Furthermore, although members of the Belizean middle class might earn significantly lower wages than their American counterparts, they gained more in social and other fringe benefits (such as access to greater opportunities to affordable housing far superior to that which can be afforded in the US), making migration less attractive.

[33] Thus, Mahler and Ugrina (2006, p. 4) suggest that although the emigration rate of Belize had fallen, more educated Belizeans were still leaving. They note that in a Belizean census report half of emigrants held high school degrees while the percentage with post-high school education rose 64% above the rate recorded in 1991. (It should be noted that while a greater percentage of Belizeans now have a high school education, education at the tertiary level is still low.)

on how family members were sponsored made it difficult for some to adjust their residency status. It also became more difficult for the undocumented to obtain "alternative documentation" (such as a social security card and drivers license). Belizeans who were legal residents were also affected by the passage of new legislation. Until the 1980s the rate at which Belizeans became naturalized US citizens was relatively low. This changed in the mid-1990s when more Belizeans acquired US citizenship. (The naturalization rate increased in the mid-1990s and then declined in the early 2000s). Some were Belizeans who were granted amnesty almost a decade earlier. A few also became citizens because of fears concerning changes in US immigration and social welfare laws. By the 1990s there was also an effort at stepping up the deportation of immigrants who committed crimes in the US. This resulted in many Belizeans being sent back to Belize.

In the 1990s Belizeans continued to migrate to other countries as well. Because Belize was gaining more international exposure and becoming a tourist destination, Belizeans were more in contact with nationals from countries other than the United States. Nationals from other countries were also residing in Belize. And as Belizeans emigrated to a greater number of countries, the chain migration process followed. Some Belizeans, in particular Mestizos, emigrated to other Central American countries, such as Costa Rica, where the economy had improved.[34]

Emigration in a new century: 2000 and beyond

Six years into a new century, many Belizeans continue to emigrate to the United States and increasingly to other countries.[35] But there are questions about the extent to which they will continue to emigrate. There has been an ebb and flow of this emigration, but it will continue because of economic as well as social factors. Furthermore, Belize still cannot fulfill the raising aspirations, expectations, and goals of many would-be-migrants. One doesn't have to search too hard in Belize for anecdotal stories of Belizeans who recently arrived or migrated in the last five years. More concretely, while the number of Belizeans applying for the US immigration lottery indicates the desire of many Belizeans to emigrate, statis-

---

[34] Writing about regional migration to and from Belize Mahler and Ugrina (2006, p. 4) note that during the early 1990s five percent of Belizeans who emigrated moved to other Central American countries. This was slightly higher than in the past.

[35] Barry (1995) writes, "There is no reason to believe that emigration to the US will not continue to be a distinguishing feature of Belizean life" (p. 126). He also notes that even in the best of times Belize cannot offer its young women and men the kind of wage, educational, and vocational opportunities available in the United States (Barry, 1995, p. 125).

tics on the number of Belizeans granted permanent residency indicate that Belizeans are still migrating in significant numbers. Of course this does not take into consideration the undocumented. Despite difficulties in acquiring alternative documentation and stricter enforcement of US immigration laws (especially since 9/11), many still choose to reside in the United States illegally.

Certain features distinguish Belizeans who wish to, and those who do, emigrate. America still appeals to younger Belizeans, and many have the urge to emigrate. Some are recent school leavers who find it difficult to obtain employment. Although Belize now has a lot of what these young people want in America (in terms of consumer goods), many are still lured by the experience (and excitement) of living in America. Older Belizeans are primarily seeking employment opportunities. Even if they hear that America "is not like it once was," they are willing to gamble since many have little to lose. With little hope of obtaining a US visa—because they are un- or underemployed—some still contemplate going to the US "tru di back." Reuniting with family is also a desire of many of these Belizeans who would like to emigrate, and in many instances obtaining an immigrant visa is also out of their reach.

In contrast, other Belizeans have little or no desire to emigrate because they have a career or a stable job, some with good wages and benefits. They are not willing to, as Belizeans would say in Creole, "let guh di the bone fi di shadow." Many know that America now has a tighter labor market and that even if they get jobs, it might not be commensurate with their education and skills. For the US Embassy, these people are prime candidates for visitors' visas, and for most in this group becoming undocumented in the US is no longer acceptable. Since the late 1980s, they and other Belizeans (who are able to obtain US visas) are choosing to just visit the United States, primarily to spend time with relatives and friends. With many Belizeans getting a month's vacation, some make regular visits. But it should be noted that although many of these people have secure jobs, Belize is not in the best of economic times.

When the PUP won by a landslide in the 1998 general election, it promised to abolish the value added tax of the UDP administration. And with its agenda of growth economics, the PUP administration also promised to make possible greater prosperity (jobs and housing). Since those early heady days the PUP administration has been plagued by a series of scandals and financial crisis because of corruption, mismanagement, and waste. These actions have contributed to an upward spiral in Belize's external debt of over one billion dollars. Despite this, growth in tourism has made it Belize's number one industry. A few other businesses and industries have also experienced growth (or been revived), and in 2006 the discovery of oil in Belize led to it being exported. But most Belizeans have yet to see the benefits of tourism, much less oil; and in this economic climate many Belizeans compete for jobs with Central American immigrants. Beyond construction, agriculture, and other sectors of the economy, the immigrants

are a preferable source of labor (cheaper and more compliant) for employers, especially those who engage in selective hiring practices. This has contributed to a general lack of employment opportunities and an exodus of Belizeans from certain industries, for example banana (Moberg, 1996), because they refuse to work for
lower wages. And to add to the economic woes of Belizeans, government recently
instituted a General Service Tax (similar to the VAT) to help service its debts.

While Central Americans, Chinese, and other immigrants flock to Belize,
this economic climate has created conditions for Belizeans to emigrate. In Belize
Central Americans seek employment opportunities and higher wages they
would otherwise not earn in their home country. Similarly, Chinese immigrants
seek out opportunities to start businesses and have been successful in doing so.
The case is similar for Indian immigrants. Then there are immigrants from the
United States and few from Europe who are in various business activities, namely tourism and real estate. In this economic climate some Belizeans are getting
rich or have become wealthy, a few because of government connections. Others
are economically doing well. But many Belizeans are economically marginalized,
especially those with little human capital. "Things haard out yah" is the Creole
refrain some Belizeans are saying to convey the general mood about economic
conditions in the country. (Some have also resorted to saying "nuttin nuh deh
dah Belize") (Central Statistical Office, 2004).[36]

Belizeans in the United States

Estimates of the number of Belizeans in the United States have varied, and
there is no way of knowing the exact population figures. As a result, there have
often been wild estimates about the number of Belizeans in the US. Vernon
(1990, p. 7) noted that the poor state of data collection concerning the migration and settlement of Belizeans in the United States is one reason why it's difficult to estimate the number of Belizeans in the US. It is also difficult to make an
estimate because of the significant (and unknown) number of undocumented
Belizeans in the US. A reasonable estimate is that there are between 110,000 and
120,000 Belizeans in the United States, including US raised children (about
30% of the Belizean-American population is native born).[37]

Largely as a result of chain migration Belizeans in the United States are still
concentrated in a few states and metropolitan areas. Until the late 1970s New

---

[36] The CSO report indicates that 33.5% of Belizeans live below the poverty line; 10.8%
live below the indigent line. The rates vary by district: Toledo has the highest percentage
of its population who are poor-79%; Orange Walk has 34.9%; Stann Creek has 34.8%;
Cayo has 27.4%; and Belize has the lowest at 24.8% (p. 39). See the full report at
http://www.cso.gov.bz/publications/poverty_asses_rep2002.pdf.

York followed by Chicago was the home for the largest concentration of Belizeans in the US, and these populations reflected the early years of Belizean migration to the United States (Babcock, 2003 & 2006; Cornebise, 2005; and Morrissey, 2005 have written about Belizeans in Chicago). Indeed, pioneering Belizeans settled in places such as New York as early as World War I. In terms of characteristics, the New York population included a significant number of middle class Belizeans from the City, while the Chicago population included a significant number of rural Belizeans from villages in the Belize District such as Crooked Tree. Greater Los Angeles now has the largest concentration of Belizeans outside of Belize. With over 45% of the Belizean population in the US, estimates of the number of Belizeans in greater Los Angeles range from 50,000 to as high as 55,000. A significant number of Belizeans also reside in metropolitan areas such as Miami (southern Florida), New Orleans (until the hurricane), and Houston. Belizeans are becoming more dispersed as they seek employment opportunities and affordable housing in others areas of the US (Arnold, 1988; Lemmel, 2001; and Straughan, 1992 & 2004 have written about Belizeans in Los Angeles).

The increasingly diverse Belizean population in the United States represents virtually every sector of Belizean society. Although Belize City has been the main provider of immigrants, Belizeans in the United States have come from nearly every village and town. But Belizeans from urban areas, namely Belize City south side, predominate. Women seem to slightly outnumber men in the Belizean immigrant population. This population is also characterized by the significant presence of entire families. The intent of most of these families is to remain in the United States instead of being sojourners.

The diversity of Belizeans in the United States somewhat mirrors the diversity of ethnic groups in Belize. Creoles constitute the largest ethnic group in the US, most coming from Belize City.[38] With a history of migration, the Garifuna,

---

[37] An estimate of individuals of Belizean ancestry in the United States was arrived at through my interpretation of all data in the annual reports issued by the Immigration and Naturalization Service, US Census data, previous estimates that have been made on the number of Belizeans in the United States (Vernon, 1990), and in general the informed judgments of several Belizean sources. The 2000 census recorded only 37,688 individuals claiming Belizean ancestry (the 1990 census recorded 21,205), which is a gross undercount of the number of Belizeans in the United States. This represents an ongoing flaw in census undercounts of minority (Black and Latino) and immigrant population for a number of reasons.
[38] In the mid-1980s Roser, et al., (1986) estimated that Creoles made up as much as 65% to 75% of the Belizean immigrant population in the United States. Today, that percentage has decreased, as Belizeans from other groups (namely Garifuna and Mestizo) have migrated in significant numbers. And in a study of Belizeans in Los Angeles in the early 1990s Straughan (1992) noted that the majority of Belizeans in L.A. came from Belize City (the majority came from the south side of the city) followed by Dangriga.

coming from primarily from Dangriga, were once the second largest ethnic group in the US (DeFay, 2004; Grizzle Huling, 2004 have also written about Garifuna emigration and settlement in the US).[39] Until the late 1980s, Creoles and Garifuna, both with African roots, were an estimated 75% of the Belizean population in the United States (see Vernon, 1990). Today, with increased US emigration, Mestizos are a greater percentage of the Belizean population. Correspondingly, Mestizos are perhaps now the second largest ethnic group of Belizeans in the US, surpassing Garifuna. (Few Maya have emigrated to the United States.).

The impact of emigration on Belize

Emigration, especially to the United States, has had a significant impact on Belize; and Belizeans abroad have had a significant impact on Belize, in terms of both their absence and presence.[40] In the early 1970s, an editorial written by Homero Escalante (1973) in a Belizean journal *National Studies* noted the exodus of Belizeans to the United States and the impact it was having on the country (p. 1). Escalante listed the names of several Belizeans families who were no longer in Belize. Of great concern to many Belizeans is the impact that emigration has had on Belizean families and the resulting split that many families have experienced. Belizean emigration essentially progressed from single migration to partial family unit migration, which meant that children often were left with grandparents or other relatives. This phenomenon often resulted in social problems, such as an increase in delinquency.[41] But this issue is often more complicated as other factors need to be taken into consideration such as the length of time parents were separated from their children and the economic resources available them. Overall, the impact of emigration is a lot greater than the absence of a few families or split families.

In a short time, emigration (and immigration) helped change demographically the face of Belize. As stated above, until the early 1980s the majority of Belizeans who emigrated were Creole and Garifuna. A significant number of Mes-

---

[39] The Garifuna population in the US has been of great interest to scholars and others in the US, perhaps because of the name. In turn, the Garifuna are still the focus of most research relating to Belizeans in the United States, in terms of Belizeans collectively and other Belizean ethnic groups. It seems that many of these studies have focused on this group because of the great interest of academics in an "indigenous" group that seems "exotic."

[40] In the early 1980s Everitt (1984, p. 319) noted that emigration profoundly altered Belize within a short time.

[41] In her study of Garifuna migration Miller (1993) discusses the role of women in emigration. She also notes that the social costs of migration have been high and resulted in a sharp increase in social problems among Garifuna youths in Los Angeles and Belize.

tizos followed. But the greater emigration of Creoles and Garifuna contributed to (instead of caused) a demographic shift in the country (from Black to Mestizo). This coincided with, starting in the early 1980s, the widespread immigration from Central America into Belize. Some Belizeans, such as the publisher of the local *Amandala* newspaper, reasoned that "if only more Black Belizeans had stayed at home," Creoles would still be the largest ethnic group and Belize would still be a Black majority country. This view found support in the writings of Woods, Perry, and Steagall (1997) and Cornebise (2004) who, in their analysis of Belizean migration patterns, focused on how significant emigration and immigration led to the demographic shift in Belize. This view can be rather simplistic and doesn't take into consideration that regardless of how many Creole and Garifuna Belizeans emigrated, this ethnic shift was perhaps inevitable because of factors such as the greater integration of Belize into Central America, government's immigration policy (or lack thereof), wage differentials, and employers' appetite for cheap labor.[42] No longer an unlikely destination, Belize has been incorporated into a regional pattern of migration (Hamilton & Chinchilla, 1991; Repak, 1995; Mahler & Ugrina, 2006). In turn the settlement of a significant number of Central Americans led to chain migration and the continued flow of Central Americans. What is undeniable is that the influx of Central Americans to Belize was complemented by an emigration of Belizeans, primarily Creole and Garifuna, to the United States (Mahler & Ugrina, 2006). Lastly, because of significant emigration (and immigration) Belize has become a more transient country and the social connections Belizeans once experienced from living in a smaller country and knowing each other are diminishing.

Correspondingly, Belizeans living abroad continue to have an impact on the country in various ways. They have an economic impact when they send remittances, invest, visit, or eventually return to live.[43] Many Belizeans from abroad were in Belize for the 25th anniversary of Belizean independence (and the Battle of St. George's Caye Day). As tourists in their own country, over the years they have had collectively an impact on the Belizean economy. Correspondingly, a recent Inter-American Development Bank report indicated that in 2005, Be-

---

[42] Like Belizeans, since the early 1980s Central Americans (namely Salvadorans, Guatemalans, and Hondurans) were emigrating to the United States in significant numbers, but in part for different reasons, such as political instability and civil unrest (Hamilton & Chinchilla, 1991; Mahler, 1991; Mahler & Ugrina, 2006; Repak, 1995). Indeed, some Central Americans who initially settled in Belize moved on to the United States. Furthermore, like their ethnic brethren in other parts of Central America, native Mestizos are just as prone to emigration. And if not for a late start their rate of emigration would be just as high as that of Creoles and Garifuna.

[43] The emigration of Belizeans resulted in a "brain drain," as recently noted by Mahler and Ugrina (2006). But in a functional way, emigration kept down the unemployment rate in Belize.

lizeans in the United States sent remittances to Belize at the value of BZ$160 million. In the current economic condition that Belize is in, such remittances have economically propped many Belizeans. A tour of Belize City quickly reveals new and well kept houses with all the amenities of an American lifestyle and bushy, overgrown lots where dilapidated houses once stood. Both the past and current government officials have bought or "seized" some of these properties and in turn built houses on them. The "states house" or states property stands out.[44] While some Belizean sever their ties with Belize, others return and buy property, build houses, and/or renovate the ones they have. This contributes to the building boom Belize City has experienced. As stated, with the money they have earned, some Belizeans return to invest in the country and start businesses. But to date there has not been the formation of an Overseas Belizeans Investment Company that is collectively investing in Belize.

For the most part Belizeans abroad have been a positive socio-cultural force on Belize. Over the years, they have had an impact in music, more recently in sports, and in other avenues.[45] But some of the emigrants have also had a negative impact on the country. Some who have returned have brought back certain attitudes and behavior that encourage Belizeans to mimic an American life style that is not always positive. In terms of transnational ties, Belize experienced a gang problem in the early 1990s when Belizeans emulated a gang lifestyle from the streets of Los Angeles with the help of Belizean youth who had lived in South Central and other areas of L.A. (Hayden, 1995; Matthei & Smith, 1996). Ethnicity and class factored into the Belizean gang problem. (While Creole and Garifuna Belizeans have been involved in the African-American Bloods and

---

[44] A marked difference exists between Belizeans who return to Belize to build and/or renovate houses (often on property that they inherited), and Belizeans who live abroad and have inherited property, but don't consistently return to Belize to take care of their property, or who return periodically—if at all-and let the property and/or houses fall into disrepair. Thus, while some Belizeans are economically successful and are able to build "states houses," others who might not be financially secure, do not take care of their property. For a variety of reasons—numerous family concerns in the US, disagreements with family members about ownership/responsibilities, etc., many Belizean immigrants have severed their ties to Belize. Also, both the past and current government officials have sold, bought, or "seized" some of these properties and in turn built houses on them.
[45] In terms of transnational ties, technology has had a significant impact on the way that Belizeans at home maintain contacts with Belizeans abroad. Up until the mid-1970s few Belizeans had phones (mostly only more affluent Belizeans). But by the early 1980s many Belizeans installed phones in their home in order to keep in touch with relatives abroad. The Internet had a similar effect. In the early days of the Internet when web pages were still "primitive" many Belizeans made web pages, primarily to advertise tourism in Belize. Through their messages boards and forums, Belizeans abroad began to communicate with Belizeans at home. Indeed because of these web pages Belizeans were one of the first immigrant groups to make greater use of the Internet.

Crips, there is no report of Mestizos involvement in the Latino Mara Salvatrucha and the 18th Street gangs). From deportees to retirees some Belizeans are returning to Belize. As Belizeans abroad grow older, some are returning (at times on a semi-permanent basis) to Belize after they retire. Meanwhile, other Belizeans are returning involuntarily. Stricter enforcement of US immigration laws resulted in the stepped up deportation of Belizeans even for minor offences. "Eh get dip," some Belizeans now say in Creole about deportees. (With citizenship being somewhat of a shield against deportation, this reflects the low naturalization rate of Belizeans in the US).

References

ARNOLD, FAYE WILLIAMS. (1988). *Ethnic identification, ethnicity, and ethnic solidarity in Los Angeles County's West Indian-American Community.* Doctoral dissertation, University of California Los Angeles. (ProQuest/UMI No. 8727806: http://gateway.proquest.com/openurl?url_ver=Z39.88-2004&res_dat=xri:pqdiss&rft_val_fmt=info:ofi/fmt:kev:mtx:dissertation&rft_dat=xri:pqdiss:8727806).

ASHCRAFT, N. (1973). *Colonialism and underdevelopment: Processes of political economic change in British Honduras.* NY: Columbia University Press.

BABCOCK, ELIZABETH COOLING. (2003). *Belizean transnationalism: The role of migrant voluntary associations* (in Illinois). Doctoral dissertation, Indiana University. (ProQuest/UMI No. 3094160: http://gateway.proquest.com/openurl?url_ver=Z39.88-2004&res_dat=xri:pqdiss&rft_val_fmt=info:ofi/fmt:kev:mtx:dissertation&rft_dat=xri:pqdiss:3094160).

BABCOCK, ELIZABETH COOLING. (2006). The transformative potential of Belizean Migrant Voluntary Association in Chicago. *International Migration* Vol. 44 (1).

BARRY, TOM (with DYLAN VERNON). (1995). *Inside Belize: The essential guide to its politics, economy, society, and environment.* Albuquerque, New Mexico: Resource Center Press.

BOLLAND, O. NIGEL. (1986). *Belize: A new nation in Central America.* Boulder: Westview Press.

BROCKMANN, C. THOMAS. (1985). Ethnic participation in Orange Walk economic development. *Ethnic Groups* 6, 2-3, 187-207.

BROOKS, D. (1975). *Race and labor in London transport.* London: Oxford University Press.

BYRON, MARGARET. (1994). *Post-War Caribbean migration to Britain: The unfinished cycle.* Aldershot: Avebury.

CENTRAL STATISTICAL OFFICE (2004). 2002 *Poverty assessment report.* Belize: CSO/National Human Development Advisory Committee. Full report can be accessed at http://www.cso.gov.bz/publications/poverty_asses_rep2002.pdf.

CORNEBISE, MICHAEL. (2004). *An analysis of Belizean international in- and out-migration trends.* The Association of American Geographers 100th Annual Meeting, Philadelphia, PA, 14-19 March. See http://www.eiu.edu/~geoscience/presentations.html#Cornebise.

CORNEBISE, MICHAEL. (2005, Spring). Belizean population and migration trends: Examining the supply side of Chicago's Belizean migration story. *Bulletin of the Illinois Geographical Society* Vol. 47, No. 1.

DAVIDSON, ROBERT B. (1962). *West Indian migrants: Social and economic facts of migration from the West Indies.* London: Oxford University Press for the Institute of Race Relations.

DAVIDSON, ROBERT B. (1966). *Black British: Immigrants to England.* London: Oxford University Press.

DEFAY, JASON BRADLEY. (2004). *Identity matters: Immigration and the social construction of identity in Garifuna,* Los Angeles (California). Doctoral dissertation, University of California, San Diego. (ProQuest/UMI No. 3158470: http://gateway.proquest.com/openurl?url_ver=Z39.88-2004&res_dat=xri:pqdiss&rft_val_fmt=info:ofi/fmt:kev:mtx:dissertation&rft_dat=xri:pqdiss:3158470)

DONOHOE, WILLIAM A. (1946). *A History of British Honduras.* Montreal, Canada: Provincial Publishing Company.

ECHEVERRI-GENT, ELISAVINDA. (1992). Forgotten workers: British West Indians and the early days of the banana industry in Costa Rica and Honduras. *Journal of Latin American Studies 24,* 275-308.

ESCALANTE, HOMERO. (1973, July). Belizean exodus? Editorial, *National Studies* Vol. 1 No 4.

EVERITT, JOHN C. (1984). The recent migration of Belize, Central America. *International Migration Review 18* (2), 319-325.

FAWCETT, JAMES T. & ARNOLD, FRED. (1987). Explaining diversity: Asian and Pacific immigration systems. In JAMES T. FAWCETT & BENJAMIN V. CARINO (Eds.). *Pacific bridges: The new immigration from Asia and the Pacific Islands.* Staten Island, NY: Center for Migration Studies.

FONER, NANCY. (1978). *Jamaica farewell: Jamaican migrants in London.* Berkeley: University of California Press.

FORD, AMOS A. (1985). *Telling the truth: The life and times of the British Honduran Forestry Unit in Scotland (1941-44).* London: Karia Press.

GMELCH, GEORGE. (1992). *Double passage: The lives of Caribbean migrants abroad and back home.* Ann Arbor, MI: University of Michigan Press.

GRANT, C.H. (1976). *The making of modern Belize: Politics, society, and British colonialism in Central America.* Cambridge: Cambridge University Press.

GRIZZLE HULING, PATRICIA KAYE. (2004). *Unbecoming Black: The case of the Garifuna* (Belize, California). Doctoral dissertation, The Claremont (California) Graduate University. (ProQuest/UMI No. 3147304: http://gateway.proquest.com/openurl?url_ver=Z39.88-2004&res_dat=xri:pqdiss&rft_val_fmt=info:ofi/fmt:kev:mtx:dissertation&rft_dat=xri:pqdiss:3147304)

HAMILTON NORA & CHINCHILLA, NORMA STOLTZ. (1991). Central American migration: A framework for analysis. *Latin American Research Review 26* (1), 75-110.

HAYDEN, TOM. (1995, 30 Jan.). L.A.'s Third World Export: Gangs. *Los Angeles Times* B, 5:1.

HONDAGNEU-SOTELO, PIERRETTE. (1994). *Gendered transitions: Mexican experiences of immigration.* Berkeley, CA: University of California Press.

HYDE, EVAN. (1995). *X Communications.* Belize City, Belize: The Angelus Press Ltd.

JAMES, WINSTON & HARRIS, CLIVE. (Eds.). (1993). *Inside Babylon: The Caribbean diaspora in Britain.* edited by Winston James and Clive Harris. London: Verso.

LEPAGE, R.B. & TABOURET-KELLER, ANDREE. (1985). *Acts of identity: Creole-based approaches to language and ethnicity.* Cambridge: Cambridge University Press.

LEMMEL, DAVID ANTHONY. (2001). *Racial socialization and Black identity formation in the initial postsecondary school pathways choices in three African-descended groups.* Doctoral dissertation, University of California, Los Angeles. (ProQuest/UMI No. 3032883: http://gateway.proquest.com/openurl?url_ver=Z39.88-2004&res_dat=xri:pqdiss&rft_val_fmt=info:ofi/fmt:kev:mtx:dissertation&rft_dat=xri:pqdiss:3032883).

LENT, JOHN. (1989). Country of no return: Belize since television. *Belizean Studies* Vol. 17, No. 1, pp. 17-41.

MACDONALD, JOHN S., & MACDONALD, LEATRICE D. (1964, Jan.). Chain migration, ethnic neighborhood, and social networks. *Milbank Memorial Fund Quarterly 42*, pp. 82-97.

MAHLER, SARAH J. (1995). *American dreaming: Immigrant life on the margins.* Princeton, New Jersey: Princeton University Press.

MAHLER, SARAH J. & UGRINA, DUSAN. (2006, April 1). Central America: Crossroads of the Americas. *Migration Information Source: Fresh Thought, Authoritative Data, Global Reach.* Full report is at http://www.migrationinformation.org/Feature/display.cfm?id=386.

MATTHEI, LINDA M. & SMITH, DAVID A. (1995). Women, households and transnational migration networks: The Garifuna and global economic restructuring. In ROBERTO P. KORZENIEWICZ & WILLIAM SMITH (Eds.) *Latin America in the World Economy* (pp. 133-150). Westport, CN: Greenwood.

MATTHEI, LINDA M. & SMITH, DAVID A. (1996). Belizean boyz 'n the nood?: Garifuna labor migration and transnational identity. *Comparative Urban and Community Research 6*, pp. 270-290.

MOBERG, MARK. (1992). *Citrus, strategy, & class: Politics of development in Southern Belize.* Iowa City: University of Iowa Press.

MOBERG, MARK. (1996). Myths that divide: Immigrant labor and class segmentation in the Belizean banana industry. *American Ethnologist 23* (2), 311-330.

MILLER, LINDA R. (1993). *Bridges: Garifuna migration to Los Angeles.* Doctoral dissertation, University of California, Irvine. (ProQuest/UMI 9317878: http://gateway.proquest.com/openurl?url_ver=Z39.88-2004&res_dat=xri:pqdiss&rft_val_fmt=info:ofi/fmt:kev:mtx:dissertation&rft_dat=xri:pqdiss:9317878).

MORRISSEY, ROBERT. (2005). Belizeans. *Encyclopedia of Chicago (Online version).* Chicago Historical Society. Retrieved from http://www.encyclopedia.chicagohistory.org/pages/127.html.

OLIVEIRA, OMAR SOUKI. (1985). *Analysis of the differential effects of exposure to Mexican and US television on consumer attitudes in Northern Belize.* Doctoral dissertation, The Ohio State University.

OLIVERIA, OMAR S. (1986). Effects of transborder television in Corozal Town and surrounding villages. *Belizean Studies* Vol. 14, No. 3, pp. 31-51. (ProQuest/UMI 8510793: http://gateway.proquest.com/openurl?url_ver=Z39.88-2004&res_dat=xri:pqdiss&rft_val_fmt=info:ofi/fmt:kev:mtx:dissertation&rft_dat=xri:pqdiss:8510793).

PALACIO, JOSEPH. (1992, Dec.). Garifuna immigrants in Los Angeles: Attempts at self-improvement. *Belizean Studies* Vol. 20, No. 3, 17-26.

PALACIO, MYRTLE. (2002). Dangriga BZ or USA? Out-migration of a Garifuna Community in post-independence Belize. Paper delivered at UWI School of Continuing Studies Belize Conference, Nov. 21-24, 2001. http://www.cave-hill.uwi.edu/bnccde/belize/conference/paperdex.html. Belize City: UWISCS Centre.

PASTOR, R. (Ed.). (1985). *Migration and Development in the Caribbean: The Unexplored Connection.* Boulder: Westview Press.

PEACH, CERI. (1968). *West Indian migration to Britain.* London: Oxford University Press Institute for Race Relations.

PORTES, ALENDRO & RUMBAUT, RUBEN. (1996). *Immigrant America: A portrait.* Berkeley, CA: University of California Press.

PURCELL, TREVOR. (1993). *Banana fallout: Class, color, and culture among West Indians in Costa Rica.* Los Angeles: UCLA Center for African-American Studies.

REPAK, TERRY A. (1995). *Waiting on Washington: Central American workers in the nation's capital.* Philadelphia, PA: Temple University Press.

ROSER, C., SNYDER, L. B., & CHAFFEE, S. H. (1986). Belize release me, let me go: The impact of mass media on emigration in Belize. *Belizean Studies* Vol. 14, No. 3, 1-30.

SETZEKORN, WILLIAM DAVID. (1975/1981). *Formerly British Honduras: A profile of the new nation of Belize.* Athens: Ohio University Press. (Original work published in 1975 by Newark. NJ: Dumbarton Press.)

SHOMAN, ASSAD. (1995). *Thirteen chapters of a history of Belize.* Belize City, Belize: The Angelus Press Ltd.

SNYDER, LESLIE, CONNIE ROSER, and STEVEN CHAFFEE. (1991, Winter). Foreign media and the desire to emigrate from Belize. *Journal of Communication 41*, No. 1, 117-132.

STRAUGHAN, JEROME. (1992). *Factors affecting community cohesion and Belizean immigrants in the Los Angeles area.* Masters thesis, California State University, Los Angeles.

STRAUGHAN, JEROME. (2004). *Belizean immigrants in Los Angeles.* (Doctoral dissertation, University of Southern California; ProQuest/UMI No. 3145295: http://gateway.proquest.com/openurl?url_ver=Z39.88-2004&res_dat=xri:pqdiss &rft_val_fmt=info:ofi/fmt:kev:mtx:dissertation&rft_dat=xri:pqdiss:3145295).

SUTHERLAND, ANNE. (1998). *The making of Belize: Globalization in the margins.* Westport, Connecticut: Bergin & Garvey.

THOMPSON, MEL E. (1990). Forty-and-one years on: An overview of Afro-Caribbean migration to the United Kingdom. In RANSFORD W. PALMER (Ed.) *In search of a better life: Perspectives on migration from the Caribbean* (pp. 39-70). New York: Praeger.

UEDA, REED. (1980). West Indians. In STEPHAN THERNSTROM, ANN ORLOV, & OSCAR HANDLIN (Eds.) *Harvard Encyclopedia of American Ethnic Groups* (pp. 1020-1027). Cambridge, MA: Harvard University Press.

VERNON, DYLAN. (1990). Belizean exodus to the United States: For better or for worse. *SPEAReports 4*: Second Annual Studies on Belize Conference, pp. 6-28. Belize: SPEAR.

VERNON, DYLAN. (1992). Ten years of independence in Belize: An analysis of the socio-economic crisis. *SPEAReports 8*. Belize: SPEAR, pp. 38-50.

WADE, SELVIN. (1986-1987). "Smokey Joe." *Amandala* newspaper. Belize City: Amandala.

WESTERN, JOHN. (1992). *A passage to England: Barbadian Londoners speak of home*. Minneapolis: University of Minnesota Press.

WOODS, LOUIS, PERRY, JOSEPH & STEAGALL, JEFFREY. (1994, March). Tourism as a development tool: The case of Belize. *Caribbean Geography 5*, No. 1, pp. 1-19.

WOODS, LOUIS A., JOSEPH M. PERRY & JEFFERY W. STEAGALL. (1997). The composition and distribution of ethnic groups in Belize: Immigration and emigration patterns, 1980-1991. *Latin American Research Review* Vol. 32, No. 3, pp 63-88.

YOUNG, ALMA H. (1990). Belize. In JAMES M. MALLOY, EDUARDO A. GAMARRA (Eds.). *Latin America and Contemporary Record*, B215-B225. NY/London: Holmes & Meier.

Part 4

Culture

11. Coming of Age: Reflecting on the Past 25 Years at Archaeology

Jaime J. Awe

When the declaration of independence was announced in front of the National Assembly building in Belmopan on the 21st of September 1981, it was made only a few meters away from the previous headquarters of the Department of Archaeology (DOA). I remember the day vividly for it came just two months after my return from Canada following the completion of undergraduate studies at Trent University. At the time the DOA, as we called it, was housed in the basement of the East Block building in Belmopan, and we served the country under the portfolio of the Ministry of Trade and Industry. Our headquarters consisted of four offices, a small library, and a large vault with a metal door in which were kept the nation's most valued artifacts.

In 1981 the entire staff of the Department of Archaeology consisted of 12 people. These included five officers who were stationed in Belmopan, six caretakers who served as custodians at the Cerros, Lamanai, Altun Ha, Xunantunich, Lubaantun, and Nim Li Punit reserves, and a conservation foreman. The five staff members in Belmopan included the late Harriot Topsey who served as Commissioner; I was the chief Archaeologist; Allan Moore and John Morris were archaeological assistants; and the late Winnel Branche was an archaeologist. With bachelors degrees, Harriot and I had the highest academic qualifications. Allan and John had high school and sixth form diplomas respectively, and Winnel was pursuing her B.A. at Trent University in Canada.

Life at the DOA was quite frugal in the early 1980s. The few pieces of equipment at our disposal could best be described as antiquated (no pun intended). We had two typewriters for producing reports and correspondences, a beat-up SLR Canon camera, an old slide projector, some cave equipment that included a few carbide lamps, a cable ladder and about six helmets. Two very beat up vehicles served our transportation needs. Harriot had a Ford truck that had been donated to us, and I had "Old Betsy," a seemingly indestructible Land Rover whose legendary feats are still retold among the older heads at the present-day Institute of Archaeology.

In Belize during the early 1980s, only five foreign projects were directed toward archaeological research. Three of the projects were located in the Orange Walk District, one in the Belize District, and the other in Toledo. The only field work that DOA conducted was minor salvage operations in response to land development in the Valley of Peace, which is located near Belmopan at the Ponces Site south of Blackman Eddy. Occasionally I would also take John Morris and Allan Moore to explore new caves or surface sites that were reported to us.

Despite the fact that we had six major sites opened to the public in the 1980s, there was little for visitors to see at these reserves. The two most developed sites at the time were Xunantunich and Altun Ha, and even these were a far cry from spectacular. At Xunantunich only the Castillo, the stela house, and structures A13 and A11 had undergone minor levels of conservation. Exposed to the elements since the late 1950s, the East Frieze on the Castillo was rapidly deteriorating and the topmost section of the building had some large cracks due to diverse natural causes. At Altun Ha structures A1, A3, and B4 had been partially consolidated, while at Lubaantun and Lamanai the only architecture that was visible was that left exposed by previous excavations. At Nim Li Punit all that visitors could see were the carved stelae strewn about the plaza, while at Cerros the large beautiful stucco masks, previously discovered by archaeologists from Southern Methodist University in the late 1970s, had to be reburied because of a lack of knowledge on how to conserve these types of monuments. During this time the maximum number of visitors at all our sites combined was no more than about 5,000 per annum, and except for Altun Ha, we had no guidebooks or brochures for any of the parks.

And so it was in 1981. We were a fledgling department, similar in many respects to our small country that was about to embark on its most dramatic right of passage. We were, in fact, in the process of adapting our own unique identity within a governmental system, while at the same time forging ahead with ambitious ideas, great plans, and the hope of strengthening and developing the human resources that would take us into the future.

The latter part of the 1980s and the early 1990s were equally as benevolent as they were detrimental to the fortunes of the DOA in Belize. I say this because some of the events that unfolded during this decade and a half represent major accomplishments of the department, some represent hard blows and setbacks, while others greatly influenced the direction we would eventually take.

In 1983, having been denied leave to pursue graduate studies, I resigned my post with the DOA and returned to do graduate work in North America. But my departure did not affect the department's ability to attract new recruits, such as George Thompson, Brian Woodye, Theresa Batty, and Paul Francisco, who brought fresh energy and new ideas to the DOA and ensured that we would continue building on the achievements of the past. Eventually several other members of staff received study leave under better terms to continue training in archaeology. Some, such as Winnel Branche and Harriot Topsey, subsequently returned to Belize, but Winnel left the DOA shortly thereafter to take over the newly established Department of Museums.

The late 1980s and early 1990s also witnessed the first two major conservation projects in Belizean archaeology. A grant from the United States Agency for International Development (USAID) allowed the DOA to focus particular attention on Cahal Pech, Caracol, Xunantunich, Santa Rita, and Lamanai. A few years later with funds from the European Union, the Maya Archaeological Sites Development Program (MASDP) allowed us to conserve much of the site cores at Lubaantun and Nim Li Punit. Although broader in scope than the MASDP project, the overall conservation accomplishments of the USAID project were considerably less than that of the former, most likely because much of the funds were spent on research rather than architectural stabilization. The MASDP project is significant because it is the first project of its kind ever to be directed by our own Belizean archaeologists.

During the late 1980s and throughout the 1990s, the DOA was moved from one ministerial portfolio to another. After finally leaving Trade and Industry the DOA spent time with the Ministries of Natural Resources, Education, Culture, and eventually Tourism. These periodic moves greatly affected our operations, hindered our progress, and often influenced our mission. But despite the uncertainties associated with these constant transitions, these moves were far less damaging than the two hard blows that fate had reserved for us. First Winnel Branche was diagnosed with advanced malignant cancer and quickly succumbed to the disease. Then returning one night from Roaring Creek, Harriot Topsey was killed in a traffic accident on the Ring Road in Belmopan. In a relatively short period of time we lost two of our pioneering Belizean archaeologists, both in the prime years of their careers.

The loss of senior key personnel was quite devastating, but the DOA refused to "lie down and lick its wounds." The younger members quickly stepped up to the plate and continued to forge ahead. During the next few years Allan Moore, John Morris, George Thompson, and Brian Woodye all served the department well in the capacity of commissioners. Each of them also managed to continue their studies in archaeology and to contribute to the establishment of one of the most highly qualified and proficient institutions in the government of Belize. Under their direction several new reserves were added to our growing number of parks, many new research policies were introduced, and the management of our park system was vastly improved. Toward the end of the 1990s

Allan Moore and John Morris also left to pursue postgraduate studies at the University of London and at the University of California, Los Angeles. Both returned to Belize just before the second millennia, but John was subsequently transferred to redevelop the Department of Museums while Allan stayed with Archaeology.

Major events occurred in the year 2000 that were destined to transform who we were and to subsequently define the DOA as major contributors to national programs that fostered the preservation of our cultural heritage and the dissemination of cultural knowledge. The first of these major events was the launching of the Tourism Development Project (TDP). The major purposes of this incredibly ambitious project were to develop the tourism potential of Belize's premier archaeological sites and to improve the human resources of the DOA. Then the Ministry of Tourism and my friend and colleague Allan Moore lured me away from my position as a professor of anthropology at the University of New Hampshire, and I headed back to Belize. During the next four years the TDP greatly transformed all of our major archaeological parks. The monumental architecture at many of the sites was excavated, then subsequently conserved. Other works focused substantial efforts on improving the infrastructure at all the parks. This included the construction of new visitor's centers, modern bathrooms, water systems, ranger quarters, and the improvement of many old facilities. In addition to these changes, the access roads to Xunantunich, Caracol, and Altun Ha were greatly improved and several community projects provided training in the production of handicrafts and the construction of gift shops where these and other souvenirs could be sold.

To improve our ability for sustainable management of our resources the project provided funding for training several of our officers. George Thompson and Brian Woodye successfully pursued masters degree programs in park management and Paul Francisco completed a B.A. program in conservation. Other staff members such as Jorge Kan, Enrique Itza, and Matias Meneses received practical training on the conservation of ancient monuments and in the design and construction of park-related architecture. In 2003 amidst all these changes came the most momentous event of the new millennia–the passing of the National Institute of Culture and History Act. With a stroke of the pen the archeology department was dissolved and a new Institute of Archaeology (IOA) was established as its replacement. Along with three other new sister institutions, the IOA was to operate as a branch of the National Institute of Culture and History (NICH), a statutory board whose primary focus was the preservation and promotion of Belizean culture.

Since the passing of the NICH Act, the new IOA has grown considerably. From five permanent staff members and six caretakers in 1981 we now have 17 officers stationed at our new headquarters in Belmopan and 50 rangers and park managers. Among the office staff two have Ph.D.'s, three have M.A.'s, two with B.A.'s and all the others have associate degrees. Today we manage 13 first class archaeological parks and have signed agreements for the co-management of four cave sites. Since 2003 we organize and host an annual international symposium on Belizean Archaeology and have successfully published the proceedings of all these meetings in an accredited journal-style volume. In addition to these scholarly publications we produce a quarterly newsletter entitled "The Underground," and we present a television series known as "Glimpses of the Past." The staff is involved with the publication of several books on Maya prehistory, regular newspaper and magazine articles, and numerous papers in scientific reports, journals and books. Our highly qualified staff members also conduct extensive outreach programs at primary, secondary, and tertiary institutions with the purpose of educating students about the prehistory of Belize. Other similar programs focus on the professional training of tour guides in an effort to improve their level of presentation to local and foreign visitors at our sites.

In the area of research and conservation the IOA now supervises between 15 and 20 annual foreign projects that are conducted across the country. In 2000 we began our own archaeological investigations at Baking Pot, Cahal Pech, and the Roaring Creek and Caves Branch River valleys. In addition to these research projects our staff continues to conduct reconnaissance of new sites, and we have been recording the national collection of antiquities and known archaeological sites in an electronic medium.

Participation in the Tourism Development Project has given us the capacity and technical expertise to conserve all forms of monumental architecture, and we are the leading Central American nation in the production of fiberglass replicas of ancient Maya stuccoed monuments. During the last two years we have also enjoyed great success with acquiring foreign grants that have allowed us to preserve fragile monuments at several of our archaeological parks. Over the past several years, we have created a well-stocked library on Maya and Mesoamerican archaeology and the facility now has the potential to serve the research needs of both local and foreign academics. Our present plan is to establish the first archaeology museum in Belize. This facility will not only house some of the nation's crown jewels, but will also serve important educational purposes and be a venue to display the great achievements of our ancient predecessors.

The last 25 years have been challenging at the IOA. During the last few years we have gained much greater visibility and prestige as an institution. Thus, in the year 2006 we can say with confidence that we have come of age. We now supervise cutting edge research, maintain world class management of our archaeological parks, organize an annual international symposium in archaeology, and we are leaders in the integration of archaeology and tourism development. Under NICH we continue to be dedicated to the research, protection, preservation, and sustainable management of Belize's cultural and archaeological resources. In spite of these achievements however, much work still needs to be done. And so, on this our 25th anniversary of independence, we are able to assure the nation that we shall continue expending every effort to achieve our goal and mission–to preserve our past for future generations of Belizeans and all those who come to visit our archeological treasures.

12. Cultural Policy, Local Creativity and the Globalization of Culture in Belize

Michael Stone

Introduction

This essay considers post-1981 changes in the production, circulation, and consumption of local and foreign forms of cultural expression; reviews local responses to internationalization and cultural globalization; examines the case of Belizean music's success in regional and international markets for what it may suggest in terms of possible cultural policy initiatives; addresses the potential of regional integration strategies in relation to national cultural policy; and outlines areas for further consideration vis-à-vis Belize's socioeconomic and political commitment to elaborating a comprehensive cultural policy strategy in coming years.

Culture

Without delving into the long intellectual history of social science debates over the meanings of culture, two connotations are particularly relevant to discussions of cultural policy. Most broadly, culture refers to an entire way of life, a people's shared perception of what is essential to the human condition, a dynamic set of ideas expressing a common sense of place, history, and social belonging, framed in terms of language, values, norms, customs, traditions, spiritual orientation, and the like. Culture simultaneously refers to the aesthetic orientation and judgment that informs the relationship between creative people, their expressive creations and their audiences–the mediated circulation, evaluation, and consumption of creative work in a particular social context (Lewis & Miller, 2003; McGuigan, 2003).

Culture concerns how people create and sustain their sense of identity and give meaning to social life. It informs how people from diverse backgrounds interact and live together. There is a tension between conceptions of culture as a "conservator" of identity versus an encounter in which diverse local styles, genres, and historical sensibilities find points of articulation capable of addressing national, regional, or global registers of cultural identification simultaneously (Bhabha & Stimpson, 1998; Prott, 1998). In addition to its creative capacity, culture has the potential to exacerbate divisions between people and reinforce inequities in power and political participation that marginalize some groups while benefiting others. This is a matter of paramount importance in cultural policy debates.

Cultural policy

Traditionally, the national framework is where cultural policy has been conceived and undertaken. However, following World War II, the United Nations Educational, Scientific and Cultural Organization (UNESCO), through its various conventions regarding cultural property and cultural and national heritage, became a key focus of cultural-nationalistic claims, when many developing nations gained independence in the 1960s and thereafter. More recently, regional organizations such as the European Union and the Mercado Común del Sur (MERCOSUR) have addressed the shortcomings of an exclusively national approach to questions of economic and cultural development (McGuigan 2003).

But such top-down approaches are often bound up with commercial concerns. In response, non-governmental organizations (NGOs) have sought to emphasize the civil-society framework, and the importance of grassroots organization and popular mobilization (Miller 2003). Cultural policy implies an engagement in the politics of culture and the creation of a culturally educated citizenry. This in turn speaks to the question of governmentality and cultural citizenship, the daily conduct of citizens, and the state's concern with social and artistic relations and the governing thereof. From a grassroots perspective, cultural citizenship entails more than the consumer's assigned role to purchase goods and services—including cultural commodities, because social problems are remarkably resistant to the injunction to consume and otherwise "behave"; they require concerted cultural analysis, political organization and social action, all predicated on an ideal of citizenship in which a sense of belonging and "having a future" is paramount (García Canclini, 1996; Lewis & Miller, 2003; McGuigan, 2003).

Cultural policy emanates from bureaucracies and institutions charged with systematically regulating, evaluating, and supporting creative production, those organizations (governments, foundations, corporations, NGOs, private initiatives, community groups, etc.) that "fund, control, promote, teach and evaluate 'creative persons'," and the processes of distributing financial and educational resources in the name of art and artistic production (Lewis & Miller, 2003, p. 3). Cultural policy thus concerns those entities that actually determine, impose, and enforce (i.e., police) the very measures of what constitutes cultural creativity in any given social and political context.

While private, corporate, and philanthropic enterprises also play a role in cultural policy, the state has been the primary actor in the formulation, support, and dissemination of creative activity, as part of its broader project of modernization, including the conversion of its various socioeconomic, racial, and ethnic sectors into normative citizens. From the foregoing discussion of internationalization and globalization, it should be clear that, given technological developments and their application by the multinational communications industries, across the board, all the arts are treated similarly as "product" and evaluated according to fundamental economic criteria, an approach reinforced by international trade and copyright laws (del Corral & Abada, 1998; McLeod, 2003).

Against this view, across the region, social movements have organized to contest the dominance of mass industrial commercial culture and the corporate, profit-oriented practices that govern cultural production, circulation, and consumption. This is seen in home-grown efforts beginning in the 1980s and 1990s to identify, document, and promote the unique expressive work of Belizeans, and the economic barriers encountered in the process. That work has been supported by multilateral organizations, foundations, and NGOs, which have sought to expand the definition of cultural heritage beyond the purely material to the intangible.

Such is the case with UNESCO's declaration on Garifuna language, music, and dance (2001). Similarly, the growing deterritorialization of production (as with music and videos produced by Belizean artists in the United States) represents a response to the worldwide broadcasting capabilities of the new communications media, the availability of new technologies, rising production costs, and the near monopoly of the entertainment majors in regional and international markets. A certain paradox is also inescapable, insofar as national cultural initiatives and activities cannot but respond to the socioeconomic logic of the tourism industry—as evident with the Mundo Maya network, the Central American museum network, and the many ecotourism ventures established in Belize and elsewhere in neighboring countries in the 1980s and thereafter.

Culture, internationalization and globalization

Traditionally, cultural transmission at the national level has been a function of the social and political elite's educational preparation and capacity to travel, making their aesthetic orientation and consumption patterns both locally dominant and international in character. As a historical artefact of colonialism, in

291

Belize as elsewhere this condition has tended to privilege Western cultural norms and goods, while marginalizing local, national, and regional expressive cultures, both popular and folkloric (Yugar, 1999).

However, industrialization, the expansion of international relations, post-colonial societies' commitment to fostering literacy, the increasing geographical mobility of populations at large, the spread of mass-communications technology, and the consolidation of free-market capitalism in the absence of a viable alternative model for social and economic development have entailed the world-wide elaboration of a complex set of developments often referred to as the globalization of culture. This phenomenon has important consequences for the viability of local cultural traditions.

In cultural policy discussions it is worth distinguishing between two prevailing analytical formulations, internationalization and globalization. The period following World War II, particularly after the demise of the Soviet bloc, has been one of intense international convergence, marked by increasing interaction between people and societies of different cultures, nations, and regions. This has opened societies around the world to foreign goods, technologies, information, and ideas, together with population influxes, regardless of the particularities of any given society's cultural, socioeconomic, political, and religious foundations (Appadurai, 1990; García Canclini, 1998; Patterson, 1994).

However, increasing circulation of Western popular cultural production in diverse and widely dispersed consumer markets has taken particular transnational form, reflecting globalization's prevailing functional organization of and structuring of cultural and social interactions between societies. Free-market capitalism in the global political economy emphasises the speed and ease with which goods and information can be distributed locally to consumers via a system seen as having no theoretical limits on multinational's corporate capacity to distribute ideas, goods, and services and to accumulate wealth.

With respect to culture and the arts, internationalization, globalization, and regional integration have effectively reorganized national cultures via three powerful, ubiquitous, and closely related phenomena: (1) the consolidation of global economic and financial systems, (2) the elaboration of global information systems, and (3) the reach of global entertainment systems (Bhabha & Stimpson, 1998). This is not the place to rehearse these phenomena, but it should be apparent that they have practical implications in debates on creativity and cultural policy.

The idea of "global" creativity only makes sense in relation to an associated conception of the "local." While creative work always originates in and speaks to the contemporary context, it retains critical spatial and temporal perspectives informed by a particular sense of local history (in normative cultural, intellectual, aesthetic, and technical terms). Conversely, the global perspective entails a sense of universal cultural space wherein human beings are seen as capable of interacting regardless of heritage or geographic location (Bhabha & Stimpson, 1998). While incapable of resolution, the tension between globalism versus local, national, or regional sensibilities requires a nuanced sense of history and cultural distinctiveness and a flexible, balanced, and creative cultural policy strategy.

Culture and development

While presenting new opportunities, globalization also has adverse consequences for multicultural societies whose very composition is a product of internationalization; this can undermine the ability to advance a broadly democratic, plural social and political project. As elsewhere, in Belize the close relationship between culture and development has socioeconomic and political implications with respect to sustaining cultural diversity. UNESCO's 2001 Universal Declaration on Cultural Diversity frames cultural rights as human rights, and thus prioritises the need to protect cultural diversity and pluralism world-wide (HIVOS, 2002; cf. Prott 1998). UNESCO's nomination of Garifuna language, dance, and music as "Masterpieces of the Oral and Intangible Heritage of Humanity" is a particular expression of this commitment (UNESCO, 2001; Cayetano & Cayetano, 2005).

Highlighting issues of cultural representation within national heritage is only one of several pertinent issues, however. Policy debates also have emphasized the political organization and control of a national heritage administration; the allocation and equitable distribution of cultural financing and support services, goods, and information; and the engagement of a representative range of interested local, national, and regional actors in policy debates, decision-making, and implementation (HIVOS, 2002; Prott, 1998). All of these issues obtain and warrant consideration in Belize.

Internationalization and cultural globalization in Belize

The economically driven global circulation of Western popular cultural production and ideology exerts strong influence in Belize upon local traditional forms of cultural expression. The rapid expansion of multinational mass communications really took hold in the 1980s with the introduction of TV, video and recording technology, the commercial-scale piracy of video and music recordings, and, somewhat later, the introduction of personal computers. Simultaneously, in the 1980s the demographic composition of the newly independent nation shifted markedly with the sustained influx of refugees from economic crisis and political conflict in Guatemala, Honduras, El Salvador, and Nicaragua, and continuing emigration to the United States by Creole and Garifuna Belizeans.

The preceding occurred precisely as regional integration initiatives took shape, advanced by co-operation among the government of Belize, multilateral organizations, and other actors, including the United Nations Development Programme (UNDP), the UN High Commissioner for Refugees, UNESCO, the Mexican Consulate, Casa de las Américas, the Inter-American Development Bank (IDB), European and North American government development agencies (e.g., VSO-England, SIDA-Sweden, HIVOS-Holland, CIDA-Canada, USAID, Peace Corps), an array of western and Belizean NGOs, various church-based initiatives, and Belizean enterprises such as Stonetree Records and Cubola Productions. All have played a role in the shifting field of cultural production and transmission.

The reconfiguration of Belizean culture under the regime of globalization presents new challenges and opportunities with respect to articulating and implementing nationally viable, democratically oriented cultural policies. As elsewhere, these shifts have fostered new connections between culturally diverse individuals and communities, bringing their locally informed creations to new audiences at home and abroad. Digital technology's broad availability and relative affordability have facilitated local creativity in TV, video, filmmaking, photography, music, and the arts, while aiding the dissemination of creative productions. These trends present lessons that may serve to counter the aggressive expansion of transnational communication conglomerates and the cultural industries, under conditions of near-monopoly commercialisation and standardisation of global cultural fare, at the expense of local, national, and regional forms of cultural expression.

The deterritorialization of culture is also a consequence of the industrialization of mass popular culture and its international distribution. This has given rise to a dynamic global youth culture repertoire characterised by homogenised information, styles, and commodities that cross societal boundaries regardless of national cultural, socioeconomic, political or religious context, animating and informing youthful consumers from very different cultural and social backgrounds (García Canclini, 1998).

But the apparent uniformity of global youth culture is not a one-way process that imposes Western norms and practices everywhere in mass-produced fashion. Nor should global cultural interactions be seen as an irrevocable threat to the diversity and particularism of the world's cultures (Patterson, 1994). For Belize, the best practical refutation of such pessimistic views (and an illustrative case of the kinds of cultural policy strategies that are likely to succeed in Belize) is manifest in the example of Belizean music, which over the past two decades has emerged as a significant artistic influence in Central America and the Caribbean, in North American expatriate communities, and on the burgeoning world-music scene (Shuker, 2003; Stone, 2006; Throsby, 1998), as discussed below.

Some readers will recall the "Buy Belize" campaign that followed independence. The desire to reinforce national production spoke to an old dilemma—Belize's profound dependency on imported manufactured goods, a problem widely faced by ex-colonial societies after World War II. Internationally, cultural policy debates of the post-war period grappled with an analogous set of questions regarding the degree to which industrialised cultural production from the global North should be accepted, and how much the influence of international artistic and cultural fashions should be embraced. A linked concern was the national protection, development, and promotion of local traditions and creative pursuits.

But whether seen as a foreign cultural invasion or an opportunity to experiment with and meld uniquely local creative inspirations with cosmopolitan innovations, the economic, technological, and ideological shifts enforced by the market logic of cultural globalization remain pervasive and inescapable. Belizean smallness is only part of the explanation, which more fundamentally concerns structural features of the complex, globally extensive developments already described. In common with its Latin American and Caribbean neighbors, Belize is limited in its ability to compete in the current regime of industrialized global cultural production, as evident in an overview of its positioning in such areas as publishing and literature, the visual and plastic arts, and the audiovisual realm of film, TV, video, radio, and music production.

Even so, a number of post-independence developments present examples whereby creative efforts have exploited comparative advantages inherent in the uniqueness of Belize's plural cultural heritage and vibrant local creative efforts. Summarizing some of these innovations can point the way to cultural policy initiatives geared to the creative possibilities embodied in local, national, and regional contexts vis-à-vis cultural development.

Cultural development in Belize

The National Institute of Culture and History

The National Institute of Culture and History (NICH) was created in 2003 by the government of Belize to bring together and rationalize the efforts of diverse government departments that were historically dedicated to preserving and promoting Belizean culture, among them the National Arts Council. NICH's mission is to craft and implement cultural policy to enhance Belizeans' understanding of their cultural and historical roots and to instill collective pride in the country's unique cultural diversity, fostering a shared sense of national identity. NICH's founding was marked by the conversion of Government House into the Belize City House of Culture and the Museum of Belize in Belize City.

NICH is charged with preserving Belize's ancient and historical monuments and artefacts; interpreting documents, photographs, and oral history; promoting contemporary visual, literary, and performing arts; and carrying out research and community outreach to facilitate cultural access and participation for all Belizeans. Its four main branches are the Institute of Creative Arts, the Museums of Belize and Houses of Culture, the Institute of Archaeology, and the Institute of Social and Cultural Research. In its short existence, NICH has drafted a national cultural policy, overseen the building of both the new Bliss Centre for the Performing Arts (Belize City) and the Museum of Belize, and the establishment of the various district-level Houses of Culture and Visitors' Centres.

Heritage preservation

Cultural heritage concerns the tangible manifestations of a given people or cultural tradition, including immovables (buildings, monuments, archaeological sites, natural features of the landscape) and movables (artwork, material objects, etc.). It also includes a culture's intangible elements—its intellectual heritage, artistic and philosophical creations, traditions and rituals, etc., together with the unique cultural information—and the transmission thereof, the process that makes heritage comprehensible and reproducible in cultural and historical context (Prott, 1998).

The Regional Museum Project in Central America (RED CAMUS) is the product of a recent Swedish International Development Cooperation Agency (SIDA) initiative that has produced concrete results, suggesting possibilities for future regional collaboration. Pursuing a coordinated strategy similar to the Mundo Maya cultural tourism project (which seeks to develop and promote Maya sites in Mexico, Guatemala, Belize, and Honduras), since 2001, RED CAMUS constitutes a national network for museums in every Central American country, with a mission to train personnel and to promote the network. A regional executive committee is comprised of national museum coordinators, and a steering committee convenes the national directors of cultural heritage offices from Belize, Costa Rica, El Salvador, Guatemala, Honduras, Nicaragua, and Panama (Belize joined the network in 2005).

At the project's inception, Guatemala and El Salvador were the only countries with museums that already had some sort of association in place. Belizean sites assisted by RED CAMUS include the House of Culture (formerly Government House), the Museum of Belize, Cahal Pech Visitor Center, Lamanai Visitor Center, and Nimli Punit Visitor Center (Markensten, 2006; Red Centroamericana de Museos, 2006). The five-year project funding cycle ended in September 2006, and the resulting report should help to formulate future cultural policy and assess further prospects for regional collaboration.

Publishing

Since the nineteenth century, the most dynamic publishing realm in Belize has been its newspapers, although they have been geared strictly to a national audience, often linked to a particular political party, and reliant on advertising and the reprinting of material from abroad. Newspapers have not branched out into book publishing or assumed a broader role in literary affairs, and prominent Belizean authors such as Zee Edgell have been published overseas. Nor is there a local tradition of literary criticism. Apart from the Roman Catholic Church's support of *Belizean Studies* and its predecessor *National Studies*, the most successful contemporary literary and documentary publishing enterprise remains Cubola Productions, whose roots extend back into the pre-independence struggle. Cubola is committed to promoting and publishing Belizean writers and scholars in Belize and internationally. Apart from ready national appeal, Cubola's success demonstrates an ability to make the most of a very small market by producing a diversified catalogue that includes literature, essays, textbooks, and a variety of publications that address the interests of international visitors.

Cubola is also a founding member of the Caribbean Publishers Network (CAPNET), a non-profit organization whose mission is to support and promote indigenous publishing throughout the region. Seeing publishing as a cultural enterprise, CAPNET seeks to foster cultural and socioeconomic development by building a vigorous Caribbean publishing industry. CAPNET has organised numerous events across the Caribbean, has developed a joint member catalogue, and has encouraged regular attendance at book fairs worldwide.

Poetry also has enjoyed some success in Belize. Beyond his appeal to local audiences, spoken-word artist Leroy Young, "The Grandmaster," has demonstrated the potential to link Belizean folklore, oral literature, street politics, and local music in ways that attract international audiences, as evident in the critical overseas acclaim accorded his debut recording, *Just Like That* (Stonetree Records), and his summer 2006 Canadian tour. Of course, his overseas success reflects the artist's musical appeal more than his status as a traditionally published literary figure, underscoring how differently local artists may be received by international audiences and indicating the potential to develop different strategies to promote local artists in overseas markets.

Visual and plastic arts

The 1990s were a decade of change, and Minus 8, by Ivan Duran and Yasser Musa (at the Bliss Institute in 1992), marked the opening of a new perspectives on the Belizean visual arts scene. The Second Annual Conference on Arts and Culture was convened in Belize in 1992 (National Arts Council, 1992), setting the stage for subsequent activity in this realm. The 1990s also saw the development of the Poustinia Land Art Park (1992), the Cubola New Art Foundation (1993), and the Image Factory Art Foundation (1995). The latter was created by Yasser Musa, an artist and teacher at the St. John's College arts training program.

At the culmination in 2000 of the Minus 8 project, ZERO, a new Belizean art project emerged, curated and directed by artist Joan Duran with the support of the Image Factory and NICH, along with international agencies and the hosting institutions. ZERO (1995) featured the work of Belizean artists, including Santiago Cal, Alfonso Galvez, Michael Gordon, Damian Perdomo, Gilvano Swasey, and Yasser Musa. Comprising installations, video, sound, photography, paintings and visual poetry, it was shown again in Mexico, in 2000 upon Mérida's declaration as the Cultural Capital of the Americas. The exhibit also travelled to Barcelona, Lisbon, San José Costa Rica, Guatemala City, Antigua Guatemala, Caracas, Santo Domingo, and Kingston, Jamaica. Then, in 2001, the exhibit was hosted in Havana by Casa de las Américas (Casa de las Américas, 2001; Rondón Gutiérrez, 2000).

The successful ZERO project metamorphosed into Landings–a series of ten international exhibitions in which Belize's artists teamed with young artists from more than a dozen countries, from southeastern Mexico to Central America and the Caribbean. Landings opened in 2004 in a restored 17th-century Franciscan convent in Conkal, Yucatan. The project is scheduled to finish late in 2008, having exhibited over 500 works by more than 50 artists in Mexico, the Dominican Republic, Costa Rica, Cuba, Spain, the United States, and Taiwan.

HIVOS, the Dutch development assistance agency, maintains an active arts and culture programme in Latin America, dedicated to fostering local contemporary artistic productions, concentrating on the performing and visual arts, gaining international exposure for supported work, and facilitating artistic exchange. Belizean organizations receiving HIVOS support have included the National Dance Company, the Image Factory, Stonetree Records, and the nonprofit Music Industry Association of Belize (MIAB), among others.

However, HIVOS has had difficulty in identifying activities by indigenous organizations that correspond with its cultural funding priorities, namely to support expressive culture initiatives related to contemporary cultural and social issues. Understandably, ethnic minority initiatives often focus on conserving traditional heritage objects, customs, knowledge, and traditions. In response, HIVOS has announced its intention to develop alternative strategies in this area (HIVOS, 2002). In a plural society such as Belize, of course, especially with respect to its Maya and Garifuna populations, this dilemma has broad consequences for cultural policy planning and implementation. This is true not only nationally but also regionally, given ethnic mobilizations by these populations in neighboring Mexico and in nearby Central American countries.

Such activity must be seen, moreover, in the global context of the visual arts' overall assimilation into world markets, via networks of galleries, museums, international scholarship, and media coverage. Thus nationally and regionally distinctive art is likely to continue to thrive in the context of the new global cultural milieu, increasing the importance of combining national support of artistic development with extra-national collaborations.

Dance

Dance has been a dynamic form in Belize, drawing on traditions of the nation's various ethnic groups, in some cases combining those elements with classical and modern influences. Most prominent has been the Belize National Dance Company (BNDC), formed in 1990 with government support and training by teachers from the National Dance Theatre of Cuba. Guest instructors also have come from Mexico, Costa Rica, Honduras, Jamaica, and the United States. The company grew throughout the 1990s, established its own training program in 1997, and apart from performing around Belize, has taken part in various regional and international dance festivals (Vernon, 2000). More recently, however, the cessation of funding by the government of Belize adversely impacted BNDC's activities, reducing it to a volunteer folkloric ensemble and bringing an end to visits by international instructors.

A number of community and school-based dance groups also have sought to offer training and performing experience at the local level. In 1998 YAA! (Young Artists Association) coalesced to serve as an umbrella organization to connect clients with performers, producers, and technicians, to provide dance and music performances at public and private events, along with radio, music, and stage production services (Vernon, 2000). The group's effort to organize the creative community of artists, producers, and technicians was in part a reaction against the common attitude that artistic entertainment is not something for which people should have to pay, countering the pernicious idea that cultural production somehow operates (or should operate) outside the remunerative logic of regular everyday economic relations. YAA!'s underlying message and motivation were that artists should be able to make a living pursuing their talents, their creative pursuits constitute serious and culturally valuable work, and creative workers should be actively supported for the benefit of society at large. Cultural policy strategies must confront this issue.

YAA!'s global youth culture orientation also challenged more traditional views about cultural authenticity and the proper focus of cultural preservation efforts and cultural policy initiatives. Tellingly, without sustainable support, YAA! dissolved, and William Neal, one of its founders, went on to become director of the Institute of Creative Arts (ICA), a division of NICH, founded in 2003 by the government of Belize.

The dynamic character of the relationship between local and international youth culture remains very much in play. This reflects the continued dominance of North American mass media in Belize, ongoing migration to the United States, and the return of young Belizeans from abroad. These facts inevitably influence local tastes, styles, and cultural orientations, and thus have policy implications.

The many lively dance and music initiatives in expatriate Creole and Garifuna communities in the United States—often oriented to preserving and celebrating Belizean culture—also warrant mention, one more manifestation of cultural deterritorialization via globalization. The issue calls for revising the scope and conceptual framework of cultural policy and thinking outside boundaries more traditionally construed in terms of geography and a static view of national culture. The National Dance Company's history of working with artists from other countries (especially those from within the region) and its past interaction with HIVOS underscore the value of articulating coordinated regional strategies to achieve common objectives of cultural development and to enhance intercultural understanding.

Audiovisual arts

Belizeans have been avid consumers of cinema and recorded music ever since British and North American mass media first became available in Belize. The arrival of television in the 1980s enabled Belizeans to consume TV, video, and recorded music as never before. However, as throughout Latin America and the Caribbean, local TV, film, and music production is quite limited when compared to consumption levels. Moreover, there is a lively unregulated exchange of home-recorded video and music in the country and with expatriate communities.

In sum, Belizean audiovisual production does not begin to meet local consumption levels, and it commands a tiny export market, mostly in the realm of music. That imbalance reflects the overwhelming presence of news and entertainment emanating from the United States, a condition that Belize shares with Latin America and the Caribbean at large. The cultural and economic significance of this should be clear, but structurally, insofar as the multinational communications industries are among the most dynamic in terms of global investment, corporate earnings and employment, these media are (or in the Belizean case, might become) critical actors when it comes to questions of economic development and intercultural exchange (García Canclini, 1998). Like most developing countries, Belize is at a distinct disadvantage in the global marketplace, where societies from around the world effectively meet and interact to an increasing degree via mass communications technologies, and via corporate mass communications networks. However, past success with such Hollywood productions as *Dogs of War* (John Irvin, 1981) and *The Mosquito Coast* (Peter Weir, 1986) illustrates Belize's potential draw as a film location, a potential that deserves further consideration.

Partly at issue are Belize's small size and questions of economic scale, but even the largest southern hemisphere media producers (i.e., Mexico, Argentina, Brazil, Chile, and Colombia) compete with the global North on markedly unequal terms. These circumstances underscore the need to formulate coordinated regional strategies to bolster audiovisual production and distribution closer to home. But that approach can only work when effective controls on distribution and consumption are also enacted, and such protective mechanisms are applied comprehensively to all forms of media. This will require a concerted commitment of human and financial resources to elaborate the necessary regional institutional frameworks and operating protocols, which at present exist only in nascent, scattered form in the region.

The case of music, in which Belize has enjoyed a modest degree of international success, presents an illustrative case study; an overview of recent Belizean musical history and what that experience might have to say vis-à-vis cultural policy is the subject of the next section.

Belizean music in the post-independence era

The most dynamic sector of Belizean cultural production continues to be music. The colonial encounter between indigenous, African, and European music and dance gave rise to a dynamic popular music culture by the early nineteenth century. Elites worried that African drumming carried coded messages to coordinate the revolt of the enslaved, but the same musicians and dancers participated enthusiastically in the raucous annual bramming and street festivities between Christmas and the New Year. The vitality of popular culture also extended into official ceremonies and parades, with music provided by military and police bands.

If Belizean elites looked to western European classical models as the supposed universal inspiration for local cultural aspirations, popular music-making and dance continued to animate work in the logging camps, plantations, and urban neighborhoods of the post-emancipation political economy well into the twentieth century. While colonial administrators, newspaper commentators, and religious authorities may have decried the alleged degeneracy of Maya and Mestizo fiestas, Garifuna sacred and secular music and dance, and Creole brukdown and boom-and-chime music, taken together, were truly the music of the land.

The pre-independence period reveals a lively if poorly documented history of music-making, from the annual classical performance competitions judged by visiting English music teachers who handed out rare and coveted scholarships to study in Britain, to concerts by police bands and school choirs, liturgical music and gospel singing, Maya harp and marimba performances, Garifuna drumming, and Creole string-band and accordion music.

The advent of recording technology and radio broadcasting initiated fundamental changes in local popular tastes and, indeed, the way music was conceived of and enjoyed, furthered by the entrepreneurship and shifting tastes of the Creole elite. Business figures and club owners financed and managed dance hall bands bearing the sponsor's name, supplying them with imported instruments and repertoires influenced by recorded music heard on the radio from the United States, Mexico, Cuba, Jamaica, Trinidad, and elsewhere in Latin America. Typically, musicians did not own their own instruments and were hired like interchangeable day labourers, paid by the job, and subject to dismissal at the whim of the band owner. An itinerant class of musicians worked the urban club scene from Chetumal, Mexico, south to Guatemala (Livingston, Puerto Barrios), and Honduras (Tela, La Ceiba).

The first commercial recordings and international tours of Belizean bands were produced by Compton Fairweather's CES label. Beginning in the mid-1960s, Fairweather, who had lived and worked in the United States, organized tours in Belizean expatriate communities taking North groups such as Lord Rhaburn, Jesus Acosta and the Professionals, and numerous others, arranging recording sessions in New York when the bands performed there. Some of these recordings can be heard on the recent Numero Group-Stonetree compilation, *Belize City Boil Up*.

Expatriate Garifuna musicians also made LPs, prominent among them John Mariano in New York and "Don Justo" Flores in Los Angeles. Originally released in very limited quantities, these are now collector's items; one newly available example, reissued in 2006 by Delvin "Pen" Cayetano, is *Garifuna Punta Anthology*, a collection of John Mariano's recordings of Dangriga's Isabel Flores, the renowned Garifuna drummer, and Lady Lord, considered by many to have been the best Garifuna singer of her generation. These early private recording efforts illustrate the readiness of Belizean musicians and promoters to operate in the international realm and to adapt their music to and disseminate it via newly available technologies.

The 1980s marked a new era in Belizean music, sparked in part by innovations in the Garifuna community of Dangriga. A group of young artists and musicians coalesced around the Moho Road studio of Garifuna painter, musician, and composer "Pen" Cayetano. Inspired by the traditional music of Isabel Flores, Lady Lord and John Mariano, Cayetano and friends began to experiment by mixing Garifuna drumming and turtle shell percussion with the amplified R&B, rock, jazz, country, calypso, reggae, and Latin music that they had grown up listening to on the radio and playing as musicians on the coastal club circuit.

After a series of successful "roadblock" performances in Dangriga, Cayetano and company took a bus north to try their luck in the Belmopan market. Drawing an enthusiastic crowd and passing the hat, they collected enough to continue to Belize City. There they played a free concert in the park, retiring to the Belize Radio One studios when rain ended their outdoor performance. The Original Turtle Shell Band went on to garner an invitation to perform at the New Orleans Jazz and Heritage Festival (1983, with a reprise in 1989), and punta rock, as the new genre came to be called, caught on quickly, not only in Belize but also in neighboring Mexico and Central America. Soon every self-respecting band was adding punta rock to its repertoire.

Ethnomusicologist Ronnie Graham, while heading VSO, liked what he heard in Belize and helped to organize the Sunrise recording project, which documented the music of Andy Palacio, Bredda David, Children of the Most High, and Mr. Peters Boom-and-Chime, along with titles featuring police brass bands, Maya Kekchi harp music, and an anthology of punta rock. While the masters from those sessions are now lost, the emerging world-music scene in England got word of these developments, which led to a summer 1986 tour of Garifuna drummers, singers, and dancers. The group played several concerts sponsored by the now-defunct Commonwealth Institute and capped their time in England with an appearance at Peter Gabriel's then-nascent World of Music, Art & Dance (WOMAD) festival. All these performances are preserved at the British Library's National Sound Archive and are important documents of Belizean popular music history.

After "Pen" Cayetano moved to Germany in 1989, Andy Palacio became the standard bearer for punta rock and Garifuna music. In 1995, Ivan Duran's newly founded Stonetree Records took Palacio into the studio to record his first full-length release, *Keimoun*, still considered by the world-music press to be among the top 100 albums of the genre. Stonetree has gone on to document major Belizean roots artists and traditions, winning international acclaim for *Paranda* (1998), its Garifuna ballad compilation, and for more recent recordings by spoken-word artist Leroy Young "The Grandmaster" and Garifuna singer Aurelio Martínez, whose 2006-2007 tour of Canada and the United States promised to open a new era in the history of music developed and produced in Belize. Belizean roots music is now well established in the world-music press and on touring circuits in Western Europe and North America. Because of the efforts of Stonetree, along with expatriate recording projects and live music scenes primarily situated in Los Angeles and New York, Belizean music has also developed a higher profile in Mexico, Central America, and elsewhere in the Southern Hemisphere.

Stonetree's latest recording, *Wátina*–and Andy Palacio and the Garifuna Collective's 2007 North American and European tour–marks the company's first worldwide release since *Paranda*. By teaming with the Cumbancha label and Alia Agency (a booking agent)–both based in the United States–the project was conceived to overcome the structural constraints imposed by the international music market on local production. Enthusiastic critical reception at GlobalFest in New York (Lipp, 2007; Pareles, 2007) suggest that Stonetree has crafted a fruitful combination of high-quality, superbly produced, traditionally inspired Belizean music with the necessary logistical strategy to bring the music to a keen international audience.

Belizean music, the international market, and copyright

Stonetree's vision has brought a new degree of professionalism to homegrown Central American music, and documented important–in some cases, quite elderly–artists whose work was not generally known outside their home communities. As the only independent recording enterprise in Belize, and one of very few in Central America, Stonetree represents a real departure. But this achievement has not come without problems.

Small, local, independent cultural producers operate in an economic context that strongly favors the handful of multinational entertainment giants whose financial resources and global reach enable them to dominate international markets, while distorting local markets in the process. The structural features of globalization make it extremely difficult for small independent labels to gain international exposure for its artists, or to secure favourable licensing and touring agreements for locally based, locally produced creative efforts. This in turn prevents talented local musicians from developing their art and becoming full-time performers and touring artists, a situation exacerbated by local audiences unaccustomed to paying full value for entertainment, whether live or recorded. Likewise, when there is no local tradition of music criticism and little serious coverage of local music, these conditions combine to discourage artist development, and to impede the ability of local entrepreneurs to gain traction for their artists locally and internationally.

Simultaneously, the open and uncontrolled commercial piracy of recorded music–whether produced by local firms or multinational entertainment conglomerates–speaks to the practical debility of Belizean copyright law, drafted in the late 1990s and enacted in 2000 to meet stipulations of the General Agreement on Tariffs and Trade (GATT) enforced by the World Trade Organization (WTO). Artists were, of course, quite concerned about the copyright issue, and Belizeans will recall their own confusion regarding what the new law would mean vis-à-vis the then-rampant piracy, whether of recorded music, videos, or the unauthorized capture and redistribution of satellite TV programming.

Government can now cite its conformance with international copyright and industrial and intellectual property law. But as artists would soon discover, lawyers understood from the beginning that, compared to the case volume and fee structure associated with criminal law, copyright is not where the money is. To say the least, artists were deeply disillusioned with the non-enforcement of the legislation, finding few lawyers willing to take on copyright cases or facing legal fees far beyond their financial reach.

Copyright is conceived as a means to protect individual expressive and creative activity. The Universal Declaration of Human Rights, Article 27.2 recognizes "the right every human being enjoys to the protection of his or her moral and material interests related to the scientific, literary, and artistic works vested in a given person" (del Corral & Abada, 1998, p. 211). Copyright law came into existence in seventeenth-century England to protect the work of publishers from unauthorized reproduction (Prott, 1998), and from its inception, it was formulated to recognize only individual creations. At stake is "a historically and culturally situated notion of authorship and ownership that is rooted in Western Enlightenment philosophy that emphasizes individualism, originality, and property rights" (McLeod, 2003, p. 241).

The law defines creative authorship in favour of property conceptions inscribed in the legal codes that govern the developed Western economies. This arrangement facilitates the flow of cultural resources from less-developed centres of production into the international marketplace, where those resources gain "protection" for its new owners via mechanisms of privatization and enforceable copyright. Under extant law, the only way oral heritage can gain protection is to be extracted from collective folk knowledge and be converted into private–thus copyrightable–property (McLeod, 2003; Shuker, 2003, Throsby, 1998).

These individualistic and highly competitive conditions are antithetical to the preservation of local cultural heritage. By definition, international copyright law excludes the oral and intangible cultural heritage of native peoples such as the Maya and Garifuna of Central America. UNESCO's 2001 declaration regarding Garifuna language, music, and dance implicitly recognizes the disadvantaged position of cultures whose collective heritage is denied the protections inscribed in international copyright law. Hence, copyright and intellectual property law is at best a partial remedy to preserve local cultural expression (Prott, 1998).

These same constraints impact local cultural production activities of firms such as Stonetree, and thus undermine the ability of local musical talent to achieve broader international recognition and the accompanying rewards. Economies of scale and the lack of access to international financing impose undue costs on local production when compared with the legal advantages, financial resources, and global market access enjoyed by multinational corporate entertainment entities (the so-called "majors"). Fostering local music production, promoting artist development, working actively to expand local music exposure via live performances and radio and TV broadcasting, seeking ways to expand global market access for local music, taking seriously the spirit of copyright law and protecting artistic rights are all areas where the government of Belize is positioned to play a much more engaged and proactive role in bringing the nation's unique cultural creations to far wider audiences and protecting the ability to continue to produce uniquely local music.

Cultural policy considerations in Belize

It is clear, the older model of cultural policy as a national project overseen by government is today insufficient to the challenges posed by multidirectional globalization, market integration, and the tensions inherent in the pull between processes of cultural homogenization and heterogeneity. It should be evident, moreover, that the interdependent process of transnational cultural homogenization is asymmetrical in its effects. Likewise, a tension exists between the invocation to respect cultural diversity and the global application of international standards of cultural preservation, production, circulation, and consumption. All of this can act very quickly to undermine any given unique cultural heritage (Prott, 1998).

The universalizing trend represented by the consolidation of global economic and financial systems, the primacy of global information systems, and the massive expansion of global entertainment systems all work to reduce or erase real cultural differences. As cultural homogenization shuffles, blends, reorganizes, and re-presents cultural differences, it creates new, unequal relations of production, circulation, and consumption that are more amenable to market dictates than to sustaining existing cultural and territorial identities and traditions. This observation applies equally to regional and ethnic differences within nations, and to differences between nations, reflecting inequitable access to the global economy of cultural production (Bhabha & Stimpson, 1998; García Canclini, 1998).

Peripheral nations and regions are well advised to elaborate cultural policies designed to maximize their comparative cultural advantages, while recognizing the impossibility of competing on all global fronts. One version has been to retreat into established local traditions that emphasize the radical uniqueness of expressive culture associated with particular nations, ethnic groups, and minority populations. But a separatist celebration of difference can produce an artistic insularity and radical conservatism that may well reinforce existing inequalities and forms of discrimination, while also stifling artistic innovation and openness.

Yet few nations or ethnic groups are truly autonomous in cultural, economic, and political terms. Indeed, those with especially resilient expressive traditions often find that their art—whether domestically produced or generated as a consequence of expatriation—is well received in international markets. This, of course, further exposes endogenous traditions to all the influences contributing to global cultural hybridization, and new, culturally heterogeneous forms are the typical result. The sustenance of cultural heritage in fact entails an ongoing process of dialectical change, and preservation through innovation is more culturally productive than resistance to change. The positive reception of Garifuna music on the world-music stage illustrates this observation.

Still, the material constraints on policy options are considerable. Local cultural production is insufficient to satisfy local consumer demand, while the global entertainment and communications majors continue to extend their international reach and domination of worldwide markets. While this expansion produces an apparent multicultural array of consumer offerings, it is hardly representative of actual global cultural diversity. The aesthetic organization of multiculturalism reflects the universalizing construction of Western tastes and perceptions. Globalism's affectation of equalizing all world cultures constitutes what García Canclini (1998) calls "a process of tranquilizing hybridization" that

306

fosters "the pretence that we can be close to others without trying to hear or understand them" (p. 173). Cultural policies need to combat this tendency by emphasizing the depth and complexity of uniquely local creative traditions.

As already discussed, in the current global context, the prevailing set of relationships between government, private enterprise, and independent organizations requires fundamental rethinking. The immediate strategy should be to support, revitalize, and expand local artistic development and cultural production, and especially to facilitate the distribution and consumption of cultural products closer to home, nationally and regionally.

This will require a concerted commitment involving investment in training and technological advances, together with a careful restatement of public commitment to and interest in the formulation and pursuit of cultural policies crafted in the public interest. A most insidious trend, nationally and internationally, is the transfer of cultural programs and institutions (e.g., Belize Radio One) to private corporate hands, while sidelining civil society organizations that take into account a multiplicity of factors, in which the overall public good and the more intangible aspects of cultural heritage take primacy over profitability.

Instead of exiting the field altogether, the government has a critical role to fulfill, to ensure the growth of a democratic, plural society wherein cultural expression can flourish as something far more than a commodity for sale to those who can pay. Government can and should play a strong role in sustaining arts education, artistic development, artistic research and scholarship, and cultural institutions, in partnership with private corporate interests, non-profit organizations, and regional consortiums. Important initial steps have been taken in Belize in this direction. As a universal human right, the arts deserve and require support for artistic development, creative production, and public enjoyment, and the collective construction of a shared sense of history informed by a simultaneously local, national, regional, and global perspective.

Belizean experiments to date with cross-national artistic alliances (as outlined above) point the way to innovative, mutually supportive possibilities with respect to regional integration and economic development. It bears repeating that the culture industries represent one of the most dynamic sectors worldwide in terms of generating investment, employment, and economic growth. Cultural expression is far more than a non-compensated "free-time" activity, and ample possibilities suggest themselves for bilateral and regional development initiatives focused on libraries, museums, educational institutions, the news media, publishing, film and video, music, dance, theatre, the graphic and plastic arts, and cultural research. The recognition of diversity and a renewed commitment to the principles of democratization and human rights vis-à-vis cultural expression fundamentally concerns the kind of access that groups enjoy to the resources and capabilities that define their cultural uniqueness and foster their ability to give artistic expression to their sense of cultural identity.

Given Belize's geographical and cultural location in a diverse geopolitical milieu, it also is essential to cultivate an informed dialogue regarding what is of cultural value in the expressive work of neighboring societies. Much work remains in order to overcome a mutual historical legacy of cultural prejudice and misunderstanding and to acknowledge the cultural convergence of countries in the region. Belize has taken key steps to begin to redress such issues, cooperating with such organizations as CIDA, HIVOS, SIDA, VSO, UNDP, UNESCO, and the UN High Commissioner of Refugees. It will continue to be important to identify and overcome the constraints inherent in insular, purely nationally oriented cultural policies, developing a more critical understanding of how globalization processes continue to alter the conditions for cultural development, a phenomenon that has raised the stakes, and that now requires a broader, more ecumenical and regional orientation dedicated to producing mutually beneficial results in the realm of cultural expression and identity.

References

APPADURAI, ARJUN. (1990). Disjuncture & Difference in the Global Cultural Economy. In MIKE FEATHERSTONE (Ed.), *Global culture: Nationalism, globalization, modernity* (pp. 295-310). London: Sage Publications.

BHABHA, HOMI, & STIMPSON, CATHERINE R. (1998). Global Creativity & the Arts. In UNESCO (Ed.), *World culture report* (pp. 183-192). Paris: UNESCO. See http://www.unesco.org/culture/worldreport/html_eng/index_en.shtml.

CASA DE LAS AMÉRICAS (2001). *Recientes y próximas de La Casa*. Casa de Las Américas 224, 173-175.

CAYETANO, MARION, & CAYETANO, ROY. (2005). Garifuna, language, dance & music: A masterpiece of the oral & intangible heritage of humanity. In Joseph O. Palacio (Ed.), *The Garifuna: A nation across borders* (pp. 230-250). Benque Viejo del Carmen, Belize: Cubola Productions.

DEL CORRAL, MILAGROS, & ABADA, SALAH. (1998). Global & economic development through copyright in the information society. In UNESCO (Ed.), *World culture report* (pp. 210-221). Paris: UNESCO. See: http://www.unesco.org/culture/worldreport/html_eng/index_en.shtml.

GARCÍA CANCLINI, NÉSTOR. (1998). Cultural policy options in the context of globalization. In UNESCO (Ed.), *World culture report* (pp. 157-182). Paris: UNESCO. See:http://www.unesco.org/culture/worldreport/html_eng/index_en.shtml.

HIVOS. (2002). Policy document: Arts & culture. The Hague: HIVOS (Humanistisch Instituut voor Ontwikkelingssamenwerking). Retrieved June 2006 from www.hivos.nl/english/english/themes/arts_culture.

LEWIS, JUSTIN, & MILLER, TOBY. (2003). Introduction. In JUSTIN LEWIS & TOBY MILLER (Eds.), *Critical cultural policy studies: A reader* (pp. 1-9). Oxford: Blackwell Publishers Ltd.

MARKENSTEN, KARIN. (2006). *The regional museum project in Central America: Review of regional museum & theatre projects*. Stockholm: Swedish International

Development Cooperation Agency (SIDA). Retrieved June 2006: www. sida.se/shared/jsp/download.jsp?f=Review+museum+project.pdf&a=20251.

MCGUIGAN, JIM. (2003). Cultural policy studies. In JUSTIN LEWIS & TOBY MILLER (Eds.), *Critical cultural policy studies: A reader* (pp. 23-42). Oxford: Blackwell Publishers Ltd.

MCLEOD, KEMBREW. (2003). Musical production, copyright & the private ownership of Culture. In JUSTIN LEWIS & TOBY MILLER (Eds.), *Critical cultural policy studies: A reader* (pp. 240-252). Oxford: Blackwell Publishers Ltd.

MILLER, TOBY. (2003). Introduction to part VIII: International organizations & national cultures. In JUSTIN LEWIS & TOBY MILLER (Eds.), *Critical cultural policy studies: A reader* (pp. 267-271). Oxford: Blackwell Publishers Ltd.

NATIONAL ARTS COUNCIL. (1992). *Proceedings of the Second Annual Conference on Culture & the Arts*. Belize City: National Arts Council.

PARELES, JON. (2007, January 23). Individualists, straddling cultures & exporting ideas. *New York Times*.

PATTERSON, ORLANDO. (1994). *Global culture & the American cosmos*. Paper Series on the Arts, Culture & Society. Paper No. 2. New York: The Andy Warhol Foundation for the Visual Arts.

PROTT, LYNDEL V. (1998). International standards for cultural heritage. In UNESCO (Ed.), *World culture report* (pp. 222-236). Paris: UNESCO.

RED CENTROAMERICANA DE MUSEOS (RED CAMUS). (2006). Belize. Retrieved June 2006: www.museoscentroamericanos.net/museos_belice/belice_info.htm.

RONDÓN GUTIÉRREZ, DENISSE. (2001). *Con el nuevo arte de Belice*. Casa de Las Américas 224, 141-144.

SHUKER, ROY. (2003). "We are the world": State music policy, cultural imperialism & globalization. In JUSTIN LEWIS & TOBY MILLER (Eds.), *Critical cultural policy studies: A reader* (pp. 253-263). Oxford: Blackwell Publishers Ltd.

STONE, MICHAEL. (2006). Garifuna song, groove locale & "World-Music" mediation. In NATASCHA GENTZ & STEFAN KRAMER (Eds.), *Globalization, cultural identities & media representations* (pp. 59-79). Albany: State University of New York Press.

THROSBY, DAVID. (1998). The role of music in international trade & economic development. In UNESCO (Ed.), *World culture report* (pp. 193-209). Paris: UNESCO.

UNESCO. (2001). *Proclamation of the masterpieces of the oral & intangible heritage of humanity: The Garifuna language, dance & music.* www.unesco.org/bpi/intangible_heritage/belize.htm.

VERNON, DYLAN G. (2000). *The state of the arts: Culture & cultural expression in Belize*. San José, Costa Rica: HIVOS-Central America.

YUGAR, ZULMA. (1999). Report of the Latin American & the Caribbean Regional Seminar. In PETER SEITEL (Ed.), *Safeguarding traditional cultures: A global assessment of the 1989 UNESCO recommendations on the safeguarding of traditional culture & folklore*. Washington, DC: Center for Folklife & Cultural Heritage, Smithsonian Institution. Retrieved June 2006: www.folklife.si.edu/resources/Unesco/yugar_eng.htm.

13. Independence, Globalization, & Rice and Beans

Richard Wilk

Belize has never been isolated and its history has always been deeply affected by events taking place far away. Therefore globalization is not something new to the country, for Belize has always been a "globalized" nation. This chapter traces the changing history of Belizean globalization, from its beginnings as a buccaneer's outpost, to its recent transformation into a stop on the tourist "Ruta Maya." What will happen in the future? This article ends with three possible futures for Belize at its fiftieth anniversary of independence.

Is it a Happy Birthday?

The 25th birthday of the nation of Belize is a good time to think about what independence really means, and how much Belize has changed during this dramatic quarter-century.[1] How is Belize today different from the Belize of 25 years ago? Has it truly become an independent nation? What has really changed, and what do these changes mean as we look into the future? This paper presents evidence that Belize has become both more and less independent over the last quarter-century. Despite the widespread influence of television, tourism, and con-

[1] I wish to acknowledge the help of the many Belizeans, too numerous to list here, who have educated me about their country, as well as fed me, over much of my lifetime. I also wish to thank the best cooks I know, Aurora Mendez from San Pedro Columbia in the Toledo District, and Miss Gloria Crawford in Crooked Tree Village, for feeding me the delicious meals that sparked my curiosity about Belizean cuisine. Thanks especially to Joseph Palacio who has generously shared his wisdom about anthropology and Belize with me since I was a teenager. My research has been financially supported by a Fulbright fellowship, the Wenner-Gren Foundation, USAID, the Economic and Social Research Council of the UK, and Indiana University.

sumerism, Belize has successfully forged itself into a nation. Today the Belizean people have a real national identity, reinforced and reflected in art, history, its press, and its unique position on the borderlands between the Caribbean and Latin America. On the other hand, this cultural independence rests uncomfortably on shaky economic foundations. Local culture has been built almost entirely from imported raw materials. This disconnection between the economy and the culture of Belize is a problem faced by many small countries in the world today; it is a symptom of the phenomenon many scholars call globalization (see for example Appadurai, 1990; Arizpe, 1996; Wilk, 1995).

Clearly it is impossible to do justice to all these complicated issues in a short paper. Some narrow but revealing examples of globalization in Belize help to focus the question. Globalization is a terribly overused word, and like all popular concepts its meaning is sometimes so stretched and general that it has no real significance. In being very specific about the meaning of globalization some risks occur because globalization emphasizes the important connections between small places such as Belize and the rest of the world. Unlike other countries, in Belize globalization is not new or recent; it is a phenomenon with a long and deep history. With this framework in mind, history can be conceived of as a series of types of globalization, as each kind of globalization connects places together in different ways (Wilk, 2006).

The view of globalization in Belize presented here is based partially on historical records, especially newspapers, travelers' accounts, and several decades of government reports, and the outstanding work of many scholars who have worked in Belize, especially Nigel Bolland and Assad Shoman. My analysis has also been shaped by the transformations seen during a long acquaintance with Belize, starting when it was still called British Honduras.

My memories of Belize are similar to those depicted in movies that condense into a few seconds the growth of a seed to a flowering plant. While I have lived in Belize for about seven years altogether, those 85 or so months have been spread out over 33 years. Changes in a place seem much more dramatic when seen in this fashion. Instead of seeing an old building being gradually demolished and a new one rising slowly, the building exists during one visit, and a different one magically appears in its place on a return visit. In 1984 when I was working on a USAID/Ministry of Works roads and bridges project, I was lucky enough to spend three months traveling every single road in Belize and visiting every village and town in the country. Traveling to those same places today is a very different experience. New roads, bridges, electricity, cell phones, piped water, and the construction of new houses and shops have transformed many areas "beyond recognition." Urban Belize and places such as San Ignacio and Belmopan have grown enormously in physical size and population. Equally important are the less visible changes in peoples' consciousness of belonging to their own country, rather than to the British Empire.

311

Nationhood and globalization

Nationhood, the culmination of more than fifty years of struggle and uneven progress towards political self-determination has also led to dramatic changes in Belize. A seat in the United Nations, a national flag, a military force, and a set of unique legal codes, and political processes–these are the kinds of things that country after country has taken as the goalposts of identity, of reaching the global stage as a member of the club of nations. But many skeptical observers of independence in the Caribbean and Africa have argued that nationhood is not all it seems at first glance, that it ushers in a new era of dependency and neocolonialism (for example, Sheller, 2003; Barongo, 1980; Henke & Reno, 2003). The balance of power has not changed, they say, it has just become less visible.

Even the proponents of neo-liberalism at the World Bank would agree that nationhood cannot deliver all the promises of independence, for the simple reason that globalization makes independence impossible in the world today. This is especially true for small countries with few energy resources. National boundaries are after all, imaginary lines on a real world, a world where immense amounts of material goods and all kinds of intangibles from television signals to electricity, e-mail and wire transfers move around with little respect for imaginary lines or border guards. In this new world, industry goes wherever it wants, tourists travel freely, but average working people face border guards and legal penalties when they try to move across borders to find work (Hannerz, 1996; Barndt, 2002).

Faced with multinational corporations, huge and powerful neighbors, international laws and organizations of all kinds, smugglers and the Internet, and institutions such as the World Bank and the International Monetary Fund (IMF), the powers of nations appear diminished and weak. In truth, the ideal of the culturally unified nation, firmly defended behind national borders, was never more than an ideal type, even during the 18th century in Europe where the modern idea of the nation was first invented. So let us look beyond appearances and ask how Belize has been global in different ways at different times, and think about what kind of future globalization might bring to the jewel of the Caribbean.

Globalization through food

This essay draws on material presented in my recent book *Home cooking in the global village*, which uses the medium of food as a means to discuss Belize's relationship with the rest of the world. While this book and this article are ostensibly about Belizean food and cuisine, food is a metaphor for describing Belize's relationships with the rest of the world. Food is a particularly good vehicle for this because it always has both cultural meaning and economic significance. This is especially so in a country such as Belize where so much of the food people eat is, and has always been, imported from elsewhere. Depending on someone else for daily meals is a dramatic form of dependence, for food is simultaneously substance and symbol, a daily necessity, and also a source of identity and pleasure. Many recent studies describe how important a local cuisine is to the process of building a nation, with scholars focusing on particular foods that have become "national dishes" (e.g., see the 14 articles in Belasco & Scranton, 2002).

The history of colonialism and global empire can equally well be studied through the medium of food (for example, Andrae & Beckman, 1985; Super, 1988; Trentmann & Just, 2006). Ever since the beginnings of European colonialism, food products such as coffee, sugar, spices and tea were the lifeblood of trade, matched by a counterflow of rations of flour and meat to feed sailors and workers, and a highly profitable trade in wine, beer, and liquor. The regulation of food trade continues to be one of the hottest and most difficult global issues; for example, disagreements over agricultural subsidies led to the breakdown of the last meeting of the World Trade Organization. Belize faces these problems daily as both a food exporter facing export quotas and large agribusinesses and as an importer of cheap subsidized food from rich countries, providing unfair competition to local farmers.

This short paper uses a dish of rice and beans to tell part of the story of Belizean globalization. Steaming on the plate, surrounded by stewed chicken, potato salad, and fried plantain with a dash of habanero pepper, rice and beans can tell us about the complicated way that Belize is caught up in the many complications of global trade and global culture. All the contradictions of globalization and independence are there in plain sight, just waiting to be digested.

The prehistory of rice and beans

Rice and beans looks today as if it is traditional and timeless dish that has defined the country since time immemorial, a bedrock of everything which makes Belize completely unique. All the guidebooks define rice and beans as Belize's staple food, eaten daily by everyone. One even claims that everyone in Belize has eaten rice and beans since the time of the ancient Maya (Ritz, 1994, p. 61), which is unlikely considering that rice was unknown in the New World until the Spanish invasion.

In the not-so-distant past, the place of rice and beans in Belize has changed pretty dramatically. In the early 1970s, before the Mennonites began their poultry industry, chicken was expensive, much more so than pigtail, canned meat, or fresh pork and beef. For those who could afford it, rice and beans with stewed chicken was a Sunday dinner dish, not the everyday meal it has now become. Going back further in time, rice and beans becomes less and less important as a part of the Belizean diet. The first time it is mentioned is in 1895 in an issue of the Catholic Church Monthly, when it was served as part of a New Year's dinner for the inmates of the Belize City poorhouse and asylum. To be sure in the 19th century, rice and beans were imported in small quantities, and some were undoubtedly grown in the colony, but not in the volume needed to be staple foods. None of the 19th century travelers who visited Belize ever mentioned either rice or beans, and certainly not as any kind of particular local or even regional dish. So if rice-and-beans is only a bit more than a hundred years old, what were the previous "national dishes"?

The Baymen who settled along the coast in the 17th century ate all kinds of things, especially game meat, but one visitor claimed the favorite dish was called "pig and pease," a stew of salt pork with dried green or yellow peas (Dampier, 1717/1906, p. 123). Both were brought from Europe on ships, and they were part of the regular diet of sailors on board ships, so it makes sense that Baymen would eat the stew, given that many had been sailors at one time in their lives. Dried peas and salt pork were spread all over the world by British sailors, and they became part of many local cuisines.

Later on in Belize, as in many other parts of the Caribbean, African slaves in the mahogany camps were also fed imported rations of salted meat or fish and white flour. They cooked these foods into a dish called "pork and doughboys," which consists of boiled salt pork and white flour dumplings, washed down with the cooking broth. Over time, however, many slaves began to make plantations to supplement their rations and to get produce to sell in town markets. All the evidence show that their favorite crops were ground foods and plantains, rather than rice or beans. If there was a common staple dish in the 18th and 19th century, it would have been saltfish and plantains, which many travelers reported to be the daily diet of rural Creoles and the urban poor. This is probably the ancestor of today's "boil up," still a popular Creole dish. A lot of the fish may have been caught and dried (corned) in coastal villages, making this dish the first entirely local cuisine, and if it had remained Belize's staple food, Belize would have been able to feed itself. Instead another kind of cultural globalization led many Belizeans to abandon salt fish and plantains.

While poor and rural people were eating salt fish and plantains, the better-off urban dwellers, including the emerging Creole middle class and the British colonial officials, ate imported European food as much as possible. When they did eat local meat or vegetables, they drowned them in imported sauces and gravies. By the beginning of the 20th century, huge amounts of packaged and tinned foods supported a substantial population who were living in tropical America, but eating as if they were in London. They even imported tropical fruit and fish in tins, in preference over the fresh articles available in local markets.

This history exposes two of the most damaging legacies of colonialism for both Belizean culture and the Belize economy. Foreign food products were always ranked above local ones. Tinned, processed, sterilized food from England and other parts of the empire were thought to be more healthful, more cultured, more civilized than the products of the local oceans, forests, and fields. Because foreign products were "superior," local production for the market was stunted and disadvantaged. Those people in Belize who had the money to spend on food were the ones who sneered at local products, even when they were cheaper and fresher than imports. Generations of historians have blamed Belizeans for being "uninterested in agriculture," when the blame should properly belong to urban consumers who would pay more for a single tin of British spinach than they would for ten pounds of fresh callaloo (see for example Waddell, 1961; Tripartite Report, 1966; Rogers, 1885). Fancy olive oil in beautiful tins and bottles from Italy was sold in all the large shops in Belize City, while local coconut and cohune oil were exiled to street markets, where they were sold in old bottles sealed with corncobs.

These entrenched ideas about the superiority of foreign food had dire economic consequences for the colony as a whole. The balance of trade shifted sharply to the negative in the 1880s and was never positive again until after 1919. Since then the value of imports has continued to grow at a faster pace than the value of exports, making Belize a net debtor. Even during World Wars I and II, when food and fuel were scarce and expensive in the British Empire, British Honduras food imports continued to grow, shifting the source of supply to the United States. The constant growth in the cost of imports allowed governments to depend on import duty as their main source of revenue, instead of levying reasonable land or income taxes. This legacy continues to the present day. In March of 2006 the government of Belize reported that import and export duties on international trade were still the largest source of tax revenue (GOB, 2006).

Anyone living in Belize knows the effects that import duties have on both businesses and daily life. The high cost of imported fuel works its way through the entire economy, raising the sales price of every item, even those produced within the country. The high cost of fuel makes all kinds of domestic activities and transportation expensive. Farmers find that the high cost of imported equipment, chemicals, parts, and fuel makes it very difficult for them to compete with farmers in neighboring Latin American republics, not to mention rich countries that subsidize their own farmers and food exports.[2] The cost of living is higher in Belize than anywhere else in Central America.

The legacy of colonialism contributes to a perception among many Belizeans that imported goods have higher quality than local ones. This makes it very difficult for those who are thinking about local production of competing goods, even with tax incentives and some tariff protection. It is always much less risky to go into the import-export business than into local production, a lesson many Belizean ambitious businesspeople have learned to their regret.[3] At the same time, as Belizeans become more cosmopolitan consumers, through travel, residence abroad, education, and television, they are constantly developing tastes for many new kinds of packaged, processed, frozen, and canned foods that cannot be produced in Belize at all.

---

[2] American farmers and food processors collect about $24 billion a year from the US Government in direct subsidies.

New markets and growing variety

An examination of the import records at the beginning of the twentieth century indicates that most of the rice and the beans eaten in the country were imported from the USA. Rural Creole villages grew corn, rice, and beans and raised livestock for their own consumption, but little of this trickled into urban markets. The Spanish–and Maya-speaking people of Belize–grew and ate their own beans as part of a traditional diet, but these were mostly black beans, which few people in the city wanted to eat.

Facing a financial crisis brought on by the great depression, in 1932 the colonial government began to actively promote local farming when it opened an Agricultural Board (later the Marketing Board), which paid farmers fixed prices for corn, rice, and red kidney beans. Eventually they built two rice mills and drying facilities, and gradually farmers began to increase their production of these crops. Later the British even financed a mechanized rice plantation at Big Falls on the Belize River, but as Belizeans began to eat more rice and beans, production could not keep up, and special licenses were issued to merchants to import rice and beans to make up the difference (Dumont, 1963).

After Belize achieved independence, the government continued to encourage local production of rice and beans, and a number of foreign aid programs and projects over the years have tried to increase production and efficiency. In the early 1980s, by spending large amounts of money for development and research, as well as providing subsidies to farmers, which made local rice and beans much more expensive to consumers, Belize finally reached its goal of self-sufficiency in rice and beans and got very close to providing all its own fresh beef, pork, chicken and fish. Did this mean that finally Belize was reducing its food imports and becoming economically more independent?

One walk through the supermarkets in Belize City reveals why the answer is "no." Rice and beans are no longer the staple foods they were back in the middle of the 20th century. Instead, urban consumers are turning increasingly to processed and pre-prepared "convenience" foods, as are consumers in most countries around the world. They are eating more baked goods made from wheat flour (which must be imported), and as their tastes broaden, a lot more cheese, beverages, prepared meats, and varieties of fish such as tuna and salmon,

---

[3] The Mennonites have, unlike many other Belizean farmers, had great success in producing food for the local market. While many people believe this is entirely due to their cleverness and hard work, I would point out that they also started out with large amounts of good land in Spanish Lookout and good mechanical skills, that they have access to cheap credit through their community, and have had a number of valuable concessions from government, which have allowed them to out-compete many other equally smart and hard-working farmers in Belize.

which are not local. As more and more women have entered the formal job market, they no longer have time to prepare dishes such as rice and beans or tamales. The price of many local ingredients, for example ground foods, have also gone way up. With more rushed family schedules, convenience foods, snacks, and small shops and restaurant meals are becoming more common all the time, and many of these meals are based on imported ingredients.

A number of recent positive developments, particularly in the supply of high quality fresh vegetables and fruits to urban markets, have occurred. Central American immigrants have brought a wider variety of crops to market and have branched out into producing cheese and prepared snack foods from their home countries. Chinese and Taiwanese immigrants, who initially lived only in cities, have moved into rural areas, where they are growing new fruits and vegetables, such as pitahaya and guava, which have been rapidly accepted by Belizean consumers. Small Chinese grocery stores have diversified the choices of food available to Belizean consumers in some areas, and the government is still willing to offer protection from imports to fledgling local food production and processing.

Still, farmers and food processors can never keep up with the avalanche of new food products from the USA [4] Even as high-quality local products such as bacon and ham appear on the market, they are buried by hundreds of new varieties of imported meat products, everything from turkey bacon to cheese-stuffed hot dogs. For every new vegetable that Belizean farmers painstakingly learn to grow and bring to market, supermarkets can import ten new kinds of American vegetables in microwave bags and herbed butter sauce. Yet, at the same time Belizean food and food products have never been more popular in the marketplace. What should we make of this contradiction? How did Belizean cuisine emerge?

Ethnic and national food

The British colonial policy tended to divide the different ethnic groups of the country from one another, encouraged them to stay in their own communities, and emphasized their differences. There was a good deal of mixing in Belize City, where the term "Creole" came to include many people of very diverse cultural backgrounds. Rice and beans, the Kriol language, and much of what is now thought of as "Belizean" culture emerged from this mixed urban Creole community. But right up to the time of self-government, most of the rural people of the country lived in relatively uniform ethnic communities, eating their own traditional foods and diets.

When I first started working in Corozal and Orange Walk districts in the

---

[4] According to Lang and Heasman (2004), about 20,000 new food and beverage products are introduced into US supermarkets each year.

early 1970s, very few people in the villages ever cooked rice and beans at home. Their diet was still based on tortillas and other corn products in a cuisine that could be traced to their Maya and Mestizo ancestors in Quintana Roo and Yucatan. Rice and beans was still considered a Creole food or city food, not a food for every Belizean. In 1978 in Kekchi communities in Toledo, most people had never eaten rice and beans together, even though they grew both crops to sell to the marketing board. Many Mopan and Kekchi people doubted that rice and beans could be a nourishing food capable of sustaining hard working people.

On a superficial level, it might seem that independence made few changes in the ethnic mosaic of Belizean culture and cuisine. A revival of some ethnic cuisines has spurred these offerings to emerge from kitchens into the public eye of the restaurant trade. So today one can sit down to a Garifuna meal of hudut in Hopkins, a Mopan Maya dinner of fish steamed in obel (bullhoof) leaves in Maya Centre, and an East Indian feast of chicken tacari in Punta Gorda. At the same time, however, something that can really be called Belizean cuisine has emerged and is eaten readily by all ethnic groups in the country.

In 1990 I conducted a survey of the tastes and preferences of hundreds of Belizeans of all backgrounds in urban, suburban, and rural areas. Over a thousand high school students responded to another questionnaire that asked them, among other things, to name their favorite foods. Across every ethnic group, rich and poor, young and old, the overwhelming favorite food was rice and beans with stewed chicken and potato salad. More than three-quarters of Belizeans of all backgrounds would rather eat this dish than anything else (Babcock & Wilk, 1998). Interviews I conducted in 2004 confirmed that Belizeans of all backgrounds are much more positive towards local food than before, a trend that can be seen in the constantly growing number of restaurants that proudly serve Belizean food, and a growing number of cookbooks[5] and the popularity of Belizean cooking shows on television.

The time since independence, then, has been a period during which Belizean food, as other aspects of Belizean culture, has shaken off some of the colonial legacy of low status. As in other parts of the world, travel, migration, tourism and other kinds of cultural globalization have not wiped out local culture. Instead, exposure to all these global influences has made many people more aware of what they have at home and encouraged them to recognize that it is something precious worth preserving, protecting, and developing. Presenting that culture to foreign visitors has become an increasingly important business as well, as tourism continues to grow, and tourists demand at least some version of a distinctive Belizean experience. There is even a rapidly-growing industry catering to "culinary tourists" who want to eat exotic local foods and learn how they are made.

So in many ways rice and beans, as part of the Belizean national culture, has

---

[5] For example two cookbooks by Cubola Productions *Mmmm...* and *Aaaah...*

never been more widely valued, more loved as part of Belizean life, and a symbol of cultural independence. But this value has not been translated into economic independence. While in the colonial past Belize was both culturally and economically dependent and dominated by foreigners, today cultural independence has grown, while economic dependence has, if anything, become deeper and more complete. Even if the rice and beans themselves are grown in Belize, they are raised with imported tools, fertilizer, pesticides, and fuel, cooked on an imported stove with imported propane, and served on imported plates with potato salad made from imported potatoes, salad crème, and mixed vegetables.

Conclusion: the future of rice and beans

What will happen to Belizean food culture and the food economy in the next 25 years of independence? Even if people continue to value and cultivate Belizean cooking and cuisine, the raw materials that are so much a part of Belizean food are themselves in danger of disappearing. Rural people in Belize find it harder and harder to make a living farming, and they have less time to raise their own gardens or hunt and gather in the Belizean bush. All over Belize today are the younger generations who are being raised not learning much of what their parents know about all the diverse flavors of wild foods like river crayfish, bocatora, and cohune cabbage. Old gardens with fruits like baboon cap, sorrel, and star apple may not be replanted. A generation of cooks may grow up not knowing how to make fish tea, darasa, or relleno blanco, unable to brew cashew wine or judge a ripe custard apple. In 1980 in Aguacate village in Toledo, the people knew more than 30 edible wild plants and herbs; what will happen to that knowledge in the coming years? When people are working long hours, they are more likely to buy their food in a shop, and outside of a few staples, most of that food is likely to be imported from somewhere else.

It is quite possible that in 25 years Belize will be a land of supermarkets and fried chicken stands, where Belizean families sit down to American frozen dinners, hamburger helper, and canned vegetables. After all, rice and beans can be made with canned beans, minute rice, and a cup of powdered coconut milk. Or frozen factory-made tamales can be defrosted and canned refried beans can be smeared on a factory tortilla. A future generation may even be importing plantains and cho cho if they are no longer produced in Belize.

This is not an unrealistic prediction. Large multinational supermarket chains are taking over a large part of the world's retail trade in food, because they can deliver processed food at such cheap prices. In 1991 Wal-Mart entered Mexico, and by 2004 it controlled almost 30% of all supermarket food sales there and about 6% of all retail sales, while directly owning almost 300 restaurants. Even in Guatemala, the number of supermarkets has more than doubled in the past decade, and the share of food they retail has reached 35%. In Brazil more than half of all fresh produce is now sold through supermarkets. The demands of standardization and bulk drive out small producers; small scale food processing has to grow and become industrial, and thus become part of an increasingly centralized and capital-intensive food sector dominated by global food processing giants with close connections to retailers. It is true that the Belize market is too small to be a target for a giant such as Wal-Mart, but smaller international players are waiting in the wings to pick up what the giants don't care about, like the pilot fish that follow sharks.

This is a serious economic development problem for small countries. The global trade system constantly pushes countries to specialize in the things they can produce most competitively. Large firms can pressure producers and play them against each other to get the lowest prices, and they can take advantage of economies of scale. That means buying food from the cheapest source, not the source that is best for national independence. Countries such as Belize that give in to these pressures in the future will have much less choice about the origin of their food. Their national food production and consumption will be out of their control.

The global mega-food industry therefore undercuts any nation's aspirations for a measure of economic and political independence. Huge food companies can swing a great deal of economic and political power, so they can run roughshod over local environmental and labor regulations. Instead of losing sovereignty to other countries, a place like Belize can be dominated by foreign corporations (as already happened in the last century with Standard Fruit in the banana trade). Allowing Belize's very food supply fall under the control of foreign corporations makes the country vulnerable in some dangerous ways.

For countries such as Belize, maintaining viable local food production and building a local food-processing industry is going to require flying in the face of this powerful economic force. Farmers and food businesses will require some protection and encouragement from government (despite what the International Monetary Fund has to say), and they will have to take advantage of any possibilities to expand by exporting specialty products such as Marie Sharp's pepper sauces. There is certainly a potential for Belize to capitalize on its ecological reputation to export more specialty products such organic candies (especially coconut and chocolate products), spices, and exotic preserves or food and spice mixes. But this cannot solve the larger problems of what will happen to Belize as more and more of its food is imported.

A real revival of local food production, which would benefit both rural farmers and the tourist industry, could draw some inspiration from the worldwide movements towards organic and local foods, and especially what is now called "slow food." This encourages people to pay extra for foods that have a particular local quality, for rare varieties of fruits and vegetables, and to value the flavors that are so often lost when food is highly processed and packaged. The same inspiration can be seen in the farmers' market movement in the USA and in public health campaigns that emphasize the health problems, particularly diabetes and high blood pressure, which result from eating processed foods that are typically high in fats and sugars.

The tourist industry in Belize has historically tended to rely on imported foods. Today most of the expensive restaurants that cater to tourists are serving Italian, Thai, French, or some other style of food. Belizean dishes may appear on a menu as a side dish, or a Belizean raw ingredient like venison or lobster may be featured in a non-Belizean dish. Some of the eco-tourist lodges have made great strides in adapting Belizean ingredients and dishes to the often-finicky tastes of tourists, but still a great deal can be done to elevate Belizean food to the same level of respect that is granted to, for example, Italian cuisine. Unfortunately, most of the chefs who come to Belize to teach the restaurant trade do not really know anything about Belizean cuisine. They teach the important techniques that are needed to produce consistent and reliable restaurant meals, but they can only provide the tools needed to create a Belizean cuisine that could compete at an international level.

So, in my estimation, the future of rice and beans holds many dangers. If the wonderful diversity and variety of Belizean food and cooking are going to survive to Belize's 50th birthday, people will have to pay much more attention to where their food comes from and how it is produced. Consumers, producers, and government will need to take action to demand accountability from food importers and encourage and protect local food production and processing. It may not be enough to just buy the Belizean product when it is as good and as cheap as the imported one. People may have to think about going out of their way to find and value foods, which are presently half-hidden and little-known.

But after all, this is a lesson known to everyone. Nothing tastes as good as "Mother's cooking." It would be a great tragedy if the special flavor of the mother country were lost.

References

ANDRAE, GUNILLA & BECKMAN, BJORN. (1985) *The wheat trap: Bread and underdevelopment in Nigeria.* London: Zed Books.

APPADURAI, ARJUN. (1990). Disjuncture and difference in the global cultural economy. *Theory, Culture & Society 7*, 295-310.

ARIZPE, LOURDES. (Ed.). (1996). *The cultural dimensions of global change: An anthropological approach.* Vendome, France: UNESCO.

BABCOCK, ELIZABETH & WILK, RICHARD. (1998). International travel and consumer preferences among secondary school students in Belize, Central America. *Caribbean Geography 8*(1), 32-45.

BARNDT, DEBORAH. (2002). *Tangled routes: Women, work, and globalization on the tomato trail.* Boulder, CO: Westview Press.

BELASCO, WARREN & SCRANTON, PHILLIP (Ed.) (2002). *Food nations: Selling taste in consumer societies*. New York: Routledge.

BARONGO, YOLAMU R. (1980). *Neocolonialism and African politics: A survey of the impact of neocolonialism on African political behavior*. New York: Vantage Press.

DAMPIER, WILLIAM. (1717/1906). *Dampier's voyages: Two voyages to Campeachy, Vol. II. Edited by John Mansfield*. London, UK: E. Grant-Richards.

DUMONT, RENE. (1963). *A development plan for British Honduras, Part 2; The modernization of agriculture*. UN Commission for Technical Assistance, Dept. of Economic and Social Affairs.

GOVERNMENT OF BELIZE. (2006). Ministry of finance: monthly report on fiscal operations, March. Retrieved from the Government of Belize webpage: http://www.belize.gov.bz/monthly_report_march2006.html.

HANNERZ, ULF. (1996). *Transnational connections*. London: Routledge.

HENKE, HOLGER & RENO, Fred. (2003). *Modern political culture in the Caribbean*. Mona: University of West Indies Press.

LANG, TIM & HEASMAN, MICHAEL. (2004). *Food wars: Public health and the battle for mouths minds and markets*. Washington DC: Earthscan Publications.

RITZ, STACY. (1994). *The new key to Belize*. Berkeley, CA: Ulysses Press.

ROGERS, E. (1885). British Honduras: Its resources and development. *Journal of the Manchester Geographical Society 1*, 197-227.

SHELLER, MIMI. (2003). *Consuming the Caribbean*. London and New York: Routledge.

SUPER, JOHN. (1988). *Food, conquest, and colonization in sixteenth-century Spanish America*. Albuquerque: University of New Mexico Press.

TRENTMANN, FRANK & FLEMMING, JUST (Eds.). (2006) *Food and conflict in Europe in the age of the two world wars*. NY: Palgrave Macmillan.

TRIPARTITE REPORT. (1966). *Report of the Tripartite economic survey of British Honduras, May 1966*. Canada, UK, U.S.A.: Tri-national survey team.

WADDELL, D. A. G. (1961). *British Honduras: A historical and contemporary survey*. London: Oxford University Press.

WALMARTFACTS 2006 INTERNATIONAL OPERATIONS. (2006). Website accessed December 12, 2006, http://www.walmartfacts.com/FactSheets/1222007_International_Operations.pdf.

WILK, RICHARD. (1984). Rural settlement change in Belize, 1970-1980: The effects of roads. *Belizean Studies, 12*(4), 1-10.

WILK, RICHARD. (1995). Learning to be local in Belize: Global systems of common difference. In D. MILLER (Ed). *Worlds apart: Modernity through the prism of the local*. (pp. 110-133). London: Routledge.

WILK, RICHARD. (2006). *Home cooking in the global village*. Belize City: The Angelus Press and London: Berg Publishers.

ZARGER, R. K. (2002). Acquisition and transmission of subsistence knowledge by Q'eqchi' Maya in Belize. In J. R. STEPP, F. S. WYNDHAM, & R. K. ZARGER (Eds.) *Ethnobiology and biocultural diversity* (pp 593-603). Athens: University of Georgia Press.

Notes on contributors

Jaime J. Awe received his Ph.D. at the University of London, England and was educated at Trent University, Canada, and the State University of New York, Albany. He taught at Trent University, Ontario, Canada, and then at the University of New Hampshire, he launched and directed the Western Belize Regional Cave Project. In 2000 when he returned to Belize, Dr. Awe became the Deputy Commissioner of Archaeology in the then Department of Archaeology, and in 2003 he became the first Director of the Institute of Archaeology (IOA) and was appointed as Associate Professor at Galen University, Belize.

Dr. Awe is Belize's technical representative to the Mundo Maya Organization and Director of the Belize Valley Archaeological Reconnaissance Project, which in 2007 will host its 19th summer field school project with field work at both Baking Pot and Caves Branch Rockshelter. As the Archaeological Coordinator with the Tourism Development Project, he conducted excavations and conservation work at Caracol, Lamanai, Xunantunich, and Altun Ha. Dr. Awe has published articles on Cahal Pech, Baking Pot, the caves of Western Belize and completed several documentaries. In addition to his work at IOA and teaching, he devotes time in the field investigating Baking Pot and several caves in western Belize.

Candy Gonzalez obtained her J.D. degree, but even before she had spent most of her life as an advocate for human rights and environmental justice. Presently, she is vice-president of the Belize Institute of Environmental Law and Policy (BELPO) and as a member of the Environmental Law Alliance Worldwide (E-LAW), she considers threats to human and environmental rights as one and the same.

For six years, Candy Gonzalez has been one of two NGO representatives, either as an alternate or main representative, on the National Environmental Appraisal Committee (NEAC) for the Belize Alliance of Conservation NGOs (BA-CONGO). She is an adjunct faculty at Galen University, Belize, and serves on the Board of Governors for Cayo Centre for Employment Training.

From the early civil rights struggles in 1960s in the U.S. (as a member of the Student Non-Violent Coordinating Committee working in Mississippi), to the present, she has been devoted to the goals of justice and equity. She was a people's attorney, representing those challenging civil and human rights abuses, fighting for the rights of workers, and the poor and spent a great deal of time defending her husband (and partner, comrade, and friend) against many cases brought against him, stemming from racism.

Crucita Ken has an M.S. in Regional Development and a B.A. in Economics and is on leave pursuing her Ph.D. in Morelia. She will return to teach in the Economics and Finance Bachelors Program and in the Economics and Public Administration Masters Program at the University of Quintana Roo, Mexico. Since 1991 Crucita Ken has researched topics on Belize-Mexico economic relations, has published over 30 articles–from newspapers to scholarly journals–in English and Spanish on economics, tourism, and regional development in various sectors. Between 1995 and 1996 Crucita participated in the proposal for the creation of the Corozal Free Zone and was the Free Zone Business Association's first General Manager.

Melanie McField completed her Ph.D. at the College of Marine Science, University of South Florida, after receiving the first International Society of Reef Studies Coral Reef Ecosystem Science Fellowship. Her research explored the role of disturbance events and the impact of management actions (like MPAs) on coral reef community structure in Belize.

At present Dr. McField is the coordinator of the Healthy Mesoamerican Reef Ecosystem Initiative. The goal of this multi-institutional effort is to develop a collaborative platform to better track the health of the reef ecosystem, the human choices that shape it, and our progress in ensuring its long-term integrity. Prior to this, she worked as Belize's Senior Program Officer for the World Wildlife Fund's Mesoamerican Reef Program on a variety of conservation programs. Since 1990, Melanie has worked as a biologist with the Hol Chan Marine Reserve. In 2003 she was awarded the National Coastal Award for Marine and Coastal Research from the Belize Coastal Zone Management Authority and Institute, which recognized the relevance of this research for management.

Nadia Bood has an M.S in marine science specializing in biological oceanography and coral reef ecology from the University of South Alabama. The goal of her master's thesis research was to ascertain whether impacted reefs are able to absorb shocks, resist phase-shifts, and regenerate subsequent to disturbances, and whether protection designation (no-take protected areas) could confer recovery benefits.

At present Nadia Bood is working as the Reef Scientist for the World Wildlife Fund Mesoamerican ecoregion, but she has been working in the environmental field since 1998, as a lecturer in the natural resource management programme of the University College of Belize's (now University of Belize), an environmental technician in the Department of Environment, and a reef biologist/unit head for the national coral reef monitoring programme of the Coastal Zone Management Authority and Institute. Working in such diverse fields, she has seen first hand how limited environmental knowledge, awareness, and willingness impede the management and conservation of Belize's coral reefs.

Antoinette Moore received her J.D. degree from Loyola University, Chicago, a Master of Studies degree in International Human Rights Law from Oxford University, London, and obtained a Legal Education Certificate from the Norman Manley Law School in Kingston, Jamaica, which qualifies her to practice law in the Caribbean. Like Candy Gonzalez, Antoniette Moore is a human rights lawyer and a life-long activist committed to political social and economic justice. With her law chambers in Dangriga, Stann Creek District, she is the only lawyer practicing full time in southern Belize.

Before relocating to Belize in 1994, Antoniette Moore was the Deputy Director of Amnesty International's Midwest Regional Office in the U.S., coordinating the work of 13 states on refugee rights, death penalty abolition, and other human rights issues. Prior to that, she was a staff attorney at the Legal Assistance Foundation of Chicago, the largest agency in the city of Chicago serving the legal needs of the indigent community.

Joseph O. Palacio received his Ph.D. in Caribbean Anthropology from the University of Berkeley. Over the past 30 years he has received many fellowships and awards. His monographs, articles and reports have been published on topics including archaeology, food, ethnography, migration, refugees, urban and rural development, indigenous peoples, primary health care, child abuse and neglect and continuing studies. Dr. Palacio has taught at the University of California, Berkeley, McGill University, and Galen University, Belize, and as a Resident Tutor at UWI in Belize. His latest book *The Garifuna: A nation across borders* is a collection of essays on topics such as oral history, local government, spirituality, gender, cultural identity and the background leading to UNESCO's 2001 Proclamation of Garifuna culture as a masterpiece of the oral and intangible heritage of humanity.

Michael J. Pisani has a Ph.D. in International Business from the University of Texas-Pan American, an M.A. in Latin American Studies, and an MBA from the University of New Mexico. He is an Associate Professor of International Business at Central Michigan University, and a visiting professor at Galen University, Belize. His research interests include cross-border business issues, Western Hemispheric trade agreements, labor market informality, microfinance, and entrepreneurship with a special focus on the Latin American region, especially Belize, Mexico, and Nicaragua. Dr. Pisani has published widely, in both Spanish and English journals.

Robert B. Richardson holds a Ph.D. in agricultural and resource economics from Colorado State University and an MBA from New York University. He is an assistant professor at Michigan State University in the Department of Community, Agriculture, Recreation and Resource Studies and an adjunct professor at Galen University, Belize. His teaching, research, and outreach program focuses broadly on sustainable development and natural resource-based tourism. His research interests include economic development, the economic impact of climate change, the economic benefits of wilderness protection, and the relationship between tourism and poverty in developing countries. He has studied the economic impact of climate change on national park visitation and gateway communities in the western USA and the implications for park and urban planning. He has studied the vulnerability of economic sectors to climate change in Belize, with emphasis on tourism and coastal areas. He is presently involved in a project that examines the role of sustainable tourism development in poverty reduction strategies in southern Africa. Dr. Richardson's published work appears in *Ecological Economics, Journal of Leisure Research*, and the *Review of Regional Studies*.

Michael Rosberg has a Ph.D. in Development Studies from the Land Tenure Centre of the University of Wisconsin-Madison and a M.S.W. (Community Practice) from the State University of New York at Buffalo. Currently Dr. Rosberg is an Associate Professor at Galen University, Belize, and Director of the Galen University Applied Research and Development (GUARD) Institute, which he founded. In his recent publication, *The power of greed: Collective action in international development*, he suggests that successful development work must speak directly to the self-interest of individuals. Dr. Rosberg is also author of several journal articles mostly dealing with justice and collective action.

In addition to teaching in Colombia and Canada, Dr. Rosberg was a Development Project Officer for the Canadian University Service Overseas (CUSO), and Director of Development Programmes for the International Department of the Canadian Co-operative Association. He has done development project consulting work for the Government of Canada and for non-governmental and multi-lateral development organizations in Canada the USA and developing nations in Asia, Africa, Latin America, and the Caribbean.

Michael Stone has a Ph.D. in cultural anthropology from University of Texas at Austin and an M.A. in Latin American Studies from Stanford University. He is Executive Director of Princeton University's Program in Latin American Studies. He has worked or consulted for the United Nations High Commission for Refugees, the United Nations Development Program, the European Community, the Smithsonian Institution Center for Folklife Programs & Cultural Studies, the Institute of Texan Cultures–University of Texas at San Antonio, and Texas Folklife

Resources. He previously taught at Universität Konstanz (Germany). His research focuses on the indigenous musics of the Caribbean coast of Central America; recent essays include "Garifuna Song, Groove Locale & World–Music Mediation (in *Globaliziation, cultural identities & media representation*). He is the translator of *Beautiful flowers of the maquiladora: Life histories of women workers in Tijuana* (*La flor más bella de la maquiladora*), by Norma Iglesias Prieto, and is contributing editor at RootsWorld. His work also appears regularly in *fRoots* (London) and *Global Rhythm* (New York), on the National Geographic world-music web site, and in other world-music publications.

Jerome Straughan is a Belizean-America sociologist who resides in Los Angeles, and he is one of few Belizeans to have done research on Belizeans immigrants in the United States. His research on Belizeans in Los Angeles culminated with his Ph.D dissertation on the life experiences of Belizeans in Los Angeles. This research focused on how some of their characteristics (such as their ethnoracial background), help shape certain aspects of their lives and influence some of the types of experiences they have in a diverse and spatially defined L.A. This research also reflected Jerome's overall interest in international migration, race, and ethnicity. He also has an interest in urban sociology, and is currently writing on the transformation of Belize City, from the city of his childhood to what it is now.

Richard Wilk holds a Ph.D. in Anthropology from the University of Arizona, and an M.A. in Anthropology, University of Arizona. Dr. Wilk is a professor of anthropology and gender studies at Indiana University. He has done research in Belize since 1973, first as an archaeologist in the Corozal and Orange Walk districts, then as a cultural anthropologist, beginning in Toledo in several Kekchi communities. He has also worked as an applied anthropologist with UNICEF, USAID, Cultural Survival, and a variety of other development organizations. With his wife, archaeologist Anne Pyburn, he has lived in all the districts, and most recently has worked along with the residents of Crooked Tree village. His initial research on farming and family organization was followed by work on consumer culture, globalization, television, beauty pageants and food. Much of his recent work has turned towards Belizean history. His most recent books are *Home cooking in the global village*, *Off the edge: Experiments in cultural analysis* (with Orvar Lofgren), and *Fast food/slow food.*

Colin A. Young holds an M.A. and a Ph.D. in ecology from the University of Connecticut and has a dual B.A. degree in conservation biology and ethnobotany from Marlboro College, Vermont. Currently, he is the Director of the Environmental Science Program at Galen University, Belize, where he developed and teaches courses in sustainable development; ecology, plant and society; introduction to botany, adventure and ecotourism; environmental problems; society and environment, and he consults in both the undergraduate and MBA programs.

Dr. Young's involvement in conservation began very early in the village where he grew up, Bermudian Landing, at the Community Baboon Sanctuary; he now serves as a voluntary consultant and advisor to the Community Baboon Sanctuary Women's Conservation Group. At the University College of Belize, he co-founded the Students Concerned for the Protection of the Environment environmental club. He serves on the Board of Directors of the Katalyst Institute for Public Policy and Research and was recently elected to the board of Friends for Conservation and Development.

Robert Horwich received his Ph.D. in zoology from the University of Maryland and worked in a postdoctoral position in India with the Smithsonian Institution. For over 20 years in nine countries and sixteen cultures, Dr. Horwich has worked as the Director of Community Conservation (CC) with community conservation projects. CC's main goal is to catalyze community-based conservation projects, encouraging local rural people to become stewards and protectors of the lands and waters within or adjacent to where they live. In 1985 in Belize, CC staff initiated the Community Baboon Sanctuary to help save the endangered black howler monkey, and used it as a model to establish other community-based conservation projects throughout the country, such as the Gales Point Manatee Project and the community process for the Temash National Park. In addition, CC initiated a UN Development Program grant to further community co-management of Protected Areas. With government-community co-management agreements established, CC worked with the Peace Corps, government staff, and community members to strengthen the existing community-based organizations in Belize.

Index

340